Terrible Revolution

Terrible Revolution

Latter-day Saints and the American Apocalypse

CHRISTOPHER JAMES BLYTHE

OXFORD
UNIVERSITY PRESS

Oxford University Press is a department of the University of Oxford. It furthers the University's objective of excellence in research, scholarship, and education by publishing worldwide. Oxford is a registered trade mark of Oxford University Press in the UK and certain other countries.

Published in the United States of America by Oxford University Press
198 Madison Avenue, New York, NY 10016, United States of America.

First issued as an Oxford University Press paperback, 2023

Library of Congress Cataloging-in-Publication Data
Names: Blythe, Christopher James, author.
Title: Terrible revolution : Latter-day Saints and the American apocalypse /
Christopher James Blythe.
Description: New York, NY, United States of America : Oxford University Press, 2020. |
Includes bibliographical references and index
Identifiers: LCCN 2019044754 (print) | LCCN 2019044755 (ebook) |
ISBN 9780190080280 (hardback) | ISBN 9780197695159 (paperback) |
ISBN 9780190080303 (epub) | ISBN 9780190080310 (Digital Online)
Subjects: LCSH: Christianity and politics—Church of Jesus Christ of Latter-day Saints. |
Church of Jesus Christ of Latter-day Saints—History—19th century. |
Christianity and politics—United States—History—19th century. | United States—
Politics and government—19th century. | Christianity and culture—
United States—History—19th century. | Apocalyptic literature—
History and criticism.
Classification: LCC BX8643.P6 B58 2020 (print) | LCC BX8643.P6 (ebook) | DDC 289.3/73—dc23
LC record available at https://lccn.loc.gov/2019044754
LC ebook record available at https://lccn.loc.gov/2019044755

Printed by Integrated Books International, United States of America

For my "Nucleus of Heaven,"
Christine, Chris, Blaine, and Jack

Contents

Acknowledgments

I gratefully acknowledge the many friends, family, colleagues, and mentors who have assisted or encouraged me in this project. The core of this book was written as a dissertation, which I was fortunate to write under the supervision of John Corrigan at Florida State University. Dr. Corrigan was the ideal doctoral advisor, helping me to relate my arcane interests and research to the concerns of the academy, reading and critiquing drafts, and recommending new lines of inquiry. I was also fortunate to have Amanda Porterfield as a mentor and committee member. Early on in my doctoral career, she pushed me to have confidence in my work and to think broadly about its significance. Trevor Luke and Michael McVicar offered many suggestions that have been incorporated into this work. Amy Koehlinger introduced me to the work of scholars of American Catholicism who would, in turn, revolutionize my approach to the study of religion.

I began my graduate career in 2007 in the new Religious Studies program at Utah State University. In Utah, I became acquainted with the landscape and scenery that would inspire me to try to imagine how early Latter-day Saints thought about their world, and as importantly, I was able to learn from two men, Charles Prebish and Philip Barlow, both who kindly nurtured my interests in the study of religion. Dr. Barlow has made a particularly large impact on my life and on my work over the past decade of friendship and tutelage.

After finishing my doctorate, I was fortunate to take a position with the Joseph Smith Papers located at the Church History Library of the Church of Jesus Christ of Latter-day Saints in Salt Lake City. Life at the CHL was a wonderful three-year passage that allowed me to become immersed in nineteenth-century manuscripts and to be surrounded by passionate and knowledgeable scholars. I am particularly indebted to the "walking group" for their friendship and the time we spent working out ideas in the history of Mormonism. Thank you, Mason Kamana Allred, Jeffrey Cannon, Brett Dowdle, David Grua, Christian Heimburger, Robin Jensen, Jeffrey Mahas, Jenny Reeder, Tyson Reeder, and Jordan Watkins. Mason and Jordan were always quick to read and offer feedback on chapters of this work. There were others that read and commented on drafts of this book, including a monthly writing group at the CHL, Joe and Kay Darowski, Matthew Godfrey, Matt Grow, Scott Marianno, Spencer McBride, Mark Lyman Staker, and Richard Turley.

I am currently surrounded by wonderful scholars at the Neal A. Maxwell Institute for Religious Scholarship at Brigham Young University, who have generously read and commented on portions of this manuscript. My thanks to D. Morgan Davis, Spencer Fluhman, Deidre Green, Carl Griffin, Brian Hauglid, Kristian Heal, Janiece Johnson, and Catherine Gines Taylor.

Other scholars who have commented on chapters or complete drafts of this book, shared sources, or discussed their own research into related matters include Mark Ashurst-McGee, Edward J. Blum, Adam Brasich, Eric Eliason, Jessie Embry, Lawrence Foster, Trevan Hatch, Michael Hubbard MacKay, Joseph Spencer, Jonathan Stapley, and John Turner. Jenny Webb edited the manuscript and offered many suggestions that improved my analysis. At the Maxwell Institute, I have had excellent research assistants who were essential for the completion of this project: Liel Maala, Jamie Mortensen, and Jenessa Lynn Soutas.

I owe a particularly monumental debt of gratitude to my parents, Michael and Carol Blythe. I fondly remember my father introducing me to many of these ideas long before I had ever heard of Mormonism. This volume is the product of over a decade of research and writing, during which my parents have been a constant source of encouragement and support as I faced the cold uncertainties of modern academia. This is doubly true of my wife, Christine, who has shared in the struggles and joys of this journey. She has listened to my ideas, read drafts, and debated theories ad nauseum. Thank you.

Introduction: Vernacular Religion and Mormon Apocalypticism

A terrible revolution will take place in the land of America, such as has never been seen before; for the land will be literally left without a supreme government. And every species of wickedness will run rampant. Father will be against son, and son against father, mother against daughter, and daughter against mother. The most terrible scenes of murder and bloodshed and rapine that have ever been looked upon will take place. Peace will be taken from the earth and there will be no peace only in the Rocky Mountains.

—A prophecy ascribed to Joseph Smith[1]

I was next in the City of Baltimore and in front of the square whare [*sic*] the Monument of 1812 Stands, in front of St. Charles and other Hotels I saw the Dead piled up so high as to fill the square. I saw Mothers Cut the throats of their own Children for the sake of their blood, which they drank from their veins, to quench their thirst and then lie down and die. The waters of the Chesapeake and of the City were so stagnant and such a stench arose from them on account of the putrefaction of Dead bodies that the vary [*sic*] smell Caused Death and that was singular again I saw no man except they were dead, lying in the streets and vary few women, and they were Crazy mad, and in a dying condition. Ever whare [*sic*] I went I beheld the same all over the city, And it was horrible, beyond [*sic*] description to look at.

—A vision ascribed to Wilford Woodruff, Joseph F. Smith, or John Taylor[2]

Terrible Revolution. Christopher James Blythe, Oxford University Press (2020). © Oxford University Press.
DOI: 10.1093/oso/9780190080280.001.0001

The Latter-day Saints of the nineteenth century belonged to an apocalyptic tradition. Their very identity was entangled with the belief that society was headed toward cataclysmic events that would uproot the current social order in favor of a divine order that would be established in its place. These expectations were largely, although not exclusively, expressed in an American context. Latter-day Saints read in the Book of Mormon how God had led the way for European immigration in the New World. They praised the Constitution and revered the Founding Fathers. Their religion was one of the means by which these early Americans expressed their patriotism, and yet, by the end of the church's first decade, the nature of their citizenship became complicated. The Saints came to see the federal government as oppressive and tyrannical—a view that was only strengthened as tensions mounted throughout the century. Embattled, the Saints opposed their persecutors through an outpouring of apocalyptic commentary, which they produced through scriptural exegesis, as well as fresh prophecies, visions, and dreams. A wealth of oral and written apocalyptic texts emerged, each foretelling divine deliverance by way of plagues, natural disasters, foreign invasions, American Indian raids, slave uprisings, or civil war unleashed on American cities and American people. For the Saints, these violent images promised an end to their oppression. From the nation's fall, the Kingdom of God would rise to power while defending the original ideals of the republic.

The Church of Christ, later renamed the Church of Jesus Christ of Latter-day Saints, was a highly organized new religious movement. The complexity of its hierarchy and local leadership grew with each passing year. From its founding, Joseph Smith served as the institution's Prophet, Seer, and Revelator, and more ranks and officers were gradually added until the church was led by a First Presidency consisting of the prophet-president and two counselors, twelve apostles, a high council, bishops, presiding elders, and various other authorities. The priesthood itself—which Smith stated had been bestowed by angelic ministration—consisted of two major tiers, the Aaronic and Melchizedek priesthoods, which were subdivided into different offices. The priesthood office that a man held depended on the responsibilities he held within the church. On one hand, the church had a non-professional clergy and all men could be called to serve in one position or another for a time; on the other, the faith clearly had its elites. In the nineteenth century, those who served as leaders often continued in leadership the remainder of their lives, as was almost always the case with the highest authorities.[3]

In contrast to this explicit hierarchical structure, apocalypticism was a communal project not confined to any one segment of the Mormon body. End times auguries were reported both by "ordinary" men and women without ecclesiastical station as well as members of the hierarchy. Not surprisingly, the laity took church leaders' apocalyptic commentary seriously, but leaders could also take seriously the visions of their flock. So long as the church existed in tension with both the state and the broader American culture, then the laity's production and circulation of apocalypticism were beneficial. Conjuring images of divine justice was a useful tool of resistance that strengthened a separatist identity. As long as defiance was a key strategy of their public relations, church leaders had little incentive to interfere with the Saints' vibrant expressions of apocalypticism. When the hierarchy sought to lessen the tensions between themselves and the American political and cultural powers, however, visions of a violent end to the nation became a liability. At such times, apocalypticism within Mormonism was strictly regulated to prevent it from undermining the institutional agenda of accommodation.

This book is about how these two sets of relationships between the church and the state and between the Latter-day Saint hierarchy and the laity have informed Mormon history. It examines how through the nineteenth and early twentieth centuries the hierarchy's regulation of or non-interference with apocalypticism impacted the tradition's relationship with the United States. The book also addresses how a sense of "official" and "unofficial" versions of the faith developed out of the strict regulation of apocalypticism that occurred at the turn of the century. This distinction has been crucial in fostering a dominant suspicion for all expressions of the faith that do not explicitly originate with the church's hierarchy.

Apocalypticism

Scholars have used a variety of terms in their study of end of the world beliefs. I employ "apocalypticism" in part as an allusion to the rich Jewish–Christian literary tradition of the Apocalypse (e.g., Daniel, Revelation). This literary form, as characterized by John J. Collins, "involves a narrative framework that describes the manner of revelation. The main means of revelation are visions and otherworldly journeys, supplemented by discourse or dialogue and occasionally by a heavenly book. The constant element is the presence of an angel who interprets the vision or serves as a guide on the otherworldly journey."[4] These apocalyptic writings suggest that "human life is bounded in the present by the supernatural world of angels and demons and in the future by the inevitability of a final judgment."[5] While Mormons did not use the language of "apocalypse" to describe their dreams and visions, their end times revelations often fit the genre. Thus, the literary form of apocalyptic is a useful means through which to view Mormon writings on the last days because it helps us to see how content from disparate sources and divergent social contexts are not only thematically related, but also evolutionarily connected. Utilizing this terminology thus allows us to trace the larger historical contours at work in the Mormon apocalyptic impulse.

For the purposes of this volume, apocalypticism is synonymous with what Religious Studies scholar Catherine Wessinger refers to as *catastrophic millennialism*, in which

> there is belief in an imminent and catastrophic transition to the millennial kingdom. Catastrophic millennialism involves a pessimistic view of human nature and society. Humans are regarded as being so evil and corrupt that the old order has to be destroyed violently to make way for the perfect millennial kingdom. Catastrophic millennialism involves a radically dualistic worldview. Reality is seen as involving the opposition of good versus evil, and this easily translates into an "us versus them" outlook.[6]

My use of apocalypticism is not meant as a corrective to historian Grant Underwood's rendering of Mormonism's eschatology as millenarian. Underwood influentially placed the conversation in terms of Christian theology; however, my hope is to avoid the now well-trod discussion as to how well the Latter-day Saint tradition fits post-millennial or pre-millennial/millenarian models. The astute reader will find elements of both views in the material presented here. The Saints understood they had a responsibility to prepare the world for the millennium—that at some level God awaited their successful efforts to spread the Gospel and build Zion—but the emphasis was on God's impending deliverance from their enemies. It was only with the Second Coming that the full utopian implications of the millennium could be enacted. This book focuses on the Latter-day Saint anticipation of what would happen before the millennium begins, specifically on the destructions that would pave the way for the promised reversal of powers.

Vernacular Religion and Mormon Studies: Methodology

It is frequently claimed that the Latter-day Saint tradition does not possess a theology, at least not a systematic theology. In its place, the church's construction of history—its mythologies of a sacred past—defined official Latter-day Saint belief. Historian Kathleen Flake has credited Smith's success to his use of narrative "to challenge the Christian tradition in ways not possible through discursive debate or speculative theology."[7] Unlike other Christian leaders of the time who exchanged "creedal statement and dogmatic restatement" in order to define their communities, Joseph Smith "wrote stories."[8] A key premise of this study is that Mormon narrative theology was crafted and spread not through hierarchical voices alone, but also through missionaries, regional leaders, and lay women and men. Grant Underwood cautioned that the Book of Mormon and by extrapolation other Mormon scripture cannot necessarily "be used as evidence of early Mormon belief." The scholar must instead look to the "crucial mediating link between the written text and the actual life and teaching of the church—interpretation."[9] In practice, this meant that Underwood looked to the words of a theologian class of Latter-day Saint characterized by apostles like Parley P. Pratt, Orson Pratt, or John Taylor. Building on Underwood's suggestion, I have selected a broader range of interpreters including recognized exegetes, those whose ideas diverged into the realm of heterodoxy, as well as those who only shared their ideas privately in domestic settings.

Latter-day Saint historiography is weighted heavily toward narratives centering on the direction of the church and the lives and views of its most elite members. Scholars have focused on leaders' presentations of belief and doctrine, rather than the imagination of the laity; official ritual, rather than lived practice; and orthodoxy, rather than heresy. Such historiographical privileging of elites has been observable in the broader study of American religion as well, although with the rise of lived religion, historians have made good progress in correcting it.[10] This has not been the case, however, in the study of the Mormon past where very few have attempted to tell the tradition's history while emphasizing the lived religion of the Mormon people.[11] Of course, if historians have shown a preference for elites, folklorists have focused on the stories of the church's laity.

Mormon Studies scholars have largely overlooked this material, rarely engaging with even well-respected scholars of Latter-day Saint folklore Hector Lee, William Wilson, or Austin and Alta Fife.[12] Historians have made some contributions to our understanding of the birth and development of Mormon legends, although they have tended to, in the words of Tom Mould and Eric A. Eliason, made their "primary objective to distinguish fact from fiction."[13] In contrast, folklorists prefer cultural analysis to debunking. William Wilson explained that the "narratives shared by members of a like-minded group serve as a mirror for culture, as a reflector of what members of the group consider most important. Thus the stories we Latter-day Saints tell provide valuable insights into our hopes, fears, dreams, and anxieties."[14] In 2007, Wilson gave the thirteenth annual Leonard J. Arrington Lecture Series in Mormon Studies and was the first nonhistorian to do so. At that time, he pleaded for the inclusion of folklore in the newly minted Mormon Studies program at Utah State University where the lecture was held: "If we want to understand Mormon hearts and minds . . . we must know their stories."[15] As noted previously, there has been a narrative turn in Mormon Studies that should not be ignored. Yet, the sophisticated studies of narrative that scholars like Kathleen Flake or Samuel M. Brown have brought to Joseph Smith's theology and institutional history-making have rarely been extended to the stories of the laity.[16] Perhaps Jared Farmer's historical study of cultural geography has made the greatest strides in writing history that emphasizes story and the broad swath of Latter-day Saint people.[17]

At the same time that folklorists have led the way in the study of the everyday Latter-day Saint, there has been a major push in the field of folklore to avoid speaking of the "folk" in distinction from the elite (i.e., the well-educated, the wealthy, the refined). Folklorist Alan Dundes described this outmoded definition of the folk as "a group of people who constituted the lower stratum, the so-called *vulgus in populo*—in contrast with the upper stratum or elite of that society."[18] In distinction, folklorists now conceive the object of their study—the folk—as any group that shares a culture. Leonard Primiano has applied this concern regarding elitism to the subject of religious folklife, calling for an end to terminology such as "folk religion," "popular religion," or "unofficial religion," which imply a "two-tiered model with 'official' religion."[19] The implication of this two-tiered model is that "religion somewhere exists as a pure element which is in some way transformed, even contaminated, by its exposure to human communities."[20] In contrast, Primiano defines his preferred term, vernacular religion, as "religion as it is lived: as human beings encounter, understand, interpret, and practice it. Since religion inherently involves interpretation, it is impossible for the religion of an individual not to be vernacular."[21] The same methodological concerns would underlie the move from "popular religion" to "lived religion" among American religious historians.

Even before historian David D. Hall became an advocate for "lived religion," his brilliant *Worlds of Wonder, Days of Judgment* modeled how to conceive of such a study. One of his crucial methodological points was that it would be a mistake to assume "'popular religion' refers only to the ways in which lay men and women broke with what the clergy said."[22] By imagining a constant struggle between hierarchical voices and lay ones, scholars are prone to miss the less exceptional expressions of lay religion that seek to reproduce, translate, and localize the faith to their own experiences. As we will see, dissent and protest are key to the story of Mormon apocalypticism, but it is far from the most pronounced response to hierarchical voices. A key point shared by both Hall and Primiano is that clergy and laity are dependent on interpretation by which to practice their faith. A member of the clergy does not practice the official religion—they, too, must interpret it for their own uses.

So, what then is the rationale behind recognizing a distinction, albeit complex and permeable, between laity and leadership in the context of this project? There are historical trajectories that are only made visible through such a distinction. By taking the hierarchies of Latter-day Saint (LDS) culture as a structure worthy of analysis, we can see within the hierarchy the development of processes of regulation, as well as the effects of such regulation within the general populace. It is this regulation that creates the contrast between "unofficial" and "official" versions of a tradition. This is the case regardless of how successful such regulation efforts might be.

Neither advocates for vernacular religion nor of lived religion mean to suggest that scholars should overlook an institution's role in the making of an "official religion." The construction of orthodox belief and practice is one of the key functions of institution, after all. However, from a scholarly perspective, there is not a single authentic version of a faith to which the institution has unique or exclusive access.

While I disavow any scholarly notion of a singular authentic version of a religion, there is a master narrative from which the apocalypticists in my study draw. Joseph Smith and other early members of the hierarchy established a master narrative that was then replicated on the ground by lay members, who localized their apocalyptic expectations. The vernacular narrative tradition is dependent on Mormonism's broader master narrative. Scripture and other official representations—such as that articulated by the founding prophet Joseph Smith—offered ideas, frames, images, motifs, and stories that provided a blueprint for the reproduction of this discourse on the ground and in the Latter-day Saint imagination. As the reader will discover, this assertion holds true both when the hierarchy interprets these narratives as well as when the laity does so. Significantly, a consensus in Mormon thought regarding how these ideas were received never emerged. Apocalypticism remained a vibrant force within Mormonism as it went through transitions both small and large. And wherever it appeared, Mormon apocalypticism was always contested, pluralistic, and dynamic.

This is a study of how apocalypticism developed in conversation with the U.S. government. To be sure, Latter-day Saints believed that no nation would escape the destructions of the last days. Yet, I do not address in any real depth the apocalyptic events that missionaries anticipated would occur in foreign lands, and I make only passing references to the place of Palestine, Russia, or Great Britain for Latter-day Saint ideas of the apocalypse. Wherever Latter-day Saints imported their beliefs, especially in the nineteenth century, they have sought to incorporate prophecy. I hope other scholars will chart the development of Mormon apocalyptic on the international stage.

Chapter Organization

This volume begins in the first chapter with a presentation of the tradition's apocalyptic master narrative from the appearance of an angel in Joseph Smith's bedroom in September 1823, to Smith's institution of a theocratic legislature that would govern the world in the coming millennium. Over this twenty-year period, a robust vision of the last days took shape. This vision included the gathering of the righteous to safety before the coming of end times destructions, the establishment of the New Jerusalem in Missouri, warfare in the United States (both among citizens and against invading armies), the establishment of the Kingdom of God, and the return of Jesus Christ. I also examine how Latter-day Saints who were not part of the hierarchy responded to this narrative and thereby contributed to the apocalyptic worldview.

The second chapter considers the significance of martyrology for Mormon apocalypticism. The narrative continues with the assassinations of Joseph Smith and Hyrum Smith in 1844, an event that would color Mormon feelings for and reaction to the United States for the next several decades. With this act, the Saints came to believe that the nation had sealed its doom. John the Revelator's image of martyrs pleading for God to avenge their murders became a prominent element in Mormon apocalypticism. The Mormons fled Nauvoo and eventually the United States itself in order to distance themselves from their persecutors but also to escape the very land that had been primed for judgment. Before departing, through verbal, written, and ritualized means, the Saints cursed those complicit in their persecution, including various politicians and an uncaring populace. The chapter considers how the elements of martyrology and cursing play out in Mormon apocalypticism.

Chapter 3 documents how Latter-day Saints in the late 1840s and 1850s found an interpretive lens available in the faith's master narrative that they could then deploy to make sense of the lands they colonized in the American West. Drawing on the apocalyptic geography of the Bible, the Saints came to believe they resided in the "wilderness" of the Book of Revelation where they would be protected from persecution. They recognized the region's peaks as the mountain setting for Isaiah's prophecies of a last days temple and an ensign to the nations. This chapter continues—abandoning a strict chronology—to examine how in the late nineteenth century Canada and Mexico would also be incorporated into the era's apocalyptic geography.

Chapter 4 focuses on the Utah territorial period—a time marked by hostility between the Saints and the federal government. Throughout the latter half of the nineteenth century, Mormon visionaries deployed prophecies of Gentile invasions on the Saints, as well as judgments on the major cities of the nation. The assurance that God would intervene against their enemies' aggressions offered catharsis to the anxieties brought on by the U.S. Army's occupation of Utah during the 1850s, the Civil War, and federal enforcement of anti-polygamy laws—what was known as "the raid." While it was during the territorial period that many of the most influential vernacular apocalyptic prophecies were written down, it was also during this period that Joseph Smith's prophecy of a future American civil war circulated widely in Mormon and non-Mormon circles. As would be expected, the apocalyptic prospered as tensions festered between Mormons and the federal government.

The fifth chapter examines the impact of Americanization on apocalypticism. The relationship of the Church of the Latter-day Saints with the federal government changed radically when Utah obtained statehood in 1896. Church leaders had pursued national respectability since the First Presidency issued the Manifesto six years earlier. With such a drastic transition, the reining in of dissenting voices became essential. It was in this era, I argue, that church leaders opposed prominent themes in vernacular apocalypticism in an effort to engender conformity to the Americanizing project within Mormonism. Apocalyptic themes that were embraced in the 1880s were now seen as a threat. Instead of disavowing the apocalyptic master narrative or their own statements from years past, church leaders criticized the same themes when they appeared in vernacular prophecy among the laity. New institutional discouragement from sharing dramatic visions, dreams, and other manifestations also limited the influence of apocalypticists.

Chapter 6 documents the fracturing of end-of-the-world belief in the twentieth century. Church leaders re-envisioned apocalypticism as a "moderate millenarianism," to borrow a term from Grant Underwood. At the same time, Mormon fundamentalists—deemed heretics by many church leaders—deployed apocalypticism to challenge Americanization, adding the church's own apostasy as a distinctive part of their last days chronology. Finally, what I describe as radical apocalypticism continued to find resonance with a contingent of committed Latter-day Saints. This chapter wrestles with how this final group has been able to negotiate their apocalyptic sentiments and Latter-day Saint affiliation even in the face of continual criticism. Most importantly, it is in this chapter that I demonstrate how apocalyptic ideas of any variety continued to be perpetuated in private and family circles.

A Note on Sources and Voices

My goal has been to write a history that makes use of insights from both folklore and religious studies; however, my research was largely conducted through traditional archival work. This volume contains references to hundreds of manuscripts, including newspapers, journals, memoirs, correspondence, pamphlets, broadsheets, and folklore items. Over the past three years, as a documentary editor for the Joseph Smith Papers, I have been uniquely positioned to benefit from the holdings of the Church History Library of the Church of Jesus Christ of Latter-day Saints and to immerse myself in nineteenth-century records. My interest in the spiritual narratives of Latter-day Saints began many years before that—long before I envisioned this volume. Over the past two decades, I have spent substantial time at the major archives of Mormon Studies: the Church History Library in Salt Lake City, the Community of Christ Library and Archives in Independence, Missouri, and the special collections at Brigham Young University, Utah State University, and University of Utah. My time at these archives has centered around collecting the visions and spiritual manifestations that Latter-day Saints circulated among each other or recorded in their own private records.

One of my methodological priorities—a priority shared by modern folklorists—has been to allow my subjects to speak for themselves. While I have not been averse to paraphrasing when necessary, my desire has been to present personal narratives in the words of those who spoke or wrote them. Admittedly, some readers will find the length of certain quotations distracting. I have aimed to include only what is salient to the discussion; however, in some cases, I have used longer quotations so as not to obscure their voices.

My goal has been to present the full range of voices in the Latter-day Saint tradition. While women did not hold the same types of hierarchical positions in the church as men, they were deeply influential in private circles. They were more likely than men to possess spiritual gifts, but less likely for the content of their manifestations to be recorded and circulated among church members. I have drawn on their dreams, visions, and defenses of apocalypticism in this study, yet I have also come to realize that the most extensive apocalyptic texts were authored by men. It was not until the twentieth century that women visionaries began to author their own writings describing their visionary gifts.

Whenever possible, I have cited accessible documentary editions of primary sources. The one exception to this is with prophecy literature. Since a critical edition of Latter-day Saint apocalyptic texts has yet to be published, I quote from the manuscript sources instead of contemporary devotional collections. When citing the Joseph Smith Papers, I use the published volumes except when the sources are only available on the website of the Joseph Smith Papers. I cite Joseph Smith's revelations according to their original manuscript form in the Joseph Smith Papers and include the references in the most recent edition of the Doctrine and Covenants of the Church of Jesus Christ of Latter-day Saints in brackets. I have opted to remove crossed out words when quoting from original sources without notifying the reader. I note archaic spellings or misspellings with [*sic*] or occasionally modify the spelling with a bracket.

Segments from two chapters have appeared elsewhere. A portion from chapter 3's section entitled, "Holy War in Utah Territory," has previously appeared as "The Exorcism of Isaac Russell: Diabolism and Nineteenth-century Mormon Identity Formation" in the *Journal of Religion*.[23] A portion of chapter 5 appeared as "The One Mighty and Strong(s): Messianism and the Rise of Mormon Fundamentalism" in *The Persistence of Polygamy: Fundamentalist Mormon Polygamy from 1890 to the Present*.[24]

Portions of this book have appeared in print previously. A section in chapter four entitled, "Holy War in Utah Territory," was developed from a portion of an article, "The Exorcism of Isaac Russell: Diabolism and Nineteenth-Century Mormon Identity Formation" that appeared in the *Journal of Religion*. A section in chapter five entitled, "A Twentieth-Century Hierarchical Response to Messianic Prophecy," was developed from "The One Mighty and Strong(s): Messianism and the Rise of Mormon Fundamentalism" that was published in *The Persistence of Polygamy*, Vol. 3.

1
The Apocalyptic Tradition in Early Mormonism

> Ye hear of wars in far Countries & you say in your hearts there will soon be great wars in far Countries but ye know not the hearts of they in your own Land.
>
> —Joseph Smith, Revelation[1]

On the night of September 21, 1823, in Palmyra, New York, an angel appeared in the bedroom of a 17-year-old Joseph Smith (see Figure 1.1). Smith was in prayer when he noticed an otherworldly light begin to brighten the room until it "was lighter than at noonday when immediately a personage appeared at my bedside standing in the air for his feet did not touch the floor."[2] When Smith first looked at the angel, he was frightened but then felt a sense of calm as the being spoke. "He called me by name and said unto me that he was a messenger sent from the presence of God to me and that his name was Nephi [*sic*—Moroni]. That God had a work for me to do."[3] According to a secondhand account, Moroni explained that this work had to do with "the great preparatory work for the second coming of the Messiah, [which] was speedily to commence; that the time was at hand for the gospel, in its fulness, to be preached in power unto all nations; that a people might be prepared with faith and righteousness, for the Millennial reign of universal peace and joy."[4] Moroni, who in life was a fifth-century proto-Amerindian prophet, told Smith about a record engraved on gold plates interred near the Smith family's home. The record included the story of the "former inhabitants of this continent, and the source from whence they sprang." Its words contained "the fulness of the everlasting Gospel." Moroni told Smith that when he retrieved these gold plates, he would also find spectacles that would enable him to translate the record into English.

Terrible Revolution. Christopher James Blythe, Oxford University Press (2020). © Oxford University Press.
DOI: 10.1093/oso/9780190080280.001.0001

Figure 1.1 Lewis A. Ramsay, "Visit of the Angel Moroni." Originally included in William A. Morton, *From Plowboy to Prophet: Being a Short History of Joseph Smith, for Children* (Salt Lake City, UT: Deseret Book, 1912). Courtesy of Everett Historical, Shutterstock.

Still in his bedroom, the angel spent the remainder of the vision reciting passages of scripture concerning the last days. Sometimes Moroni's versions included "a little variation from the way it reads in our [King James] Bibles," as was the case with his recitation of Malachi 4. He started with identical phrasing: "For behold the day cometh that shall burn as an oven, and all the proud yea and all that do wickedly shall burn as stubble, for they that cometh shall burn them saith the Lord of hosts, that it shall leave them neither root nor branch." Continuing, Moroni amplified the prophecy of Elijah's return to include his bestowal of priesthood. "Behold I will reveal unto you the Priesthood, by the hand of Elijah the prophet before the coming of the great and dreadful day of the Lord. . . . And he shall plant in the hearts of the Children the promises made to the fathers, and the hearts of the children shall turn to their fathers, if it were not so, the whole earth would be utterly wasted at his coming."[5]

Moroni continued to recite apocalyptic verses, Isaiah 11, Acts 3:22–23, and then the final five verses of Joel 2:

> And it shall come to pass afterward, that I will pour out my spirit upon all flesh; and your sons and your daughters shall prophesy, your old men shall dream dreams, your young men shall see visions: And also upon the servants and upon the handmaids in those days will I pour out my spirit. And I will shew wonders in the heavens and in the earth, blood, and fire, and pillars of smoke. The sun shall be turned into darkness, and the moon into blood, before the great and the terrible day of the Lord come. And it shall come to pass, that whosoever shall call on the name of the Lord shall be delivered: for in mount Zion and in Jerusalem shall be deliverance, as the Lord hath said, and in the remnant whom the Lord shall call.[6]

After reciting and expounding on these and other verses, Moroni ascended through "a conduit [that] open[ed] right up into heaven . . . and the room was left as it had been before this heavenly light had made its appearance."[7] The angel appeared twice more that night to recite these same verses and impart additional instructions. On his second visit, Moroni told the teenage visionary about "great judgments which were coming upon the earth, with great desolations by famine, sword, and pestilence, and that these grievous judgments would come on the earth in this generation." After the third appearance, Smith heard the rooster crow and realized "our interviews must have occupied the whole of that night."[8] The next day Smith saw the angel again, as well as a vision that would lead him to the location where Moroni had deposited the record 1,400 years before. For four years, Joseph Smith returned to this spot annually until in September 1827 the angel permitted him to recover the plates and begin translating.[9]

Although Smith would sometimes relate an earlier theophany, which has come to be known as his "first vision," most frequently it was this experience with Moroni through which he explained the origins of his prophetic gift. The scene highlights both Mormonism's peculiar idea of Christian primitivism, in which ancient Christianity could be restored through the aid of additional scripture and new revelation, as well as the tradition's rich apocalypticism. When Smith wrote about this angelic visitation in 1838, he noted that the angel stated the Book of Mormon contained the "everlasting Gospel."[10] The phrase, which appears only once in the Bible, linked Smith's interactions with Moroni to John the Revelator's description of an angel flying through the "midst of heaven, having the everlasting gospel to preach unto them that dwell on the earth, and to every nation, and kindred, and tongue, and people."[11] Smith likely made this connection years before he recorded this account in 1838, since an 1832 revelation declared that this angel had already made its flight.[12]

Joseph Smith was not the only visionary among those who would become Mormons. On the same night that he finally obtained the gold plates, future converts in New York watched a heavenly army march through the sky. Heber C. Kimball recalled, "We could see distinctly the muskets, bayonets and knapsacks of the men, who wore caps and feathers like those used by American soldiers in the last war with Britain; and also their officers with their swords and equipage, and heard the clashing and jingling of their implements of war, and could discover the form and features of the men." The group recognized the start of a battle not only from the visual but also because "we could distinctly hear the report of the arms and the rush." They continued to observe the skies for hours until the soldiers disappeared. Vilate Kimball was frightened by the display. Turning to the elderly John Young, she asked, "What does all this mean?" He responded "in a lively pleased manner, 'why, its one of the signs of the coming of the Son of Man.' "[13] In another New York village, John's son and daughter-in-law, Brigham and Miriam Young, also watched the heavenly spectacle.[14] Only a few years later, the Church of Christ would bring together the Kimballs, Youngs, and many other apocalyptically minded Christians. While it might be argued that Smith's voice was particularly influential in establishing the master narrative of this new apocalyptic community, there were always an abundance of voices experiencing and responding to that master narrative on their own terms.

This chapter examines the development of the master narrative of Latter-day Saint apocalypticism that took shape during Joseph Smith's lifetime. Readers will learn about the major eschatological themes detailed in the Book of Mormon and other early Latter-day Saint texts. The chapter then concludes with a discussion regarding how Joseph Smith and other early church leaders responded to accounts like the one just described. I argue that while Smith established a policy that only he could receive authoritative revelations for the church as a body, he simultaneously facilitated the communal project of apocalypticism among his disciples.

The Book of Mormon and American Apocalypse

The Book of Mormon is an apocalyptic text, continually drawing on themes of destruction and renewal. The text opens in Jerusalem with Lehi, an Israelite prophet, and his vision of the coming Babylonian invasion. More precisely, following a pattern established in Isaiah, Ezekiel, and Revelation, a divine messenger handed Lehi a book and Lehi "read concerning Jerusalem—that it should be destroyed, and the inhabitants thereof; many should perish by the sword, and many should be carried away captive into Babylon."[15] Finding few willing to heed his warning, Lehi abandoned his wealth in the city and led his family into the wilderness. One of his sons, Nephi, from whose perspective the first two books of the Book of Mormon are narrated, came to believe his father's teachings. When praying about his father's dreams, he had his own vision of the future—a vision that served to provide readers with an overview of the major events within the text as well as the prophecies that Book of Mormon prophets expected to occur in the future after the text's completion. Interestingly, his vision also followed the conventions of apocalyptic literature, including its most telling feature: the presence of an angelic guide.[16]

After a vision of Jesus's incarnation and ministry in Palestine, Nephi was shown a future with his and his brothers' descendants in the "land of promise." For generations, they "gathered together to battle, one against the other; and I beheld wars, and rumors of wars, and great slaughters with the sword among my people."[17] Nephi witnessed the coming of future destructions, including cities destroyed by sinking, fire, and earthquake. In the wake of these calamities, a mist of darkness that Nephi had seen "on the face of the land of promise" lifted and Jesus descended from the heavens to appear before the survivors.[18] Nephi saw that Jesus called twelve disciples, the New World equivalents of the Old World apostles. For three generations after this event, the people lived peacefully, "pass[ing] away in righteousness."[19] While, as literary scholar Grant Hardy has noted, the Second Coming and millennium are only directly referenced four times in the Book of Mormon, the similarities between Christ's appearance in Bountiful and expectations for the Parousia are unmistakable.[20]

Nephi witnessed the return of war after a period of peace, and watched the demise of his offspring and the spiritual decline of his brothers' descendants. I will return to this pivotal moment, what literary scholar Jared Hickman refers to as the Book of Mormon's "Amerindian apocalypse."[21] At this point, Nephi was briefly left waiting to know what would happen to his brother's posterity as his vision turned to "the nations and kingdoms of the Gentiles," where he saw the "formation of a great church . . . most abominable above all other churches, which slayeth the saints of God, yea, and tortureth them and bindeth them down."[22] He saw that this apostate body was founded by the devil and referred to it as "the great and abominable church." Its "desires" included the pursuit of wealth and "the praise of the world." It would be responsible for the persecution of the true Saints.[23] The great and abominable church would also remove "many plain and precious things" from the Bible.[24] This scene was one of the earliest Mormon representations of the great apostasy, a term that Latter-day Saints used to describe the era after the death of the apostles when Christianity became corrupted.

At this point in Nephi's vision, it becomes clear that his view of the future is in direct conversation with that of John the Revelator.[25] At one point, he called the great and abominable church the "whore," pointing readers to Revelation's "Whore of Babylon," a figure that is seen riding the beast that is sometimes identified as the Antichrist. Protestant commentators had long seen the beast and sometimes the whore as apostate Roman Catholicism. Many early Mormons understood the whore of Babylon and the great and abominable church as synonymous, identifying them with Roman Catholicism and its Protestant offspring.[26] Some interpreted the beast's number—"666"—as a representation of the 666 denominations they believed emerged from the original apostasy.[27] Here right in the initial chapters of the Book of Mormon was the corruption of primitive Christianity.

Nephi's vision turned from the apostasy to the Gentile (i.e., European) discovery of the New World initiated by an unnamed man inspired to go "forth upon the many waters."[28] Others followed him and "went forth out of captivity, upon the many waters."[29] Mormons would come to see this description as a prophecy of Christopher Columbus's voyage and the eventual arrival of the Puritans. In a seeming allusion to the Revolutionary War, Nephi saw that later "their mother Gentiles were gathered together upon the waters, and upon the land also, to battle against them."[30] The settlers in the promised land "were delivered by the power of God out of the hands of all other nations."[31] Crucial to Mormonism's conception of the United States was this understanding that the earliest Americans were gathered by God and inspired in the creation of the republic. A later revelation noted that God "established the constitution of this Land by the hands of wise men whom I raised up unto this very purpose and redeemed the Land by the shedding of blood."[32] Mormons understood this narrative in terms that cast the United States as a special land central to the tradition's restoration project: the religious freedom available in the United States—limited as it might have been in practice—had made it possible for God to restore his church.

Nephi's vision introduced the idea of the Americas as "a land of promise" in the vein of ancient Canaan. The Book of Mormon revealed more of the secret history of this "choice land," hidden from the rest of the world save those "brought by the hand of the Lord."[33] At least five civilizations emerged from small groups that found their way to its coasts—the Jaredites, the Mulekites, the Nephites, the Lamanites, and in the future, the Gentiles. According to the Book of Mormon, each nation resided on the Promised Land under the condition of righteousness. If they kept the commandments, "they would prosper on the face of this land."[34] If they did not, they would be "swept off."[35] The Book of Mormon depicted the fulfillment of this promise in several societal collapses—the destruction of the Jaredites through warfare around 600 BCE, the destruction of the wicked via natural disasters at the death of Jesus, and the Lamanite slaughter of the Nephites around 400 CE (see Figures 1.2 and 1.3). These past destructions served as a warning for what would occur in the last days among the Gentiles.

Despite the grave penalties for transgression that the inhabitants of the Promised Land faced, it was also here that the prophesied New Jerusalem would be built. The Book of Mormon distinguished between two last days Jerusalems. The original Jerusalem in Palestine would be "built up again, a holy city unto the Lord," but was not the New Jerusalem of Revelation, because "it had been in a time of old."[36] The New World capital would be a New Jerusalem, identified as such in the same way New England and New Hampshire were named after their Old World counterparts. It would be "a land of peace[,] a City of refuge[,] a place of safety for the saints of The most high God."[37] Latter-day Saints also used the term Zion to describe this American last days city—a term they would come to use more broadly to refer to "all N[orth & S[outh] America" as well as "any place where the Saints gather."[38]

Figure 1.2 "Destruction of Zarahemla," illustration from George Reynold's *Story of the Book of Mormon* (1888). This image depicts the Book of Mormon's account of destructions in the Americas following the crucifixion of Jesus Christ.

Figure 1.3 Arnold Friberg, *Mormon Bids Farewell to a Once Great Nation.* © By Intellectual Reserve, Inc. One of the concluding passages in the Book of Mormon depicts the prophet Mormon reflecting on the collapse of the Nephite civilization.

Many Americans shared the Saints' providential interpretation of the United States and the larger continent.[39] Even the Book of Mormon's positioning of the biblical apocalypse onto New World geography was not exceptional. America had a long history of apocalypticists dating back to its European discovery. On April 6, 1503, Christopher Columbus experienced a vision in which a disembodied voice declared that God "gave you the keys to the gates of the Ocean which were held with such great chains."[40] He would later describe his journeys in eschatological terms. "Of the New Heaven and Earth which Our Lord has made, and as St. John writes in the Apocalypse, after had told of it by the mouth of Isaiah, He made me the messenger for it and showed me where to find it."[41] Columbus believed the New World would provide the necessary wealth for the conquering of the Holy Land, which was then under Muslim rule, and the restoration of Jerusalem in fulfillment of prophecy.[42]

Although scholars today debate whether the first generation of Puritans were motivated by their apocalyptic pretensions to migrate to the New World, there is no question that later generations understood their New World experience in this vein. Puritan divines compared their journey across the ocean to the Israelites' flight from the Egyptians across the Red Sea. Some saw in their migration the fulfillment of John's vision of the woman—a symbol of the church—who would flee into the wilderness where she would find refuge from a pursuing dragon identified as the devil.[43] As Cotton Mather noted, "[T]is thought by Some, that *America* might be intended, as a Place where the Worshippers of the Glorious JESUS, may be Sheltered, while fearful Things are doing in the *European* World."[44]

Most commentators believed, like Columbus, that the New Jerusalem referred to the restoration of Jerusalem in Palestine, and that the event would correspond with the national conversion of the Jewish people.[45] Yet, there were also those who hoped the millennial capital would be in New England. In an exchange between William Twiss and Joseph Mede, Twiss recounted his having "wondered in my thoughts at the providence of God concerning that world; not discovered till this Old World of ours is almost at an end. . . . Sometimes I have had such thoughts, Why may not that be the place of the New Jerusalem?"[46] In response, Mede insisted the Americas were the habitation of the devil, who had fled there after the Christianization of Europe.[47] Twiss conceded his error, although some were not so easily persuaded. Numerous Puritan divines argued against Mede's dismissal of the New World as Gog and Magog, identified as the residence of the final enemies of the

New Jerusalem described in prophecy.[48] In 1697, Samuel Sewall published a tract referencing various proofs, including scripture, that the New Jerusalem would be established in New Spain. Sewall connected his views with the proposition that Native Americans had descended from ancient Israel as had been laid out in two books published in 1650 written by Menasseh Ben-Israel and Thomas Thorowgood, respectively.[49]

The idea of America's apocalyptic significance continued into the rise of Evangelicalism. Jonathan Edwards, a proponent of post-millennialist thought, argued that the "great work of God" leading to the conversion of the world was imminent and that "there are many things that make it probable that this work will begin in America." He interpreted a verse in Isaiah, "Surely the Isles will wait for me, and the ships of Tarshish first, to bring my sons from far," as a reference to the coming of the gospel to the Americas.[50] He believed there was significance in the timing of European contact: "about the time of the Reformation, or but little before: which Reformation was the first thing that God did towards the glorious renovation of the world." Echoing Columbus, he argued that the Old World would not only benefit from American wealth and material goods but that it was also from the Americas that they would receive "religion in its most glorious state." In short, from the western hemisphere, "God presently goes about doing some great thing to make way for the introduction of the church's latter-day glory, that is to have its first seat in, and is to take its rise from that new world."[51]

The Revolutionary War was a further step in America's providential history. Historian Ernest Lee Tuveson has famously described the new republic's self-perception as a "redeemer nation."[52] Guyatt has cautioned that while this interpretation of American destiny was widespread, it did not always express itself in an apocalyptic style.[53] Historian Nathan O. Hatch has coined the term "civil millennialism" to describe "a subtle but profound shift in emphasis [from] the religious values that traditionally defined the ultimate goal of apocalyptic hope—the conversion of all nations to Christianity—became diluted with, and often subordinate to, the commitment to America as a new seat of liberty."[54] In other words, after the American Revolution, apocalypticism in the United States was less marked, but the new republic's identity—its drive to influence the world toward democracy and Western culture, even its residual anti-Catholicism—were genetic markers of a more pronounced apocalyptic past.

Connected to the belief that America's destiny had apocalyptic dimensions was a persistent, if not always mainstream, thread that Native Americans were ethnically Jewish. In this line of thought, the Native Americans were understood as descendants of the "lost ten tribes of Israel" who had forgotten their traditions and history. The "lost ten tribes" referred to the legendary body of Israelites who survived the eighth-century BCE Assyrian conquest of the northern kingdom of Israel and the subsequent relocation of its inhabitants.[55] According to 2 Esdras, this population traveled from their captivity into "a further country, where never mankind dwelt. That they might keep their statutes, which they never kept in their own land."[56] For centuries, Jews and Christians alike had speculated on the whereabouts of this lost people; with the discovery of America, its inhabitants became the most likely candidates. Believing Native Americans were, in fact, Jews and that Jews must convert before the Second Coming motivated Protestant conversion efforts.[57] One of the most popular and late arguments in favor of the Jewish-Indian theory, Elias Boudinot's *A Star in the West*, appeared in 1816. In Boudinot's mind, "[U]ncovering the true Hebraic identity of the Indians would lead to another kind of unveiling, namely the apocalypse of the Book of Revelation."[58] He even posited that the United States' significance might lie in its role of transporting these New World Jews back to their Palestinian homeland: "Who knows but God has raised up these United States in these latter days, for the very purpose of accomplishing his will in bringing his beloved people to their own land." America, and perhaps some nations in Europe, were particularly suited to this task because they were "a maritime people—a nation of seafaring men."[59]

Situating Mormonism within three centuries of Christian speculation on the Americas and its inhabitants demonstrates how familiar Smith's narrative was to the culture of nineteenth-century Euro-Americans. In some ways, the Book of Mormon canonizes and therefore preserves the speculation on the apocalyptic significance of America, which was already in decline in the nineteenth century. On the other hand, this positioning also highlights distinctive elements within Mormon apocalypticism. These include peculiarities like prophecies that both a New Jerusalem in the Americas and a restored Jerusalem in Palestine would be critical to the last days chronology.[60] Another key example, as historian Mark Ashurst-McGee has argued, is that Zion appears in the Book of Mormon as a distinctive national identity from that of the "Gentiles" and by extension the United States. The Book of Mormon included "elements of American nationalism, but always turned them to the service of Zion instead of the United States."[61] Perhaps what most starkly sets apart the apocalypse foreseen in the Book of Mormon from other apocalyptic expectations for the

New World is its inclusion of what literary scholar Jared Hickman has called "Amerindian apocalypse."[62]

Unlike American apocalypticism rooted in redeemer nation ideas and Anglo-Saxon triumphalism, the Amerindian apocalypse of the Book of Mormon "keyed the formation of an alternative chosen people—Mormons and Indians."[63] The Lamanites, according to the Book of Mormon, would build the New Jerusalem and the righteous Gentiles (i.e., Mormons) would only assist in this effort. The Book of Mormon promised that if the Gentiles repented and became righteous, that God would "establish my church among them, and they shall come in unto the covenant and be numbered among this the remnant of Jacob, unto whom I have given this land for their inheritance."[64] As Hickman notes, "It is not the Indians who will be gathered into the benevolent fold of white Christian America, but rather repentant white Americans who will be gathered into the American house of Israel."[65] While this reversal was spelled out in the text and would have its advocates throughout the nineteenth century, it was always the most controversial and neglected element of Mormon apocalypticism.

Another element of the Amerindian apocalypse, the Native slaughter of the American Gentiles, proved more popular in the early Mormon imagination. In the Book of Mormon text, the resurrected Christ himself prophesied that the "remnant of Jacob shall be among the Gentiles, yea, in the midst of them as a lion among the beasts of the forest, as a young lion among the flocks of sheep, who, if he go through both treadeth down and teareth in pieces, and none can deliver."[66] That Indian raids signaled God's wrath was not original to the Book of Mormon as it dated to the colonial era.[67] Mormon apocalypticism seemed to resonate with these older interpretations of Natives as the agents of divine judgment, but they were also akin to Nativist prophets among American Indians themselves. These prophets and their followers believed the divine would enable them to defeat their enemies and sometimes employed the language of apocalyptic.[68]

The Saints expected these events to develop in the near future. The apostle Parley P. Pratt contextualized Andrew Jackson's efforts to relocate Indians west of the Mississippi in his influential *A Voice of Warning*. Addressing the "Red Men of the forest," he wrote:

> The Gentiles shall not again have power over you; but you shall be gathered by them, and be built up, and again become a delightsome people, and the time has come; yea, the work has already commenced; for we have seen

> you gathering together, from all parts of our land, unto the place which God has appointed for the Gentiles to gather you; therefore lay down your weapons of war, cease to oppose the Gentiles, in the gathering of your various tribes—for the hand of your Great God is in all this; and it was all foretold by your Forefathers, ten thousand moons ago.—Therefore suffer them peaceably to fulfill this last act of kindness, as a kind of reward, for the injuries you have received from them, for the very places of their dwellings will become desolate; except such of them as are gathered and numbered with you; and you will exist in peace, upon the face of this land, from generation to generation. And your children will only know, that the Gentiles once conquered this country, and became a great nation here, as they read it in history; as a thing long since passed away, and the remembrance of it almost gone from the earth.[69]

Of course, Pratt only sympathized with the government's agenda because he believed it would bring about a Native American confederation that would be able to reclaim their rightful inheritance and ultimately bring about their own removal of non-Mormon Euro-Americans.[70] Still, Pratt's words provide a useful example of the ways in which the apocalypticism of the Book of Mormon extended beyond the themes and motifs of the narrative itself and into the sociopolitical worldview of the early Mormons themselves.

Other Israelites and Zions in the Last Days

Mormonism's master narrative revolved around lineage and civilization. The Book of Mormon established American Indians as Israelites and critical players in the apocalyptic drama. It referred to Europeans as Gentiles and only differentiated between non-Israelite Mormons and non-Mormons in terms of "believing Gentiles" and "unbelieving Gentiles." In the years after the Book of Mormon was published, Smith revealed more about the peoples of the last days, Mormon ethnic identities, and prophesied the return of other lost civilizations.

While the Book of Mormon traced the genealogies of Native Americans to a family that departed Jerusalem after the Assyrian conquest scattered the ten tribes and did not associate them with the lost body discussed in 2 Esdras, the legendary ten tribes would also play their part in Mormon apocalypticism. First, Mormons believed the ten tribes had, in fact, dispersed among many nations. Lehi's family descended from a remnant of these tribes that were not scattered but continued to reside in Jerusalem. Smith would explain how Europeans might also be descendants of this group of Israelites.[71] Yet, unlike the Native Americans who were universally descended from Israel, only those Europeans who converted to the Mormon tradition were considered Israelites. Smith assured those who were not literally descended from Israel that they were adopted into the lineage at the time of their conversion. The Holy Ghost would "purge out the old blood & make him actually of the seed of Abram."[72] Certain Mormon males were ordained as patriarchs and in charge of discerning—through laying their hands on an individual's head and pronouncing a blessing—the tribal lineage of a Latter-day Saint. In most cases, then and now, they discovered that the recipient of a patriarchal blessing descended from the tribe of Ephraim.[73] Just as identifying Native Americans as genealogically linked to Israel brought them into the apocalyptic drama, by identifying Mormons with Ephraim, they claimed "a special connection to the whole redemptive history and destiny of God's chosen people."[74] Mormons would come to see the Americas as the inheritance of Joseph, just as Palestine was the inheritance of Judah. Their kinship with Native peoples explained why, as designated descendants of Joseph through Ephraim, they shared in the destiny of America, whereas the unbelieving Gentiles would eventually be removed from the land.

Second, Mormons expected the lost ten tribes would return en masse. Smith's revelations described their epic return from the "north countries" at the Second Coming: "Their Prophets shall hear his voice & shall no longer stay themselves & they shall smite the rocks & the ice shall follow [flow] down at their presenc[e] & an high way shall be cast up in the midst of the great deep." At the end of their journey, "shall th[e]y fall down & be crowned with glory even in Zion by the hands of the Servents [*sic*] of the Lord even the children of Ephraim."[75] In 1840, Smith taught that "this earth was the largest panat [planet] that ever was made and that there has been parts taken from it several times and at the time the 10 tribes were lost there was a part taken from it and that they would all come back and be joined to it again." The resulting collision would, according to Smith, fulfill Isaiah's prophecy that "the earth shall reel to and fro like a drunkard."[76] Other reminiscences would claim that Smith had taught that the ten tribes were living in the "north pole."[77] While there was much discussion on the lost tribes' whereabouts, as far as apocalyptic elements were concerned, the importance of their return overshadowed that of their hiding place.

The ten tribes were not the only lost civilization that Mormons expected would miraculously return before the millennium. There was also the ancient city of Enoch that had been "translated"—made immortal—and removed from the Earth before the flood. Smith had introduced the history of this community in an expansion of the verses about Enoch in Genesis, which he published under the title, "Extracts from the Prophecy of Enoch." The city was named "the City of Holiness, even Zion." In vision, Enoch saw that his city "in process of time, was taken up into heaven," before destructions swept the earth. His vision included various other scenes, including the survival of Noah, the incarnation and ascension of Jesus, and the last days. It was then that Enoch's vision juxtaposed his own city with that of the New Jerusalem that would be constructed before the Second Coming. Enoch was promised a joyous meeting between his city—which would return to the earth—and this last-days New Jerusalem.[78] Zion's return also featured in another expansion to the biblical text dictated by Smith: Following the flood, when Noah was told about the sign of the rainbow, he was informed that the bow also served as a reminder that when Noah's posterity became righteous, then "Zion should again come on the earth."[79]

According to the Book of Mormon, the Latter-day Saints—the believing Gentiles—were to assist Natives in constructing the New Jerusalem—the earthly city of Zion. In September 1830, one of Smith's revelations declared that the city would be built "among the Lamanites." Not coincidentally, the same revelation called a group of missionaries to preach to the American Indians.[80] While the missionaries were initially optimistic after meeting with the Delaware who then resided west of Missouri, the mission ultimately failed after opposition from the federally appointed Indian agent. Yet, their efforts were not all a loss as the location of the New Jerusalem was identified in the region of the mission. A summer 1831 revelation declared "this [i.e., Missouri] is the land of promise & the place for the City of Zion . . . the place which is now called Independence is the centre place." The revelation even identified "the spot for the Temple" on a lot near the city's courthouse.[81] Thus, the apocalyptic theme of Zion's return at the Second Coming began to be associated with the literal geography of the United States. Mormonism's ability to concretize apocalypticism within both living people and material sites helped to ensure an ongoing engagement with the apocalyptic both theologically and culturally within the faith.

The newly identified "spot for the Temple" played an important part in continuing to ground Mormon apocalypticism in real-world locations.

Jackson County was the frontier and Independence, the county seat, was sparsely populated. Responding to further revelations from Smith, the Saints purchased land, dedicated a temple site, and established a printing press. By 1833, over a thousand Mormons had gathered to help establish the city of Zion. Hostile relationships developed with their neighbors over matters of slavery, politics, and, class. Rumors and prophecy that Mormons intended to incite the Indian population or possibly even organize a slave revolt only fomented these tensions. Violence came to Jackson County in July 1833, but the Mormons were not the aggressors. A group of armed men ransacked the church's printing press and razed the building. They tarred and feathered church leaders. The Saints were eventually driven from their homes in November 1833.

In response, the Saints organized the "Camp of Israel," more commonly referred to as Zion's Camp, a 200-man military force. Smith intended for the camp to accompany the displaced Mormons as they reclaimed their property in Jackson County. While members of the camp were armed and ready to defend themselves, they hoped to avoid altercations, particularly since they expected Missouri Governor Daniel Dunklin to provide them with militia support. Ultimately, Dunklin declined to do so. Smith was determined to move forward with their plan to enter Jackson County but eventually he dictated a revelation on June 22, 1834, that commanded them not to do so: "Therefore it is expedient in me, that mine elders should wait for a little season for the redemption of Zion, For behold I do not require at their hands, to fight the battles of Zion."[82]

The redemption of Zion, however, remained a crucial component of Mormon eschatology. Even though the Saints would not return to Jackson County in the nineteenth century, Mormon millenarianism did not die out. Instead, its frame was reworked within the context of the Mormons' western migration. In 1838, they were driven from Missouri altogether under Governor Lilburn Boggs's infamous "extermination order." Thereafter, the Saints understood themselves as exiles from the Promised Land—a key pillar to Mormon millenarianism.

Fleeing Babylon

Joseph Smith was an apocalyptic prophet. As much as his teachings emphasized moral living, restoring ancient rites, and establishing a contemporary utopia, his revelations also pronounced God's wrath on an immoral society. A March 7, 1831, revelation described impending natural disasters and "an overflowing scourge . . . a desolating sicknes [*sic*]" that would precede the Second Coming.[83] The righteous would "see signs & wonders for they shall be shewn forth in the heavens above & in the Earth beneath & they shall behold blood & fires & vapors of smoke & before the day of the lord come the sun shall be darkened & the moon be turned into blood & some stars shall fall from Heaven." Most strikingly, Smith described the total collapse of social ties and the rise of violence in the last days. The prophecy declared: "[I]t shall come to pass among the wicked that evry [*sic*] man that will not take his sword against his Neighbour [*sic*] must needs flee unto Zion for safety . . . the only people that shall not be at war one with another."[84] In 1833, he wrote a letter to a newspaper editor in New York, warning that "not many years shall pass away before the United States shall present such a scene of *bloodshed* as has not a parallel in the history of our nation pestalence [*sic*] hail famine and earthquake will sweep the wicked of this generation from off the face of this Land. . . . Repent ye Repent, ye and imbrace [*sic*] the everlasting Covenant and flee to Zion before the overflowing scourge overtake you."[85]

Smith did not only record prophecies of coming events but told of witnessing these future destructions in apocalyptic dreams and visions. In the summer of 1839, he described a vision of "men hunting the lives of their own sons, & brother murdering brother, women killing their own daughters & daughters seeking the lives of their mothers. I saw armies arrayed against armies I saw blood. desolations, fires &c,—" The murderous scene was "at our doors."[86] Jedediah Grant seems to have recalled a telling of this same vision when, in 1854, he remembered being with a small group in the prophet's home:

> He told several of us of the night the visions of heaven were opened to him, in which he saw the American continent drenched in blood, and he saw nation rising up against nation. He also saw the father shed the blood of the son, and the son the blood of the father; the mother put to death the daughter, and the daughter the mother; and natural affection forsook the hearts of the wicked; for he saw that the Spirit of God should be withdrawn from the inhabitants of the earth, in consequence of which there should be blood upon the face of the whole earth, except among the people of the Most High. The Prophet gazed upon the scene his vision presented, until his heart sickened, and he besought the Lord to close it up again.[87]

The distress that Smith and other visionaries suffered at the sight of last days violence would become a popular motif in Mormon apocalypticism. It enhanced the audience's sense of dread, while reminding them to respond with compassion when faced with human suffering.

Smith's use of such intense imagery was meant to encourage the Saints to flee Babylon—their homes, their lives, and sometimes their families—and gather in Zion. Zion or the New Jerusalem, the place of righteousness and refuge, was often juxtaposed with Babylon. In terms of loyalty to the divine, John set the New Jerusalem as "the bride, the Lamb's wife" against the prostitute Babylon.[88] When Daniel used the term in his own last days prophecy, he likely meant it as a literal reference to the Babylonian empire, the seat of power of Israel's arch-enemy. John's Babylon seemed to invoke Rome and thereby assured his early Christian audience that God would eventually remove their persecutors.[89] For early Mormons, Babylon referred to unjust political and religious systems throughout the world. In practical terms, abandoning "Babylon" meant leaving countries of origin, relationships, family members, occupations, and lives to relocate among the Mormons.

In John the Revelator's vision of the future, he saw an angel herald the fall of Babylon. A voice speaking over his vision warned, "Come out of her, my people, that ye be not partakers of her sins, and that ye receive not of her plagues."[90] In September 1830, Smith declared a revelation to gather the Saints "unto one place upon the the [*sic*] face of this land to prepare their Hearts & be prepared in all things against the day of tribulation."[91] Other revelations were more explicit regarding the relationship between this command to gather and the revelation of John. A November 1831 revelation read: "Go ye out from among the Nations even from Babylon From the midst of wickedness which is spiritual babylon."[92] As the world became increasingly dangerous through persecution, natural disasters, and social decay, the gathered Saints trusted the prophet could identify sites of refuge. Historian Grant Underwood observed that the practice of the gathering in Mormon eschatology functioned like the rapture did within John Nelson Darby's influential dispensationalist eschatology. For Darby, the rapture would entail the heavenly removal of the righteous from the earth before the tribulation commenced. This explained how the Second Coming could be imminent (for believing Christians) and yet still delayed such that there was time for the major events expected to precede the apocalypse to occur before Christ's general appearance. Underwood pointed out that in the same manner through which the righteous would be in their raptured state during these events, Latter-day Saints believed they would be weathering the apocalypse in their "cit[ies] of refuge."[93]

Mormons saw themselves as tasked with preparing a populace to survive the coming cataclysm. Missionaries left the safety of Zion to seek the righteous and warn them of impending destruction, even as their presence also served as a catalyst for such destruction. As a December 1832 revelation explained, "[A]fter your testimony [*sic*], cometh wrath, and— indignation, upon the people."[94] Missionaries visited distant cities and foreign lands to warn and, when rejected, to condemn. The apocalypse would be a global event; however, as in the Book of Mormon, specific visions and prophecies tended to be localized in the American continent and usually within the confines of the United States. The March 7, 1831, revelation assured readers that the last days violence would not be confined to distant lands, but would be "nigh even unto your doors & not many years hence ye Shall hear of wars in your own lands."[95] This chapter's epigraph includes a similar pronouncement in a January 1831 revelation.

On Christmas day, 1832, a revelation provided Smith with details on the impending war. It would be the first of a series of escalating conflicts that would eventually result in "war [that] will be poured out upon all Nations."[96] The Mormon prophet specified that the war would begin "at the rebellion of South Carolina which will eventually terminate in the death and misery [*sic*] of many souls."[97] The "southern states shall be divided against the Northern States, and the Southern States will call on other Nations even the Nation of Great Britain as it is called and they shall also call upon other Nations in order to defend themselves against other Nations."[98] More and more nations would be drawn into the conflict, "until [*sic*] the consumption decreed hath made a full end of all Nations."[99] A decade later, Smith repeated the prophecy and suggested that "it probably may arise through the slave trade."[100] Mormons saw the Civil War as a fulfillment of this prophecy, whereas skeptical interpreters have suggested that the prophecy reflects a larger sense of foreboding and anxiety leading up to the start of the war. Either way, Smith believed these regional conflicts would lead to the "commenceme[n]t of bloodshed as preparat[o]ry to the coming of the son of man."[101]

The Mormon response to the perceived imminence of the Second Coming was a specific gesture: that of fleeing Babylon. While this flight occurred, in part, through the literal geographic dispersion and gathering of the Mormons as they sought repeatedly to build a Zion upon the American continent, it also occurred through missions meant to gather converts from out of a worldly Babylon and bring them to Zion. In either configuration, the geography of the Mormon Zion remained grounded within the United States. Smith himself reflected this geographic preference in multiple revelations, which promised coming violence in apocalyptic terms—to flee Babylon, then, became both a physical relocation of the Mormon people, and a promise that a necessary pre-millennial violence would be visited upon the lands of the American Babylon from which the Mormons fled.

The Second Coming

As with other millenarian Christians, Mormons expected the apocalypse to conclude with the return of Christ in glory. Yet, for Latter-day Saints, the Second Coming was not a single event during which Christ would appear to the world, but a series of appearances to the Saints, to the Jews in Palestine, and finally, a universal Parousia that would usher in the millennium, the judgment of the wicked, and the resurrection of the dead. While the Saints eagerly anticipated the resurrection and judgment, they expected Christ to appear privately to the faithful long before the general Parousia. Smith emphasized two earlier appearances based on passages in the Old Testament. First, the Saints expected that Christ would "suddenly come to his temple" as prophesied by Malachi.[102] Later Mormons have posited that Christ's visitation with Moses, Elias, and Elijah in the Kirtland Temple fulfilled this prophecy. Whether or not that experience was understood in terms of this particular prophecy, it was certainly understood as a significant apocalyptic event in which the three Old Testament–era prophets bestowed the authority or "keys" on Joseph Smith for the last days.[103] Elijah's appearance explicitly fulfilled Malachi's prophecy of Elijah's return—the same prophecy that Moroni recited to Joseph Smith in 1823. Yet, if Smith conceived of this event as the start of the Second Coming, he kept it to himself. The event was not publicized among the Saints until the 1850s.[104] The vast majority of nineteenth-century Saints would look forward to a future appearance in the temple. It was presumed that the temple in Jackson County would be the site of these prophecies.

A second appearance of Jesus would fulfill a prophecy of events described in the Book of Daniel. The relevant scene depicted a figure, the Ancient of Days, seated on a throne judging a vast body of people. A second figure, one "like the Son of Man," descended from the clouds before this celestial monarch, who then bestowed on him "dominion, and glory, and a kingdom that all people, nations, and languages, should serve him."[105] According to biblical scholar John J. Collins, the "meaning or identity" of this second figure "is perhaps the most celebrated question in all apocalyptic literature."[106] Joseph Smith identified him, like most Christians, as the resurrected Jesus Christ. He deviated from traditional interpretations when he identified the Ancient of Days, a figure traditionally recognized as deity, as the first and therefore oldest man, Adam. In Smith's reading of the scene, Adam, once invested with a responsibility over the planet, would at this pivotal moment return it to Jesus Christ.[107]

In 1838, Smith identified a location in northern Missouri as Adam-Ondi-Ahman, a site named in the original "Adamic" language for the place Adam dwelt and the future location of this divine appearance.[108] Although Smith believed in a universal Parousia, the gathering at Adam-Ondi-Ahman was limited to the righteous. Once the Mormons were exiled from Missouri, the expectation of their return there was configured through an underlying apocalypticism as it often corresponded with hopes of attending this future meeting of the living and the dead.

Another preliminary appearance would occur in Palestine. Joseph Smith's revelations confirmed that the ancient city of Jerusalem was the site of the battle of Armageddon and the miraculous deliverance that would follow. Christianizing a passage in Zechariah,[109] Jesus would appear at the battlefield to defend his chosen people, before revealing himself as the messiah:

> Then shall the Jews look upon me & say what are these wounds in thine hands & in thy feet then shall they know that I am the Lord for I will say unto them these wounds are the wounds With which I was wounded in the house of my friends[.] I am he that was lifted up I am Jesus which was crucified [sic] I am the Son of God.[110]

Although there would be some Jewish converts in early Mormonism, Smith believed that this moment would lead to the national conversion of the Jewish people. As noted previously, Jerusalem would serve as a second capital of Christ's millennial government, alongside the New Jerusalem in America.

Mormons believed the Second Coming was imminent. The anticipated appearance was, in the words of Smith's December 7, 1830, revelation, "nigh at hand."[111] On February 14, 1835, he declared that "even fifty six years, should wind up the scene"—placing the apocalypse in 1891.[112] Smith made similar remarks on a few other occasions, but for the most part he focused on the chronology of events that would precede the Second Coming rather than the specific timing. For instance, he argued against William Miller's prediction that Christ would return between 1843 and 1844, contending that the Jews would have to first return to Jerusalem and that such an imminent Second Coming did not leave sufficient time for this event to occur.[113]

On April 2, 1843, Smith first explained why he had come to believe there was a special significance to 1890–1891. He recalled sometime in the past having "earnestly desir[e]d to know concern[in]g the coming of the Son of Man & prayed. when—a voice said to me, Joseph, my son, if thou livest until thou art 85 years old thou shalt see the facce [*sic*] of the son of man. therefore let this suffice & trouble me no more on this matter."[114] Smith reflected publicly on the revelation four days later: "I was left to draw my own conclusions concerni[n]g this, & I took the liberty to conclude that if I did live till that time ~~Jesus~~ he would make his appeara[n]ce.—but I do not say whether he will make his appearance or I shall go where he is."[115] Smith would have turned 85 years old on December 5, 1890. Unlike earlier statements that seemed to suggest the apocalypse would occur between 1890 and 1891, in 1843, he did not posit a date for the Second Coming. He only discounted the possibility that it could occur before 1890.[116]

Smith provided his followers with signs to look for before the Second Coming. Most of the portents he identified echoed biblical signs, but he sometimes added to these expectations. For example, Smith revealed that during the year Christ would return, there would be no rainbows.[117] He was particularly fixed on heavenly signs. In November 1833, like numerous other Americans, he was awed by the Leonid meteor shower (see Figure 1.4). Joseph Smith reflected on the experience in his journal. "I arose, and to my great joy, behold the stars fall from heaven like a shower of hailstones; a literal fulfillment of the word of God, as recorded in the holy scriptures, and a sure sign that the coming of Christ is close at hand."[118] At the end of his life, he placed great significance in Christ's prophecy that "the sign of the Son of Man in heaven" would precede the Second Coming.[119] In February 1843, Smith challenged one man's claim of having personally seen this sign because he believed it was scheduled to occur "after the sun shall be darkened and the moon bathed in blood."[120] The sign, like these other celestial phenomena, would be visible to all. In 1843, he declared that the "world" would try to dismiss the sign when it eventually appeared by claiming "it is a planet. a comet. &c."[121]

Figure 1.4 Engraving of the 1833 Leonid meteor shower by Adolf Vollmy. From *Bible Readings for the Home Circle* (1888).

Destructions would occur until the time Christ would make his appearance and his very presence would destroy the wicked who remained. One of Smith's revelations explained that at the time when "all flesh shall see me together" that "evry [*sic*] coruptable [*sic*] thing both of man, or of the beasts of the field or of the fowls of the heavens or of the fish of the sea that dwells upon all the face of the earth shall be consumed And also that of element shall melt with fervent heat and all things shall become new that my knowledge and glory may dwell upon all the earth."[122] Christ's presence would institute a new global ecosystem—what Smith referred to as its "paradisiacal glory."[123] From that point, the righteous dead would be resurrected and the living would grow old, die, and then "be changed in the twinkling of an eye, and shall be caught up." Humans and animals would universally forsake their carnivorous pasts.[124] Christ would inaugurate his personal reign by binding Satan, thereby ridding the world of temptation. A thousand years later, violence would return when Satan would be "loosed, for a little season." The archangel Michael would lead the hosts of heaven to defeat the armies of Satan once and for all.[125]

Smith provided signs of the Second Coming by drawing on the traditions of biblical apocalypticism while simultaneously expanding on and going beyond the tradition. The signs were varied in terms of scope and scale, but their repeated appearances within Smith's work underscore the continual apocalyptic pulse that fed his prophetic imagination. The Second Coming in Smith's hands became not a single event, but instead an ongoing redemptive project whose beginning and end points remained conspicuously nebulous, despite the many prophecies and comments on the subject. As a project, apocalypticism was thus embedded within the greater Mormon context of ongoing revelation: In other words, it was a concept open to further development.

The Apocalypse in Nauvoo

In 1839, the Saints arrived in Illinois as refugees from Missouri and, after a period finding sanctuary in Quincy, settled along the Mississippi River in a city named Commerce. In November 1840, the Saints petitioned the state legislature for incorporation of the city of Nauvoo, with their petition officially approved the following month.[126] Smith explained that Nauvoo was a name of "Hebrew origin, and signifies a beautiful situation, or place, carrying with it, also, the idea of *rest*; and is truly descriptive of this most delightful situation."[127] As Smith's phrasing implied, Nauvoo became a gathering place for the Saints. Thousands relocated there from missionary efforts throughout the United States and especially in Great Britain.

Nauvoo has long been considered the setting of Mormonism's first transformation. It was there that the tradition evolved from a church steeped in Christian primitivism to a "half-Hebraicized church-kingdom."[128] This was not to suggest that the change was not gradual. Historian Marvin S. Hill demonstrated that even before Nauvoo, "dreams of a theocratic empire were solidifying" in Mormon thought.[129] Mormons had long held that they would play governing roles Coluduring the millennium, but it was only in Nauvoo that they collaborated to imagine and enact an alternative America. Having founded a city from what began as a swamp, the Saints developed new confidence. By the time of Smith's death, they had come to see themselves not only as a church pointing to the proper form of religious belief and practice, but also as a political messianic movement that could revolutionize the world regardless of the populace's religious faith.

The Temple

Mormon temples were apocalyptic spaces. This was true of the Saints' initial plan to build a temple in Jackson County, the completed temple in Kirtland, Ohio, and the temple in Nauvoo that would not be dedicated until after Smith's death. The temple's architecture was rich with millenarian symbolism. From the perspective of non-Mormon Josiah Quincy, it was a "grotesque structure . . . with all its queer carving of moons and suns."[130] Thirty pilasters surrounded the temple, each with a crescent moon at its base and a rising sun at its crown. Five-pointed stars lined the frieze—some in stained-glass windows and others engraved into the stone (see Figure 1.5). Wandle Mace, a laborer on the temple, would later describe these symbols in his journal, referencing clear apocalyptic images: "The architecture of the temple was purely original and unlike anything in existence, being a representation of the Church, the Bride, the Lambs wife." Mace believed the temple memorialized a passage from Revelation 12, in which John described " 'a great wonder in heaven; a woman clothed with the sun, and the moon under her feet, and upon her head a crown of twelve stars.' This is portrayed in the beautiful cut stone of this grand temple."[131] Joseph Smith's "inspired translation" identified the woman as a symbol of the church. In the passage, she would birth a child, which Smith's translation referred to as the "kingdom of our God and his Christ."[132]

The temple's tower also bore symbols of the last days. Although it would not be placed on the structure until January 1846, an angel positioned horizontally to depict it in a state of flight adorned the temple's weathervane. According to Perrigrine Sessions, the angel donned "his priestly robes with a Book of Mormon in one hand and a trumpet in the other which is overlaid

Figure 1.5 William Weeks's architectural drawing of the Nauvoo Temple, 1846. The temple included symbolism adapted from Revelation 12's depiction of the woman in the wilderness and Revelation 14's portrayal of a last days angel "fly[ing] in the midst of heaven." Courtesy of the Church History Library.

with gold leaf."[133] The scene was significant to Mormons due to the angel's attire as he wore the same clothing as temple initiates, as well as its allusion to biblical prophecy. The figure invoked Revelation's last days angel—which Smith had already connected to Moroni—bearing the everlasting gospel.

As Smith introduced the rituals that would be performed in the temple, he associated them with the fulfillment of apocalyptic prophecy. He pronounced vicarious baptism for the dead, the first of these rites to be publicly theologized and practiced, as the fulfillment of Malachi's prophecy that Elijah would "before the coming of the great and dreadful day of the Lord . . . turn the heart of the fathers to the children, and the heart of the children to their fathers."[134] In October 1841, Smith declared the performance of this rite "as the only way that men can appear as saviors on mount Zion," a reference to a prophecy in the Old Testament book of Obadiah.[135] In October 1840, Smith also anticipated that animal sacrifices would take place in the temple in response to Malachi's prophecy of the "sons of Levi . . . may offer unto the Lord an offering in righteousness."[136]

In 1842, Smith began to prepare for the performance of the endowment, a series of new rituals, in the temple. The endowment, as performed in Nauvoo, would entail a lengthy drama, inspired by Smith's recent initiation into Freemasonry, in which initiates symbolically entered the presence of the divine. By the summer of 1844, thirty-seven men and twenty-nine women had received this rite and would meet together regularly as part of a fraternal society referred to as the Quorum, Anointed Quorum, or Holy Order.[137] In 1843, Smith introduced this group to the new and everlasting covenant of marriage, a "sealing" rite that promised the perpetuation of marital relationships after death. According to a July 1843 revelation, such a sealed union was necessary to achieve exaltation in the hereafter.[138] Smith had already taught select individuals this concept of eternal marriage, including those he entrusted with knowledge of the nascent practice of plural marriage.

A higher anointing referred to as the fullness of the Melchizedek priesthood was also revealed at this time. Smith hinted at the rite when, in an August 1843 sermon, he argued that the biblical Melchizedek held "greater power [than Abraham] even power of an endless life . . . which was not the power of a prophet nor apostle nor patriarch only but of King and Priest to God."[139] These rites were framed in the context of the Revelation of St. John and other apocalyptic texts. Revelation's first chapter introduced the idea of Christ having made his followers kings and priests, titles traditionally linked to the selection of the 144,000 servants of God in Revelation 7. This chapter opened with four destroying angels positioned "on the four corners of the earth" set "to hurt the earth and the sea." A fifth angel prevented them from moving forward, "saying, Hurt not the earth, neither the sea, nor the trees, till we have sealed the servants of our God in their foreheads."[140] This commanding angel, whom Joseph Smith identified as John the Revelator himself, wanted God's servants—the 144,000—protected from the coming onslaught.

Historian Samuel Brown has noted that Mormons, like other millenarians, understood this seal to be "an actual mark upon the foreheads of believers."[141]

There were preliminary ideas about how one could be sealed in early Mormonism, but by the Nauvoo period, Smith explicitly associated the sealing of the 144,000 with the sealing performed in the Anointed Quorum. In August 1843, he explained, the "covenant sealed on the foreheads of the Parents secured the children from falling that they shall all sit upon thrones as one with the God-head Joint Heirs of God with Jesus Christ."[142] He again confirmed the connection between the 144,000 and Nauvoo esotericism during a February 3, 1844, meeting of the Anointed Quorum. Discussing Revelation 7, Smith showed "that the selection of persons to form that number had already commenced," presumably among those who had received the fullness of the Melchizedek priesthood rite.[143] These teachings had a significant impact on their hearers, who recalled them decades later. Wandle Mace remembered hearing Smith encourage the Saints to "Pray, that you may live to go into the Temple and be sealed in your forehead."[144] Levi Richards also recalled Smith pointing to "the necessity of the temple that the Servants of God may be sealed in their foreheads," noting that "the 4 angels [would] not be permitted to destroy the earth till it was done."[145]

The Nauvoo Temple was an apocalyptic monument—a material fulfillment of Old Testament prophecy. The building itself was replete with the imagery drawn from Revelation: suns, moons, and stars, and an angel wearing priestly robes, carrying the gospel to the four corners of the earth. The apocalyptic symbolism of the exterior reflected the underlying apocalypticism of the temple rituals themselves. Joseph Smith's desire to share his vision concerning the earth's millenarian destiny and mankind's role therein led him to form rites and rituals that would, in essence, place his followers within a salvific narrative contextualized by an understanding of sealing drawn from Revelation 7. The rituals performed within the temple walls transformed recipients into players in the last days drama. It would continue to do so in more subtle ways until the present, placing the ongoing millenarian project at the center of Mormon ritual worship.

Political Messianism and Mormon Americanism

Mormon apocalypticism developed to include a strain of political messianism during the Nauvoo period (1839–1846). After the city's incorporation in 1840, Mormons continued to actively seek influence in local, state, and federal politics.[146] It was also during this period that Mormons became convinced that the current political establishment was corrupt and ultimately that only Latter-day Saint intervention could reform a nation in decline.

Mormon faith in the United States declined rapidly after Smith petitioned the federal government for redress and reparations for the loss of life and property in Missouri. While away from Nauvoo between October 1839 and February 1840, Smith lectured and met with politicians, hoping to gain sympathy for the Mormon plight. He even spoke with President Martin Van Buren in the parlor of the mansion that would later be called the White House. For Smith, Van Buren's response was gut-wrenching: "What can I do? I can do nothing for you,— if I do any thing [*sic*], I shall come in contact with the whole State of Missouri."[147] Smith took this as an admission of Van Buren's own corruption, not wanting to do what was just if it would cost him the support of Missouri voters. Later, in February and March 1840, the U.S. Senate deliberated and rejected an official petition for redress, determining that the decision was not under their jurisdiction.[148]

In July 1840, Smith prophesied that the Saints would preserve American liberties. He referred to a future when "eeven [*sic*] this Nation will be on the very verge of crumbling to peices [*sic*] and tumbling to the ground and when the constitution is upon the brink of ruin this people will be the Staff up[on] which the Nation shall lean and they shall bear the constitution away from the very verge of destruction."[149] Although no contemporary records explained how Smith expected the Saints would preserve the constitution, the image of Latter-day Saints salvaging the imperiled constitution became a standard component of Mormon last days prophecy.

Mormons also expected to provide military assistance to the United States during a future invasion. The Nauvoo Charter had given the city the rights to form an extension of the state militia, known as the Nauvoo Legion. Smith commanded the legion as lieutenant general by the commission of Governor Thomas Carlin.[150] On March 11, 1843, Joseph Smith related a dream in which he was approached by an elderly man who sought his protection as the lieutenant general from "a mob force coming upon him, and he was likely to loose [*sic*] his life." Smith consented and assured the stranger that he was "a patriot" willing to help the "innocent" among his fellow countrymen. The nameless man, in turn, promised Smith that he would put "any amount of men" under his command.[151] Smith again shared the dream on April 2, when Orson Hyde provided an interpretation. The old man symbolized the

"Govermnt [*sic*] of these Unit[e]d States, who will be invaded by a foreign foe. probably England. U.S. Goverment [*sic*] will call on Gen Smith to defend probably all this western territory and offer him any am[ou]nt of men he shall desire & put them under his command."[152] The dream promised Smith that he would one day be recognized as the lieutenant general of the army in very deed. Perhaps there was an attempt at fulfilling this hope when Smith sought approval from Congress for raising troops in order to defend settlements in the "uncivilized portions of our continent."[153]

Mormon messianic expectation might also have come to fruition through political involvement. From Nauvoo, the Saints had already sought and succeeded in influencing regional elections. After failing to convince President Van Buren or Congress to grant their petition for redress, Smith believed the Saints' hope was in the outcome of the 1844 election. In October 1843, he proposed a plan to select a candidate "who will be the most likely to render us assistance in obtaining redress for our grievances--and not only give our own votes, but use our influence to obtain others, and if the voice of suffering innocence will not sufficiently arouse the rulers of our nation to investigate our case, perhaps a vote from fifty to one hundred thousand may rouse them from their lethargy."[154] The following month, Smith drafted letters to five of the presidential candidates to seek such a man, querying how they would respond to the plight of the Mormons.[155] The candidates who responded confirmed they would offer Smith no special favors.[156]

In January 1844, Smith announced his decision to run for the U.S. presidency. He presented his candidacy as a last resort to defend the Mormons' rights. Smith and his advisers developed a platform that weighed in on many of the major issues of antebellum society. His solutions were, as historian Richard Bushman described them, "idealistic but politically impractical."[157] Smith addressed slavery, political corruption, the formation of a national bank, western settlement, and prison reform. He called for the president to have command of a standing army able to go into states to put down mobs whether they had the consent of the state governor or not.[158] An advocate for national unity, Smith insisted the greatest ill of antebellum society was its political and social fracturing. He differentiated himself from self-interested candidates who played party politics: "We have had democratic presidents; whig presidents; a pseudo democratic whig president; and now it is time to have a president of the United States."[159]

Smith's candidacy reshaped the way Mormons thought about their religion. Ultimately, Mormons would see Smith's political campaign as the nation's final chance to escape divine judgment. Looking back on his campaign from the vantage point of Smith's death, which followed soon after, Mormons would come to view his candidacy as a martyr's final witness to his killers. If they had accepted the prophet's vision for America's future, Smith would have been able to redeem the nation.

The Kingdom of God and Mormon Separatism

According to a late and secondhand account, one of the scriptures Moroni discussed with Joseph Smith on the night of September 21, 1827, was Daniel 2. In this often discussed passage, "[T]he God of heaven [would] set up a kingdom, which shall never be destroyed . . . it shall break in pieces and consume all these kingdoms [i.e., the four kingdoms shown in Nebuchadnezzar's dream], and it shall stand for ever."[160] In the words of Wilford Woodruff, "When the angel of God delivered this message to Joseph Smith he told him the heavens were full of judgments; that the Lord Almighty had set his hand to establish the kingdom that Daniel saw and prophesied about, as recorded in the second chapter of Daniel; and that the Gospel had to be preached to all nations under heaven as a witness to them before the end should come."[161] Latter-day Saints tended to see biblical prophecy about the Kingdom of God fulfilled in the organization of the Church of Jesus Christ of Latter-day Saints. Smith frequently used the term "kingdom" as a synonym for "church." This was true despite the fact that Smith's rendering of Revelation 12, described here, presented the millennial kingdom as the metaphorical offspring of the church.

On July 15, 1842, the Mormon prophet articulated his growing cynicism for secular governments in an editorial entitled the "Government of God." Throughout history, he declared, "nation has succeeded nation, and we have inherited nothing but their folly."[162] Man-made political systems, Smith posited, would continue to fail until the emergence of a divinely instituted millennial government:

> It has been the design of Jehovah, from the commencement of the world, and is his purpose now, to regulate the affairs of the world in his own time; to stand as head of the universe, and take the reigns [sic] of government into his own hand. When that is done judgment will be administered in righteousness; anarchy and confusion will be destroyed, and "nations will learn war no more."[163]

This government would not be the church, although both organizations would be directed by revelation. In March 1844, Smith established a political institution, named by revelation: "The Kingdom of God and his Laws, with the keys and power thereof, and judgement in the hands of his servants. Ahman Christ."[164] Those involved also referred to the Kingdom as the Council of Fifty or the Quorum of Fifty. Bound by an oath of secrecy, members went so far as to obscure references to the Council in their own diaries, writing "Council of YTFIF," "Council of —," or "the K."[165]

The Kingdom was the culmination of Mormonism's apocalyptic and religio-political thought. During the Nauvoo period, ideas of an earthly government with a mortal king—a latter-day King David—were regularly entertained.[166] Latter-day Saints were not passively awaiting Christ's triumphant return for the fulfillment of these expectations. They saw themselves tasked with the ongoing project of building and operating the same structures that Christ would personally govern at a future day. An apocalyptic scenario would eventually bring about the sort of social upheaval necessary to instill a new worldwide government. In the meantime, the Kingdom would be established over any territory that would recognize its authority.

The Kingdom would give birth to Mormon separatism but was not necessarily designed for a traditional revolution. During the three months Joseph Smith held meetings of the Kingdom, his candidacy for the U.S. presidency became a major component of the group's agenda. One Council member recalled that the Fifty's goals would be accomplished "if we succeeded in making a majority of the voters converts to our faith and elected Joseph President, in such an event the dominion of the kingdom would be forever established in the United States." Because this was an unlikely feat, the Council developed a backup plan to negotiate with the Republic of Texas for land bordering the United States. In this situation, assuming the Republic complied, "we could but fall back on Texas, and be a kingdom notwithstanding."[167] This was an oversimplification, but captured the general attitude of the Council—they intended to find a way to establish Mormon self-rule in one way or another.

The Fifty considered several possibilities for Mormon gatherings. The official minutes for March 11, 1844, read: "All seemed agreed to look to some place where we can go and establish a Theocracy either in Texas or Oregon or somewhere in California &c."[168] Yet, Nauvoo had not been forgotten. On April 18, 1844, Lorenzo Wasson expressed himself "in favor of moving the seat of government to Nauvoo" in the event that Smith was elected. Smith remained in favor of "establish[ing] independent [*sic*] governments" in Texas, but admitted he had no desire to go there himself. For the Mormon prophet, the great apocalyptic reversal of powers had already taken place in the Council of Fifty: "We consider ourselves the head, and Washington the tail. We can make laws and send them abroad and not say anything to them about it, untill [*sic*] we get ourselves firmly set beyond their power."[169]

A week before these bold words, the Council officially recognized Smith as "our Prophet, Priest & King, and uphold him in that capacity which God has anointed him."[170] He was already Christ's mortal representative as prophet of his church, and now he was recognized as his mouthpiece in a religio-political role as well. Those present performed the collective "hosanna shout" reserved for only the most sacred moments.[171] At Smith's request, Council members avoided referring to their prophet as "king" even within the Fifty's meetings.[172] Council members and others in the know would sometimes allude to his title without being explicit. For example, a letter to Joseph Smith from Heber C. Kimball and Lyman Wight, who were then campaigning in the eastern states, assured him that he was "already President Pro tem of the world."[173] Reuben Miller, who would have heard of this event secondhand, provided the earliest published reference: In "the quorum of Fifty . . . Joseph himself, by the powers of the priesthood which he revealed and conferred in the quorum, was anointed and ordained a leading minister and director over the whole House of Israel forever."[174]

One of the first responsibilities Smith gave to his new political advisors was to draft the constitution for the Kingdom of God, utilizing the American Constitution as a guide. We know of only one piece of counsel Smith provided for the task: "No laws can be enacted but what every man can be protected from."[175] As Smith had earlier "translated" the Bible as a preliminary task in founding a restored church, he sought a divine version of the constitution as a preliminary task in founding the Kingdom of God.[176] On April 18, the committee assigned to draft the constitution presented the start of such a document, beginning:

> We, the people of the Kingdom of God, knowing that all power emanates from God, that the earth is his possession, and he alone has the right to govern the nations and set in order the kingdoms of this world; that he only has a right to institute laws and establish decrees for the government of the human family; that he is our Father in heaven; and we, his legitimate children, inhabiting his footstool, and that no rule, law, government, dominion

> or power, unless instituted by him, can be productive of the greatest happiness, prosperity, exaltation and glory of his subjects.[177]

It continued by stating that no other nation "acknowledge[d] the *creator* of the *Universe* as their Priest, Lawgiver, King and Sovereign, neither have they sought unto him for laws by which to govern themselves." There was no "original kingdom" set up by the divine: Instead, they had all "obtained their power, rule and authority by usurpation, rebellion, bloodshed, tyranny and fraud." No nation truly had "the disposition and power to grant that protection to the persons and rights of man, viz. <u>life</u>, <u>liberty</u>, <u>possession</u> of <u>property</u>, and <u>pursuit</u> of <u>happiness</u>, which was designed by their creator to all men."[178]

After the lengthy preamble, the document included three articles written in the voice of God. The first article declared the powers of government in the hands of God—"[T]o me alone belongs the right, the power, the majesty, the glory, and the dominion; I alone am King of Kings, and Lord of Lords." The second article acknowledged the place of Smith as the mortal prophet to "whom I will reveal my laws, my statues, and my ordinances, my Judgements [*sic*], my will and pleasure concerning my kingdom on the earth." The final article stated that the prophet would "appoint Judges and officers in my kingdom, And my people shall have the right to choose or refuse those officers and judges, by common consent."[179] The document clearly laid out Mormon issues with the United States, including Mormonism's recent skepticism with the manner by which politicians were elected: by popular vote.

On April 25, 1844, Smith ended further consideration of the constitution of the Kingdom of God by dictating a short revelation. "Verily thus saith the Lord, ye~~a~~ are my constitution and I am your God, and ye are my spokesmen. From henceforth do as I shall command you. Saith the Lord."[180] The revelation envisioned a worldwide government without a set of universal laws but one that would instead be governed by ongoing revelation.

Even though it was not adopted, the proposed constitution captured Smith's notion of a "theodemocracy, [a government] where God and the people hold the power to conduct the affairs of men in righteousness."[181] Smith had introduced the novel term for Mormonism's political philosophy in an April 15, 1844, editorial. On one hand, the Council of Fifty was a theocracy, instituted by God with leaders appointed by revelation. On the other hand, Mormons believed that it was only through this means that true democratic ideals could be maintained. For example, the Council of Fifty held to the concept of a representative form of government. Council member

Benjamin F. Johnson wrote that the millennial kingdom would consist of "a government formed of representatives from every nation, principality or tribe upon the earth."[182] This was signified in the makeup of the Council of Fifty itself, in which three of the members were non-Mormons. The Council of Fifty conformed to Smith's conception of a millennium in which pluralism remained.[183]

Smith also saw the Kingdom of God as "democratic" in that its reign was not forced upon its citizens. The popular image of Smith as an American Muhammad intent on seizing political control by the violent aid of his fanatical flock did not accurately reflect the future Smith saw in his own prophetic imagination.[184] As one Council of Fifty member explained, "[T]he people will leave all other notions and flow unto this government."[185] Mormons believed that the crumbling of modern political systems would lead the remnants of humanity to recognize the only stable government that remained. The apocalypse would expose the false sense of security held by the citizenry of other nations, which would, in turn, lead to their willingly and peacefully becoming citizens of the Kingdom of God. In fact, many would have to flee to the borders of the Saints' gathering places to avoid the spreading violence and disease.

During the Nauvoo period, many Mormons saw themselves as witnesses of unfolding prophecy. William Clayton memorably reflected on the April 18, 1844, meeting of the Council: "It seems like heaven began on earth and the power of God is with us."[186] The Council of Fifty became a symbol of Mormon nationalism and had become a permanent fixture in the imagery of Mormon apocalyptic. While the institution itself may have become less important once the Saints arrived in Utah, the hope for a worldwide government led by the Mormon priesthood endured.

Regulating Mormon Vernacular Religion

So far, this chapter has examined the master narrative of Mormon apocalypticism, emphasizing the major anticipated events and motifs, and also considered how Smith came to express these beliefs at the end of his life in Nauvoo. Given this focus on the master narrative, the discussion has concentrated on sources that have clarified and emphasized the institutional hierarchy of the Mormon Church itself. However, lay members also had their own complicated interactions with the last days. Like Kimball and Young who watched soldiers march and battle in the skies of New York, many early Mormons had already been immersed in the millennialism of the Bible and the apocalypticism of the Second Great Awakening's fringe.

While the church's hierarchy framed life in terms of the apocalyptic, the general membership also participated in the apocalyptic project. Looking for "signs of the times" in local or global events was part of a Latter-day Saint's lived religion. The sense that destructions would soon commence and that God would act in miraculous ways was constructed through a variety of practices. The Saints turned to scripture study, dream and vision telling, reading local newspapers, and following local gossip. We have already seen how Smith himself, although the prophet of the church, permitted others to interpret his dreams and seek revelation for the constitution of the Kingdom of God. Smith at times embraced, at times rebuffed, and in some instances merely allowed apocalyptic revelations and speculation among his flock. To grasp the range of Smith's reactions to church members' involvement in apocalypticism, a few more historical examples will be discussed.

In 1830, before Smith had selected the site for the New Jerusalem, another early Mormon revelator tried to divine the location. Hiram Page had no reason to think he was transgressing when he, like Smith, dictated revelations through the medium of a seer stone. The same was true when Oliver Cowdery excitedly brought Smith news of Page's revelation, seemingly unaware that a controversy might ensue. Cowdery, Page, and others among the first Mormons viewed Smith as a chosen vessel, but not necessarily as the sole prophetic voice for the movement. In response to Page's dictations, Smith countered with a revelation decrying Page's prophetic gifts. The revelation commanded Cowdery to return to Page and inform him that his revelations were "not of me [God] & that Satan deceiveth him."[187] According to one source, the stone was shortly thereafter "Broke to powder and the writing [i.e., his revelations] Burnt."[188]

By marginalizing Page's revelatory gift, the revelation clarified Smith's role in the church. According to the revelation, "[N]o one shall be appointed to Receive commandments and Revelations in this Church excepting my Servant Joseph for he Receiveth them even as Moses."[189] While Oliver Cowdery, as the "second elder," could give commandments to the church when inspired to do so, even he was forbidden from "writ[ing] by way of Commandment."[190] It was only after this revelation that Smith was fully recognized as *the* Prophet, Seer, and Revelator over the church.[191]

The revelation rebuking Page exposed underlying tensions in the faith. For example, David Whitmer, who would remain loyal to Smith at the time, would, half a century later, describe the recognition of Joseph Smith as "Prophet, Seer, and Revelator" as the church's "first error." He believed it was a misrepresentation of how the faith had once operated. Smith received a number of true revelations, "but this is no more than many of the other brethren did." Whitmer recited the names of several "who gave great prophesies," including among them Hiram Page.[192]

Yet, Smith was a part of the early Mormon community of apocalypticists. While his revelations declared that others should not direct the church through written revelation, he did not discount their individual prophecies unless they contradicted what he considered the proper direction of the movement. He was particularly cautious about portrayals of Amerindian apocalypse. This caution may have played into why in 1831 Smith cracked down on charismatic performances in Kirtland, Ohio. These performances included speaking in Indian languages, impersonating fighting with a tomahawk and scalping, and preaching to invisible Native audiences. In 1832, in a private letter, Smith criticized the prophecies of "ignorant & unstable Sisters, & weak members . . . which excites many to believe that you are putting up the Indians to slay the Gentiles which exposes the lives of the Saints evry where [*sic*]."[193] In this case, Smith explained why he sought to regulate the Amerindian apocalypse—because it would foster suspicions of an Indian–Mormon military alliance.

Indeed, Smith's reaction to the Nauvoo High Council's deliberation over one Latter-day Saint's peculiar teachings on the apocalypse puts these more rigid examples of Smith regulating apocalypticists in perspective. On March 19, 1843, Pelatiah Brown was brought before the Nauvoo High Council, the church's ecclesiastical court, for the charge of "teaching false doctrine,"[194] specifically for promoting a novel interpretation of "the four beasts and four and twenty Elders mentioned in Rev. ch 5 v. 8."[195] That such discussions could raise controversy among the Saints was not new. Four years earlier, the Twelve Apostles issued an epistle warning missionaries against teaching "the further mysteries of the kingdom, till God shall tell you to preach them, which is not now." They cautioned against seeking to unravel the meanings of "the horns of the beast, the toes of the image, the frogs and the beast mentioned by John"—suggesting that some had made such speculation a component of their ministries.[196]

Yet, rather than chastizing Brown, Smith defended him over the pulpit the following month. "The old man has preached concerning the beast which was full of eyes before and behind and for this he was hauled up for trial. I never thought it was right to call up a man and try him because he erred in doctrine, it looks too much like methodism and not like Latter day Saintism. Methodists have creeds which a man must believe or be kicked out of their church. I want the liberty of believing as I please, it feels so good not to be tramelled [*sic*]. It don't [*sic*] prove that a man is not a good man, because he errs in doctrine."[197] Smith was concerned about "speculation" and "contention" when either related to the symbols of Revelation. For that reason, he provided his own exegesis of the passage, employing a literalist reading that the beasts were actual heavenly animals in contrast to Brown's belief that they represented the kingdoms of heaven.[198] When he finished preaching, he again warned Brown not to publicly speculate on these symbols while away from Nauvoo proselytizing.[199]

Smith's interactions with Brown here demonstrate the ways in which Smith was concerned by controversy but preferred not to restrain church members from developing individual interpretations of scriptural passages. This reaction recalls his more cautious warning to those taking stock in Miller's prophetic dates. In each of these examples, Smith opposed lay visionaries when he believed they tried to direct the church's movements or its membership. He corrected them when their revelations or apocalyptic interpretations created contention among their fellow Saints or provoked outsiders. Yet, the very nature of nineteenth-century Mormon religious practice allowed for a degree of individualized speculation. Smith's goal was not to stifle conversation, but to police the acceptable contours of that conversation in his role as the tradition's institutional prophetic voice. Ultimately, Smith's goal was to establish his authority to trump individual interpretations while still facilitating the project of communal apocalypticism among his followers. While he corrected Brown's interpretation of the beasts of Revelation, he defended Brown's right to present such ideas without censure.

2

"Long Shall His Blood . . . Stain Illinois"

Martyrology and Malediction

> But why did the people murder this prophet? What were they afraid of? O if he lives he will take away our power of government get the rule in his own hands and we will be destroyed. But they were mistaken. If they had let him alone or had received him he would have saved the nation from ruin and destruction. But now the nation has got to answer for his blood and the blood of his brother both of which were the Lords anointed.
>
> —Orson Hyde[1]

In death, Joseph Smith entered the cosmology he had outlined during life. He became the final martyr, whose murder would unleash the full magnitude of God's wrath upon the persecutors of the Saints.[2] Mormons understood this pattern—prophet testifies; prophet is killed for his testimony; destruction follows—through their reading of scripture. Thus, although Smith's assassination took the Saints by surprise, they would come to remember it as expected, necessary, and providential—another major event on the millennial timeline.

This chapter proposes an expansion on the standard interpretations of the Mormon trek from the United States. When Mormons marched en masse, leaving the borders of the United States, they sought a place where they could practice their religion unmolested. Mormons imagined their trek as a reenactment of the Israelites' exodus to the Promised Land. Theirs, too, was the story of an unwanted people guided by a prophet to an elusive land of prosperity and refuge by way of an imposing wilderness. Yet, this comparison needs further unpacking to bring out the on-the-ground significance for those who abandoned the city they had built from a swamp and marched into the frontier with a hope for greener pastures.

Terrible Revolution. Christopher James Blythe, Oxford University Press (2020). © Oxford University Press.
DOI: 10.1093/oso/9780190080280.001.0001

Historian Jan Shipps enhanced our understanding of the Latter-day Saint exodus when she suggested the similarities between these two journeys extended not only to the organization of the "Camps of Israel" (the name Brigham Young gave to the pioneer companies), but also to the initial Mormon escape over the Mississippi River. Shipps described the Mormons' sense of the miraculous as they made their way over the recently frozen river, an unlikely journey across a waterway similar, in this sense, to the parting of the Red Sea.[3] In this chapter, I will turn our attention away from what lay before the Mormons to what lay behind them—*from* their epic journey to the Promised Land and *to* the not-so-symbolic pursuing army led by a hostile and unmerciful pharaoh. While this image has been neglected in scholarly portraits of the exodus from Nauvoo, it was a common motif in contemporary sermons and prose.

Mormons employed other scriptural "types" or metaphors to describe their flight as well. Some spoke and wrote of the Saints figuratively closing the ark doors against the United States and taking refuge within as the flood waters rose. More often the Saints compared their departure to Lot and his family scrambling from Sodom moments before "brimstone and fire" lay waste to the city.[4] In distinction to the punishment dealt to Pharaoh and the Egyptians, the heavenly assault on Sodom and Gomorrah and the antediluvian world were not simply designed to coax a political leader to end persecution—they were acts of divine justice. From a nineteenth-century Mormon perspective, the United States was cursed when they took Smith's life and rejoiced in its aftermath. The "righteous" were no longer safe among the "wicked"; and in the former's absence, God would deal with the latter as he had so many earlier civilizations.

* * *

On June 27, 1844, Joseph and Hyrum Smith were both assassinated when the jail at Carthage, Illinois, was overrun by an "armed mob—painted black—of from 150 to 200 persons."[5] At 5 p.m., Joseph Smith, Hyrum Smith, John Taylor, and Willard Richards were located in a bedroom on the second floor, when multiple gunmen charged up the stairs as others aimed into the window from the courtyard below. The four Latter-day Saints endeavored to stave off their attackers by blocking the door with their bodies and, when that proved futile, by deflecting the muskets that appeared through the partially opened door with the aid of a cane. Hyrum Smith was the first to fall, shot in the face. Taylor recalled the patriarch's final words as he collapsed to the floor, "I am a dead man!"[6] Taylor was next to be shot, taking a bullet to the left thigh. He took shelter under the bed, although he was hit three more times. The final bullet struck him "on the fleshy part of my left hip . . . dashing the mangled fragments of flesh and blood against the wall."[7] Both Taylor and Richards would survive the attack.

Sometime during the action, Smith emptied his six-shooter into the hallway.[8] With no other means of defense, he tried to leap from the window, but, according to some accounts, while he did so he was shot dead, exclaiming: "*O Lord my God!*" The Mormon prophet was struck a total of four times. One bullet "entered his right hip and exited through the lower body," another "entered his right chest and exited below the shoulder blade," a third "hit under the heart," and the final "shot may have hit the right collarbone."[9] There are contradictions in the sources and a debate in the historiography about whether these bullets all found their mark while Smith was still standing in the second floor of the jail or after he had fallen from the window and landed on the ground below.[10] John Taylor, for example, noted that the bodies of both Hyrum and Joseph were, in an act of brutality, shot after they were dead. Other accounts suggest that Joseph survived the fall only to then be killed by firing squad while propped against a well in the jail's courtyard.[11]

Even before the bodies of Joseph and Hyrum were returned to Nauvoo, before any orators had eulogized them and before any individuals mourned their deaths, Latter-day Saints already had a robust and distinctive martyrology by which to make sense of their loss. The Smith brothers were not the first Mormon martyrs. There was Andrew Barber, killed in an 1833 Jackson County skirmish, whose body Mary Elizabeth Lightner Rollins described as "a more heavenly corpse I never saw or expect to see on the face of the earth. His face was so happy."[12] There was also David Patten, who was killed at the Battle of Crooked River and whose slow death had been memorialized in the *Journal of Heber C. Kimball* (1840). There were the seventeen men and boys slaughtered (and in some cases dismembered) at Hawn's Mill. The count of martyrs rose to hundreds when Mormons considered all the deaths from exposure and disease that occurred as a consequence of their forced exiles; it amounted to thousands when the status, or at least a share in the status, was granted to those who had survived such hardships.[13]

Mormons were not the only Christians in early America to find meaning in stories of martyrdom. Quakers and Baptists still remembered their own early American persecutions. Anglo-Protestants, more generally, looked back on their persecutions in early modern England. They still imagined a Roman Catholic menace eager to shed blood, defile innocent Protestant women, and enslave the minds of the faithful. Charles Buck's popular *Theological Dictionary* included a lengthy entry on both "martyr" and "martyrology." While disparaging Roman Catholic martyrologies as full of superstition and interpolation, Buck presented the sheer "number and fortitude of those who have suffered for Christianity as a collateral proof at least of its excellency." Martyrdom might not offer conclusive evidence of Christianity's truthfulness, but the willingness of so "many wise and good men" to die for their beliefs would "certainly afford something considerable in its favour."[14]

In the antebellum era, stories of martyrdom were still occasionally used as a means of educating children on their Christian duty. The year after Smith's death, the *Child's Friend and Family Magazine* published a piece entitled "Martyrs," which opens with a child insisting that his mother keep her promise to tell him more concerning the martyrs. The mother selects "a terrible story in the apocrypha, which was almost too terrible to relate, and which is yet so glorious and inspiring that I feel that I believe I must tell you." There were great religious lessons in the martyrs and their examples of the soul becoming "supreme master, defying suffering, defying death, and still more defying the promise of all the pleasures of this life to turn from its allegiance to God."[15]

Martyr-lore could be found in the scriptures, including both testaments and the Apocrypha (still printed in most Bibles), but also in another volume regularly found in local libraries and Christian bookshelves. Like generations before them, many Americans still found inspiration in the pages of John Foxe's *Actes and Monuments*, also known in the United States as the *Book of the Martyrs*.[16] Mormons were also conversant with this Protestant classic and its themes. Edward Stevenson recalled that Joseph Smith had once borrowed his personal copy. When the Mormon prophet returned it, he told Stevenson, "I have seen those [English] martyrs by aid of the Urim and Thummim; God has a salvation for them."[17] For Joseph Smith, the content of the book and the significance of that content had been confirmed by supernatural means. Early Mormon writings occasionally borrowed from Foxe's martyrology. For example, in 1844, Parley P. Pratt used Foxe's treatise to describe the first-century apostolic martyrdoms. He described these men "crucified, beheaded, sawn asunder, burned, torn by wild beasts; betrayed, shot, Hung, boiled, roasted, imprisoned, starved, and Tortured in ten thousand nameless ways."[18]

Mormons, almost universally raised as Protestants, were already schooled in the interpretive category of martyrdom, which was easily applied to their lived experience of persecution and conflict.[19] The Saints expected casualties at the hands of the wicked. After all, the Book of Mormon had portrayed the murder of the righteous as a necessary act, bringing on civilization's destruction. Mormons were convinced that it was their own blood that would topple Gentile society. Only months after the violence at Hawn's Mill, Eliza R. Snow explained, "The nations of the world can never fill the cup of their iniquity without shedding innocent blood, and the blood of the 'Latter Day Saints' will, that of many of them be required."[20] Snow employed a phrase unique to Smith's revelations, "the cup of their iniquity," to refer to the golden cup held by the female prostitute figure of Revelation 17. This woman, "Babylon the Great, the Mother of Harlots," is "drunken with the blood of the saints, and with the blood of the martyrs of Jesus."[21] The contents of Babylon's cup consisted of the fruits of her persecution, which would be repaid to her "double" in terms of "plagues . . . death, mourning, and famine."[22] But first, claimed Snow, she would need to fill her cup, so God could, in turn, pour out the cup of his wrath.

Once the Saints had arrived in Commerce, the apostles published a statement to comfort those who had endured hardships and persecutions in Missouri and who were now refugees along the river. The statement focused their attention on the apocalypse. Drawing again on the imagery of Revelation, the apostles pointed to the martyrs under the heavenly altar found in chapter 6. The ancient martyrs pled for justice: "How long, O Lord, holy and true, dost thou not judge and avenge our blood on them that dwell on the earth?"[23] The response: They were to "rest yet for a little season, until their fellow servants also and their brethren, that should be killed as they *were,* should be fulfilled."[24] Although the apostles' epistle consoled the Saints with the assurance that "angels have gazed upon the scene, and your tears, your groans, your sorrows, and anguish of heart, are had in remembrance before God," there was no immediate promise of better times ahead. They instructed the fold to "be patient, then until the words of God [to the martyrs] be fulfilled, and his designs accomplished and then shall he pour out his vengeance upon the devoted heads of *your* murderers, and then shall they know that he is God, and that you are his people."[25] For the Mormons, to die at the hands of their oppressors was the act that would usher in the apocalypse. Further persecution and martyrdom were thus inevitable and expected.

"The Martyrdom" and Emotion in Nauvoo

There was a collective effort to construct meaning from the unexpected tragedy of Joseph and Hyrum Smith's murders. From the first eulogy offered by William W. Phelps, the Mormon prophet's martyrdom became the predominant theme in sermons and the writings of the church's leadership. Joseph and Hyrum had been willing to go to their deaths to prevent the destruction of Nauvoo. They had died for their people. Their deaths set them apart as witnesses for their faith. One account of the martyrdom, which was eventually added to Mormon scripture, eulogized Smith in no uncertain terms: "He lived great, and he died great in the eyes of God and his people; and like most of the Lord's anointed in ancient times, has sealed his mission and his works with his own blood; and so has his brother Hyrum. . . . The testators are now dead, and their testament is in force."[26]

Latter-day Saints heard and imbibed these sentiments, but they likely did not require anyone to tell them that their murdered prophet should be revered as a martyr. In fact, the rhetoric employed by hierarchical voices was only one aspect of the project of sacralizing Smith's memory. To comprehend the real impact of Smith's death, we must also look to the journal writing, dream telling, and local gossip that was so important to everyday life in Nauvoo. By so doing, we are better able to understand the contours of Smith's re-conception as a martyr, who in his death was yet perceived as consciously engaged in the divine drama. His death functioned as a hinge in the Mormon cultural conception of time around which everything now swung.

Nineteenth-century diaries, memoirs, and correspondence are replete with descriptions of the moment individuals and communities of Latter-day Saints learned of the tragedy. The Saints' grief was sometimes expressed in terms of the inability to shed tears, as with Benjamin F. Johnson who "stood up, dazed with grief, or could groan but could not weep. The fountain of tears was dry!"[27] Arza Adams, in contrast, recalled the moment as "a solemn time," in which "many a rosy cheek was wet with tears, both men and women."[28]

The impact of the martyrdom was so substantial that many claimed to have experienced an emotional wave of inexplicable sorrow that corresponded to the time of Smith's murder. In 1849, Orson Hyde recalled:

> There was an unspeakable something, a portentous significancy in the firmament and among the inhabitants of the earth. Multitudes felt the whisperings of wo and grief, and the forebodings of tribulation and

> sor[r]ow that they will never forget, though the tongue of man can never utter it. The Saints of God, whether near the scene of blood, or even a thousand miles distant, felt at the very moment the Prophet lay in royal gore, that an awful deed was perpetrated. O, the repulsive chill! the melancholy vibrations of the very air, as the prince of darkness receded in hopeful triumph from the scene of slaughter! That night could not the Saints sleep, though uninformed by man of what had passed with the Seer and Patriarch, and far, far remote from the scene; yet to them sleep refused a visitation—the eyelids refused to close—the hearts of many sighed deeply in secret, and inquired, "Why am I thus?"[29]

In memoirs, descriptions of these initial emotions are followed by descriptions of the Smith brothers' viewing. Throughout the morning and afternoon of June 29, thousands came to the Nauvoo Mansion, Smith's final residence, to pay their last respects to the prophet and patriarch as they lay side-by-side in the large dining room. Mosiah Hancock recalled the procedure for attendees: "As we came in at the door, we came to the feet of the Prophet Joseph, then passed up by his left side and around his head, then down by his right side. Next we turned to the right and came to the feet of Hyrum, then up by his left side and around his head and down by his right side; then we filed out of the other door. So the great stream of people continued until the Saints all had the privilege of taking their last look at the martyred bodies."[30]

Like the bodies of earlier martyrs, they possessed a certain sanctity even while lying in their gore. Joseph Fielding suggested that the "Noble Appearance" the two possessed in life "was by no means lost in Death."[31] Sarah Rich referred to the expressions on their faces as "peacefull."[32] Others commented on the reality of two human corpses, although washed and dressed, still lying lifeless in their coffins. Gilbert Belnap was not alone in describing the brothers' remains as "mangled bodies."[33] Multiple accounts describe Joseph as natural in his appearance, but Hyrum "had been shot in the face and therefore he did not look very natural."[34] Joseph Hovey wrote, "Joseph looked quite natural but Hyrum was so sweled [*sic*] in the face that he did not look natural."[35]

Many brought their children to see the remains of the two revered men in hopes of making a lasting impression. Mary Rich, whose father had guarded the bodies the previous night, was escorted into the mansion before the general viewing. She recalled, "I went down, saw them and laid my hand on

Joseph's forehead. The blood was oozing out of the wound in his shoulder, and the sheet that was around him was stained with blood."[36] Another guard remained with his adolescent son at the mansion following the viewing. Mosiah Hancock remembered a spontaneous ritual at the site of the bodies. His father instructed him "to place one hand on Joseph's breast and to raise my other arm and swear with hand uplifted that I would never make a compromise with any of the sons of Hell."[37] He then repeated the oath with his hand on Hyrum's corpse.

The raw interaction with the bodies underscored the experience of the martyrdom. As Lyman Littlefield wrote in 1888, "That was an hour marked in the history of this people, and although forty-four years have since passed away, the powers of memory seldom go back and review the scene—though in gleams of momentary fleetness—without sensations of pain."[38] There is little danger of exaggerating the level of grief the Saints encountered in the summer of 1844. For some it seemed to be embodied in the very landscape. As Sally Randall wrote, "[I]t seames [*sic*] all nature mournes [*sic*]."[39]

The mourning Saints also experienced confusion and doubt. Some Mormons worried that Smith had died prematurely. Because of the institutionally focused histories written about this period, the question most associated with this moment is: Who would take the lead of the church now that the Mormon prophet had died? However, it is possible that another question was of equal importance to many Latter-day Saints: Was Joseph Smith not supposed to live to see the temple completed, become the president of the United States, translate further sacred records, or, perhaps, live until the Second Coming of Christ? Smith's allegedly premature death was an important aspect to critics' assertions that he had become a "fallen prophet," but it also consumed the devout with anxiety.[40]

In contrast, Smith's confidants regularly spoke of having heard the prophet refer to intimations of his approaching death. Not all were convinced by these claims. Isaac Scott, a Mormon who had sided with William Law, a dissident member of the church's first presidency, wrote, "All these statements, I believe, are false and got up for the purpose of reconciling the minds of the church. I believe they had not the least idea that they were going to be murdered."[41] Yet, as with other charismatic Christians of the era, Mormons endowed with the gift of prophecy regularly foresaw their own deaths. In 1843, Smith eulogized James Adams, claiming that the deceased "had had revelations concerning his departure, and had gone to a more important work—of opening up a more effectual door for the dead."[42] Smith was also the recipient of revelations spelling out the timing of his death. In the days after learning of the Carthage slaying, Lyman Wight recounted that while he was incarcerated with Smith in Liberty, Missouri (1838–1839), the prophet confided to him that "he should not live to see forty years but told him not to reveal it until [*sic*] he was dead."[43]

These statements were not only confined to memoirs relayed after the fact. There were numerous expressions of such forebodings recorded in the minutes of Smith's sermons. For example, in 1842, he told a meeting of the Relief Society "that the church would not have his instruction long, and the world would not be troubled with him a great while."[44] Such pronouncements will not be surprising to those familiar with R. Laurence Moore's claim that since the beginning of his prophetic career Smith "had determined to cast himself in a martyr's role, and a considerable part of what he wrote and said was designed to further that image. By the last years of his life, his statements had become numbingly formulaic."[45] Other historians, such as Richard Bushman, have interpreted these moments as bouts of melancholy and despair.[46] Whether we interpret them as part of Smith's own psychology or as his deliberate self-portrayal as predestined martyr, Smith's predictions of his death were not only a matter of post facto fantasy.

Accounts of Smith's seeming foreknowledge of his martyrdom softened the blow that the Mormon prophet had died before he could administer the anticipated endowment within the completed temple. Often when the apostles spoke of Smith's premonitions of his death, it was in reference to him entrusting them with these rites. He had been "constrained" to pass on the most valuable revelations in order that they would not be lost.[47] Recalling his own reception of these rites, Joseph Fielding recorded his confidence that Smith had completed his earthly mission and was needed in the "World of Spirits." "These reflections in a great measure took off the edge of the grief that I might else have felt, for I thought that he had so fulfilled his own purposes, and I felt willing to say amen to it."[48]

Mormons generally assigned meaning to death by asserting that the deceased were still able to move forward with his or her mortal callings or receive additional postmortal assignments. In reference to James Adams's death, Smith had earlier explained that to die simply meant to graduate onto "a greater and more glorious work."[49] Although Latter-day Saints tended to emphasize that Smith continued his ministry after his death through his work with spirits in prison, many also believed he remained conscious of happenings on earth and could act here as well. Benjamin F. Johnson later remembered that Smith had once assured him that "if I was on the other side of the veil I could do many times more for my friends than I can do while [I] am with them here."[50]

This understanding mitigated the failed expectation that Smith was supposed to obtain the American presidency, as some of the Saints anticipated he would, or at least, that he would be alive to finish his bid for office. Although earlier we noted that Brigham Young was skeptical about whether Smith could obtain the necessary votes, there was a popular belief that their prophet was destined to hold the presidential office. As late as 1854, Benjamin G. Ferris claimed "there are those among [Smith's] followers in Utah who firmly believe he would have been elected in 1844 had not his career been cut short by an untimely death."[51] John D. Lee seems likely to have been among this number. While still campaigning in the East, he recorded an angelic visitation which he received in response to his concerns about what to do now that Smith had died:

> A Personage whose face shone as lightning stood before me!! and bid my fears depart. Your mission[,] continued He, and labors are accepted—so were the 12 and 70s that were sent out by the Son of God—they supposed that their labors were lost: when their leader was taken and crucified instead [*sic*] of being crown[ed] King (temporal) of that Nation as they fondly expected—Just so it is with you—instead of electing your leader the chief Magistrate of this Nation—they have martyred him in prison—which has hasten[ed] his exaltation to the ex[ec]utive chair over this generation—so now return home in peace and there wait your endowment from on high as did the di[s]ciples at Jerusalem—for this circumstance is parallel to that.[52]

Lee's vision spelled out the same message undergirding so many other expressions of the Mormon faith in this period: that Smith's death would enable, rather than inhibit, the prophet to fulfill these prophecies.

Fear and Vengeance

Realizing there were those eager to avenge their prophet, members of the hierarchy waged a concerted effort to alleviate the potential for further bloodshed. Leaders acted quickly to quash any attempt at organizing a military or vigilante campaign against Carthage. William Clayton wrote, "A few words would raise the City in arms & massacre the Cities of Carthage and Warsaw & lay them in ashes but it is wisdom to be quiet."[53] Mormons armed themselves, but accepted their leaders' caution not to instigate conflict. Richards articulated the Saints' approach toward their enemies when he returned to Nauvoo from Carthage. He urged the Saints "to trust in the law for redress, and when that failed, to call upon God to avenge us of our wrongs."[54] Although many believed that the Nauvoo Legion could easily ravage Carthage for its crimes, the Saints would await justice from the courts.[55]

Placing trust in the sympathies of a non-Mormon legal system did little to assuage the fears of Nauvoo's residents. Initially, some worried that the martyrdom was only the beginning of a more substantial Mormon holocaust to follow. Joseph Fielding described his thoughts as he watched the wagon carrying the Smiths' remains arrive in Nauvoo: "Is the blood of the sheep again to be shed like that of the shepherd as in former days? Father, if it be possible, let this cup pass from us, but if not, let thy will be done and let us be strengthened to endure to the end."[56] The story of the Christian martyrs seemed set to repeat in Nauvoo.

Vilate Kimball also anticipated violence. In a letter to her husband, Heber C. Kimball, still in the East campaigning for Joseph's candidacy, she related the news of the martyrs' deaths. Her account moved from a scene of grief at the viewing, where the crushing impact on the Saints was such that "every heart is filled with sorrow, and the very streets of Nauvoo seam to morn," to one of fear in its aftermath. Specifically, Vilate pointed to a frightening portent that had manifested on June 17, ten days before the events of Carthage, while the Nauvoo Legion had organized to defend the city against rioters:

> We are kept awake night after night by the alarm of mobs. These apostates say, their damnation is sealed, their die is cast, their doom is fixed, and they are determined to do all in their power to have revenge. [William] Law says he wants nine more that was in his quorum. Some time I am afraid he will get them. I have no doubt but you are on[e]. What makes me feer [*sic*], is from a circumstance that took place when the legion was first called out to defend the city. There was several Drums found with blood on, no one could account for it. They examined to see how many there was, they found tenn [*sic*], and while they were examining the eleventh there came a large drop on that. Wm has seen them; he says with all the drums have ben [*sic*] used the blood is yet plain to be seen. He has got two if he gets the nine more it will make eleven. But I try to submit all things into the hands of God.[57]

The final martyr's cry was often portrayed in legal terms. In the October 1845 conference, Smith's mother, Lucy Mack Smith, remembered that when her son returned from Washington, D.C., he announced that he had exhausted all possibility for redress, but then promised that "these cases are recorded in heaven, and I am going to lay them before the highest court in heaven."[63] The last five years of prayer might have proved efficacious, but could not compare with a personal plea from the other side. The Mormons now had a new advocate in heaven and were thus confident that it would not be long before God would act.

Phelps's eulogy cast Smith as another figure in the Revelation of St. John as well, namely, as the final of seven destroying angels armed with vials of God's wrath to be poured out sequentially on the wicked. The author of Revelation portrayed this seventh angel as issuing God's final act of justice. When the figure "poured out his vial into the air . . . there came a great voice out of the temple of heaven, from the throne, saying, It is done" (Revelation 16:17). Phelps narrated Smith's transformation to angelic status: The Mormon prophet had "escaped through blood to bliss to fire the indignation of the holy ones who wrote the destinies of men! And he is an angel now, and if ever there was a time when the 'vials of wrath,' ought to be poured out upon the wicked—*it is now and hence! and who can do it better than Joseph?*"[64] Nauvoo's general never led the armies of the United States as some had hoped, but as a destroying angel, he would take the lead in administering vengeance on the Saints' enemies. Smith had ascended to heaven to serve as witness, prosecutor, and executioner in a court that would decide the fate of the world.

"Mutilated Bodies" and Promised Resurrections

Lore surrounding Smith's material remains blossomed in the wake of his death. One set of stories concerned their persecutors' efforts to defile the corpses. Soon after the Smiths' deaths, reports circulated that while the mob had gathered around Joseph's lifeless form, onc of their number stepped forward to dismember the body. According to legend, a bolt of light prevented the sadist from severing Smith's head and sent the mob fleeing from the jail[65] (see Figure 2.1). The Saints suspected this "ruffian" would not be the last to seek their prophet's remains.[66] Those caring for the body organized a mock burial to mislead potential graverobbers. They held a public ceremony,

The implication of the bloody drums was also noticed by Sally Randall: " say there is nine more they are determined to have, and when it will I don't know."[58] Vilate Kimball identified Law's intended victims as those were "in his quorum," seemingly an allusion to the Anointed Quorum, w had eleven members at its initial meeting, although that number would l included Law himself. Undergirding this rumor was a belief that apostate their very nature would seek to prevent the sacred temple rituals from b imparted to the Saints. Smith had been inspired to give them to a select b and now bloodthirsty apostates would kill them one-by-one in order to s the rituals from being disseminated.

As frightening as the days following the martyrdom must have been, Saints found some consolation in a reading from the Revelation of St. Jo where they came to believe Smith's death promised them a rapid solution their mounting problems. Smith became an implicit but necessary figure the Saints' rendering of the Book of Revelation. In this reading, Smith w seen as the final martyr to join his comrades under the celestial altar pleadi for vengeance.[59] There was talk that Joseph Smith had even sent word fro Carthage instructing his followers to "read the 6th chapter of Revelati and take particular notice from the 8th to the 12th verse."[60] The chapt detailed the opening of the seven seals with their corresponding apocalypt events, including the appearance of the fourth horseman, Death, the marty prayer, and the heavenly phenomenon of the moon turning to blood and t sky darkening as the destruction of the wicked began.[61]

Whether Smith had drawn these verses to the attention of his fold the report merely reflected a nascent legend, W.W. Phelps articulated t imagery when preaching on the day of Smith's funeral. Phelps assured t Saints that the "souls under the altar, that John saw, hail it [Joseph's death] the harbinger of Jehovah's vengeance!" Seeing Smith as the final martyr h far-reaching implications for the emotional state of Nauvoo's residents, well as the construction of Mormon prophecy. While it had been assum in the wake of the conflicts in Missouri that many more lives would ne to be sacrificed before God would act on the Saints' behalf, now the Sai came to believe that the deaths of Joseph and Hyrum would be the crowni act that sealed the fate of the world. As Brigham Young urged the Saints remain in Nauvoo to complete the temple, he drew upon this concept: "Y will soon wake up to things as they are. Their [*sic*] has been a great dept [*s* paid. Their [*sic*] will be no need of more Blood of the Saints being Shed present."[62]

Figure 2.1 Image of the aftermath of Joseph Smith's assassination. This image depicts a reported incident in which a "ruffian" among the mob was prevented from decapitating Smith's corpse by a blinding light. William McDaniels, *A Correct Account of the Murder of Generals Joseph and Hyrum Smith* (1845).

burying two coffins filled with sandbags in the local cemetery. Meanwhile, the actual remains of Joseph and Hyrum were secretly interred "in the cellar a cross [*sic*] the street west of the 'Nauvoo House.'"[67]

A controversy emerged later that summer when Emma Smith had the remains relocated without the knowledge of the church's leadership. She refused to reveal their whereabouts, concerned that if the apostles discovered their location, they would attempt to transport the bodies to the West.[68] There were a variety of matters at stake with regard to the possession of the bodies. For Emma Smith, hiding the bodies from others may have simply been her way of asserting a widow's prerogative concerning burial. At least one sectarian group hoped to obtain the bodies in order to legitimate their movement. John C. Bennett imagined that possessing the bodies "would have an astonishing effect in congregating the people at Voree," where James Strang had established a church.[69] The average Mormon was likely more concerned where their prophet was laid to rest for theological reasons. The Saints believed in a literal resurrection of the dead, which meant that where Joseph was buried was where he would return. Young insisted that it was his intent to fulfill Smith's wishes to be buried in the Smith family tomb constructed next to the temple, where the Mormon prophet had once publicly imagined "in the morning of the resurrecti[o]n" being reunited with his father, "as soon as the rock rends. & before we come out of our graves."[70]

In October 1845, Young conveyed his intention to "petition Sister Emma, in the name of Israel's God, to let us deposit the remains of Joseph according as he commanded us. And if she will not consent to it, our garments are clear. Then when he awakes in the morning of the resurrection, he shall talk with them, not with me; the sin shall be upon her head, not ours."[71] Yet, if Young only wanted to provide Smith with the burial he had intended, others, as Smith's widow suspected, wanted the bodies removed to the West. When Emma left Nauvoo for a brief period to reside in Montrose, an overseer of the church's properties, Joseph Heywood, wrote to Brigham Young to inform him that "[i]t is known to some through Emma where [the bodies] lie. We have thought if it was wisdom to remove them that it could be effected now especially as Emma is out of the way."[72] Although the Smiths' bodies remained where Emma buried them until 1928 when the Reorganized Church of Jesus Christ of Latter Day Saints recovered them, they would become the frequent subject of the Saints' stories—some of which held currency well into the twentieth century.

Most prominently, such narratives claimed that several individuals uncovered the corpses and brought them to the Great Basin, where they deposited them in Salt Lake City. Amorah Smithson, a daughter of John D. Lee, believed her father was one of those so entrusted with bringing the bodies to Utah. Her mother had frequently told her of a miraculous event that attended the party's trip across the treacherous Missouri River while transporting the bodies: "When they were ready to starts [*sic*], the stars came donw [*sic*] like torches and shone until they could see clear across the river, so that they made a fine landing. Then the stars disappeared and it was dark as before."[73] A similar story was passed down in the William Carter family along with another that the bodies were transported via Brigham Young, Heber C. Kimball, and Walter Eli Wilcox.[74] The belief that the bodies found their final resting place in Salt Lake City carried into the twentieth century, when it was sometimes suggested that they were interred where the Joseph and Hyrum Smith memorials were constructed in 1911[75] (see Figure 2.2).

Again, the importance of where Smith was buried was not solely due to the sanctity attached to the martyrs' remains or the fact that possession of such remains seemed to legitimate any faction of Mormonism, but rather because of the belief that the resurrected Smith would play a significant role in eschatological events. In July 1844, Parley P. Pratt heard the voice of God state

Figure 2.2 Photo of the Joseph Smith monument on the Salt Lake City Temple grounds, ca. 1911. Legends held that this monument, as well as the nearby Hyrum Smith monument, were placed on the grounds to memorialize where the martyrs' remains had been interred. In reality, the bodies of Joseph and Hyrum Smith remained in Nauvoo, Illinois, in a secret burial site near the home of Joseph Smith's widow. Courtesy of the Church History Library.

that Joseph Smith "shall stand in due time on the earth in the flesh, and fulfill that to which he is appointed."[76] Others recounted witnessing apparitions of the departed prophet; gradually, there were those who came to believe that Smith had already emerged from his grave.

On April 21, 1850, Brigham Young expressed his consternation with the idea, referring to the belief as "foolery" and those who propagated it as "men [who] have no understanding."[77] In 1857, he again decried the belief:

> Joseph is not resurrected; and if you will visit the graves you will find the bodies of Joseph and Hyrum yet in their resting place. Do not be mistaken about that; they will be resurrected in due time. . . . I do not know that any news would come to my ears so sad and discouraging, so calculated to blight my faith and hope as to hear that Joseph is resurrected and has not made a visit to his brethren . . . As quick as Joseph ascends to his Father and God, he will get a commission to this earth again, and I shall be the first woman that he will manifest himself to. I was going to say the first man, but there are so many women who profess to have seen him, that I thought I would say woman. I should feel worse than I now do, if I knew that Joseph was resurrected and had not paid us a visit, which he most assuredly will do, when that period arrives.[78]

Young's jab at Mormonism's lay visionaries is ironic given the Gospel of Matthew's assertion that the resurrected Jesus first appeared to Mary much to the chagrin of Peter, Brigham Young's counterpart in the narrative. It was apparent that Young had specific ideas for what Smith's eventual resurrection and reunion with the Saints would entail.

In the former 1850 sermon, Young promised, "Bye and bye there will be a Resurrection of the Just. Jesus will be here. Joseph[,] Hyram, and Father Smith and others will be here, but will the world know it[?] They will not."[79] Young set the temple apart as a place in which resurrected beings would instruct the Saints in performing ordinances for the dead and eventually to organize the resurrection of others. When he argued against theories of the resurrection that were then popular after Smith's death, he contended that no one could comprehend the doctrine unless they had the "keys" of the resurrection. Young insisted, "Joseph will hold the keys of the Resurrection . . . and lead this people out of their graves."[80] On another occasion, in 1854, he referred to Joseph as the "President of the Resurrection in this Dispensation," who would "be the first to rise from the dead. When he has passed through it, then I reckon the Keys of the Resurrection will be committed to him."[81] Smith was a "secondary savior": He did not supplant Jesus Christ in Mormon cosmology, but served below him as the immediate instigator of the resurrection.[82]

William Appleby took Young's assessment of Smith's future resurrection seriously. A few pages after he drafted the cited 1850 sermon in his journal, he recorded a dream of Smith's resurrection that he had experienced. The scene opened with Appleby in a room set for the performance of an esoteric rite:

> I saw myself in a building with walls and a bench setting against the North wall and near the East wall about the middle of the Room there appeared to be something resembling a case of these containing Embalmed Mummies. A person appeared in the room with a Rod in his hand, he struck the case two or three times when at his command Joseph appeared to come forth. He was resurrected. He walked and sat down on the bench against the wall at this time two men appeared with him on the Bench one sitting on the right and the other on the left of Joseph. He then commenced telling about the principles of the Resurrection and what he had passed through the one sitting on this left hand (and on the right of me as I stood facing them) moved towards Joseph and made a motion to touch him, when Joseph moved away from him and told him not to touch him. He then desisted while Joseph detailed the principles of the Resurrection.[83]

In this setting steeped with ritualized mystery, as evidenced by the presence of mummies and unnamed figures, Smith appeared in his role as the source and revealer of knowledge concerning the resurrection, just as Young suggested he would. The inclusion of a reprimand for someone eager to touch him recalled Mary's encounter with the resurrected Jesus in the Gospel of St. Matthew. The dream also hinted at another reason for why one might be eager to experience a manifestation from Joseph Smith. Not only did Smith teach Appleby about the resurrection, but in the remainder of the dream, Appleby discovered that he was also to teach these principles to others. He found himself in another room where several men, including the apostle Amasa Lyman, waited for him. He recalled, "I went to Br. Amasa put my mouth to his ear and communicated to him the principles Joseph had revealed and also concerning the Resurrection of Joseph that I had witnessed for I then recollected the same; it was glorious."[84] Thus, such a recipient did not only bypass the channels of the apostleship, but was also placed in a position to teach them. Appleby believed that Joseph Smith had actually visited him while in his dream. When he awakened, he "could remember some part of" Joseph's instruction, but after falling back to sleep, these teachings "in regard to the Resurrection that Joseph had taught were gone from me."[85]

Smith's resurrected millenarian role continued in turn-of-the-century vernacular prophecy. In a particularly popular prophecy, the female visionary Amanda Wilcox, with the assistance of Heber C. Kimball, saw the "secret" location of Smith's body, after gazing on a scene of the future Salt Lake City temple. Later she commented that "the Prophet Joseph and others will make their appearance and those who have remained faithful will be selected to return to Jackson County, Missouri."[86] Fitting into this narrative tradition, Newman Bulkley recalled a vision in which the resurrected Joseph Smith consulted with Jesus Christ in the temple before Smith and Jesus would take the lead of an army of 50,000 to reclaim Jackson County. [87] The Saints envisioned Smith in a number of apocalyptic roles—foremost among them, destroying angel to the wicked and a "secondary savior" to the righteous.

Naming the Guilty

Mormons were not solely concerned with the millenarian eventualities of Smith's death. They were also immersed in the quest to unravel what they perceived as a conspiracy at the core of their prophet's assassination. This conspiracy included but went beyond the five men charged and then acquitted for the murders—Mark Aldrich, Jacob Davis, William Grover, Thomas Sharp, Levi Williams—as well as the up to 200 who were present at the assassination but were never prosecuted.[88] The Saints believed divine wrath would be levied against apostates, government officials, and eventually the citizenry of the nation at large.

Mormons came to believe that the conspiracy was connected to Freemasonry. Smith had held the fraternity in high esteem and had even joined their ranks himself in March 1842, three months after a lodge was organized in Nauvoo.[89] Through his encouragement, within six months of his induction, there were more Masons in the Nauvoo Lodge than the rest of the state combined.[90] Smith's promotion of Freemasonry was likely part of his effort to establish security and even respectability for Mormon settlements in Illinois. Freemasons were well known for their loyalty and support of fellow Freemasons and the Saints welcomed the chance to build new friendships. The fact that several Illinois politicians were also part of the fraternity made membership particularly appealing.[91]

However, in the wake of the martyrdom, the Saints became disenchanted with Freemasonry, concluding that Freemasons would not extend their loyalty and fraternal affection to Mormon members. In fact, Mormons believed they had not done so on the fateful night of June 27. The July 15, 1844, *Times and Seasons* editorial entitled "The Murder" depicted Joseph and Hyrum Smith "shot to death, while, with uplifted hands they gave such signs of distress as would have commanded the interposition and benevolence of Savages or Pagans." Addressing Freemasonry, the editorial continued, "They were both Masons in good standing. Ye brethren of 'the mystic tie' what think ye!"[92] Here was the first claim that Smith had offered the "grand hailing sign of distress," a signal to Masons that one of their brotherhood was in danger. Zina D. Huntington would later state that Smith "made the Masonic sign of distress, but those signs were not heeded except by the God of Heaven."[93]

Mormons believed Masons were present in the mob to see Joseph signal for their aid, because Masons were numbered among his murderers. Heber C. Kimball later claimed "they were massacred through the instrumentality of some of the leading men of that fraternity through the States."[94] In 1860, Brigham Young asserted that Masons even held a preliminary council to deliberate on whether to take the prophet's life. Young claimed, "[T]here were delegates from the various lodges in the Union to see that he was put to death. . . . They have got the blood of the prophets upon their heads & they have got to meet it."[95] Smith's murder initiated the Mormon reconception of Freemasonry as if the lodge was a modern revival of the Book of Mormon's ancient Gadiantons. The latter secret combination had also served to protect assassins by secret oaths and esoteric signs.

Mormons viewed apostates as particularly responsible for Smith's blood. Not surprisingly, those associated with the anti-Mormon, or at least anti-Smith, press, including the *Nauvoo Expositor*, were considered culpable, but so were later dissenters who opposed the leadership of the Twelve. For example, church leaders portrayed Sidney Rigdon as complicit in the assassination based on his claim that God had willed the murders for Smith's crimes (i.e., polygamy).[96] Those whose professed support of the Twelve was suspect were also sometimes accused of supporting the mob. William Marks, who ran the Nauvoo Mansion in the months after Smith's death, was quickly ostracized. The real concern was the combination of his ecclesiastical influence as the Nauvoo Stake president and his opposition to plural marriage, but this was expressed in a shared sentiment that he had not sufficiently grieved when the martyrs died.[97] In February 1845, he was accused of housing a member of the mob and, in time, he was rumored to have been a participant himself.[98]

Mormons also placed blame for Smith's murder on the State of Illinois. The Carthage Greys were rumored to have acted as Smith's firing squad, even after Governor Thomas Ford's pledge that the Mormon prophet would be safe in custody. After the martyrdom, Mormons persistently recounted this broken promise. The Saints came to see Ford as not only inept in his duties as governor, but also as deliberately instrumental in setting the scene for their prophet's murder and carrying out a cover-up that allowed the guilty to escape justice. Ford would later express his concern that Mormons would depict him in the role of Pilate or Herod in what was for them a modern re-enactment of the Christian passion narrative.[99] W.W. Phelps had already recognized Illinois's specific guilt in a hymn he wrote the month after the martyrdom: "Long shall his [Smith's] blood which was shed by assassins, Stain Illinois while the Earth lauds his fame."[100]

Blame for the murder could be stretched over the entirety of the United States. On July 15, 1844, Parley P. Pratt, Willard Richards, John Taylor, and W.W. Phelps wrote a letter "To the Saints Abroad":

> As to our country and nation, we have more reason to weep for them, than for those that they have murdered; for they are destroying themselves and their institutions and there is no remedy: and as to feelings of revenge, let them not have place for one moment in our bosoms, for God's vengeance will speedily consume to that degree that we would fain be hid away and not endure the sight.[101]

Brigham Young went so far as to suggest that the "mob that collected at Carthage, Illinois, to commit that deed of blood contained a delegation representing every State in the Union."[102] This was in keeping with the Saints' belief that the assassination was an organized conspiracy, rather than the act of a band of enflamed vigilantes. The culpability of the United States for Smith's murder seemed verified by Governor Ford himself. Ford feared that Mormons took confidence that news of the murders had resulted in "active sympathy" from the rest of the United States. He wrote to church leaders, asserting, "The naked truth then, is that most well informed persons condemn in the most unqualified manner the mode in which the Smiths were put to death; but nine out of every ten of such accompany the expression of their disapprobation, by a manifestation of their pleasure that they are dead."[103]

When the court acquitted the five men charged with Smith's murder based on the argument that the defendants' actions reflected the popular sentiment of Illinois, the state and nation's guilt was again confirmed in the eyes of the Latter-day Saints. Orson Hyde compared this moment to the cry of the Jewish masses in the Gospel of St. Matthew, "His blood be on us, and on our children," which was traditionally thought to have been the pronouncement of a self-inflicted curse[104]:

> We see the same spirit manifested in the late trial at Carthage. Says one of the lawyers, whether they are guilty or innocent, I am not prepared to say; but if they are guilty we are guilty, and if you hang them, you may as well hang this honorable council. Jehovah says so too. We all want a hand in this matter, and if one is punished we will all be punished; and if you let one go free, we will all go free. Well, says Jehovah. I will give you the desire of your heart. Let not these men be punished, but let them go clear, and when he causeth his vengeance to be poured out, he will visit them all like, for they are all alike guilty: Amen, says Jehovah, I will fulfil [*sic*] and execute the judgment.[105]

On the day the verdict was read, William Clayton wrote in his journal that by this act "the whole State of Illinois has made itself guilty of shedding the blood of the Prophets by acquitting those who committed the horrid deed, and it is now left to God to take vengeance in His own way in His own time."[106] Many considered the entire United States guilty of the Smiths' murders for their tacit acceptance and sometimes open approval of the act. They were guilty because their representatives—at least one from each state according to Brigham Young—had organized the slaughter. Finally, Illinois and the United States had confirmed their guilt when they allowed the demand for justice to go unheard.

Vengeance

Some, perhaps many, Mormons desired vengeance, despite the efforts of the hierarchy to dissuade actual bloodshed. Some responded to Smith's death with their own personal vows of vengeance.[107] Allen J. Stout wrote that while gazing at the bodies during the viewing, "I there and then resolved in my mind that I would never let an opertunity [*sic*] slip unimproved of avenging there [*sic*] blood upon the head of the enemies of the Church of Jesus Christ."[108] Less than two weeks after the slaying, Orrin Porter Rockwell, who already had a reputation as a Mormon gunslinger, with two others, warned the apostate Robert D. Foster that if he remained in Nauvoo, they would kill him. When William Clayton tried to reason with Rockwell, the latter "swore bitterly he would have revenge and that Foster should not tarry here."[109] Foster would survive, although Rockwell was not finished. The following year, while assisting Jacob Backenstos, a non-Mormon sheriff who was in charge of protecting Mormon settlements from harassment, Rockwell killed Frank Worrell. Worrell was present at Carthage and was rumored to have stood at the door of the jail, inciting the mob.[110] Both Rockwell and Backenstos were acquitted of the charges.

More than a few Latter-day Saints fantasized about the prospect of avenging Smith's death. William Smith, who served as the church's patriarch in place of his brother Hyrum, blessed a string of individuals that they would have a hand in avenging his brothers' deaths. For example, he blessed James Rigby that he would be "an avenger of the blood of Prophets & Patriarchs thou shalt stand as a mighty warrior and contend with great strength for the cause of Zion."[111]

In 1845, during meetings of the Council of Fifty, several members expressed their desires to avenge the martyrs and perhaps to even organize a military response to persecution. These comments were particularly strident in two sessions held on March 11, following the state's removal of the Nauvoo Charter. In the morning meeting, George Miller declared that he wanted "to be where he can execute vengeance on those who have shed the blood of the prophets. He will wait for the word go, but he feels impatient."[112] In the afternoon meeting, Brigham Young stated, "If the time was come for the Saints to go forth and avenge the blood of the prophets and redeem Zion he would take one hundred men and sweep the State of Illinois so that there should not be a man left to tell the tale and he would not lose ten men."[113] Later, another Council member, Almon Babbitt, agreed that "[i]f this is the time and Nauvoo the place, then let us go to work and rise up and destroy without fear."[114]

Yet, in all this, the church hierarchy continued to insist that Mormons should not take justice into their own hands. They warned that it would cost them the popular sympathy they would otherwise receive. However, the order to wait for God to avenge the prophet's death was not intended as a passive form of waiting. Even if Mormons were forbidden from acting as military aggressors, they were encouraged to respond to their enemies with an arsenal of symbolic acts, namely, prayer, pronouncement, and esoteric ritual. The Saints had already performed these acts as a means of ceremonially calling down divine judgment on individuals, cities, and nations for their rejection of Mormonism and intolerance for its messengers.

Mormons saw themselves as tasked with preparing a populace to survive the coming cataclysm. Missionaries had scoured the United States and Great Britain to "warn the inhabitants of the earth to flee the wrath to come."[115] As a part of this effort, missionaries performed a ritual of removing the dust from their feet when their message was rejected.[116] This was a restoration of Jesus' instruction to the apostles: "And whosoever shall not receive you, nor hear you, when ye depart thence, shake off the dust under your feet for a testimony against them. Verily I say unto you, it shall be more tolerable for Sodom and Gomorrah in the day of judgment, than for that city."[117]

Although the act could be performed by shaking or wiping, which actually seemed to be the ritual's most common form, some of Smith's revelations specified that it be performed by washing. A September 1832 revelation urged rejected missionaries to "go away from him, alone by yourselves and cleanse your feet even with water, pur[e] water, whether in heat or in cold and bear testamony [*sic*] of it unto your father which is in heaven and return not again unto that man."[118] The washing of feet was a final act in which the missionary had completed his efforts to convince an individual to flee to Zion and was absolved of his responsibility to do so further. The ceremony theoretically ended the recipient's opportunity to receive the Mormon gospel and thus salvation.

Early missionaries needed reminders that they were not to be aggressors, even if only through symbolic means, while proselytizing among the "wicked." Smith's revelations warned that missionary work should not be completed "in haste neither in wrath nor with strife."[119] The revelations, likewise, forbade the practice of performing the rite in front of those for whom it was intended. Rather, missionaries were "to go away from him alone by yourselves," as just noted here. Or, as another revelation stated, the ritual should occur "not in their presence lest thou provoke them but in secret."[120]

Yet, even though from one perspective the rite could be regarded as a type of spiritual assault on those who seemed above their message or who subjected Mormons to ridicule and persecution, missionaries also sometimes viewed the rite as obligatory. Orson Hyde described the experience of dusting his feet against his own sister as akin to "piercing my heart." The ritual was conducted while tears "from all eyes freely ran."[121] In such cases, there was no reason to suspect that missionaries habitually performed the ritual out of malice. Instead, in Hyde's case, the ritual symbolically demonstrated that he had fulfilled his duty to warn others of the coming events and, by doing so, freed himself from any responsibility in the matter.[122]

Of course, even if the cleansing of one's feet was not always done in a spirit of malice or retribution, some individuals saw it as a legitimized way to instigate destruction by supernatural means. In fact, there are some cases in which Mormons washed their feet outside the missionary context, such as to punish the perpetrators of crimes.[123] For example, amidst their effort to obtain redress, William Marks, president of the Nauvoo High Council, published an epistle encouraging Mormons to "bear and forbear, as becometh saints," but after exhausting all legal channels and still not obtaining justice, "shake off the dust off your feet as a testimony of having so done."[124] Marks did not spell out the events expected to follow such a rite, but his reader was well aware of the implications of the performance.

Verbal pronouncement and localized prophecy were also important tools in bringing down maledictions. In the beginning of his ministry, Smith received a revelation that "whosoever shall lay their hands upon you by violence ye shall command to be smitten in my name & behold I will smite them according to thy words in mine own due time."[125] The Mormon prophet was again assured of his privilege to curse in an 1843 revelation, which reads: "[W]homsoever you bless I will bless, and whomsoever you curse I will curse, saith the Lord."[126] Smith usually employed the language of cursing in the context of revelation in which God warned a general group of individuals of the potentiality of their future judgment if they did not repent. However, Smith also singled out curses on individual apostates such as Joseph Jackson, whom he publicly cursed "in the name of the Lord Jesus Christ for his evil designes & wickedness."[127]

Others, including those without hierarchical rank, also felt enabled to curse. For example, Chapman Duncan recalled that in 1836, while at the Kirtland Temple, he "pronounced a curse upon Lieutenant Gov. Boggs, the first and last curse up to this date except washing my feet when preaching according to commandments."[128] In each of these cases, Mormons cursed those they saw as guilty of active persecution; thus, a distinction existed between such curses and the more common washing of feet associated with missionary efforts. For this reason, Duncan distinguished between the sort of curse he pronounced on Boggs and "washing my feet when preaching according to commandments." He had conducted those ceremonies as an obligation, but pronouncements against persecutors were a different matter.

As missionaries visited distant cities and foreign lands, they imagined themselves as millennial harbingers and, as such, they often fantasized about the fate of their enemies. The itinerant preachers declared that whole cities would be the recipients of divine punishment. For example, in 1836, when Parley P. Pratt departed from Toronto where he had been proselytizing, he "declared the Sword and Blood awaited that Place."[129] In 1832, another missionary, Newel K. Whitney was given an assignment, which was later canonized in Mormon scripture, to "go unto the city of New York and also to the city of Albany and also to the city of Boston and warn the people of those cities with the sound of the gospel with a loud voice of the desolation and utter abolishment which awaits them if they do reject these things, for if they do reject these things the hour of thei[r] Jodgment [*sic*] is nigh and there [*sic*] house shall be left unto them desolate [*sic*]."[130] Destructions in these three cities would appear regularly in subsequent depictions of the apocalypse.

Finally, prayer was an important aspect of cursing, both before and after the martyrdom. Although Smith denied any involvement in the attempted assassination of former Governor Lilburn Boggs in 1842, he believed that his prayers had led to Governor Thomas Reynolds's suicide in 1844. A month after Reynolds's death, Smith referenced the suicide in a sermon:

> The Lord once told me that what I asked for I should have, I have been afraid to ask God to kill my enemies lest some of them should peradventure repent[.] I asked a short time since for the Lord to deliver me out of the hands of the governor of Missouri & if it must needs be to accomplish it to take him away, & the next news that came pouring down from their, was Governor *Reynolds had shot himself*, and I would now say beware O earth how you fight against the Saints of God & shed innoce[nt] Blood, for in the days of Elijah his enemies Came upon him & fire was called down from heaven & destroyed them.[131]

Mormons well understood that prayer could be a weapon to force the hand of God against their enemies. Years earlier, after David Patten and Warren Parrish had been arrested by a sheriff's posse in Benton County, Arkansas, and released three days later, they secluded themselves in the woods for secret prayer. There, on his knees, Patten "asked God to curse them, and destroy them off the face of the earth for their wickedness and abominations, to which [Parrish] heartily responded, Amen."[132]

All these forms of cursing were quickly integrated into Mormon practice as a means to respond to the martyrdom. With the exception of verbal curses, prayer was the most common malediction performed. The Anointed Quorum met several times specifically for this purpose. On June 19, 1845, they met to pray "especially that the curse of God may fall upon Judge Richard M. Young and the Lawyers who have justified the murderers, and that they may not be able to hold court."[133] Eight days later, on the one-year anniversary of the martyrdom, they met again to offer a prayer "that God would curs[e] those that had spilt [Joseph and Hyrum's] blood and all those that percicute [*sic*] the Saints."[134] These petitions occurred regularly thereafter, often performed in the temple itself.

In July 1845, Apostle Wilford Woodruff held an impromptu meeting while visiting the nearly completed temple. With those policemen guarding the site and other friends, he climbed to the top of the building and knelt in prayer. Woodruff prayed "that [God] would speedily [*sic*] avenge the blood of Joseph the Prophet Seer and Revelator, and Hiram the Patriarch, which had been shed by the hands of the American gentile nation, upon all the heads of the Nation and State that have aided, abeted or perpetrated the hor[r]id deed, of shed[d]ing the blood of those righteous men even the Lords anointed."[135]

If Mormons were careful to hold prayers and ritualized cursings outside of the gaze of non-Mormons, they did little to conceal verbalized pronouncements of curses or descriptions of their persecutor's cursed state. In fact, Mormons employed the language of cursing in dozens of sermons from the period. Thomas Ford exaggerated only slightly when he wrote that in 1845 "the zealous and infuriated preachers now indulged only in curses and strains of abuse of the Gentiles, and it seemed to be their design to fill their followers with the greatest amount of hatred to all mankind excepting the 'saints.' . . . Curses upon their enemies, upon the country, upon government, upon all public officers."[136]

Written curses and expectations of divine vengeance fill Mormon diaries from the mid-1840s. For example, Wilford Woodruff appended a note to the June 27, 1844, entry of his journal in which he wrote, "They were martered [*sic*] by An American Gentile mob And may the Lord Avenge there [*sic*] blood in his own time & way."[137] Warren Foote, in his ultimate journal entry for 1844, wrote:

> This year has witnessed the murder of two of the best men that this generation could boast of. Joseph and Hyram Smith were murdered in cold blood in Carthage Jail, and their blood is now crying from the ground to God for vengeance, which He will avenge in His own due time, for he will avenge the blood of His saints, when their enemies are fully ripened in their iniquities.[138]

Mormons expected all this cursing—pronounced both in public and private—to be fulfilled. In the next two sections, we will look at images of their fulfillment: first on individuals and then the nation at large.

"The Mormon Curse" on the Mob

Pronouncing curses was one way in which the Saints addressed their grief and appeased their desire to seek retribution. After the acquittals of Smith's assassins, the church hierarchy assured the Saints that the murderers were better off dead than alive by depicting the guilty in a perpetual state of physical and psychological suffering. Killing them would be an act of charity. This robust practice of graphically describing the fate of their persecutors promised the Saints that God's vengeance was already in progress. For decades, Mormons told stories of encountering a member of the mob and observing what it was like to live after killing one of God's servants. The stock figure of the cursed persecutor was represented as living in poverty on the fringe of society and afflicted by strange maladies. He was bereft of political influence and friends of any sort. Rather than appearing as the object of Mormon abuse, the cursed (usually) elderly men tended to survive only through receiving Mormon charity.

Throughout the nineteenth century, these stories were essential components in Mormon vernacular prophecy. Mormons believed God really had avenged his people of their enemies. In 1882, Lyman Littlefield compiled accounts in a well-known collection entitled *The Martyrs*. Seventy years later, another popular Latter-day Saint book, N. B. Lundwall's *The Fate of the Persecutors of the Prophet Joseph Smith*, appeared, reintroducing these narratives to a new generation.[139] Scholars have consistently questioned the historical accuracy of these legends.[140] Richard C. Poulson argued that these stories were a branch of a more extensive set of American myths, foretelling divine retribution for murder and religious persecution.[141] This section examines the particular Mormon textures of these stories and the ways they reflect the wider scope of the Saints' curses on the nation at large.

Early on in these narratives, descriptions of their persecutors' lots focused largely on the details of their internal lives. Even before they killed the Smiths, the villians' hatred had engendered a thirst for blood that only the murder of the righteous could quench. These apostates seemed to be resigned to an eternal recompense, but in the meantime they were anxious to do as much damage as possible. This monstrous quality confirmed that such men were irredeemable and thus, despite Mormonism's semi-universalist soteriology, were excluded from salvation for the murder of the prophets.

Mormons imagined the Smiths' killers living in a constant state of anxiety and fear. In some statements, their supernatural punishments entailed psychological torture instigated by Joseph Smith himself. In an April 1845 sermon, Orson Hyde promised the guilty that "the angel of God will persecute you, and evil angels will torment and affriget [*sic*] you in your night visions; and in your expiring moments when sinking in the agonies of death, let the bloody ghosts of the martyred prophets appear before you."[142] Because the righteous sought an appearance of Joseph Smith's spirit as a sign of their continued relationship with the prophet, in June, Brigham Young was careful to nuance the nature of these types of crisis apparitions. He explained, "I bel[ieve] that Ghosts will haunt them, but Jos[eph] will not take the pains to haunt them in his visions [and] dreams but he will send one of the meanest sp[irits] in the Et[ernal] worlds—I say let them [the accused and acquitted members of the mob] be, let them alone—for they will be more troubled to live than to die."[143] Whether the actual ghosts of Joseph and Hyrum would visit them or whether the martyrs would depend on more sinister henchmen, the murderers would be subject to the hauntings of their departed victims.[144]

Although Hyde's portrayal of the ghastly revenants would occur at the offenders' death beds, both he and Young agreed that the mob would find no solace even in their dreams. Such a prediction was based on a belief that individuals could more easily experience spiritual realities while asleep, when "the outward organs of thought and perception are released from their activity, the nerves unstrung, and the whole of mortal humanity lies hushed in quiet slumbers."[145] Parley P. Pratt explained that the content of one's dreams were influenced by the type of spirits a person's good or evil actions had attracted. While the slumbering righteous were "susceptible of converse with Deity, or of communion with angels, and the spirits of just men made perfect," evil men were not so fortunate.[146] Their departed loved ones, "good angels," and "the spirit of the Lord . . . has left them to themselves to struggle alone amid the dangers and sorrows of life; or to be the associates of demons and impure spirits. Such persons dream of adultery, gluttony, debauchery and crimes of every kind. Such persons have the foreshadowing of a doleful death, and of darkness, and the buffetings of fiends and malicious spirits."[147]

In their waking hours, the persecutors would crave the release of death, yet be unable to bring their suicide to fruition. Mormons assured each other that the lives of their persecutors were more of a punishment than their deaths could ever be. God would not allow these murderers to die until they suffered for their deeds in mortality. Hyde made this point before a congregation of Saints in Nauvoo, drawing on the same symbolism previously employed in Jonathan Edwards's famous sermon, "Sinners in the Hands of an Angry God." Unlike Edwards, it was the anticipation of hell, rather than the fiery pit itself, that was the ultimate in divine punishments. Hyde depicted the Carthage murderers in a state of "dreading hell all the time." If one were to kill them, it would thereby "cut the thread and let them drop in, [and therefore,] they would not have pleasure of that torment."[148] Rather than Edwards's God, who would cut the thread to cast the wicked to hell at his own pleasure and only did not do so as an act of mercy, Mormons must not cut that thread so the wicked might experience the full weight of hell in the present. In truth, Mormon imagery of the afterlife did not hold the same terrors as those they expected the murderers would face as they continued living.

That being said, in some versions of the persecutors' lament, part of the terror was the inevitable justice that awaited the wicked after death. Robert D. Foster, a disaffected Mormon aligned with William Law at the time of the martyrdom, reportedly confessed, "I have not seen one moment's peace since that time [i.e., the Carthage slaying]. I know that Mormonism is true, and the thought of meeting (Joseph and Hyrum) at the bar of God is more awful to me than anything else."[149] Latter-day Saint sermons throughout the nineteenth century captured the anxiety of the guilty in the image of a triumphant Joseph Smith standing at the judgment bar. For Mormons, this moment promised to be an eschatological event akin to the righteous dead meeting Jesus. Yet, for the wicked, this moment was horrific. If no justice was to be found in the here and now, there would certainly be justice in the hereafter.

Mormon legends often depicted the guilty as cursed with an uncontrollable wanderlust. As with haunting, this imagery had ancient as well as more modern influences. Most pertinent was the medieval legend of the Wandering Jew cursed with immortality for his harassment of Jesus while the

Christian messiah marched to his crucifixion. This dual curse of immortality and wandering seems to have first made its appearance in Mormon circles in reference to Cain. Although a more sinister creature, the Mormon Cain echoes the most basic elements of the "Wandering Jew": In popular Mormon lore, the first murderer became an immortal, cursed to spend the duration of the earth's existence as "a fugitive and a vagabond in the earth" (Genesis 4:12).[150]

After David W. Patten's death in 1838, stories circulated that the apostle had personally encountered Cain, who was still wandering in the nineteenth century. Abraham O. Smoot reported that he heard the experience directly from Patten himself when Patten visited his home. Decades later, he quoted Patten as having said:

> As I was riding along the road on my mule I suddenly noticed a very strange personage walking beside me. He walked along beside me for about two miles. His head was about even with my shoulders as I sat in my saddle. He wore no clothing, but was covered with hair. His skin was very dark. I asked him where he dwelt and he replied that he had no home, that he was a wanderer in the earth and traveled to and fro. He said he was a very miserable creature, that he had earnestly sought death during his sojourn upon the earth, but that he could not die, and his mission was to destroy the souls of men. About the time he expressed himself thus, I rebuked him in the name of the Lord Jesus Christ and by virtue of the Holy Priesthood, and commanded him to go hence, and he immediately departed out of my sight.[151]

Patten's encounter with Cain presented the villain as a wicked man turned demonic. This was apparent by the identification of Cain's mission "to destroy the souls of men," from his vulnerability to being cast out by the same formula as a traditional evil spirit, and by his choice of words. Cain parroted the dialogue of the adversary, a figure read by Christians as Lucifer, who appeared before the heavenly council in chapter 1 of Job. When asked by God, "Whence comest thou?" Satan responded, "From going to and fro in the earth, and from walking up and down in it."[152]

As Mormons imagined the fate of Smith's assassins, they seemed to find inspiration from the image of Cain's divine punishment. Mormon leaders quickly introduced the idea that these murderers would spend their lives with an acute awareness of the weight of their deed. In 1845, Hyde claimed that, despite their efforts to physically escape, they would find "their conscience is as a black locust tree in the stomach, and wherever they go they are oppressed with it." Eventually, he prophesied they would seek refuge in Texas or Oregon, but warned they would not "get rid of that black locust tree you have in your stomachs."[153] Legends describing the fate of the persecutors provided examples of this prediction of wandering fulfilled. Two years after the martyrdom, a Mormon watched "a man whose clothes were white with frost, walking slowly among the trees." When he told the stranger he would happily provide him with shelter, the man responded, "I have a farm on the other side of the river, at Warsaw, as good as any farm, but I can't stay in it. . . . I was in that Smith scrape. Now I can rest nowhere."[154]

In 1881, a missionary reported meeting a man who claimed to have participated in the assassination and had been afflicted with a need for "wandering from place to place ever since, as though in search of an asylum for a troubled conscience."[155] Those who professed having crossed paths with the guilty often found them in the Rocky Mountains, living on the outskirts of predominantly Mormon communities. They lived as hermits or, when in families, appeared as the objects of abuse. Ironically, as mentioned here, these stories often portrayed the murderers' survival as possible only through the charity of Latter-day Saints.

In one variant of this narrative, the murderer claimed he was drawn westward by a desire "to know how the Mormons made out without Joseph Smith to lead them." When the devout Mormon narrator of this story discovered the man deteriorating while residing "in an abandoned cabin situated in a grove of aspens," he provided him with food and "mutton tallow to put on his sores."[156] There was poetic justice in the assassin's fate. Mormons had "made out" just fine, while their persecutor had not. Now the man was made to recognize just how ineffective were his efforts to harm God's people, while simultaneously allowing Mormons a glimpse of the corrosive effect of persecution. Such stories in which former persecutors depend on Mormons for nourishment call to mind Orson Hyde's admonition not to kill them, because they could only experience the full weight of their dread in this life. Thus, the Mormons in these narratives unintentionally perpetuated justice through their charitable kindness. For Mormons, there was no mercy in the biblical reference to God's assurance that a curse would follow any who killed Cain.[157] After all, to ensure Cain's (or the Smiths' murderers') continued life was to ensure their continued suffering.

While many narratives that described the "Mormon curse" emphasized psychological horrors, others centered on physical torments inflicted on the guilty and leading to their deaths. The trek west was the ideal occasion to witness human suffering and hardship—sometimes interpreted through Mormon eyes as God's wrath on their persecutors. An 1849 letter drafted from an expedition to Utah claimed that

> many has been the grave of the gold seeker we have seen whose bodies have been disinterred by the wolves; and the bones, pantaloons, hose, and other things laying strewed around with the head board laying near, informing the traveller [*sic*], who had been buried, wherefrom, the day they died, age, disease, etc. But we have not seen a solitary instance where one of the Saint's tombs have been disturbed by the wolves. Among the graves of those whose bones lay around their graves, bleaching in the sun, their flesh being consumed by the ravenous wolf, we recognized the names of several noted mobocrats from the states of Missouri and Illinois, who took an active and prominent part in persecuting, mobbing, and driving the Saints from these States.[158]

Brigham Young saw these deaths as a fulfillment of Joseph Smith's prophecy "that the bones of hundreds of the Missouri and Illinois mobocrats, who drove the Saints from those States, should bleach on the plains, and their flesh should be meat for wolves."[159] The key to understanding this portrayal of the murderers' final moments is the juxtaposition between the deaths of the righteous and the deaths of the wicked in Mormon thought. While the Saints were at peace even when dying on the plains, the wicked died in a state of despair. While the Saints "have had friends to condole with and comfort them in their dying moments and to mourn for a season with their bereaved relatives," the persecutors "were left in the bitterness of death without a friend and without mercy." The Saints' graves tended to be undisturbed, at least in these portrayals, but the murderers' remains were "scattered over the plains—gnawed and broken by wild beasts and are there bleaching to this day."[160] In other accounts, former persecutors were buried at sea, the recipients of a pauper's funeral, or with bodies so putrefied that there were little remains of which to dispose.

Their deaths never came easy—the guilty underwent a variety of physical torments. Parley P. Pratt recalled that one man, identified only as "Townsend," whom Joseph Smith had shot in the "arm, near the shoulder" at Carthage Jail, afterward developed a strange case of rotting. Even after the affected limb was removed, his shoulder would not heal. Nine months later, he reportedly, died, "having literally rotted alive!"[161] Townsend, like other persecutors Pratt knew from Missouri, "stank so previous to their deaths that they had to be placed in rooms by themselves, and it was almost impossible to endure their presence, and the flies could not be kept from blowing them [i.e., laid larvae in their flesh] while they were alive!"[162]

In 1881, Martha Jane Cragun Cox, a Mormon woman, became acquainted with another unfortunate murderer near a Latter-day Saint settlement in St. Thomas, Nevada. The man went by the name Jack Reed, but the narrative seemed to imply this was a false identity. Reed had attended a public meeting in St. Thomas, where he declared his involvement in the Carthage mob and in the aftermath of his confession faced a similar affliction as that of Townsend. "He was literally eaten alive by worms. His eyeballs had fallen out, the flesh on his cheeks and neck had fallen off and though he could breath [*sic*] he could only take nourishment through an opening in his throat." When asked about his strange malady, he responded, "It is the Mormon curse that is upon me. I cannot live—I must utterly rot before I die."[163] He credited Brigham Young for placing the curse on the mob and recalled that thirteen of his compatriots had met similar fates before their deaths.

Due to his central role in the martyrdom narrative, Governor Thomas Ford was frequently depicted as the cursed persecutor. An 1874 story set in 1850 claimed that a former Mormon had inadvertently attended the funeral of Ford's wife at a Methodist church in Peoria, Illinois. When the unnamed former Mormon entered the building, she noticed that a pauper's funeral was already underway with a casket "supplied at the public's expense" positioned at the front of the chapel. The importance of the account was not in the death of Ford's wife, but in the anonymous witness's recognition of Governor Ford himself. She described his appearance as "gaunt and miserable, and his bones appeared ready to pierce through the skin." Two weeks later, the woman read a notice that Ford had also passed away. It was then that she recalled "hearing Elder John Taylor say in Nauvoo that 'Governor Ford would live until the flesh would wither from his bones and he would die a pauper.' "[164] Stories of Ford's suffering as a victim of the "Mormon curse" emphasized the collapse of the former governor's social influence as well as the deterioration of his finances. Ford, like members of the mob, could not escape God's judgment. He, too, suffered from the degenerative malady that plagued the guilty.

Mormons in such narratives projected their own negative experiences and unwanted emotions onto their persecutors. Socially, these wicked men became the objects of scorn. Just as the Mormons were deprived of their material possessions at the hands of mobs, their persecutors would die as paupers. Unlike the righteous, who died with confidence of their eternal reward, the wicked were terrified of dying and what lay beyond. They were filled with regret, guilt, and unrelenting anger. While a divine hand guided the Mormon people to the West to prosper as a community, in these narratives guilt, curiosity, or greed had lured their enemies to the frontier to face their deaths.

The nature of the "Mormon curse" drew from apocalyptic imagery. This strange affliction—usually described as rotting but always degenerative—that appeared so frequently within these narratives had its basis in a prophecy first articulated by Joseph Smith on September 26, 1830:

> Wherefore I will send forth flies upon the face of the Earth which shall take hold of the inhabitants thereof & shall eat their flesh & shall cause magots [*sic*] to come in upon them & their tongues shall be stayed that they shall not utter against me & their flesh shall fall from off their Bones & their eyes from their sockets & it shall come to pass that the Beasts of the forest & the fowls of the air shall devour them up.[165]

The gruesome details of Smith's revelation blended different biblical references to God's judgments. The first element, the plague of flies, paralleled the Exodus account of Egypt's plagues. Similar descriptions of corporeal affliction were detailed in the Old Testament book of Zechariah, speaking of those who would fight against Israel at the Battle of Armageddon: "Their flesh shall consume away while they stand upon their feet, and their eyes shall consume away in their holes, and their tongue shall consume away in their mouth."[166] Finally, these graphic images were integrated into Revelation's "supper of the great God," in which an angel invites "the fowls that fly in the midst of heaven" to scavenge on the flesh of God's enemies destroyed at Christ's appearance.[167]

Historian Samuel Brown has compared the 1830 prophecy with its description of wicked men rotting away while still alive with the Saints' own hopes for a future resurrection. "This threat framed the promise of bodily integrity and corporeal resurrection as the ultimate gift of God and its loss to decomposition as God's greatest punishment."[168] This logic would seem to be borne out by a similar interest in descriptions of the state of the persecutors' burials, such as the accounts of bleached bones scattered on the prairies. Brown traced this curse of living putrefaction to older strains of divine judgment present in both John Foxe's *Actes and Monuments* and Buck's *Theological Dictionary*. Several nuances in the martyrdom curses such as the stench of the afflicted and of worms, rather than maggots, devouring the flesh could also be traced to this extra-biblical tradition.

By pulling from biblical and Mormon millenarian imagery, these individual examples of Mormon curse-lore functioned as a microcosm of the judgment that would soon be poured out on all of the wicked and the United States as a whole. The unrighteous would face famine, disease, and violence, all elements present in the individual malediction accounts. Even the murderers' paranoia and desire for death had parallels with last days' prophecy. The suffering of the guilty was only the beginning of the destructions to be enacted on the larger populace. Each story served as an assurance that God kept his promises to avenge the Saints. These curses were often encapsulated into other narratives regarding the suffering brought about by the Civil War, in which the United States as a whole faced God's wrath for their involvement in the murder of the Smiths.

The Fullness of the Gentiles and the Fate of the Nation

In April 1845 at the semi-annual general conference, the assembled Saints voted to acknowledge "that the Gentiles were cut off."[169] There would be no more missionaries assigned to minister in the United States. Of this moment, one Mormon, Reuben Miller wrote, "[L]et it be known and remembered among the Saints of God throughout this vast republic and in all the world, that the fullness of the everlasting gospel of the Son of God, is legally taken from this nation."[170] At the next conference, held within the still unfinished Nauvoo Temple, the sermons reinforced this idea. Heber C. Kimball proclaimed an additional prohibition against working for nonmembers in the region: "Why do you want to labor for them. Inasmuch as the Gentiles reject us, lo! we turn to the Jews."[171] Although not part of the published account, Joseph Hovey remembered that during his discourse, Kimball addressed the Gentiles directly: "All we ask is that they wipe up the blood of the prophets and that will be preaching enough for them for the present."[172]

In these meetings, church leaders announced their intention of relocating from the United States. A few weeks before the announcement, Young sent a message to the vigilantes that if they would stop the systematic burning of Mormon homes and other forms of harassment, then the Mormons would leave Nauvoo in peace.[173] He subsequently addressed an epistle to those Saints living outside of Nauvoo, in which he cited the rise of persecution as the immediate cause for their exodus. Yet, ultimately following in the path of his predecessor, he presented specific examples of intolerance as mere symptoms of the larger diseased state of the nation. Appealing to the Mormon sense that the nation was in rapid decline and expressing a thorough exasperation with American political wrangling, his announcement read:

> The ranklings of violence and intolerence and religious and political strife that have long been waking up in the bosom of this nation, together with the occasional scintillations of settled veageance [*sic*], and blood-guiltiness cannot long be supressed. And deplorable is the condition of any people that is constrained to be the butt of such discordant and revolutionary materials.[174]

Americans would reap what they had sown. Young insisted that "the direful eruption must take place. It requires not the spirit of prophecy to foresee it." That such was the case was not only accepted by Latter-day Saints, who seemed to face the brunt of the nation's unrelated dysfunction, but, Young continued, "Every sensible man in the nation has felt and perhaps expressed his melancholy fears of the dreadful vortex into which partizan [*sic*] ambition, contempt of the poor, and trampling down the just as things of nought, were fast leading the nation."[175] From Young's vantage point, Mormons would only temporarily remain isolated from the United States. They would "hide [themselves] until the indignation be overpast [*sic*]."[176]

The decision to abandon the United States was understood through a fatalistic—so far as the United States was concerned—apocalyptic logic. Mormons saw the significance of their march into the wilderness through two related concepts: the "gathering of the elect" and the "fullness of the Gentiles." Both of these ideas were intertwined with the progressive unfolding of the apocalyptic timeline.

Historian Grant Underwood observed that the practice of gathering in Mormon eschatology played essentially the same role as that of the rapture within John Nelson Darby's highly influential dispensationalist eschatology. Underwood pointed out that just as Darby expected the raptured Christians would be safely removed from the earth during the tribulation, Latter-day

Saints believed they would be weathering out the apocalypse in their "cit[ies] of refuge."[177]

Although Smith had pointed to gathering places in Kirtland, Ohio, and Jackson County, Missouri, and later to Lee and Hancock Counties, the Saints search for a new homeland was the first time the gathering was intended to truly isolate the Mormon people. Mormons understood the act of leaving the United States through the lens of missionaries who turned from the homes of those who would not hear or abide their message. Joseph Hovey imagined this moment of "exit[ing] from the United States":

> We then can shake the dust from our garments . . . leaving this nation alone in her glory while the residue of the world points the finger of scorn until indignation and consumption decreed make a full end. In our patience we will possess our souls and work out a more exceeding and eternal wate [*sic*; weight] of glory. Preparing by withdrawing the power and priesthood from the Gentiles for the great consolation of Israel when the wilderness shall blossom as the rose and Babylon fall like a mill stone cast into the sea.[178]

Like ancient Lot leaving Sodom just before the sulfur rained from the sky, Mormons had now allowed the destructions to commence.

Latter-day Saints often used the language of leaving the Gentiles. They intentionally alluded to the "fullness of the Gentiles," a phrase drawn from Romans 11:25–26 and associated with apocalyptic thought. The dominant Mormon position was that one should read " 'fullness' of the Gentiles as the *apostasy* of the Gentiles."[179] As Mormons emphasized the rejection of the nation, they underscored an ethnic distinction between Mormon converts and non-Mormons, who would never convert. Heber C. Kimball explained the hierarchy's desire "to take you to a land, where a white man's foot never trod." After all, he reasoned, "We are not accounted as white people, and we don't want to live among them."[180] Mormons had their own ethnic identity distinct from other Anglo-Americans. A hymn that first appeared in 1846 captured Mormon sentiment both in this regard and in reference to matters of the exodus:

> The time has come, we must away,
> To distant lands, where God shall say;
> No longer let us linger here;
> The world is doom'd to woe and fear—

This Gentile race the priesthood hates;
We have no home within these States,
Let us away and seek our rest.
Our home's not here, it's in the west.
Come then, oh come, no more delay,
The spirit whispers haste away;
This nation now has seal'd its doom.
And soon with wrath will be o'erthrown[181]

With the rejection of the Gentiles, Israel—Mormons but also Native Americans and other native peoples, as well as Jews—would become the major actor on the apocalyptic stage. The prospering of both Native and Jewish peoples was tied to the prophecy of destruction. In the Old World, the Jews would return to Palestine where they would rebuild a kingdom in Jerusalem, leading to the battle of Armageddon and the divine slaughter of their Gentile aggressors. In the Americas, Native Americans would become the hand of vengeance on the American Gentiles.

While Mormons spoke regularly about their excitement to seek Native American converts, the apostles were careful not to bring attention to their expectations for "the remnant of Jacob" to head a future massacre. The Mormon proselytization of Indians had already engendered suspicions among some parties.[182] On the other hand, the militaristic role of the Lamanites was a major thrust in the internal conversation about the fullness of the Gentiles. In time, some would remember Joseph Smith had prophesied that the Saints would be instrumental in preparing a Native army. One account of Joseph Smith's final sermon to the Nauvoo Legion included the prediction that the church would "gather the red men to their center from their scattered and dispersed situation to become the strong arm of Jehovah, who will be a strong bulwark of protection from your foes"[183] (see Figure 2.3).

Joseph Lee Robinson remembered interpreting the gift of tongues in a meeting sometime within the year following the martyrdom, in which he prophesied that God "would raise a mighty army of the Lamanites and that they should come forth in the mountains and that they should fall upon the Gentiles with mighty power and that a trembling and fear should fall upon these Gentiles that they should have no power to resist them, that as well might the puny arm of man be raised to stop the mighty Northwest winds, for the Gentiles to stop this mighty army." As Robinson spoke, he began to see a vision in which "I could see them coming over the hills across the river west

Figure 2.3 John Hafen, *Last Public Address of Lieutenant General Joseph Smith*, 1888. Hafen's lithograph depicts Smith's last address before the Nauvoo Legion in which he preached on ministries to Native Americans. According to one account, Smith prophesied the Saints' relocation to the Rocky Mountains. Courtesy of the Church History Library.

of Nauvoo. They looked terrible as a dark cloud." He told the congregation that "they [the Native Americans] should avenge the blood of the prophets that was shed in Carthage Jail," predicting that the then current hunt for the Smiths' assassins would not result in any executions.[184]

The patriarch William Smith foresaw this moment in a blessing he pronounced on the head of Abigail Abott on June 23, 1845:

> One of thy posterity named after the name of his father . . . shall be a mighty warrior, and be led on to avenge the blood of Prophets and Patriarchs, he shall lead a mighty people from the wilderness and one mighty among them who shall be also a mighty warrior by the name of Nishcosh, he shall be a descendant of one of the name of Nimrod, who was also a descendant of that Nimrod, who was a mighty hunter in days of old, by way of the Jaredites upon this continent, who founded a city and called it the city of Gnoalum, this city now lying in ruins the wreck of which only appears as the last descriptive monument of a people that has fallen, and the remnants of whom have become barbarous, wild and uncultivated.[185]

While Smith regularly promised the recipients of his blessings that they would take part in avenging Joseph and Hyrum, this blessing provided additional details revealing how the patriarch expected such would occur. He envisioned Abott's descendant as a missionary to the Native Americans who would lead a group from the wilderness to seek vengeance. William presented a new messianic figure, Nichcosh, descended from the Jaredites. This particular ancient American lineage was, according to the Book of Mormon, entirely wiped out around 600 BCE, but allowed the patriarch to suggest descent from the biblical Nimrod, as well as a prince named Nimrod in the Book of Mormon text.

While William Smith's account suggested that vengeance might wait generations, rumors were in circulation that such an army of American Indians was already in preparation. On January 15, 1845, a Mormon woman repeated the belief that "there is all ready [*sic*] ten hundred thousand of the lamanites baptized into the Church and thay [*sic*] are waiting verry [*sic*] impatient to avenge the blood of Joseph and Hirum. We have to keep men among them to keep them back or thay would [have] ben [*sic*] here before this time."[186] The image of a Lamanite army calmed nerves and fortified resolve while the Saints remained in Nauvoo completing the temple and making preparations for the trek west.

When more careful representatives from the Mormon hierarchy spoke on themes of Amerindian apocalypse, they clarified that the warriors of this future massacre would not be Latter-day Saints. For example, in 1841, the *Preston Chronicle*, a non-Mormon paper, announced that the Saints intended to form such a military alliance. An article in the *Millennial Star* countered, "[T]he Lord may see fit to make use of the Indians to execute his vengeance upon the ungodly, before they (the Indians) are converted by the record of their forefathers, yet it is certain that if they once became Latter-Day Saints they will never more use weapons of war except in defense of their lives and liberties."[187]

Members of the church's hierarchy may have shared the concern that some Mormons would try to build an unauthorized military alliance with American Indian groups. This concern seems to have been one of the reasons that church leaders monitored and eventually rejected a mission to the Delaware Indians in the late 1840s.[188] Just as curses functioned to alleviate the drive for Latter-day Saints to take it upon themselves to kill Smith's murderers, images of an impending Indian massacre of whites were meant to assure justice without having Latter-day Saints bring it about themselves. This image of Lamanites as the "battle axe of the Lord" would recur throughout the nineteenth-century vernacular prophecy.

Pharaoh's March

The Nauvoo era ended with both the long-awaited completion of the temple and increasing persecution. Male and female members of Smith's Anointed Quorum, including those apostles in Nauvoo, spent weeks performing the endowments and sealings late into the night. The performance of so many endowments served to allay fears that visible or invisible sources of evil would prevent the transmission of Nauvoo esotericism to the body of believers. Recall that rumors of serial murderers intent on slaying members of the Anointed Quorum was a persistent fear after Smith's death. Apostle George A. Smith rejoiced after 500 were endowed because, he reasoned, "if half of them should be like the foolish virgins, and turn away from the truth, the principles of the Holy Priesthood, would be beyond the reach of mobs and all the assaults of the adversaries of the Church."[189] Brigham Young assured the Saints that although they would have to abandon the building once it was completed, "there will be thousands and thousands of men that can go into any part of the world and build up the kingdom, and build temples."[190] Their hard work guaranteed the rites would continue in perpetuity.

During these final moments in Nauvoo, the Saints believed they were the beneficiaries of divine blessings and spiritual aid. The endowment allowed the faithful to share in common the mysteries that Smith imparted at the end of his life. Once endowed, one was now enabled to be sealed into a family unit and to perform greater miracles. George A. Smith envisioned that endowed couples could now "hold their children by prayer and faith and will not be obliged to give them up to death until they are fourscore years old."[191] Heber C. Kimball told a temple assembly to "refer your minds to the covenants you have made" and promised that "by an observance of these things, you will have dreams and visions."[192]

Yet, this period also had its own anxieties. Brigham Young later recalled that construction of the temple was accomplished through "the aid of sword in one hand, and trowel and hammer in the other, with fire arms at hand, and a strong band of police, and the blessings of heaven, the Saints, through hunger, and thirst, and weariness, and watchings, and prayings."[193] An armed police force was stationed outside of the temple patrolling all hours of the day. Joseph Fielding captured the anxiety of the time when he wrote, "[I]t seems as tho Earth and Hell are mad to see the Work of the Priesthood processing so rapidly[.]"[194]

The Saints felt safe inside the temple walls. By preventing non-Mormons from entering the edifice, the temple was reserved as a Mormon-only space. Brigham Young and others used the temple as a hiding place to avoid U.S. marshals seeking their arrest. On one occasion, Joseph Fielding noted, they "searched the temple through but in vain[.] The brethren have had to disguise themselves to escape them."[195] Sermons in the temple emphasized the protective, even defensive, function of temple prayer. Brigham Young credited these prayer circles as the means by which "the Church had been kept together [despite their persecutors], and not the power of arms."[196] The sacred act of ritualized prayer had kept the Saints' persecutors at bay so that they might move forward with building the temple and endowing all the Saints.

Divine protection was bestowed as part of the endowment in connection with ceremonial undergarments, which initiates were instructed to wear at all times. As religion scholar Colleen McDannell has noted, these garments provided a physical and psychological boundary between the Saints and outsiders.[197] By wearing such garments Mormons had a material reminder of vows made and promised spiritual aid. The garment's revealed origins and its bestowal of supernatural protection would become the subject of much discussion in Nauvoo and thereafter. James Allred recalled that when Joseph Smith approached his mother, a seamstress, to make the garment, "he told her that he had seen the Angel Moroni with the garments on."[198] Like the angel on the temple's weathervane, Moroni had donned the ceremonial garb.

When we contextualize this period as one of great anxiety, it makes sense that Mormons would regularly associate such garments with providing physical protection. On December 21, 1845, a meeting in the temple included several lecturers who spoke on this theme. In reference to the martyrdom, the speakers explained that Joseph and Hyrum Smith, as well as John Taylor, were not wearing their garments at the time of the raid on the jail. Only Willard Richards escaped unscathed "being protected at Carthage Jail, having on the robe."[199] Although this meeting is the earliest known discussion of the garment's role at the assassination, there had already been much conversation among the Saints on the subject.

This was particularly apparent in the many explanations given for why the Smiths and Taylor were without their garments. Taylor "corrected the idea that some had, that they had taken them off through fear."[200] With the belief that apostates were set on killing members of the Anointed Quorum, some had come to believe that the martyrs removed their garments because they did not want to be identified as endowed Mormons. Indeed, this seems to be in response to the rumors of the bloody drums. Heber C. Kimball recalled in the same meeting that "word came to him and to all the Twelve about that time to lay aside their garments, and take them to pieces, or cut them up so that they could not be found."[201] However, Taylor and Kimball did not see this as an effort to avoid their fate, but as a means to protect the sanctity of the garment, which they did not want exposed to the view of outsiders.[202]

Joseph and Hyrum Smith, as well as John Taylor, may have not worn garments for the same reason, since these well-known faces could hardly have expected to avoid recognition as Nauvoo insiders. In contrast, some interpreted the call to hide the garment as a means to avoid detection. Decades later, Sarah G. Richards recalled the order to hide the garments, acknowledging the fear "that in every habitation where any of the endowment clothes were found, [it] would [mean] death to the inmates." She remembered that her husband's garments were divided into parts and then hidden "among the articles of linen."[203] At the December 21, 1845, meeting, W. W. Phelps provided an alternative third possibility for why the martyrs removed their garments: "on account of the hot weather."[204] Smith had personally told him so.

Whichever was the case, Mormons assured one another that Willard Richards was protected because he refused to take off his garments. Just as the temple offered Mormons within a protected space, the righteous brought that same space with them wherever they went via the garment. Bishop George Miller also spoke at the December 21, 1845, meeting and referred to a time when persecutors shot at him, when "the Sentinel who was near him was killed, but he escaped unhurt, having on his garment."[205] These stories of protection were regularly featured in Mormon lore thereafter.[206] Although in Nauvoo the Saints focused on material dangers, later stories highlighted the garment's dual role in providing both spiritual and physical protection. For example, in 1854, non-Mormon Benjamin G. Ferris wrote, "The person thus invested [with the garment] is supposed to be safe against the arts of the devil to bring harm upon him, and in a condition to escape danger from shipwreck, disease, bullets, &c. Some of them are so embued [*sic*] with this idea, that in changing the garment, they will keep one leg in the old one until they invest the other with the new, lest the devil or some of his imps should obtain a temporary advantage."[207]

As we will see and as should be expected from the eschatological context of temple building introduced in the previous chapter, the temple frequently appeared in Mormon prophecies in the West, where it or its rites were portrayed as shielding the Saints from apocalyptic destructions as well as invading armies. Before Newman Bulkley's prophecy referred to the consultation between the resurrected Jesus and Joseph Smith in the Salt Lake Temple, it portrayed a future scene that mirrored the winter of 1845–1846. Outside the temple, an army stockpiled "combustibles," ready to strike against the Saints. Instead of preparing for a military defense against their invaders, "our people were laboring in the Temples day and night, endowing the Elders of Israel with the fullness of the blessings of the Holy Priesthood, until they got the number of fifty thousand endowed."[208] Meanwhile, "when the enemy had fired their combustibles, these men, endowed with the Holy Priesthood, walked along, like sentinels at their posts, and waved their hands, and the flames, smoke and ashes that were intended for the destruction of the Saints, turned upon our enemies."[209] In post-bellum Utah, the temple and its rites still checked anxieties just as it had in Nauvoo.

In February 1846, the first segment of Saints began to leave the city and head into Iowa. Ultimately, there would be no safety for the last of the

Mormons remaining in Hancock County. Rumors that some of the Saints were too destitute to relocate angered those who were eager to possess the city as their own. As a result, a makeshift army organized the forced removal of the remaining Saints, along with those friendly to the Mormons who had already purchased their lands. The final moment of resistance was September's Battle of Nauvoo, a conflict between a body of several hundred vigilantes and approximately 200 remaining Mormon males and other new non-Mormon residents. By the end of the fighting, there were three Mormon casualties and perhaps no more than one of the invading forces, although Mormons hoped that the amount of blood on the battlefield signaled that they had taken more lives than the rival forces wanted to admit. Joseph Fielding believed "it is probable that 150 fell in Battle."[210] Most historians accept the official statistics of one invading vigilante's death and a dozen wounded.

Fielding's journal provides one of the best accounts of the Mormon expulsion:

> The Mob found themselves in Possession of the City and they proceeded to capture, rob, and plunder in the most fiend like and unlawful manner they rendivouzed [*sic*] in the Temple, we had guareded [*sic*] it by Night and Day a long time feeling unwilling to leave it in their Hands, but they now had it to themselves, they even Preached in it and cursed the Saints but did no great Damage to it thinking it would add to the Value of their Property they treated the Saints with various kinds of Indignity some they pushed over the River in haste some they took and tried some they baptized &c.[211]

The temple would serve as headquarters and provide lodging for the troops. Mormons remembered that their enemies celebrated with alcohol-fueled blasphemy. Upon first taking the temple, "a mob preacher ascended to the top of the tower and standing outside proclaimed with a loud voice 'Peace, Peace, Peace to all the inhabitants of the earth, now the Mormons are driven,'" recalled Thomas Bullock.[212] They "defaced the Temple considerably, inside and out, such as knocking horns from the oxen in the [baptismal] font, running about the streets and imitating the blowing of horns with them and doing other acts of sacriledge [*sic*] too numerous to mention . . . the mob has torn down the altars and pulpits in the Temple, and converted that edifice into a meat market."[213] When one Latter-day Saint woman Mary Haskin Parker Richards learned of these incidents, she wrote, "will not the Lord pity his Saints and do unto them that have injured his House even as they have done unto it."[214] Mormons had expected the taking of their temple. Inside the building, in the east wall of the main assembly room, the intruders found a message engraved in "a circular line corresponding to the circle of the ceiling": "The Lord has Beheld Our Sacrifice, Come After Us."[215] The taunt was designed to be seen by Gentile eyes. The inscription invoked imagery from the biblical story of pharaoh's army pursuing the Israelites into the wilderness. While Mormons would not see their persecutors drowned in the Red Sea, they expected curses and plagues to fall upon the nation in their absence. When eventually federal troops would be commissioned to pursue the Saints in their mountain home as part of the Utah War, this imagery would again be invoked.

On the other side of the river, the Mormons were greeted by a sympathetic group from Quincy, who had brought clothing and provisions. As they continued on their journey, the miraculous occurred, as in the Israelite exodus, in the form of "a shower of quails." Fielding recalled the flocks that "came into the houses where the Saints were, settled on the tables, and the floor and even on their laps, so that they caught as many as they pleased." The Latter-day Saint memoirists of this period utilized the rhetoric of the miraculous to relay their history: "Thus the Lord was mindful of his people, and it was truly a matter of astonishment that in all this persecution, etc., only three of our brethren lost their lives."[216] Again taking on the role of exile and refugee, Latter-day Saints maintained a moral superiority over their critics and an assurance that all their sufferings were part of an eschatological narrative already written in the pages of prophetic scripture.

Conclusion

In this chapter, we have examined the impact of Smith's death in the development of the narrative of Mormon apocalyptic prophecy. Seeing the martyrs' bodies resting in their own blood, witnessing a lawyer justify the murder by arguing that all of Illinois agreed that the Smiths needed to die, and subsequently the mystery of the missing bodies all had real consequences on how Latter-day Saints viewed those outside their communities. The trauma of Nauvoo's final years held ramifications that lasted throughout the century.

Mormons followed a strategy identified by historian David D. Hall in reference to the seventeenth-century Puritans in which "very human feelings of anger and revenge were absorbed into religion via wonder stories, holy curses, and witch-hunting."[217] Wonder stories of martyrdom, apparitions, resurrection, spiritual empowerment, and protection assured Mormons of their place in a divine plan. Instead of literal "witch-hunts," Mormons lay blame on apostates and critics, who were, in their understanding, just as evil and conspiratorial.

Uniting in prayer against the nation or imagining curses on individual persecutors strengthened the bonds of insiders and demanded real distance from outsiders. It would not be long before Mormons began to take seriously both their isolationism and their rhetoric of ethnic distinctiveness. They were to become a new people, but it would first require discarding many links to the people of the United States. Curses created the force necessary to disassociate the metaphorical Mormon psyche from its American identity.

The development of a post-American Mormonism was at the heart of a new understanding of Mormon geography. In the mid-1840s, the Saints came to see themselves as ethnically distinct from other Euro-Americans through their understanding that Mormons came from a noble descent from ancient Israel. From this vantage point, Mormons had more in common with Native Americans than they did their Anglo-American persecutors. They came to see the act of leaving Gentile soil as the fulfillment of biblical and Book of Mormon prophecy. In the next chapter, we will examine how this refashioned ethnic identification affected the claiming of a new land unsullied by American influences.

Concerning the relationship between "official" and "lay" voices within Mormonism, this chapter has offered us a snapshot of just how erratic and unregulated prophecy was in the period immediately following Smith's death. With the exception of claiming to see the resurrected Joseph Smith, no attempt seems to have been made to silence non-hierarchical prophetic voices. This was not the case when it came to sectarian voices, as we will note in the following chapter, but talk of curses fulfilled and destructions on the United States were well received. The prophetic was a communal project, where the hierarchy acted to instill a greater emphasis on prophetic imagination rather than on-the-ground action. The hierarchy employed prophecy as a balm to salve a people wounded by despair and driven by a desire to seek revenge.

3
The Geography of Mormon Apocalyptic

> The Lord informs His people that He is coming out of His [hiding] place to punish the inhabitants of the earth for their inequity, and calls upon His people to enter into their CHAMBERS and hide themselves until the indignation is overpast. . . . In referring to the awful judgments of the latter days, Joel says, ii:32 that in Mount Zion shall be deliverance, and in the remnant whom the Lord should call. In the inspired Books the descendants of Joseph the son of Jacob are called the remnant. Then in the Mount Zion which will be among that people will be deliverance. In the destruction of Jerusalem, we read, Math. Xxiv:13, that the righteous were to flee to the mountains for deliverance. So in the bringing in of the fulness of the gentiles in the latter times: the righteous on this continent will have to flee to the mountains for deliverance.
>
> —George P. Dykes[1]

For Latter-day Saints, the apocalypse was as much about place as it was about time. Joseph Smith's revelations had presented Missouri as the setting for key eschatological events. Smith had identified Jackson County as the future location for the New Jerusalem. He envisioned the physical construction of the last days temple there, where Christ would "suddenly come."[2] The Ancient of Days and Jesus Christ would hold a council of mortals and angels in a valley in northern Missouri in order to install the millennial government. The providential connection between Missouri and the millennium was disrupted first with the Saints' exile from Missouri and again when Smith himself was murdered and violence precluded the Mormons from remaining in Illinois. As the body of Mormons fractured around several claimants who each sought to succeed Smith as head of the movement, the subject of geography and apocalypticism became increasingly significant.

Terrible Revolution. Christopher James Blythe, Oxford University Press (2020). © Oxford University Press.
DOI: 10.1093/oso/9780190080280.001.0001

While Brigham Young and the apostles promoted a continuation of Mormonism, first in Nauvoo and then in the mountain West, others presented variant Mormonisms with proposed futures in geographic settings throughout the United States. The leaders of these alternative gathering places anticipated a time when God would command them to lead the Saints back to Jackson County for the establishment of Christ's millennial reign. Missouri comprised the geographic center of Mormon apocalypticism. Mormons recognized that the trek west meant postponing their destiny in the Midwest. Relocating to the Rocky Mountains with Young meant traveling 1,300 miles west only to—if prophecy proved correct—return to Missouri presumably in the near future. Despite violence in Illinois, for obvious geotheological reasons, some Mormons were reluctant to leave behind such integral future sites of the millennium as they traveled west.

In response, those aligned with Young and the apostles developed a robust prophecy tradition, presenting the exodus to the Rocky Mountains as a pivotal part of God's plan for his last days people. This tradition developed, in part, to answer dissenting prophecy that promoted alternative gathering places, but it also replicated the method of Mormon colonization that had sacralized Missouri and Illinois. Adherents mapped scriptural expectations onto the landscape of the West just as they had in earlier Mormon settlements.

Geography and Rival Prophecy-Making

With the death of Joseph Smith, numerous would-be successors emerged to take the reins of the church.[3] The earliest rumblings of the succession crisis centered around three figures. First, Brigham Young argued that the Quorum of Twelve Apostles should take the lead of the church as a substitute first presidency. Young stressed the need to fulfill "the measures of Joseph" by finishing the projects Smith had begun—such as the completion of the Nauvoo Temple and the performance of rites therein.[4] In Nauvoo and the surrounding areas, the vast majority of the Saints sided with the apostles. Although Young was de facto president of the church by virtue of his position as president of the Quorum of the Twelve, he did not assume the head of the newly organized First Presidency until December 5, 1847.[5]

Second, Sidney Rigdon, who was Smith's first counselor in the three-man First Presidency as well as his running mate, presented himself as a "spokesman" for the deceased prophet.[6] After failing to acquire many converts in Nauvoo, Rigdon relocated to Pittsburgh, Pennsylvania, where his followers recognized him as the "first president of the church."[7] His movement numbered several hundred members before its collapse in 1847.[8]

James Strang emerged as the third figure of importance in the summer of 1844. Although he was a recent convert, Strang alleged to have received a letter from Smith appointing him as the prophet's successor.[9] While Rigdon gained a following among those who suspected and disapproved of the Twelve's still concealed practice of plural marriage, Strang surpassed Rigdon as the apostles' most threatening prophetic rival. For a decade, Strang led a successful movement numbering into the thousands with its headquarters initially established at a settlement near Burlington, Wisconsin, and later on Beaver Island in Lake Michigan.[10]

The list of would-be prophets multiplied quickly over the next decade. In 1845, the apostles expelled one of their own number, William Smith, after a feud related to his succeeding his brother Hyrum Smith as church patriarch. William Smith eventually founded an institution in favor of the eventual succession of Joseph Smith's eldest son, Joseph Smith III.[11] Later, William Smith disavowed the future ministry of his nephew in lieu of the realization that he himself was the last days Elijah prophesied in Malachi.[12] In 1847, relations soured between the Twelve and the leaders of two Mormon colonies—Lyman Wight in Texas and Alpheus Cutler in Iowa—resulting in new schismatic incarnations of Mormonism. In 1849, early Mormon convert and follower of James Strang after Smith's death, Charles B. Thompson broke with Strang and founded a new movement while claiming to be a spokesman for a greater and hidden prophet, Baneemy.[13]

Adopting a messianic apocalypticism, these less populous movements conceived of their leaders as messiahs who prepared the faith for the Second Coming. These men would pave the route back to Jackson County even if it was a circuitous route through other gathering places. In the meantime, they would reveal how the Saints could withstand the apocalypse, convert Native Americans and others, and prepare the Saints for the Second Coming. Yet, each of these messiahs sought to redeem Zion in fulfillment of the numerous references to messiah figures that permeated early Mormon revelations. For example, in 1832, Smith had referred to a figure designated as "on[e] mighty and strong," who would "set in order the house of God" and bestow the Saints' inheritances—or property—in Zion.[14] Other revelations pointed to a related but distinct figure, "a man who shall lead them like as

Moses led the children of Israel."[15] This figure would guide the Saints back to Jackson County in a journey that mirrored the Israelites' travel through the wilderness to the Promised Land.

Messianic prophecies endured in Brighamite circles as well, despite the efforts of leaders to discourage the belief that they would fulfill them. For example, Brigham Young confronted W. W. Phelps for preaching that he (Brigham) was "the man like unto Moses." Wilford Woodruff recorded the details of Young's rebuke in his journal:

> President Young asked Wm. W. Phelps by what authority he had proclaimed in Public that He (Brigham Young) was the man that the Lord said he would raise up like unto Moses. Phelps said Joseph was gone & you are left to lead the People. B.Y. That is no Argument at all. I may die & others be left. That does not prove that I or they would be the one refered to. If I thought I was the man I would not tel[l] of it. But I think I am the great man that none of the prophets eve[r?] thought of or spoke of.[16]

Ironically, Young also believed in the imminent return to Jackson County. In 1862, he privately expressed his belief that the Saints would not complete the Salt Lake Temple for some time and that the Saints would return to Missouri within the next seven years to complete that temple first.[17]

Young's insistence that such matters, even if they were true, should be concealed from the Saints suggests his concern over the prophecy's impact. He worried that his flock would neglect their practical duties—settling colonies, building temples, evangelism—if they became too immersed in apocalypticism, particularly if those prophecies pointed to an imminent return to the East. More importantly, the routinization of authority into the office of apostle and subsequent reorganization of the First Presidency had already settled Young's position within Mormon institutional life. Stable power structures benefit from a moderate faith. Young had little to gain by asserting additional apocalyptic roles. On the other hand, those outside of the priestly power structure had much to gain from messianic posturing. Without the ecclesiastical clout of the chief apostle and his quorum, such men employed messianic claims to legitimate their prophetic leadership outside of the regular channels of the church institution.

Many of these new prophets claimed that the failure of the Saints to complete the temple in a timely manner had led God to reject the church. Critics of the Twelve pointed to a divinely imposed deadline to finish the construction. A January 1841 revelation promised the church "sufficient time to build a house unto me," during which time they could perform baptisms for the dead outside of the structure. However, at "the end of the appointment [they would] be rejected as a church, with [their] dead."[18] The revelation did not spell out the deadline, but warned that if the temple was not completed within the "appointment," the church would become like all other churches—bereft of divine sanction.

The question of whether the Saints' efforts to complete the temple fulfilled the initial command, or if now were too little too late, became a major source of conflict during the period following Smith's death. Strang and Rigdon both predicted that the structure would never be fully constructed. After the Brighamites ceremonially dedicated the building on May 1, 1846, Strang, Rigdon, and others argued that the Saints never sufficiently finished the building to be properly dedicated in the first place. Such arguments presented a powerful barb against apostolic authority. They uprooted the apostles' platform of completing the temple and questioned their legitimacy as part of an existing ecclesiastical structure. If God had rejected the church, then he had also rejected the apostles. Likewise, because the rejection centered on the Nauvoo Temple, these dissenting parties opposed Mormons remaining in Nauvoo, the stronghold of the Twelve's supporters.

Just as the Twelve's sectarian opponents portrayed Nauvoo as a place cursed and rejected by God, they also condemned the Brighamite trek west. They argued that to relocate from the United States was to abandon the Latter-day Saint hope of redeeming Zion. They saw the migration to the Rocky Mountains as a costly and dangerous distraction from this greater redemptive objective. As an alternative to the westward migration, each group designated their own gathering place as a way station for the eventual return to Jackson County, which would in most cases allow the faithful to remain in the Midwest, rather than travel to "the wilderness." From these sites, the faithful could return to Missouri with greater ease as soon as the man like Moses received a revelation to do so.

The Cutlerites embraced that approach with enthusiasm. While still aligned with the leadership of the Twelve Apostles, Cutler established a mission among the Delaware then residing in Indian Territory (Kansas). The community imbued their evangelization with apocalyptic dynamics. In 1852, a cholera outbreak forced the Cutlerites to retreat to Iowa where Cutler had seen the site of their new colony, Manti, in a vision.[19] Still eager to return to Jackson County, he prophesied that a path through one of his adherent's farms would serve as a highway for thousands traveling to Zion when the time came.[20] The entire community came to revolve around these apocalyptic expectations. When Joseph Smith III, the son of Joseph Smith Jr., visited Manti, Iowa, in 1863, he recalled:

> They had become imbued with the idea that God would soon command them to gather to Zion. So strong was this belief among them that they had made ready wagons, tents and other appurtenances of nomadic life—and were ready, at a moment's notice, to throw their household goods into the vehicles and start for Independence [i.e., Jackson County]. . . . Among these people who held to Elder Cutler, there was so strong a belief that such a call would soon come, that they would not furnish their houses enough to even make themselves comfortable, nor make proper improvements upon their lands, notwithstanding the fact that they were located in one of the very best and most fertile parts of Southern Iowa.[21]

Cutler likely instigated this zealous preparation for the move to Jackson County after announcing a prophecy in 1861 that he would be "standing in Zion, if he lived to be 80 years old."[22] In other words, he planned to relocate to Missouri before 1864. When the year arrived, instead of returning to Missouri, Cutler died and his followers moved further north to Minnesota, where they could avoid the Civil War and the influence of missionaries from other Mormon movements.

Lyman Wight settled his colony in Texas based on a commission he had received from Joseph Smith in a meeting of the Council of Fifty.[23] Like Cutler, he believed that he would one day direct the building of Zion in Jackson County. Smith, according to Wight, had ordained him to "lead the saints of the most high God to Zion as Moses led the children of Israel."[24] Wight recalled that Smith had brushed off the idea of colonizing west of the Rocky Mountains. "He (Joseph) said that it would, at least, cost four million dollars, to transport the Church across the mountains. It will then cost four million to transport them back. This would be eight million dollars."[25] Wight insisted that the Twelve's advancement of westward migration indicated that they had altogether given up on the effort to build Zion.

James Strang became the most successful detractor from the trek just as he had been to the leadership of the Twelve Apostles. He championed the site of a colony in Wisconsin based on the letter allegedly written by Smith. The letter pointed to the location as a gathering place where the Saints would be protected and prosper, and where they could again build a temple along the Mississippi. In an interesting parallel to Smith changing Commerce's name to Nauvoo, the document—citing a revelation—pronounced "the name of the city shall be called Voree, which is being interpreted, garden of peace, for there shall my people have peace and rest and wax fat and pleasant in the presence of their enemies."[26] Strang presented Voree as a launching pad from which the Saints could later return to earlier sites. A revelation promised "if they gather to my city of Voree there will I keep them under the shadow of my wings and the cities from whence my people have been driven shall be purged with a high hand for I will do it, and my people shall be again restored to their possessions."[27] In other words, the Strangites would inhabit Nauvoo, Jackson County, and other sites after the Gentile populations had been removed by destruction or other means.

Not only had God appointed Voree as the site of a last days gathering place, but Strang soon presented the site as part of Mormonism's sacred past. Mirroring Smith's discovery and translation of gold plates in New York, Strang was led to where an ancient prophet had deposited a set of brass plates in the ground. The record's translation established the site as the former settlement of an unidentified proto–Native American civilization, which like the Nephites had experienced a societal collapse. Writing in the shadow of the events, the ancient author found hope that "the elect and faithful" would one day inhabit the same stretch of land.[28] Strangites referred to the place where Strang discovered the plates as the Hill of Promise and constructed a large tower to commemorate this event.[29]

In contrast, Strang portrayed the Brighamite exodus as evidence that God had rejected Young's followers. According to one of Strang's revelations, they were "cast out of my holy city" for their wickedness (i.e., "their usurpations and lyings and false teachings").[30] God had thrust them from Nauvoo for refusing to acknowledge Strang and to flee to the place of refuge that he had assigned. As Strang's vitriol for the Brighamites in Nauvoo piqued, he wrote and circulated a curse leveled against those who sided with the Twelve. The lengthy malediction echoed the curses then popularly uttered against the Saints' persecutors. The Brighamites would be bereft of "peace and home" and experience physical suffering. "In the name of God and the Lord Jesus Christ; may their bones rot in the living tomb of their flesh; may their flesh generate from its own corruptions a loathsome life for others; may their blood swarm with a leprous life of motelike ghastly corruption, feeding on flowing life, generating chilling agues and burning fevers."[31] Imagery of corruption, disease, parasites, and living putrefaction filled the text.

No known sources reveal how lay Brighamites reacted to this unsettling prophecy. On the other hand, the apostle Orson Hyde published his own revelation in response:

> Behold, James J. Strang hath cursed my people by his own spirit and not by mine. Never, at any time, have I appointed that wicked man to lead my people. Neither by my own voice, nor by the voice of my servant, Joseph Smith, neither by the voice of mine angels; but he hath sought to deceive and Satan helpeth him; but before of old was he one that was ordained to gather the tares of the field and mine angels have chosen him to do it because he was a wicked man even as Judas was chosen to destroy his Lord.[32]

Hyde's revelation unequivocally disputed Strang's claim to leadership. According to the revelation, Strang lied about a commission from Smith as well as an angelic ordination. Yet, his presence as a false prophet was also a sign of the times. Angels had selected Strang to fulfill a work, which Hyde described by alluding to the Gospel of St. Matthew's parable of the wheat and tares. The parable suggested that both the righteous and wicked (the wheat and tares, respectively) would intermingle, until the "harvest" at "the end of the world" when the tares would be gathered and burned while the wheat would be salvaged in the barn. In Hyde's portrayal of this parable, Mormons constituted both the wheat and the tares. Hyde depicted God as removing the tares via Strang's influence, just as God led the righteous to safety in another land. The tares would, by implication, be cast into the fire.

Once in the Rocky Mountains, the Saints started sacralizing a new place, but they remained aware of these alternatively proposed sites. Historian Richard Bennett has referred to the Saints' perception of the trek west as the fulfillment of biblical prophecy as a means by which they "would more than validate their decision to quit Missouri and Nauvoo—it would redeem it! It would give them the doctrinal ammunition they required to confront Strang and others and to convince many laboring behind in doubt and confusion."[33]

The Sacralization of the Mormon West

In the wilderness, Mormons faced trials and afflictions inherent to the mass crossing of the frontier. The uprooted Saints conceived of their hardships as part of a sacred narrative, which provided them with hope. They came to see the trek and subsequent arrival in the Rocky Mountains as key events in the eschatological timeline. Although they maintained the goal of building Zion in Jackson County, this geographic moment was not inconsequential. It, too, had been foreseen by ancient and modern prophets.

Considering the various prophetic expectations that coalesced to sacralize the West, the overarching theme was divine guidance. As church leaders deliberated on the future home of the Saints, they consulted published travel guides, held prayer meetings, and met with non-Mormons familiar with the region. Yet, the day-to-day drudgery of locating a place to settle did not overshadow the role of the miraculous. Mormon legend holds that when Brigham Young first saw the Salt Lake Valley, a location suggested previously by Jim Bridger, a western explorer and trapper, he prophetically declared, "[T]his is the place."[34]

Without question, it was the mountains that set this new gathering place apart. Joseph Smith had laid a preliminary groundwork for understanding the region's peaks during early plans for a westward trek across the Rockies to the Oregon Territory. He expected that each of the initial scouts would receive the endowment because "when he gets on the mountain he may wa[n]t to talk with his god."[35] Brigham Young also described mountains as a place of theophany. "There are places on the earth where the Lord can come and dwell, if he pleases. They may be found on the tops of high mountains, or in some cavern or places where sinful man has never marked the soil with his polluted feet."[36] For many Mormons, the mountains possessed an inherent sanctity, perhaps imbibed from their reading of the Old Testament.[37]

Young led the way in defining their new home as the site of biblical prophecy. While still in Nauvoo, on January 13, 1846, he warned that "the Prophets would never be verified unless the House of the Lord should be reared in the Tops of the Mountains & the Proud Banner of Liberty wave over the valleys that are within the Mountains."[38] In this representation of a last days temple, Young pulled from passages in the book of Isaiah that had long played a role in Latter-day Saint representations of the millennium. Specifically, Mormons viewed their mission in the mountains in light of the second and third verses of the second chapter:

> And it shall come to pass in the last days, that the mountain of the Lord's house shall be established in the top of the mountains, and shall be exalted above the hills; and all nations shall flow unto it. And many people shall go and say, Come ye, and let us go up to the mountain of the Lord, to the house

> of the God of Jacob; and he will teach us of his ways, and we shall walk in his paths: for out of Zion shall go forth the law, and the word of the Lord from Jerusalem.[39]

The Saints had applied this same prophecy to the New Jerusalem Temple in Jackson County, but its previous use did not prevent Young's re-interpretation of the prophecy to point to a last days temple in the actual mountains. He also based his reference to the "Proud Banner of Liberty" on a reading of Isaiah—a prophecy that God would "lift up an ensign to the nations from far."[40] Young expected to find two sites in the West—one for the building of the temple and the other for the planting of the "Banner of Liberty"—by which he would confirm the place for Latter-day Saint settlement. Others shared in this hope. For instance, at the end of 1846, Wilford Woodruff recorded a journal entry, expressing his prayer "to Heavenly Father to lengthen out my days to behold the House of God stand upon the tops of the Mountains and to see the Standard of Liberty reared up as an ensign to the nations to come unto to serve the Lord of Hosts."[41]

The pioneers discovered the latter site, soon named Ensign Peak, two days after their arrival in the Salt Lake Valley. Discussions of the site and the flag that was to be hoisted there were reflective of the period's Mormon nationalism. In Nauvoo, the Council of Fifty spoke metaphorically of their constitution as an "ensign to the nations."[42] Sometime before his death, Smith came to read the passage literally but, according to an 1847 council meeting, "did not give a description of size shape, & colors," although the flag was "commenced out of White cloth the day before Joseph died."[43] On January 13, 1846, Young announced that he knew "the spot" the flag would be flown, "& I know how to make this Flag. Jos[eph] sent out the coulours [*sic*] & Said wherever the coulours [*sic*] settled there would be the spot."[44] While the Council of Fifty had not finalized the design, Young's claim to know how the ensign should be made and where it would be unfurled was based on a vision or dream he had experienced as the fragmentary reference to Smith's instructions suggests.[45]

Later in 1869, George A. Smith provided further details of Young's vision. According to his account, Young had "sought the Lord to know what they should do, and where they should lead the people for safety, and while they were fasting and praying daily on this subject, President Young had a vision of Joseph Smith, who showed him the mountain that we now call Ensign Peak, immediately north of Salt Lake City, and there was an ensign fell upon that peak, and Joseph said, 'Build under the point where the colors fall and you will prosper and have peace.'"[46]

Although Young claimed to know the design of the ensign in March 1846, this claim did not produce a singular, definitive plan for the flag. Instead, imagining and proposing different versions of the flag was a process through which some Latter-day Saints participated in sacralizing the West. On February 26, 1847, there was a council meeting to discuss the flag. William Clayton suggested the "colors blue & red—letters red shaded with blue." Brigham Young agreed and also wanted "purple & scarlet." At that point, he envisioned the flag would include the motto "religious toleration."[47] That no officially recognized design existed was evident by the array of suggestions. On May 29, 1847, Young claimed that the "standard would be a flag of every nation under heaven."[48] This image of nations peacefully uniting resonated with Benjamin F. Johnson, who would later write that the day would come when "all nations will yet gladly subscribe [to the American Constitution,] blending their flags with the stars and stripes to form a representative political government to ultimately become the kingdom of 'our God and His Christ.'"[49] This exceptionally large flag would represent the universal dominion of the millennial kingdom.

Others were less drawn to this apocalyptic image. Even when Wilford Woodruff recorded Young's suggestion of a composite flag, he sketched his own design within the pages of his diary. Woodruff's pennant-shaped design included the sun, moon, an eight-sided star, as well as dots, lines, and other shapes.[50] Another flag was actually embroidered and perhaps flown on the *Brooklyn*, a ship that brought emigrating Latter-day Saints from New York to California. This flag was modeled, like the Nauvoo Temple, after the scene of Revelation 12:1, with an image of a woman with a crown with twelve stars wearing a robe embroidered with suns and standing on a crescent moon. While the design was fitting, Orson Hyde instructed the *Brooklyn*'s captain not to "exhibit" the still provisional standard "until the council of the church approved it."[51]

A dream narrative demonstrated the continued importance placed on this ensign and the remaining uncertainty over what it would look like. In 1867, William Johnstun recorded a dream in which he was commissioned as part of an expedition to the North Pole to retrieve the lost ten tribes of Israel. Johnstun's group was to identify itself as fellow Israelites by unfurling a flag that he described as "white with several emblems upon it; only two of which I remember being thereon, was the all seeing eye and the square and compass being under it."[52] These were common Mormon symbols appropriated from Freemasonry in the 1840s and signaled a sense of mystery and sanctity. Yet, another Kingdom of God flag flew at Brigham Young's funeral in 1877. As an observer described, "The so-called flag of the Stars and Stripes placed there on that occasion was a flag having in its upper hand corner a blue field with a circle of twelve stars and in the center a large white star. The stripes on that flag, instead of being red and white stripes, were blue and white stripes."[53] Perhaps this design alluded to Revelation 12 or the twelve tribes of Israel.

When, on July 26, 1847, an actual ceremony was held on Ensign Peak, there was no flag present to be unfurled. Rather, according to one man who watched the ceremony from a distance, the small group of church leaders in attendance "hoisted a sort of flag on Ensign Peak. Not a flag, but a handkerchief belonging to Heber C. Kimball, one of those yellow bandana kind."[54] Actual flags—likely both American and Kingdom of God-specific—would fly there in the future, but on that summer date the immediate objective was to mark the landscape with the symbols of prophecy unfolding. The banner signaled the sacralization of this new geography.

Two days later, Young selected the temple site at the base of Ensign Peak. The actual excavation and construction would not begin for several years. Yet, the announcement drew criticism from detractors and skepticism from his own supporters. They expected a revelation commanding the new temple. While Young considered himself divinely led in the decision and even countered that he could produce a revelation on the matter, he recalled that Joseph Smith had argued that such a command was no more necessary than was a divine mandate to build one's home.[55] It was not until 1853 when the church officially laid the cornerstones of the temple that Young described the experience he claimed set apart that specific piece of land:

> I scarcely ever say much about revelations, or visions, but suffice it to say, five years ago last July I was here, and saw in the Spirit the Temple not ten feet from where we have laid the Chief Corner Stone. I have not inquired what kind of a Temple we should build. Why? Because it was represented before me. I have never looked upon that ground, but the vision of it was there. I see it as plainly as if it was in reality before me. Wait until it is done.[56]

Young's foresight of the temple in the Salt Lake Valley paralleled Smith's own concerning the Nauvoo Temple. Smith also knew how that building should be constructed. Years later, the assistant temple architect recalled

Young sketching the design and explaining the basic structure in a private meeting.[57] The new temple would have six towers instead of only one, as had been the case in Nauvoo and Kirtland. The towers, three in the east and three in the west, represented the church's Melchizedek and Aaronic priesthoods, respectively. Young would point to different details of the building several times over the next decades.[58]

In dreams, visions, and imaginings, other Mormons anticipated this promised structure in the West. Woodruff recorded a dream on May 13, 1847, that "we had arived [*sic*] at our Journeys end whare [*sic*] we were to build up a stake of Zion. As we came onto the place there was An open vision of A temple presented before me." In the dream, he alone could see the temple, which "appeared as though it was built of white & blue stone. The sight of it filled me with Joy and I awoke & behold it was a dream."[59] In the forty years it took to complete the temple, others also spoke of miraculously seeing the finished building. In 1853, a missionary in England recorded a woman's account of her spirit leaving her body "carried away to the valley of the Salt Lake & saw the Temple of the Lord Built large & beautiful & saw many Elders come in with large companys [*sic*] of saints."[60] Another woman, Amanda Wilcox, remembered seeing a vision of the future Temple Square in 1868.[61]

The Saints finally dedicated the Salt Lake Temple on April 6, 1893—not during the presidency of Young or even his successor, John Taylor, but during the ministry of the fourth LDS president, Wilford Woodruff. The temple—the image of the temple—in the Salt Lake Valley would become a symbol of Mormon identity even before it materialized in granite on the landscape. Looking forward to the temple in Salt Lake was a collective act that positioned the Latter-day Saints in sacred time. This communal apocalyptic vision assured them that the millennium stood on the horizon.

Young's translation of biblical prophecies onto the mountain landscape of Deseret was key to sacralizing the new Mormon homeland. Yet, the Saints would have felt unsatisfied if they believed the decision to make the trek to the Great Basin was Young's genius. Even after they officially recognized Young as the church's Prophet, Seer, and Revelator in 1847, his revelatory pronouncements did not hold the weight of his predecessor. For this reason, the Saints took comfort in a new tradition that Smith had long known that the Saints would relocate to the Rocky Mountains.[62]

Smith's prophecy appeared in the official church history, a major writing and editing project that sought to reconstruct the church's past through the voice of Joseph Smith. An interpolation added to the record sometime between November 1845 and November 1855, written as if Smith authored the passage, read:

> I prophesied that the Saints would continue to suffer much affliction and would be driven to the Rocky Mountains, many would apostatize, others would be put to death by our persecutors or lose their lives in consequence of exposure to disease, and some of you will live to go and assist in making settlements and build cities and see the Saints become a mighty people in the midst of the Rocky Mountains.[63]

A better known example of this prophecy appeared in a statement written in 1854 by Anson Call (see Figure 3.1). Twelve years after the event supposedly occurred, Anson recalled that at the installation of the masonic lodge in Montrose, Smith prophesied:

Figure 3.1 Photo of Anson B. Call (1810–1890). Call was a Latter-day Saint pioneer to Utah who famously recalled Joseph Smith's "Rocky Mountain Prophecy." Courtesy of the Church History Library.

> Joseph stated many things to us concerning of our going to the mountains he said we should go and build many Cities and we should become a mity [*sic*] people in the midst of the mountains and we should perform a work that will astonish the nations of the earth he said their [*sic*] are those heare that shall help perform the work he said their is Br Roundy and Br Call and others that shall partisipate [*sic*] in it he charged us with the seal of an Angel to be faithful for sa[i]d he many before that day will come will Apostatise Multitudes will die and great over turns will take place with this people and many other things that I cannot recollect.[64]

In both these accounts, not only had Smith seen the colonization, his foreknowledge extended to detailing the hardships of the trek and the mass apostasies—perhaps referring to the schisms of the 1840s. Other accounts maintained that Smith called for a map to specifically chart out the Saints' future travels.[65]

Oliver B. Huntington recalled that Joseph Smith's father entrusted this knowledge to his family when questioned why the Saints were establishing a seemingly permanent settlement in Illinois when the New Jerusalem was to be built in Missouri. Father Smith informed the Huntington family that "the Lord has told Joseph" they would remain in Nauvoo for only seven years and then "will go into the Rocky Mountains; right into the midst of the Lamanites." Huntington remembered Father Smith's warning that "this is not to be made public; I would not like to have this word go any further."[66] The admonition of secrecy explained why so few knew such important information.

Beginning in the 1850s, the Saints paid increasing attention to a vision that Stephen M. Farnsworth had experienced previous to Smith's death in 1844 (see Figure 3.2). Farnsworth was a loyal follower of the Twelve Apostles residing in Pleasant Grove at the time his vision became popular. The vision has survived in several forms—some drafted by Farnsworth and others recorded from his public testimony—each variant sharing a basic structure. During a spring 1844 afternoon, Farnsworth walked toward the temple construction site in Nauvoo when he became suddenly enrapt in vision. The weather shifted and the sky became overcast. Farnsworth watched as the now sorrowful Saints began the trek west. After they arrived in the West, the Saints experienced a time of happiness and prosperity before dark storm clouds appeared and grew larger, plunging the entire sky into darkness. During this period, the apostles bound the Saints tightly together with hoops—according to an early version, with "three strong iron bands." The Twelve hammered the hoop tighter and tighter, causing the Saints much discomfort until it burst.

Figure 3.2 Stephen M. Farnsworth (1810–1885). Farnsworth recalled having an elaborate vision while living in Nauvoo, Illinois, which detailed the trek west, adversity there, and eventually the Saints' return to Jackson County. Frank Esshom, *Pioneers and Prominent Men of Utah* (1913).

Now freed, "something over one half of them run like frightened sheep."[67] Another variant suggested even two-thirds of the Saints could have fled.[68]

The Saints seem to have interpreted this moment in reference to the Utah War or at least to the earlier arrival of the army in Utah Territory. In a version of Farnsworth's vision narrated by Orson Hyde as part of a sermon, after the dark cloud appeared, "an army or force of the enemy came into the neighborhood and offered protection to all who wished it." Hyde explained that those who fled "went to the enemy for protection."[69] After their retreat, the dark cloud burst and "the countenance of the authorities which before had seemed so tyrannical and oppressive instantly changed to the most lovely and pleasant appearance, and all our troubles were immediately banished."[70] In most versions, the authorities held a feast, which inaugurated an era of unity among the Saints.[71] In the later versions, the righteous who remained were greeted by heavenly messengers who "blessed them with all that their hearts could desire and life was a pleasure."[72] In both early and later versions, the Spirit of God or the angels respectively informed Farnsworth that the early trials were necessary "in order to sift out those who were unworthy to enjoy the blessings that we now enjoyed."[73]

Farnsworth then saw destructions presumably outside of Utah, which he described as "a ten-fold vengeance upon the heads of our enemies." In the final scene of his vision, Farnsworth joined the Saints as they marched back to Jackson County. Just before they reached the holy city, Farnsworth encountered "a Missouri mobocrat very ma[l]icious in appearance comeing [*sic*] toward us."[74] All known variants ended with the aged persecutor, who had somehow survived up to this point, destroyed—"screech[ing] aloud, withered and passed away, as a thing of naught," after making eye contact with Farnsworth.[75]

The popularity of Farnsworth's vision demonstrated the ways in which Mormons subscribed to both hierarchical and lay representations of apocalyptic. Because Farnsworth's vision did not contradict the teachings or visions of the church's leadership, faithful prophecy enthusiasts embraced his experience. Saints even discussed the vision in church meetings, such as a Provo high priests' quorum meeting held on March 19, 1858, where one attendee spoke on symbolism from the vision.[76] Farnsworth's vision contained many apocalyptic elements that would have attracted Latter-day Saints even beyond Farnsworth's professed foreknowledge of the colonization of the Rocky Mountains: the punishment of the wicked, an end to the Saints' trials, and a return to Jackson County. His vision was elaborate. It was well written, and Farnsworth willingly shared his vision and dispersed copies. The prophecy garnered additional attention and legitimacy in 1857 when Apostle Orson Hyde relayed the vision over the pulpit at general conference.

Whether narrated by Young, Smith, or someone like Farnsworth, the message was the same: God had willed the colonization of the Rocky Mountains as part of his last days plans. He had given the faithful a foreknowledge of the sites in the Great Basin and the events that would unfold once the Saints arrived there. Each narrative connected the colonization of the Rocky Mountains with the larger narrative of Mormon apocalyptic.

Apocalypse in the Past: The Book of Mormon as a Lens for Possessing the West

The Book of Mormon also aided in inscribing meaning onto the Saints' new homeland. The Saints had fled from Gentile lands and took up residence near the descendants of Father Lehi. They came to believe they resided in Book of Mormon lands. By envisioning their new home as the setting of key Book of Mormon events, they tapped into a historical geography with its own moral warnings and meanings in place. Specifically, this Book of Mormon landscape had once been the place of an apocalyptic societal collapse. Evil spirits of the ancient Gadianton Robbers—once the cause of God's wrath on the ancient inhabitants—were understood as still present within this reinterpreted geography. At the same time, Mormons understood living Natives through the undercurrents of apocalypticism. Their conversion was a necessary part of the apocalyptic chronology.

Although the Book of Mormon was explicitly set in the New World, its internal descriptions of place gave little indication as to where on the continent the narrative actually occurred.[77] Smith provided information on some locations through his ministry. For instance, the recovery of the gold plates in Palmyra alerted Mormons that Moroni had deposited the record nearby at the Hill Cumorah, the location of the collapse of Nephite society in the book's climax. Later accounts claimed that Smith also discovered "Nephite altars" north of Far West, Missouri, and the remains of a "white Lamanite warrior," Zelph, in Illinois.[78] In 1834, he described the region as "the plains of the Nephites."[79] The Mormon prophet had likewise identified six plates purportedly discovered in Kinderhook, Illinois, as relics from the descendants of Noah's son, Ham, or as Parley P. Pratt stated, the pre-Nephite Jaredite civilization.[80]

Other early Mormons also theorized and speculated on modern locations of historic Nephite geography. Many of these historic scenes envisioned on the landscape were associated with violence. In 1832, William W. Phelps, the editor of *The Evening and Morning Star*, situated the Land of Desolation, the site of the Jaredite societal collapse, in "the section of country from the Mississippi to the Rocky Mountains."[81] Like other early Mormons, Phelps felt enthralled by the prospect of living in a land with such sacred historical presence. In 1841, Charles B. Thompson's *Evidences in Proof of the Book of Mormon* argued that the recent discovery of "fortifications" in the Allegheny Mountains served as evidence of a Gadianton Robber presence.[82] What scholar Darryl Caterine wrote of the first Mormon site in Palmyra—that it was "nothing less than a massive graveyard, the site of bloody warfare between the Nephites and Lamanites"—was true of the Mormon mental map of the entire West.[83]

From Texas, Lyman Wight paralleled the Rocky Mountains' ancient apostate inhabitants with the supposed iniquities of the Brighamite gathering. In a letter to William Smith, an ally who shared his suspicions of Young, he wrote:

> I ask when will this small valley [i.e., Salt Lake Valley], with its hot and cold lava boiling up from the bowels of hell, or some more fatal abode of those

> demon spirits that have been burried [*sic*] beneath the surface for their damnable practices among the Nephites in early days, and now mingled with the more innocent blood of those who have fallen victims to the damnable inquisition of the Brighamites, whose king and commander is of the pure lineage of Gadianton, who made his abode, for himself and followers, in places that might be considered a haven of rest for the abode of this damnable stink.[84]

Wight's claim that Young had returned to his ancestral lands in the American West marked a reversal of Mormonism's understanding that modern Israel would return to the lands they had inherited as descendants of the biblical Joseph (e.g., Mormons and Native Americans) inhabiting the millennial American continent. Using the Book of Mormon narrative to disparage the Brighamites' western setting, Wight's implication was that the wicked would be drawn to the West. The Saints in the mountain West had already imagined their new home as haunted and hellish just as they imagined it as a latter-day Zion. They seem to have embraced the contradiction and alternately used either conceptualization to construct a new cultural geography of the West.

While Young believed that demons shared the Saints' new home, contra Wight, he did not find the malevolent spirits a source of comfort. Brighamites understood the presence of these spirits as entities that could be resisted and exorcised. Before the trek from Iowa to the Great Basin, Young warned a congregation of the need for greater vigilance in the faith:

> The truth of the matter is there are many places we pass through that have been the slaughter ground of the ancient Nephites and Lamanites and the spirits of Devils are hovering around it and if you are not on your guard they will enter you and lead you captive at their will. For if you are not governed by the spirit of God you will be by the spirit of the devil. And if you are governed by the spirit of God while in such places and they cannot enter any of you they will try to enter your cattle your beast for they want to enter some tabernacle as they did the swine in ancient days.[85]

Young intended his comments to encourage greater obedience, but these types of sentiments would also color some aspects of the trek, as well as their new home. Willard Richards recorded an incident when a horse "sickened with bloating and cholick [*sic*]" was apparently under the influence of an evil spirit. Six men "laid hands on the horse and commanded the unclean and foul spirits of ev[e]ry name & nature to depart & go to the Gentiles at Warsaw & trouble the Saints no more." The ritual was effective. The horse "rolled twice over in great distress sprang to his feet squeeled vomited & purged" and was fine the following day.[86] By sending the evil entities toward Warsaw, whose citizens and press had been particularly critical of the church, the party exacted a touch of retribution against the anti-Mormon establishment.

Mormons often identified evil spirits as the ghosts of Gadianton Robbers during the Utah period. On February 19, 1865, Heber C. Kimball warned that "the atmosphere of many parts of these mountains is doubtless the abode of the spirits of Gadianton robbers, whose spirits are as wicked as hell, and who would kill Jesus Christ and every Apostle and righteous person that ever lived if they had the power."[87] These wicked spirits could cause illness and tempt one to commit sin. As in ancient times, they exhibited a particular passion to destroy and wreak havoc on righteous communities.

In the latter half of the nineteenth century, the Saints told stories of Gadianton Robbers haunting struggling settlements. While the Saints in these communities pointed to Gadianton Robbers to explain strange occurrences or unusual behaviors, they would also come to believe that the presence of these spirits doomed the settlement to eventual collapse.[88] Just as the Gadianton Robbers and their secret combinations led to the murders of ancient prophets, resulting in the destruction of past civilizations, their spirits held the potential to re-enact this history in the present. Mormons, through telling these stories, reminded one another that they, too, could meet with the same fate.

Book of Mormon geography could also imbue the West with sanctity as it had earlier sites. In 1849, an expedition to southern Utah reported their discovery of symbols "engraven on the Rocks, plenty of Hieroglyphics, or the Reformed Egyptian language, or Nephite language, as supposed the work of the ancient Nephites."[89] The exploring party benefited from the presence of W. W. Phelps, who had once aided Joseph Smith in translating Egyptian hieroglyphics in Kirtland. Phelps declared the region a "glorious country with its mineral wealth, whose history is written upon its ruins."[90] While these hieroglyphics were not inscribed on plates or papyri, he was eager to continue to act in the role of translator.[91]

He took particular interest in a set of glyphs discovered in the Sanpete Valley. Non-Mormon John W. Gunnison preserved Phelps's only remaining translation. It read, "I Mahanti, the 2nd King of the Lamanites, in five valleys in the mountains, make this record in the 12 hundredth year since we came out of Jerusalem—And I have three sons gone to the South country to live by hunting antelope and deer."[92] In 1852, Gunnison published this translation as part of his book *The Mormons*. He expressed his skepticism, noting that "those who were associated with Joseph as amanuenses pretend to have acquired sufficient knowledge of similar things to be enabled to decipher their signification, and have translated enough to confirm, in the most wonderful manner, the Nephite records."[93] Gunnison assumed, probably correctly, that Phelps intended to vindicate the Book of Mormon with his translation. Regardless, such translations imbued the West with a sacred past that influenced the way the Saints viewed their new setting.

Others also likely participated in translating petroglyphs. Gunnison's personal notes included another translation of a set of hieroglyphics discovered "100 miles South of Little Salt Lake Valley," although he left the second translator's name blank: "The Melchisedek [*sic*] Priest Toanti blew his trumpet thrice for the people to assemble & the multitude stood about him until the third hour, when the glory of the Lord appeared by the side of the burning altar & they fell on their faces to the ground while Toanti received the following commandments." A more extensive translation had existed, but Gunnison noted that the "remainder [was] not copied."[94] Whereas Mahanti's inscription merely documented his presence in sixth-century Sanpete, Toanti's narrative presented the Little Salt Lake Valley—later known as Parowan—as the site of a miraculous event harkening back to Moses's theophany on Mount Sinai.

As Mormons formed settlements throughout the Great Basin, they propagated legends associated with specific Book of Mormon figures. Two types of stories gained the most traction across time: those associated with the past wanderings of Moroni and those regarding the continuing ministry of the immortal "Three Nephites." Stories concerning Moroni often dealt with the last years of his life—a period not covered extensively in the Book of Mormon but that included his lonely flight from Lamanite pursuers following a holocaust of the Nephites. Joseph Smith allegedly recounted one such story to Thomas B. Marsh, who later told it to a man with the last name of Higginson. The story described Moroni's courageous death while trying to withstand four Lamanite attackers.[95] Other narratives relayed Moroni's final travels through the Americas in which he dedicated lands for the later use of the Latter-day Saints.

Moroni also became explicitly tied to the geography of nineteenth-century temple sites. After the completion of temples in Manti and St. George, stories depicted both locations as previously dedicated by Moroni during his flight from the Lamanites. These legends claimed that Young insisted he pick the exact locations for the temple to be built based on his knowledge of where Moroni had dedicated the land. Warren Snow, a bishop in Manti, may have instigated the tradition when he recalled that Young privately told him, "Here is the spot where the Prophet Moroni stood and dedicated this piece of land for a Temple site, and that is the reason why the location is made here, and we can't move it from this spot; and if you and I are the only persons that come here at high noon to-day, we will dedicate this ground."[96]

A similar tradition appeared in St. George where the Saints constructed the first completed post-Nauvoo Temple in 1877. David Henry Cannon remembered that as an 11-year-old boy, he heard Young identify the temple site and defend his decision when somebody suggested an alternative site: "We cannot move the foundation. This spot was dedicated by the Nephites, they could not built [*sic*] it (the temple), but we can and will build it for them."[97] Although Cannon recorded this reminiscence in 1942, the story had appeared earlier. In 1881, one Mormon referred to "Moroni dedicating the Temple site of what we now call St. George, Nauvoo, Jackson Co., Kirtland and others we know not of as yet."[98] Two hand-drawn maps of Moroni's travels captured this tradition. The maps oddly do not include Manti or St. George, but chart Moroni's trek from the land Bountiful, a major Book of Mormon city, which the map located in Central America, to the "[s]and hills in [the] southern part of Arizona," Salt Lake City, Adam-Ondi-Ahman, Missouri, Nauvoo, Kirtland, and finally Cumorah (i.e., Palmyra, New York).[99] Although the mapmaker is unknown, an inscription reveals that the details of Moroni's trek had been "got from Bro. Robert Dickson. He got it from Patriarch Wm. McBride at Richfield on the Seveir and also from Andrew M. Hamilton of same place. And they got it from Joseph Smith, the Prophet."[100]

No firsthand evidence exists that Young originated regional traditions of Moroni. Young never cited any historic Nephite dedications in any contemporary record.[101] These traditions emerged and circulated among lay Mormons. In each case, they appeared first as local stories that were recorded and then embraced by larger Mormon audiences. In the case of the Manti Temple, the story would eventually become a prominent theme in an annual local pageant and even the placement of a Moroni monument in 1983.

These legends and the ones that follow provided the Saints with a framing by which they could understand a novel and potentially fearsome landscape. This sacralizing lens transformed unfamiliar mountain ranges to the familiar or at least set apart locals of scripture. On one hand, these Book of Mormon or biblical inspired narratives were at the heart of creating a Mormon homeland. Significantly, the message of this new setting was that they had not failed in being driven far away from Jackson/Zion, but rather, their migration brought them closer to the actual point of Christ's return by depositing them where the necessary events would occur.

Although locating a legend's origin proves difficult, in some instances we can track its transmission through influential voices. In most cases within Mormonism, localized legends emerge from the master narrative. For example, the Book of Mormon portrayed Moroni as the last survivor of the Nephite civilization. Believing themselves in the lands of the Book of Mormon, Mormons associated Moroni's journeys with the region's past. These stories originated from the laity and were then popularized in regional cultures. In other cases, church leaders initiated Mormon legends that functioned as a lens on the West. For example, Young introduced Gadianton Robber narratives along the trek west. Lay Mormon settlers then localized this expectation of evil Native American spirits to their experience in settlements throughout the Great Basin. Stories of the Three Nephites on western soil also began with the church's hierarchy.

The Three Nephites share similarities with other religious Saint figures whose presence in a narrative signals divine intervention. They became immortal disciples of Jesus Christ, who, according to the Book of Mormon, "shall never taste of death; but [who] shall live to behold all the doings of the Father unto the children of men, even until . . . I [Christ] shall come in my glory with the powers of heaven."[102] They possessed power to continue their ministries and to appear to the faithful when they desired.

Mormons circulated Three Nephite stories before the Saints arrived in the Great Basin, but the wealth of such tales only appeared after a highly influential sermon delivered by Orson Pratt on April 7, 1855.[103] Pratt explained that the Three Nephites were aware of the Saints' presence in the region, but they would not "lift up their voices in the midst of our congregations," until the Saints proved worthy. Pratt emphasized the necessity of reformation among the Latter-day Saints for them to prove worthy of visits from such figures. "The very reason they do not come amongst us is, because we have work to do preparatory to their coming; and just as soon as that is accomplished they are on hand."[104]

Encounter narratives soon followed Pratt's sermon. In many cases, these stories described a visit from one or more of the Three Nephites to prominent

Mormons of the past or present. They also became explicitly connected to Mormon relations with Native peoples. In February 1855, Arapeen, the brother of Ute Chief Wakara, had a revelatory experience he relayed to Brigham Young by letter that included the appearance of "three personages and there Garments where white as Snow and as Briliant as the Sun and bye and bye all good People would Apear as they did."[105] This was the earliest Native report that Mormons likely saw through the lens of the Three Nephite visitations. In other cases, missionaries in the Great Basin believed their converts had already encountered the Three Nephites before they had made the acquaintance of Mormons. George Washington Hill attributed his success among the Shoshone to Chief Ech-up-wy's visit from "three strange men" who had an "Indian complexion." According to Hill's account of Ech-up-wy's experience, they told him that "the Mormons' God was the true God, and that He and the Indian's Father were one; that he must go to the 'Mormons,' and they would tell him what to do, and that he must do it; that he must be baptized, with all his Indians; that the time was at hand for the Indians to gather, and stop their Indian life, and learn to cultivate the earth and build houses, and live in them." After which, the three told the chief to "look," and when he did, he saw a vision of the future marked by cooperation between Utes and Mormons.[106]

When Mormons connected Three Nephite stories to Native conversions, apocalyptic dimensions became evident. Although the Saints often felt disappointed with the fruits of their missionary efforts among the Indians, they also expected the Natives to fulfill their destiny as it was laid out in the Book of Mormon. At times church leaders articulated this destiny as militaristic; even when devoid of any militaristic context, this destiny was always framed as messianic. In 1855, Brigham Young reminded his flock that the Lamanites would eventually "be the Lord's battle ax in good earnest," utilizing a figure that evoked the final apocalyptic battle to come.[107] The same year, Orson Pratt stated that the "Lamanites are to be the principal operators" in the building of the New Jerusalem. Twenty years later, Pratt explicitly tied the appearances of the Three Nephites with the redemption of Zion. After reviewing stories of the Three Nephites preparing Natives for encounters with Mormon missionaries, he warned that "the Latter-day Saints in these mountains never can have the privilege of going back to Jackson County and building that city which is to be called the New Jerusalem, upon the spot that was appointed by revelation through the Prophet Joseph, until quite a large portion of the remnants of Joseph go back with us." He reminded the

Saints that the Book of Mormon stated that they would assist the Lamanites in building Jackson County and not the other way around.[108]

Narratives about Gadianton Robbers, Reformed Egyptian, Moroni, and the Three Nephites inscribed the narrative of the Book of Mormon onto the mountain and desert landscape of Deseret. In so doing, the Saints sacralized their new setting just as they had sacralized the Midwest and East Coast by the identification of Adam-Ondi-Ahman, Missouri, or Palmyra, New York, as historically spiritual sites. Mormons came to believe that the Promised Land extended beyond the borders of the United States as the nation's boundaries stood at the time of the exodus. They had not left sacred space by fleeing into the mountains, but rather had discovered a new and crucial landscape for God's plans both past and future.

The Mountains and Defense

Even before Mormons integrated the Rocky Mountains into their sacred story by associating them with biblical and Book of Mormon prophecy, the mountains promised safety from their persecutors. A principal factor for relocating to such a remote setting was distance from the Gentiles as well as protection from the destructions awaiting the United States. As the 1850s progressed and federal troops arrived in Mormon settlements, Mormons came to believe God had chosen the peaks and valleys of the West to provide them with a defensive advantage against Gentile invaders.

The mountains were mysterious. On May 10, 1857, Heber C. Kimball told the Saints, "Holy men have been in these mountains before we came here. There are strong holds that you know nothing of at the present time."[109] On July 24, 1857, at a celebration of the Saints' ten-year anniversary in the valley held in Big Cottonwood Canyon, Young preached on how certain locations in the mountains would provide protection (see Figure 3.3). "He said, 'He had things on his mind to tell that he had never told to any people before. The time had now come he could have the privilege of revealing them. These are the secret chambers of the mountains." Young told the gathering that he had sent men through the canyon to "find any marks or signs or traces of Indians in this kanyon [*sic*], but have not been able to find any," but they had located "secret retreats, and mountain passes. The formation of the mountains around this place are such that they are calculated to ward off the traveler on the outside from coming down in here"[110] (see Figure 3.4). For Ira

Figure 3.3 "Brigham's Declaration of Independence," an illustration of the July 24, 1857, gathering.

Figure 3.4 Photo of Big Cottonwood Canyon. In 1857, Brigham Young pointed to Big Cottonwood Canyon as the "secret chambers of the mountains." Used by permission, Utah State Historical Society.

Ames, who recorded Young's remarks in his journal, the significance of this revelation became clear the following day when Young received and relayed news that Johnston's Army had begun its march to the valley. Their hopes in the region's geography would now be tested.

In October 1857, one of the militia stationed in Echo Canyon to impede Johnston's Army dreamed about a destination akin to Young's "secret chambers of the mountains." Nathaniel V. Jones (see Figure 3.5) dreamed that he was in Salt Lake City when U.S. troops invaded. Brigham Young directed the frightened masses to follow him to a retreat in the mountains. Jones noted that he was unfamiliar with the route, but they eventually "arrived at the place where we were to conceal ourselves from our enemies . . . at the junction of two small canyons." A hidden cave that "ran deep into the mountain" added to the site's mystique. Jones's dream ended with the Saints' "emerg[ing] from their hiding place" apparently after a significant time lapsed, since "their number had increased many times more than they were when they went in."[111]

The mountains, the weather, and the Saints' harassment of the troops delayed their entry into the valley through the fall and winter of 1857 and 1858. On January 3, 1858, Young's brother, John Young, expressed his gratitude "that we were surrounded by such a mountain of Rocks as we are here, for they were the means of preventing our enemies from coming into the Valley last fall."[112] As spring arrived and Johnston's Army neared, Young ordered the evacuation of the Salt Lake Valley and the northern settlements in what Mormons have

Figure 3.5 Portrait of Nathaniel V. Jones (1822–1863), ca. 1850s. Jones was a soldier stationed in Echo Canyon during the Utah War. He dreamed of a future invasion when the Saints would be protected in a secret cave. Courtesy of the Church History Library.

traditionally referred to as the "move south."[113] While Young initially considered a defensive war, he settled on a burnt-earth strategy, trusting that if the Saints could remove all crops and raze the existing structures, they could force the troops to retreat. Although the move south would be temporary, Young had considered seeking permanent settlements that the majority of the Saints from the densely populated northern settlements could inhabit. He sent an expedition to scout locations in the southern deserts in the region of the White Mountains on the border of Utah and Nevada. James Martineau, a member of the expedition, wrote that Young commissioned the scouts to locate "a place of refuge; some valley which should be surrounded by a desert requiring a five-day's [*sic*] march to cross."[114]

The expedition turned to the possibility of another mountain range for the Saints' refuge. Sufficiently removed from Euro-American civilization, the company selected a high mountain peak, later named Altar Peak, and ceremonially dedicated the surrounding land. Martineau described a sense of "liberty" on the peak. "We seemed lifted above the sinful world and to be nearer to heaven."[115] They constructed a makeshift altar from stones and prayed to "be led to the place appointed by his Holy Spirit that we might know the place when we see it."[116] On Altar Peak, they first saw the White Mountains in the distance, where they became convinced God directed them.

An exodus to the White Mountains never came to fruition; however, the belief that mountains would protect the Saints from a last days invasion continued long after the Utah War. Whether it was distance that would impede approaching armies, the difficult terrain, or secret retreats, God had directed the Saints to take their refuge in the mountains. There, they could safely await his next command. By viewing the mountains of the West as a divinely provided refuge, the Saints sacralized the landscape in a way that brought out the underlying apocalyptic dimension of the surrounding geography: Not only did the Saints find themselves in a sacred, protected land, but their preservation in that land served as a sign that they were, in fact, being kept so that they could at some future apocalyptic point in time retrace their steps and return to Jackson County.

To Mexico and Canada

After Mormons made plans to colonize settlements in northern Mexico in the 1880s, they expanded the "Rocky Mountain Prophecy" to include a foreseen second relocation south of the border. Mosiah Hancock recalled that Smith had visited his family's carpentry shop and requested that they bring him a map:

> I went and got my map for him. "Now," he said, "I will show you the travels of this people." He then showed our travels through Iowa, and said, "Here you will make a place for the winter; and here you will travel west until you come to the valley of the Great Salt Lake! You will build cities to the North and to the South, and to the East and to the West; and you will become a great and wealthy people in that land. But, the United States will not receive you with the laws which God desires you to live, and you will have to go to where the Nephites lost their power. They worked in the United Order for 166 years, and the Saints have got to become proficient in the laws of God before they can meet the Lord Jesus Christ, or even the city of Enoch." He said we will not travel the shape of the horse shoe for there we will await the action of the government. Placing his finger on the map, I should think about where Snowflake, Arizona is situated, or it could have been Mexico, he said, "The government will not receive you with the laws that God designed you to live, and those who are desirous to live the laws of God will have to go South."[117]

Reuben McBride also recalled hearing Smith point to a second exodus to Mexico. According to an account of McBride's recitation recorded in the journal of Charles L. Walker, after Smith "marked with his cane in the sand the track the saints would take to the Rocky Mountains," he described how the Saints would colonize parts of Mexico: "[W]e should make stations and build up settlements all the way to new, and old Mexico Until we crossed the Isthmus and get back to the place where the Covenant was broke by the old Nephites." McBride seemingly referenced the same place as Hancock, "where the Nephites lost their power." The prophecy referenced a Book of Mormon passage set in 200 CE, in which a 166-year utopian period ended and the Nephites no longer lived with "all things common among them," or they no longer "worked in the United Order" according to later Mormon speech.[118] McBride recalled that the Saints would go much farther south than Hancock—to a "Great Temple in Central America . . . situated by the River Copan anciently called the River of Nephi."[119]

In the twentieth century, prophecies of a mass southern exodus reappeared in a popular document referred to as the "Horseshoe Prophecy" recorded in 1951. In this signed statement, Edward Lunt recalled his mother's stories about a visit from John Taylor to their home in the 1880s. Taylor reportedly prophesied of a period of wickedness in Salt Lake City's future:

> He said that faithful Latter-day Saints would go to the south and would form a circle something like a horseshoe, before they return to Jackson County, Missouri. Said he, "Those only will be privileged to help build Jackson County who will be found willing and glad to obey the counsel and advice of the authorities who will be placed over them, and who will seek counsel that they may be guided and protected from dire want and distress. President Taylor also said that we will assist the Lamanites in building the New Jerusalem in Jackson county [*sic*]."[120]

A different set of prophecies integrated the Saints' Canadian settlements into Mormon apocalypticism. While contemplating the idea of colonizing the first Mormon settlement in Canada, Charles Card, a local church leader in Cache Valley, heard a prophecy that would shape how the next generation would understand the northern colonies:[121]

> Bro. Samuel Smith of Brigham City told me he was present in a priesthood meeting in the basement of the Temple in Nauvoo in the year 1843 and heard the Prophet Joseph Smith state that England or the nation of Great Britain would be the last nation to go to peaces. [*sic*] She would be ~~an~~ instrumental in aiding to crush other nations even this nation of the United States & she would only be over thrown by the 10 tribes from the North. She would never persecute the saints as a nation. She would gather togather [*sic*] great treasures of Gold & yet we should seek refuge in her dominion.[122]

This prophecy painted a radically different portrait of England than had previously typified Mormon prophecy. Smith had recognized Great Britain as a land once visited by prophets and that included the descendants of ancient Israel among its populace. Missionaries had often emphasized, however, that when God established his kingdom at the Second Coming, all national governments would be destroyed. In 1841, Parley P. Pratt wrote an open letter to Queen Victoria, warning her that God would make no exception for England.[123] However, Card and the new Mormon immigrants at the settlement in Cardston (established 1887) came to embrace Samuel Smith's memoir. Thus, Canada joined the series of gathering places foreseen by Joseph Smith.

On July 4, 1889, a particularly charismatic apostle, John W. Taylor, then residing in Cardston, predicted that the new colony "would become a fruitful land & yet in time of near it would be a haven of rest for those of our people who desired to serve the Lord. Those who were seeking fame of our people who flaunt so much about liberty in Utah would be put to the front of the battle when the Negroes rise up against their masters which soon would be the case. The red man would stalk through the land as the battle axe of the Lord and after they had done this work they would be changed to a skin of whiteness in a day."[124] Taylor insisted Canada would be vital for the apocalypse, whereas traitors and persecutors in Utah would face destructive violence wrought by Natives and African Americans.

Canada's inclusion in prophecy continued into the twentieth century. A Quaker woman named Sols Guardisto allegedly originated a prophecy of a Canadian gathering. She had visited the Cardston Temple before its dedication in 1921, during a period when non-Mormons could tour the building. Edward J. Wood, who served as the Alberta Stake President, subsequently popularized the prophecy. The vision began with an apocalyptic scene in which Guardisto witnessed an "international world war," as well as a "national revolution occur[ing] in every country." She described natural disasters and economic and political collapse. Her vision then shifted to a second scene in which she saw how Mormons would survive these devastations: "I saw further on, instructions given whereby places of refuge were prepared quietly but efficiently by inspired elders. I saw Cardston and the surrounding foothills, especially north and west, for miles, being prepared as a refuge for your people quietly but quickly." Mormon leaders prepared by gathering food, fuel, and other necessities in the period immediately preceding these cataclysmic events. She continued:

> I saw the inspired call sent forth to all the church, to gather to the refuges of Zion. I saw the stream of your people quietly moving in the direction of their refuge. I saw your people moving more quickly and in larger numbers until all the stragglers were housed. I saw the wireless message flashed from Zion's refuge to Zion's refuge in their several places that all was well with them, and then the darkness of chaos closed around the boundaries of your people, and the last days of tribulation had begun.[125]

Each of these stories had a known ending, whether a specific prophecy highlighted settlements in Utah, Nevada, Canada, or Mexico. These were only temporary destinations. The Saints understood that the climax of these apocalyptic narratives would end with mass movements of Saints to Jackson County, which retained its place as the center of Mormon apocalyptic geography. By emphasizing the return to Jackson County, the prophecies allowed the development of new geographies to maintain a cohesion with past expectations.

Conclusion

Mormon prophecy endowed lands with sanctity—a sense that God ordained even undesirable locations far from Euro-American civilization for the Saints' use. The Rocky Mountains became the ideal location to fulfill prophecy. There, the Saints would find refuge among the peaks and valleys, protected as much from Gentile aggressors as they were from God's wrath poured out on distant lands. With God's help, the Saints would prosper in the deserts, and Mormons could begin the Kingdom they earlier envisioned in meetings of the Council of Fifty. After the destructions and collapse of the other governments, the Kingdom would spread from the Great Basin to encompass the world.

A wide array of actors influenced the Mormon sacralization of the West. By criticizing the trek west, dissenting Mormon movements helped compel the Brighamites to articulate the prophetic landscape of the West. They came to emphasize how settlement in their new homeland comprised a necessary part of the last days. Mormons of all ranks participated in making their mountain refuge sacred through sharing stories of the Saints' foreknowledge of the West, interpreting Zionic scripture with their new setting in mind, and narrating their personal revelations.

4

The Judgments Begin

Apocalypticism in the Utah Territory

> The cardinal starting-point of Mormonism is, that the *last days* are at hand, and that the Mormons are *Latter-day* Saints. The controlling idea is, that the general judgment is to come *soon*; by which is not meant an indefinite series of ages, but within the lifetime of the present generation. . . . The *gathering* of the Saints is that they may witness the imposing exhibition of the consummation of all things, which, in fact, is to be got up for their exclusive benefit. Under this leading idea, the true believer leaves a comfortable home in the States, endures privations and encounters danger in the long and weary travel to Utah, shelters himself in a wretched mud hovel in the Valley of Salt, and patiently waits for the sound of the last trump.
>
> —Benjamin G. Ferris, secretary, Utah Territory, 1852[1]

As the nineteenth century progressed, Mormons continued to chart America's decline from their refuge in the West. They tracked the signs of the times they found in eastern papers and the stories of recent immigrants, occasionally plotting how the current moment would lead to Zion's redemption. As expected, America had become increasingly afflicted with war, disease, drought, famine, fires, and natural disasters. The religious and political divisions Mormons once witnessed firsthand had fomented in their absence. The citizens of the United States had, so the Mormons believed, become increasingly godless—stricken with an insatiable appetite for violence and self-destruction.

These sentiments toward the United States continued to fester, in part due to the presence of federal troops in Utah Territory in the 1850s, the Civil War, and anti-polygamy legislation. A new rise in apocalyptic thought in the latter half of the nineteenth century gave form to Joseph Smith's prophecies. While

Terrible Revolution. Christopher James Blythe, Oxford University Press (2020). © Oxford University Press.
DOI: 10.1093/oso/9780190080280.001.0001

these apocalyptic ideas and literature were not uniform, they illustrated a coherent religious imaginary. This chapter examines how this imaginary evolved in reference to the Mormon people's relationship with American culture, as punctuated by their tumultuous exchanges with the federal government.

The War Prophecy and the Gathering to Utah Territory

The Salt Lake Valley was not as isolated as the early Saints had believed. While there may have been portions of the region, as Heber C. Kimball stated, "where a white man's foot never trod," the Mormons soon realized that they could not escape a continued relationship with the United States.[2] On February 2, 1848, the signing of the Treaty of Guadalupe Hidalgo—which officially ended the Mexican-American War—transferred their new mountain home to the jurisdiction of the United States. By the end of the year, the Saints officially petitioned Congress for the recognition of the Territory of Deseret, but ultimately decided that territorial status would not be to their advantage. As a result, in 1849, they proposed the State of Deseret and formed a provisional state government. According to historian Brent M. Rogers, statehood would allow the Saints to "be free to elect their own officers, to be ruled by those of their own choosing, and to regulate their own marital practices, which were subject to state law under the system of divided sovereignty."[3] Mormons had originally envisioned their own independent government in the West; now that their new home had become a part of the nation they recently fled, they realized statehood was necessary if the Saints were to possess any level of political sovereignty. Unfortunately for them, in 1850, Congress rejected the proposal for the State of Deseret and instead formed the Utah Territory.[4]

Territorial status formalized a hostile relationship between the federal government and Mormonism. Even though many federal posts, including that of Brigham Young as the first territorial governor, were held by Mormons, the Saints believed that as a territory they were not simply subject to the federal government but were, in fact, dominated by a colonial power. During the next forty-six years, until Utah obtained statehood, the tensions rooted in the Mormons' desire for independence and the exertion of U.S. control ebbed and flowed.

In 1852, after several years' hiatus, Latter-day Saints again sent missionaries to the United States. Apostle Orson Pratt led this endeavour while stationed in Washington, D.C., where he published a newspaper named *The Seer*. Pratt's writings in *The Seer* focused on distinctive Mormon practices and doctrines such as plural marriage, the premortal existence of human spirits, and especially, the imminent American apocalypse. Pratt emphasized prophecy to promote Mormon emigration to Utah. In an editorial entitled "The First Epistle of Orson Pratt," he addressed those Saints who had yet to gather in the Rocky Mountains, and who, as a result, he suspected were in an "unpleasant and unhappy state of mind." He urged them to repent and make the trek:

> Awake then, O awake! flee to the mountains for refuge! For a day of trouble is at hand—a day of fierce battle and war—a day of mourning and lamentation for widows and orphans whose husbands and fathers shall fall in battle: it shall be the day of the Lord's controversy for His people—a day of recompense for the innocent blood of prophets and saints which has been shed among this nation.[5]

In April 1854, *The Seer* included what was likely the earliest published commentary on Joseph Smith's war prophecy. The revelation had only been published for the first time in 1851, when it was included in an extra-canonical collection of Smith's revelations, *The Pearl of Great Price*.[6] Pratt and other church leaders had known of the prophecy since its reception in 1832, but as Brigham Young recalled, "It was not wisdom to publish it to the world" previously.[7] In *The Seer*, Pratt reprinted the prophecy in its entirety. The revelation began:

> Verily thus saith the Lord, concerning the wars that will shortly come to pass, beginning at the rebellion of South Carolina, which will eventually terminate in the death and misery of many souls. The days will come that war will be poured out upon all nations, beginning at that place; for behold, the Southern States shall be divided against the Northern States; and the Southern States will call on other nations, even the nation of Great Britain, as it is called, and they shall also call upon other nations in order to defend themselves against other nations; and thus, war shall be poured out upon all nations.[8]

Pratt commented extensively on the revelation, interpreting the prophecy to refer to one ever-expanding war, beginning with the Southern rebellion.

The South would call on Great Britain, which would already be engaged in a war of its own. While Pratt noted that the revelation did not specify whether Great Britain would respond positively to the South's request, he believed they might "in order to secure commercial advantages" of an alliance.[9] Great Britain would then turn to other nations as the conflict expanded.

African American slaves and Native Americans would also be drawn into the violence. According to the revelation, "After many days, slaves shall rise up against their masters, who shall be marshalled and disciplined for war. And it shall come to pass also that the remnants who are left of the land will marshal themselves, and shall become exceeding angry, and shall vex the Gentiles with a sore vexation." Because the slaves were already "marshalled and disciplined for war," Pratt believed the passage suggested that slaves would be part of the Southern army and "that the calamity, arising from the rebellion of the Slaves, will not take place, until the nation has, by its previous struggles been reduced to great weakness." He also believed that the Native American invasion would not "take place until millions of the nation have already perished in their own revolutionary battles." Drawing on Book of Mormon prophecy, Pratt asserted that the Indians "will have power in a great measure over the whole nation."[10]

The apostle criticized the nation's sense of invulnerability and military might:

> Say not in your hearts that you are strong, and that these calamities will not come upon you; for though you increase your strength an hundred fold, and fortify yourselves with walls and gigantic towers; and by your wisdom invent engines of destruction that will cause the nations to tremble, yet you shall be as naught before the power of the Almighty, and your strong-holds shall be thrown down, as were the walls of Jericho, and you shall fall a prey to the devouring sword, and your carcases shall moulder away upon the face of the land, and your flesh shall become meat for the dogs and for the ravenous birds of the air ; and there shall be none left to blaspheme against the Holy One of Israel, or to fight against His holy word, upon all the face of this land.[11]

Pratt linked the prophesied Native American massacres with the "supper of the Great God," a biblical event in which devouring animals would cleanse the land of Armageddon's casualties.

Pratt made few comments on the final portion of Smith's prophecy, which ended with a more general apocalyptic conclusion. "And thus, with the sword, and by bloodshed, the inhabitants of the earth shall mourn; and with famine, and plague, and earthquakes, and the thunder of heaven, and the fierce and vivid lightning also, shall the inhabitants of the earth be made to feel the wrath, and indignation, and chastening hand of an Almighty God, until the consumption, decreed, hath made a full end of all nations." It was only then "that the cry of the Saints, and of the blood of the Saints," depicted under the heavenly altar in the book of Revelation, "shall cease to come up into the ears of the Lord of Sabaoth, from the earth, to be avenged of their enemies." To the Saints, the revelation charged: "Wherefore, stand ye in holy places, and be not moved, until the day of the Lord come; for behold, it cometh quickly, saith the Lord. Amen."[12]

These holy places were understood by Pratt to be located with the Saints in the Rocky Mountains. Within this geographic context, it was thus clear that the war prophecy was primarily intended to provoke the Saints to move West and no longer delay their flight from Babylon. Pratt explained, "In order that God may punish these nations and utterly overthrow them, he is calling upon his people to come out from them and flee far away and hide themselves in the chambers of the mountains, and purify themselves before the Lord, lest they also perish in Babylon."[13] The prophecy had not warned the Saints that they would face their own war in the mountains before conflict was unleashed on the United States.

Holy War in Utah Territory

Prior to the 1857–1858 military siege on Utah Territory (referred to as the Utah War), a history of tension between the Mormons and the U.S. military already existed. In August 1854, 325 men arrived in Salt Lake City under the command of Lieutenant Colonel Edward Steptoe. This was not the Mormons' first encounter with federal troops, but it was the encounter that most devastated relations between the Saints and the military. Mormons were outraged by the soldiers' drunkenness, brawls, and dalliances with Mormon women. On December 25, 1854, after Mormons and soldiers clashed at a Christmas dance, a riot broke out on the streets of Salt Lake City. The troops eventually left the city for California in April and May 1855. When they did so, it was rumored that they escorted as many as one hundred women to California.[14] Although the actual numbers were more modest, as Laurel Ulrich Thatcher has noted, "enough women left to reinforce prejudices and fears on all sides."[15] Young fumed over the men's conduct in the aftermath of the Steptoe affair. He expressed regret they had not "hung up their bodies as a public example and as a warning to others, or to have cast them over the city walls to the wolves, as I have felt sorry every [*sic*] since they went away that this was not done."[16] He promised the Saints would fight if they were again harassed by federal troops.[17]

In January 1857, the Utah Territorial Legislature issued a memorial announcing that they would not tolerate the federal government's improper interference with territorial affairs. While they professed their loyalty to the nation, they also declared the community would "not tamely submit to being abused by Government Officials, here in this territory; they shall not come here to corrupt our community, set at defiance our laws, [or] trample upon the rights of the people."[18] This defiant memorial, along with a sensational report from W. W. Drummond, a federal justice who alleged Young asserted control over the territory by the threat of violence, pushed newly inaugurated President James Buchanan to respond. In turn, Buchanan ordered General Albert S. Johnston, at the command of 2,500 troops, to travel to Utah Territory, where they would install non-Mormon Alfred Cumming in Young's place.[19]

As promised, the Mormons treated the expedition as a serious threat, a return of past violence. Young reinstituted the Nauvoo Legion, declared martial law, and forbid the entrance of federal troops into the territory. The Nauvoo Legion's strategy was to make the soldiers' journey as difficult as possible. They burned grazing land, stole cattle, and destroyed supply wagons with the idea that the soldiers would have to go elsewhere if they intended to survive the winter.[20] While the Saints were ordered not to return fire even if the soldiers shot in their direction, Mormons were serious about preventing the army from entering the valley, even if it meant all-out war. One legion general, George Q. Cannon, described the "formidable preparations" made in Echo Canyon, where a thousand Mormon men were stationed to face the expedition:

> Ston[e] Forts were built on the heights commanding the Kanyon, from which bullets and all kind of missiles could be showered without the least danger of their being stormed. Huge Rocks were piled up that with the slightest pry of a handspike could be precipitated into the Valley below. In the Kanyon or Valley trenches were dug clear across from one side to the other which could easily be filled with water, making the road

> impassable to the enemy and while they would be bridging them or getting across they would be fired upon from the heights above and from covered entrenchments in the Kanyon. A little below these trenches a large dam had been thrown across the Kanyon which was intended to flood the entire Kanyon for some distance up, and, our men had ditches and places of shelter constructed from which they could pour a deadly fire upon the enemy as they advanced.[21]

War never materialized. A friend of the Mormons, Thomas Kane, brokered a peace agreement and the standoff came to an end in April 1858, when Buchanan offered pardons "to all who will submit themselves to the authority of the federal government."[22] The Saints accepted the pardon, recognized Cumming as territorial governor, and agreed for Johnston's army to enter the valley. Neither side was entirely pleased with the agreement. Word that additional reinforcements would be joining Johnston's army likely played a role in Young begrudgingly agreeing to the pardon. John D. Lee recorded a secondhand account of Young's negotiations with Cumming in which the prophet told the governor "that with 50 men he could have cut of[f] Johns[t]on's whole army, by the help of the Lord; but that he did not want to Shed their blood."[23] While such a response fits well with Young's defiant personality, it might also reflect the Saints' own disappointment at the anti-climactic conclusion of the war.

Some of the federal troops were also frustrated that they would not have revenge for the Nauvoo Legion's winter raids. One soldier lamented that the Mormons were allowed a pardon when "they are as impudent and villainous as ever." He believed they should instead "hang about 100 of them, and then the rest will submit."[24] This sentiment was by no means unique.

The presence of the military in Utah was frightening. The vast majority of Salt Lake City had been vacated as part of the "move South" prior to the troops' march through its streets on June 27, 1858. One of the few Mormons who remained described it as a "death-like silence march through the deserted streets of the dead city, a few of the officers with uncovered heads, as if attending a funeral." He found "the solemnity of the march was oppressive; and glad relief came to our strained feelings, when we saw the soldiers' camp fires kindled on the 'other side of the Jordan.' "[25] The army established Camp Floyd about forty miles from Salt Lake City.

Although the camp was removed from large settlements of Saints, the Saints understood they were now living in an occupied territory. On

February 23, 1859, Heber C. Kimball recorded an optimistic personal revelation that read: "The word of the Lord to me that the Army will leave this year or most of them."[26] His calculation was a little off. The soldiers' departure would wait until the spring of 1860, when the number of troops was reduced from 2,000 to less than 300. The Civil War would eventually result in the total abandonment of the camp on July 27, 1861.[27] After their departure, Mormon Charles L. Walker expressed a sense of victory in his journal:

> To day I had the P[l]easure seeing some cannon and canister shot that was brought here to bring the Mormons into subjection by the U.S. troops, but thanks be to God tho thousands were brot [*sic*] here not one [h]as been fired and not a saint killed. For the Lord our God has held them . . . and they have not had power to hurt or harm the least one of us. And now they are going back, after being here since the Year 1858 and have not accomplished the thing they came for, besides spending some Millions of dollars.[28]

Both sides in this conflict subscribed to notions of holy war. Federal troops saw themselves on a crusade against non-Christian fanatics in rebellion against the nation. Mormons, on the other hand, understood the army's march and occupation in terms of a foretold invasion of latter-day Israel. The striking descriptions of such an invasion were found in Jewish and Christian apocalyptic literature. Ezekiel prophesied of a war in which enemy nations, including the mysterious Gog, would align against Israel. With His people under siege, God would destroy the armies through "pestilence and with blood . . . an overflowing rain, and great hailstones, fire, and brimstone."[29] John the Revelator similarly depicted the Battle of Armageddon in which armies including "the kings of the earth and of the whole world" would invade the Promised Land at Armageddon. It was Christ who would defend his people, entering the scene on a white horse, and "clothed with a vesture dipped in blood." He would slay the followers of the Beast, an anti-Christian tyrant, with a "sword [that] proceeded out of his mouth," leaving "the flesh of kings, and the flesh of captains, and the flesh of mighty men, and the flesh of horses, and of them that sit on them, and the flesh of all men, both free and bond, both small and great" to be eaten by "all the fowls that fly in the midst of heaven."[30] The conclusion of both Ezekiel and Revelation's wars ended with an invitation to these scavenging creatures to eat the dead in the aforementioned "supper of the great God."[31]

Mormon commentators also invoked Revelation's image of the woman fleeing into the wilderness in order to inscribe Johnston's army within the final scenes of divine history. Orson Hyde explained:

> The woman spoken of by John the Revelator as being driven or fleeing into the wilderness, after having brought forth the man-child, is said to be the Church by our wise orthodox commentators upon holy writ. Be it so. The Latter-Day Saints fled from the face of the serpent monster into this vast wilderness and desert, and it appears the serpent cast out a flood of water from his mouth to destroy the woman. This is highly figurative language; yet is there anyone present who can favor us with a better solution of the matter than the waters or troops which the United States are now sending here to destroy us? God grant that the earth and the heavens also may help the woman![32]

Hyde's plea to the earth alluded to the conclusion of this scenario when, according to Revelation, "the earth opened her mouth, and swallowed up the flood which the dragon cast out of his mouth."[33] He later speculated the conflict in Utah Territory might end when "the earth may kindly open her mouth in the form of an earthquake, and drink up the flood or army."[34]

Mormons also drew on apocalyptic themes of supernatural warfare in order to understand their experiences with the U.S. military. Like Daniel and John the Revelator, who witnessed angels engaged militarily against Israel's earthly enemies or demonic forces, they emphasized the support of angelic hosts in their own latter-day conflicts. In the wake of the Steptoe affair, Young had encouraged the Saints to find courage in scenes from 2 Kings where a single angel slaughtered 185,000 sleeping Assyrians and where Elisha's servant's vision of fiery chariots caused him to announce that "they that be with us are more than they that be with them." God could also defend the Saints by "invisible beings . . . millions and millions more than the inhabitants of this earth."[35]

These supernatural themes, including visions of angelic hosts, became widespread as reports of the approaching federal troops circulated throughout Utah. One Mormon widow reported seeing her husband's apparition "dressed in the most splendid military ar[r]ay." When she asked him if he was "going to fight the soldiers," he responded, "I am going into the mountains to help defend the Kingdom of God."[36] The Saints would be assisted by angels—the righteous dead—but they, too, would fight. Shortly after the war, one of the Nauvoo Legion generals, George Q. Cannon, dreamed that he saw a massive heavenly army that "descended to the earth in double file to where we were Standing, and mingled among us. Their countenance were bright and effulgent as the sun; and terrible to look upon." While still dreaming, he asked his uncle, the apostle John Taylor, to interpret the vision. Taylor "said that now the power would be with us: the hosts of heaven would be with us, and the nation who were opposing us would speedily go down."[37]

Some statements even suggested that Satan empowered the invading American troops. Wilford Woodruff described the standoff as a war "between God and the Devil."[38] Charles W. Penrose's hymn "Up Awake, Ye Defenders of Zion" was more specific:

> Up, awake, ye defenders of Zion!
> The foe's at the door of your homes . . .
> Though assisted by legions infernal,
> The plundering wretches advance,
> With a host from the regions eternal,
> We'll scatter their troops at a glance.[39]

An editorial in the *Millennial Star* referred to Buchanan as the devil's "mighty chieftain—the hero of his hosts."[40] This rhetoric characterized the U.S. troops as an evil military body led by a malevolent dictatorship that, in Heber C. Kimball's words, "designed to wipe us out of existence."[41]

The apocalyptic lens by which the Saints understood the Utah War highlighted tensions at the heart of their understanding of national identity. During the conflict, church leaders made no secret of their desire for independence from the United States. They believed they had been tasked with building the Kingdom of God in the mountains and that their sovereignty was essential for this endeavour. At the same time, church leaders vehemently defended their loyalty to the Constitution, arguing that the United States had failed to live up to the founding ideals of the nation. In 1855, Young echoed Smith's 1840 Constitution prophecy, predicting a day when the Saints would prove their affection for the United States: "[A]s you will see if you only live long enough, for that we shall live to prove it is certain; and when the Constitution of the United States hangs, as it were, upon a single thread, they [the government] will have to call for the 'Mormon' Elders to save it from utter destruction; and they will step forth and do it."[42] The apocalypse that Mormons foresaw was one in which the national government collapsed in order to allow the Mormons to step forward and restore the dignity of the Constitution. This heroic framing had been a constant theme in Mormon apocalyptic since Nauvoo and would continue throughout the century. Each of these apocalyptic elements—the Mormons' self identification as the embattled latter-day Israel foretold in Jewish and Christian apocalyptic literature, their characterization of the war as extending into and involving supernatural beings, and their application of the apocalyptic framework that understood the U.S. government and army to receive Satanic support, sanction, and even power—provided the Mormons with an extended understanding of their actions and role within history. The apocalyptic elements utilized by the Mormons allowed them to see themselves as embedded within a long prophesied holy war, thus justifying their actions as they fought not against other men, but the very powers of the devil. The advantage to this framing was clear: In addition to the prophesied war, the apocalyptic texts contained information regarding the outcome of said war. By placing themselves within a narrative where God's victory was already promised, the Mormons strengthened their own belief in their ability to overcome the natural and political elements that threatened their independence and autonomous existence.

So far as the Mormon conception of the last days was concerned, the Utah War added another temporal point in the chronology toward the nation's collapse. John H. Beadle, a popular critic of Mormonism, recalled that during the Civil War some Mormons believed that "the late war never would have occurred . . . if Johnston's army had not been sent."[43] The trauma of living with the expectation of an imminent and merciless invasion would continue to influence Mormon sentiments toward the nation and a renewed assault became one possible future that Mormon apocalypses foretold.

Civil War as American Apocalypse

In 1861, the first year of the Civil War, Mormon leaders claimed a singular type of neutrality. Young publicly stated that he "earnestly prayed for the success of both North & South . . . [that] both parties might be used up."[44] On July 4, 1861, John Taylor explained the Saints' loyalties in a sermon:

> Shall we join the North to fight against the South? No! Shall we join the South against the North? As emphatically, No! Why? They have both, as

> before shown, brought it upon themselves, and we have had no hand in the matter. . . . We know no North, no South, no East, no West; we abide strictly and positively by the Constitution, and cannot, by the intrigues or sophisms of either party, be cajoled into any other attitude.[45]

Aware of allegations that neutrality was, in fact, disloyalty to the Union, Taylor reviewed the history of Mormonism's persecutions. "No parties in the United States have suffered more frequently and grievously than we have the violation of our national compact. We have frequently been mobbed, pillaged and plundered, without redress. We have been hunted as the deer on the mountains, our men have been whipped, banished, imprisoned, and put to death." Even after fleeing to "make a home in the desert wastes . . . those who should have been our fathers and protectors, have thirsted for our blood and made an unconstitutional use of the power vested in their hands to exterminate us from the earth." Yet, in spite of all this, Taylor assured his audience, "we are loyal, unwavering, unflinching in our integrity; we have not swerved nor faltered in the path of duty."[46] Taylor, like so many other Mormon commentators of the era, spoke of the Saints' "duty" to stand firm in their patriotic support of the Constitution, even as he spoke out against the nation's corruption. From the Mormons' perspective, it was through such corruption that Americans had sown their harvest of war.

The war prophecy effectively framed the Saints' understandings of the events of 1861–1865. As tensions between the North and South intensified, Mormons became increasingly vocal regarding their confidence in Smith's prophecy. A December 1860 letter from William H. Miles, then a missionary in New York City, to a recent convert in Salt Lake City captured how the prophecy informed the Saints' response to the initial news of division in the States. Miles relayed a sermon Orson Pratt had preached the night before on "Joseph's prophecy about the rebellion of South Carolina, and pointed out with clearness wherein was being and would be fulfilled even to the very letter." Pratt declared "that no person who observed the signs of the times, could fail to be convinced, of the truth of that revelation, and that we are now upon the very eve of the greatest events of this, or any other age." Miles then explained, "Bro. Gibson, it is now universally conceded by the press of this city, that we are to have *secession*, the state of South Carolina leading off. She had called a Convention on the 17th of the present month for the purpose of resolving on secession." Miles declared, "There is no longer any hope for our beloved Country. I feel to mourn on her account, but, I know well that the prophecies must be fulfilled." He still hoped there would be many that would learn their message "in this nation and be gathered out in the midst of troublous [*sic*] times."[47]

Mormons viewed the Civil War through the injustices of the past thirty-one years. Above all, the warfare and devastation spelled out God's anger for the murder of Joseph Smith. This seemed to be confirmed in the war prophecy's prediction that it would only be at the "full end of all nations" that "the cry of the Saints and the blood of the Saints [would] . . . be avenged of their enemies."[48] In February 1861, Brigham Young compared the future collapse of the republic to the destruction of Jerusalem in 70 CE. Americans would "have to pay for [killing Joseph Smith] as the Jews did in killing Jesus."[49] In June, a Latter-day Saint named Elijah Averett argued that "the now existing troubles" had been brought on the United States because they rejected Joseph Smith, who God had sent "to govern the world."[50] In March 1861, Orson Hyde articulated a similar line of thought while preaching in Mount Pleasant;

> Joseph Smith presented himself as a saviour to the nation but was refused, they killed him but the Lord has armed him so that he will be able to conquer the nation and he will rule with a rod of iron. Lincoln and Davis are instruments in Joseph's hands to fulfill the purpose of God. He made them to come together in a convention in Charleston, South Carolina and got them to divide, and now he rules with an iron rod and breaks the nation to pieces like a potters vessel.[51]

The image of Joseph Smith directing the final destructions had been conjured on numerous occasions since Phelps first introduced the motif in Smith's funeral sermon. Hyde's reference to Smith ruling by an "iron rod" was his own original contribution, based on the promise of Revelation 2:26–27: "And he that overcometh, and keepeth my works unto the end, to him will I give power over the nations. And he shall rule them with a rod of iron; as the vessels of a potter shall they be broken to shivers: even as I received of my Father." Likewise, Hyde identified Smith as the "man child," born from the woman in the wilderness, "who was to rule all nations with a rod of iron: and her child was caught up unto God, and to his throne."[52] Whether the Saints referred to the Revelation of St. John or Smith's war prophecy, the interpretive outcome was the same: a vision of an imminent apocalypse.

Significantly, Americans on both sides of the Mason–Dixon Line shared Mormonism's conviction that divine providence led these national events. Many described the war through biblical references to the apocalypse. Only two months into the conflict, former-slave-turned-preacher Frederick Douglass related the American conflict to the Book of Revelation's depiction of a "war in heaven." He told his audience that men could take their positions as "angels" or "demons" in the "eternal conflict between right and wrong, good and evil, liberty and slavery, truth and falsehood, the glorious light of love, and the appalling darkness of human selfishness and sin."[53] In 1863, an editorial printed in the *Prophetic Times* stated that while last days believers "have been long expecting and predicting that the rotten and tottering dynasties of the Old World would fall," it had taken the events of the Civil War to reconcile them to the belief that "our government, so free, so just, so liberal, so enlightened, so Christian" would also fall as part of the apocalypse.[54]

More universal than these apocalyptic descriptions was what historian Nicholas Guyatt has termed judicial providence, that is, the idea that God punished and rewarded nations according to their deeds.[55] Both Southern and Northern preachers spoke of the suffering that accompanied the war as a punishment for the nation's sins.[56] Even President Abraham Lincoln came to believe God was behind the violence: "If God wills that [the war] continue, until all the wealth piled by the bond-man's two hundred and fifty years of unrequited toil shall be sunk, and until every drop of blood drawn with the lash, shall be paid by another drawn with the sword, as was said three thousand years ago, so still it must be said 'the judgments of the Lord, are true and righteous altogether.' "[57] Lincoln's statement, like similar interpretations and predictions that frame the war as God's punishment on the nation for slavery, did not imply that the events of the Christian apocalypse were unfolding. Yet, Americans were often careful not to suggest that God took vengeance for the sake of vengeance alone. The subtext to Lincoln's statement was that the suffering of the war would ultimately prove redemptive. It would allow the fulfillment of America's divine destiny.[58]

In Mormon thought, though, the nation's failure that God would rectify by punishment was not slavery's sin, but rather a failure to defend the Saints' constitutional rights. To the Mormons, whose religious experience centered on notions of divine accessibility and immediacy, the collapse of the nation signaled the start of a series of events that would culminate in the arrival of the millennium. Of course, the political and apocalyptic overlapped in this interpretation, in which God willed the collapse of the nation not only as punishment, but also because the Mormons could save it and in that salvation would inaugurate the millennial reign. During a February 1858 priesthood meeting in Provo, a man named Albert Williams connected the war prophecy to the prophecy "that the Constitution would fall & we would revive it again and hold it up to the nations of the earth. Hence," he continued, "we are approaching that day & when the South take up vs the North down will go the Constitution."[59]

Through the devastation of peoples and places, the Saints were free to "build up the waste places of Zion."[60] This language of "waste places" came from the King James version of Isaiah, appearing in Smith's revelations to describe the Saints' eventual redemption of Zion in Jackson County. Mormons believed that they would not be able to claim the promised site until after the space was cleansed via God's judgment. For this reason, they possessed a particular interest in what was occurring in that region during the war—an interest that could be satisfied in the pages of the *Deseret News*.[61] In 1863, the *News*' coverage included the republication of a Missouri newspaper's report entitled, "Devastation in Jackson County, Mo.": "The depopulation of the counties in Jackson, Cass, Bates, and Vernon is thorough and complete. One may ride for hours without seeing a single inhabitant and deserted houses and farms are everywhere to be seen. The whole is a grand picture of desolation."[62] The Saints also received word of the destructions from family members and fellow Mormons in the East. In November 1863, Hannah Peck Meacham, a Latter-day Saint then living in Illinois, wrote a relative in Utah, "I with you believe a great revolution has commenced for many years the Saints have prayed for this very thing. . . . Missouri is being paid off with heavy Interest."[63] On November 9, 1864, Charles Walker recorded the popular sentiment that neither side had "gained the victory yet, nor will they until the decree of the Lord has been fulfilled and the way prepared for the return of the People of God to the center Stake of Zion. . . . Missouri has been scourged and almost laid waste by the ravages of the war. Ther [*sic*] meeting out to them what they meted unto us. Great is thy justice, oh King of Kings."[64]

Yet, the war ended before the Saints expected. Beadle observed that the war "stopped so suddenly, they maintain it must soon break out again."[65] Young once predicted that the war would "take years and years, and will never cease until the work is accomplished. There may be seasons that the fire will appear to be extinguished, and the first you know it will break out in another portion, and all is on fire again, and it will spread and continue until the land is emptied."[66] This sentiment was present in a June 1865 letter a Saint named Henry J. Doremus wrote to his non-Mormon uncle living in New Jersey. Doremus pointed his uncle to a copy of the war prophecy he had sent the year before and promised "if you have it and will read it, you will have a picture of the future." He took heart that the prophecy had already accurately foretold the start of the war and the participation of African American slaves. He assured his uncle that "you flatter yourselves that the war is over, it's not over." Doremus believed the South would resort to "secretly poisoning everything," spreading disease, or "by laying powder plots, and firing on a large scale the large cities all over the North, and manufacturing establishments." His uncle had "hardly seen the commencement of the trouble that will come upon that nation."[67]

As time passed, some Mormons came to predict the coming of a second American Civil War. In 1866, the *Daily Cleveland Herald* reported that "Mr. Kelsey, A Bishop and Prophet of the Mormon Church" had predicted that "the South would again secede and the recent rebellion would be nothing in comparison to what would follow."[68] The *Deseret News* published an interview with estranged founding-Mormon David Whitmer, who spoke of a "great tribulation" consisting of "a civil war more bloody and cruel than the rebellion. It will be the smashing up of this nation."[69] Nephi Packard drafted a letter to one of the church's historians relating a prophecy Joseph Smith had reportedly told his brother, Noah Packard. Noah claimed "he heard the Prophet Joseph say that the next great (U.S. civil) war after the war of the rebellion (the Civil War of the 1860's between the North and the South) would commence in a little town now called Chicago but at that time it would have grown to be a very large city." Nephi recalled that "another brother" had told him that the conflict's cause "would be the depreciation of the currency of the United States."[70]

None could claim that the Civil War answered all elements of Smith's original war prophecy. There was yet to be a "full end of all nations." The majority interpretation was that the war had fulfilled the first elements of the prophecy—the initial rebellion, the participation of former slaves, and the South's request for aid from Great Britain—but that the prophecy still anticipated elements yet to occur. For example, while one strain of thought held that blacks who enlisted in the Union forces answered the prophecy that "after many days Slaves shall rise against their Masters who shall be Martialed [*sic*] and disaplined [*sic*] for war," others expected further race wars.[71]

Mormonism's detractors were skeptical of claims that the Civil War vindicated Joseph Smith's prophecy at all. T. B. H. Stenhouse believed these Saints declared a "hasty fulfillment" of the prophecy in the Civil War based on the "peaceable adjustment of Britain's difficulties with the United States." In other words, the world had not been consumed in violence. The prediction of an imminent Indian massacre seemed "equally obscure and improbable."[72] Beadle similarly wrote, "It will be perceived that of the thousand predictions in relation to our civil war, Joseph's was among the most shrewd, and certainly hit on two or three very curious things. But he met with the difficulty common to all prophets in these days, when he ran into particulars he missed it seriously."[73] Beadle left his reader to determine which particulars Smith had missed. Yet, Mormon apocalypticists used these unfulfilled elements to continue to point to the near future. Part of the prophecy had been fulfilled. The rest would be fulfilled soon.

Mormon Apocalyptic after the Civil War

Even though the military was largely distracted with the Civil War, the federal government had not forgotten about the infamous zealots situated on the nation's western frontier. In 1862, the territory made another unsuccessful attempt at statehood. At the same time, Congress passed the Morrill Act, which "outlawed bigamy in the territories, providing for a prison sentence of up to five years and a fine of $500."[74] Lincoln delayed enforcing the law and, as of 1874, with the test case of George Reynolds, there was yet to be a single conviction. When *Reynolds v. United States* was brought before the U.S. Supreme Court in 1878, the question was whether the First Amendment's free exercise clause would protect the Mormon practice of polygamy. The Court ruled in the negative, upholding legislation against plural marriage despite the sincerity of the perpetrators' beliefs.[75]

The decision strengthened the position of anti-polygamists within Utah Territory. As historian Sarah Barringer Gordon observed, "The Supreme Court's decision translated Mormon Utah from an alternative society (however dangerous) into unconstitutional deviance (with all the resonance of treason such a label carried.)"[76] Additional laws followed. The Edmunds Act of 1882 prohibited polygamists from serving on juries and modified the requirement to prove a marriage in order to gain a conviction. In this case, it was only necessary to prove that a man considered more than one woman his wife.

The presence of federal marshals tasked with enforcing the law revived a sense of occupation in the territory. Annie Clark Tanner, both a plural wife and daughter of polygamous parents, recalled the hardships of the "raid," in which federal agents came into Mormon communities to arrest offending males:

> It is difficult to picture the unsettled conditions in Utah and Idaho during the raid against polygamists. Homes were broken up and families scattered among relatives or friends. Thus, shelter was given them as they sought to avoid the officers who raided the towns. Some had secret hiding places in their own homes; others trained the children to watch for the Deputy Marshal, and to evade or deceive when asked questions by strangers or deputies about family relations. If people were at any public gatherings and the Federal Marshal entered the town, there was a scattering of local Church authorities. Polygamists were warned or smuggled to safety. Mothers ran with their babies to the neighbors; old men took to the fields.[77]

Not surprisingly, apocalypticism prospered in these conditions. In this regard, the Saints were aided by new editions of the scriptures edited by Orson Pratt. In 1876, the new edition of the Doctrine and Covenants added twenty-five revelations dictated by Joseph Smith and one by Brigham Young that had not appeared in earlier editions. Included in this number were several revelations that contained apocalyptic themes: the war prophecy, Moroni's 1823 statement on Elijah's coming, and two sections containing Smith's commentary on portions of the books of Revelation and Isaiah, respectively.

Yet even while the church made these older resources more widely available, many eschatological developments among the institutional hierarchy—including revelations and special ceremonies—were not disclosed to the public. These included a revelation dictated in October 1880 by the apostle Wilford Woodruff "concerning the Nation who encumber the land of promise." The revelation promised judgments on the U.S. for the murder of Joseph and Hyrum Smith, the persecution of the Saints, and the ongoing legislation that condemned plural marriage. In response, the revelation stated the following utilizing the first person voice of the divine: "I have decreed Plagues to go forth and lay waste mine Enemies and not many years hence they shall not be left to pollute mine heritage. The Devil is ruling over his Kingdom and my spirit has no Place in the h[e]arts of the Rulers of this

Nation, and the Devil stirs them up to defy my Power, and to make war upon my Saints."[78]

Woodruff's revelation commanded each of the Twelve Apostles to individually wash their feet against those who had persecuted the Saints and to meet together for a special prayer in the temple. In this prayer, they were to provide a list of those who had persecuted them, including "The Preside[n]ts of the United States, The Supreme Court, The Cabinet, The Senate & House of Con[g]ress of the United States The Governors of the States and Territories The Judges & Officers sent unto you and all men & persons who have taken part in persecuting you or Bringing distress upon you or your families or have sought your lives or sought to hinder you from keeping my Commandments or from Enjoying the rights which the Constitutional Laws of the Land guarantee unto you."[79] In December, John Taylor requested that Woodruff prepare the prayer. It was read following the ordinance of washings during a meeting of general authorities on January 19, 1881.[80] While the listing of those persons and parties who had brought grievance into the Mormons' lives can be understood in terms of straightforward revenge, the coordination between this list and the washing ordinance draws out the underlying apocalypticism of this particular event. That is, the church leaders participated together in an act that designated enemies of the church in connection with a washing that took place as a sign of judgment, and in the greater context of foot washing within Christianity more generally (see, e.g., John 13) as a foreshadowed apocalyptic final judgment that would determine those that were with Christ, and those that ultimately were not.

The laity, too, were drawn to the project of imagining and narrating the apocalypse. As was often the case in such periods of intense apocalyptic interest, they desired additional insights into the apocalypse. They wanted to know how current events would pave the way to Zion's redemption. The absence of this type of official apocalyptic texts encouraged the growth of new instances of vernacular apocalyptic literature. The period especially saw a rise in first-person testimonies of elaborate visions in the vein of Farnsworth's vision, which had gained respectability decades earlier. Following in the tradition of the classic apocalypse, these visions included the visionary being transported through various scenes of destruction, while accompanied by a visible or invisible angelic presence that interpreted the experience for the visionary. These visionaries witnessed an America ravaged with disease or war, where those who did not want to fight had to flee to Mormon settlements in the West. They watched the divine intervene during future invasions in the American West and witnessed the miraculous construction of the New Jerusalem in Jackson County.

The first instance of a post–Civil War apocalypse to be considered here was drafted in 1877. Although this vision was unquestionably one of the era's most widely circulated, little is known about its authorship or composition.[81] As copies dispersed through Mormon communities, the anonymous vision was credited first to Joseph F. Smith and then to Wilford Woodruff. One surviving copy ascribed the vision to "A Seventy," which at the time was a common priesthood office held by those outside of church leadership—a more modest and believable claim that likely ruled out the tradition's highest echelons.[82] A copy was brought to the church historian's office in 1878, which Wilford Woodruff transcribed into his journal. He left a space where he planned to record the visionary's name when he identified it, suggesting that this early document was either anonymous, credited to the nameless seventy, or had already been credited to someone that Woodruff knew was not the actual author.[83] In 1880, Joseph F. Smith issued a statement denying he authored the document.[84]

The vision began with the visionary lying in bed, when he "felt a strange stupor Come over me and apparently became partially unconscious. Still I was not asleep, nor awake With a strange far away dreamy feelings." In a visionary state, he found himself preaching in front of the Ogden Tabernacle and felt spiritually directed to prophesy concerning "some of the things which will shortly come to pass."[85] While still at the pulpit, he entered a vision within his vision, when he was transported throughout the United States from one city to another to see the effects of a last days plague. In Salt Lake City, he saw that the streets were entirely barren of people and "badges of mourning" adorned the doors of each home. "I saw no funeral [procession], or any thing [*sic*] of that kind, but the City looked vary Still and quiet as though the people were praying and had Controll [*sic*] of the desease [*sic*] what ever [*sic*] it was."[86] The badges of mourning signaled that Salt Lake City had not gone unscathed, but the righteous were quarantined and protected by a divine hand. The scene was reminiscent of the ancient Israelites who found shelter inside their homes while the destroying angel slaughtered the Egyptian firstborn sons.

The visionary's sight was transported to other American cities, each less fortunate than the next. Washington, D.C., had been abandoned after an unknown calamity. "The white House Empty, the Halls of Congress the same Every thing [*sic*] in ruins." In Baltimore, mounds of putrefying human bodies

Figure 4.1 Augustus Kollner, "Baltimore Battle Monument" (ca. 1849). In the apocalyptic 1877 vision, the bodies of the dead would have filled this usually tranquil square. Courtesy of the Library of Congress.

surrounded the 39-foot high Battle Monument, what the visionary called the Monument of 1812 (see Figure 4.1). Disposing of human remains in the Chesapeake Bay had rendered the water unsafe for human consumption. The city's desperate and depraved populace turned to any means necessary for survival. "I saw mothers cutting the throats of their own children for their blood. I saw them suck it from their throats to quench their own thirst and then lie down and die."[87]

In Philadelphia, "every thing [*sic*] was Still. No living soul was to be seen to greet me, and it seemed as though the whole City was without an inhabitant." The smell of decomposition made it "impossible for any living thing to breathe."[88] The scene shifted to Broadway in New York City, where "the bodies of Beautiful women lying stone dead, and others in a dying Condition" were scattered across the sidewalks (see Figure 4.2). Male thieves who had taken shelter from the miasma emerged from cellars to rob them or in a later variant to "ravish the persons of some that were yet alive and kill them and rob their bodies of all the valuables they had upon them."[89] The murderers and rapists would die themselves before they could make it back to safety.

Figure 4.2 Lithograph of Broadway, in New York City, 1875. In the apocalyptic 1877 vision, men victimized women on this busy thoroughfare, and female bodies in various states of injury, including death, would have been strewn along the street. Courtesy of the Library of Congress.

The final image of the people of New York City was one of parents murdering and devouring the flesh of their own offspring.[90] The visionary watched as a fire started when "a mighty East wind sprang up and Carried the flames west over the City, and it burned until [*sic*] there was not a single building left Standing whole Even down to the wharfs. And the shipping all seemed to be burned and swallowed up in the Common destruction and left Nothing but a Desolation whare [*sic*] the great City was a short time before." New York City, America's most fitting symbol of Babylon, would be reduced to ash.[91]

The vision's depictions of America's cities emphasized that no societal or familial ties would survive among the wicked during the apocalypse—it would be every person for him- or herself. The graphic treatments of rape, murder, and child cannibalism informed readers that American society was guilty of the vilest mistreatment of women and children. Predictions of last days cannibalism had not appeared in the Bible or in Smith's prophecies. There are biblical examples of parental cannibalism during war, however. According to biblical scholar Stuart Lasine, scenes of mothers eating their children in

2 Kings 6 signaled "an inverted world in which social relations have totally broken down."[92] More contemporary images of cannibalism associated the practice with that of the indigenous savage.[93] Through either lens, to depict the civilized women and men of Baltimore and New York eating their own children was to predict they would revert to a primitive state.

The 1877 vision's larger emphasis on disease had been a consistently significant element in Mormon eschatology as it was in the apocalyptic source material in the Bible. Joseph Smith dictated a revelation on March 7, 1831, discussed previously, foretelling the coming of "an overflowing scourge . . . a desolating sicknes [*sic*] shall cover the land."[94] The "overflowing scourge" recalled Isaiah's prophecy: "[W]hen the overflowing scourge shall pass through, then ye shall be trodden down by it."[95] When the cholera epidemic began in 1832, Mormons identified this scourge with the new disease.[96]

Other Americans also believed cholera was a divine judgment. Reports of prostitutes wiped out in droves and drunkards suddenly taken with the plague all seemed to confirm the belief that God had sent cholera to punish certain populations over others.[97] As historian Charles E. Rosenberg wrote, "The abrupt onset and fearful symptoms of cholera made Americans apprehensive and reflective—as they were not by the equally deadly, but more deliberate, ravages of tuberculosis or malaria."[98] Individuals who were previously healthy and energetic were stricken with severe cramping, diarrhea, and vomiting, which led to dehydration and ultimately death (see Figure 4.3). As one witness observed, "I have seen people eating breakfast apparently quite healthy, and we would have them buried before night."[99] The way the disease moved through groups of people seemed to mirror the motions of apocalyptic angels, leading some Latter-day Saints to speak of it as "the destroyer."[100]

In 1884, another disease-centric apocalypse appeared in *The Contributor*, a Utah-based Mormon newspaper. A presumably different anonymous prophet described an experience he had three or four years previously when he was awakened in the night by a "glorious messenger." Mirroring a common scene throughout apocalyptic literature, the angel handed him a book and urged him to "Look, and see what is coming to pass." The book's title was emblazoned on the front cover in gold lettering, "The Book of the Plagues." He sat up in bed and began to investigate the volume. Each linen page included a picture "printed in colors as natural as art can copy nature." Below each vivid illustration was a written description. While the book numbered over fifty pages, the visionary described only three.

Figure 4.3 "A Young Woman of Vienna who died of cholera, depicted when healthy and four hours before death," watercolor, ca. 1831. Courtesy of the Wellcome Library, London.

The first page was an image of a banquet set on the grounds of a "stately suburban villa, adorned with all the ornaments of modern architecture." "Richly dressed ladies and gentleman" gathered around a long table situated on the carefully manicured lawn. A "sickly brass hue" had overtaken the sky and disease, as represented by white specks, drifted through the atmosphere. Unknown to the party, the specks had landed in their food as they continued to eat. The serene country estate was transformed into a scene of tragedy. "Many were falling backward in the agonies of a fearful death; others drooping upon the table, and others pausing with their hands still holding the untasted food, their countenances betraying a fearful astonishment at the peculiar and unlooked for condition of their companions."[101] The sudden manner in which this unnamed disease struck mirrored cholera, known for decimating persons who seemed completely healthy moments before.

A circular vignette on the corner of the page depicted a "store of a dealer in pork" with "barrels of pork, long strings of sausages, fresh slaughtered hogs, piles of smoked bacon and headcheese." A row of twelve large hams, each with a letter painted on it, spelling out the word "abominations," lined the structure. Below the portrait was the caption: "A Feast among the Gentiles, commencement of the Plague."[102]

On the second page was an illustration of an already devastated cityscape. The streets were covered with lifeless forms. None survived to bury the dead. "Upon the balconies of the richly decorated residences, across the thresholds of the opened doorways, along the walks and upon the crossings, lay the men, women and children, who a few days before were enjoying all the pleasures of life." The visionary observed that the city's wealth filled the banks as the inventory of merchants sat purposeless on the shelves. Pigs made their appearance in the city as well. "A hungry drove of those horrible ugly slaughter-house hogs (which may be seen in the pens attached to the filthy slaughtering places in the outskirts of many cities), was tearing and devouring the dead and feasting upon the bodies of rich and poor alike with none to molest them."[103]

The Vision of the Plagues offered a glimpse of what historian Marvin Hill referred to as Latter-day Saint "class consciousness."[104] Suburban opulence and urban wealth were foreign to the vast majority of Mormon converts. Stark disparity in wealth so easily observed in the American city was particularly immoral to Latter-day Saint sensibilities. The subtext of these two scenes from the Vision of the Plagues seemed to be that status and wealth could not shield society's elites from God's wrath. Ultimately, they would meet the same fate as the world's unconverted poor.

The image of ravenous swine eating the apocalypse's victims was an updated depiction of Revelation and Ezekiel's "supper of the great god," when birds would fill themselves on the flesh of the wicked dead. The scene was fitting for post–Civil War America. During the conflict, roaming swine often uncovered hastily buried bodies.[105] These pigs were "ugly slaughterhouse hogs," but New York City was still known for its scavenging pigs that numbered in the thousands in the nineteenth century. The observation that these hogs ate the carcasses of both rich and poor may have alluded to the progress of confining pigs to slums, which would prove entirely vain during the apocalypse.[106] While it had been true that the wealthy could separate themselves from filth in their lives, they could not protect themselves from judgment.

The earlier scene of the pork dealer seemed to point readers to the cause of the last days plague. By this era, most Americans were aware that slaughterhouses and animal pollution more generally were a factor in the spread of cholera.[107] In 1868, several church leaders, perhaps concerned by the 1866 cholera epidemic, preached against the Latter-day Saint consumption of pork. Apostle George A. Smith explained that "within the past few years in some countries where a great amount of pork has been consumed the people have been afflicted with a kind of pestilence—a disease which is considered incurable."[108]

As a community entrenched in the Bible, Mormons would also have seen other significances in the pigs. The Old Testament dietary restriction against pork meant scripturally swine were unclean and, as such, were associated with the Gentiles, who ate them. Mormons were also familiar with Jesus' exorcism of the Gerasene demoniac and his allowing the devils to possess a herd of swine who, in turn, threw themselves off a cliff.[109] In 1860, Heber C. Kimball related a dream he had at the end of the Utah War, a dream that linked hogs with madness and Gentiles. In it, he saw Johnston's army depicted as a herd of rabid swine—"frothing at the mouth just like mad hogs do"—that filled the Salt Lake Valley. The hogs tried to bite the Saints but were prevented by an unseen force until they eventually disappeared.[110] In the nineteenth-century Mormon imagination, pigs already possessed the potential to appear as frightening and monstrous, the perfect inhabitants of the apocalypse.

The visionary examined "nearly fifty of these pictures . . . wherein the fearful effects of this and other plagues were almost as vividly portrayed as if I had actually seen them." He described the last illustration captioned, "A camp of the Saints who have gathered together and are living under the daily revelations of God, and are thus preserved from the plague." The scene centered on a community of "small rectangular wall tents in rows . . . each tent clean and white, and appearing to be of a size suited to the wants of an ordinary family." The tents surrounded a two-story "large cone-shaped tent of a bright purple color" and another white "round wall tent." While the visionary did not explain how the Saints used these larger tents, they likely represented a modern tabernacle complex. The protected community was surrounded by "the same atmosphere as in the previous pictures, with the atoms of poison . . . and the same time and season of the year." The visionary observed that "each family was in its tent during the hours of the day that the poison falls, and thus were preserved from breathing the deadly particles."[111] He may have intended to depict the community en route to Jackson County. The setting was not the Rocky Mountains, but a prairie with elms and cottonwood trees, both native to Missouri.

A third instance of apocalyptic was composed by Charles D. Evans, a school teacher in Springville, Utah, on December 25, 1882, and published in

Figure 4.4 Charles D. Evans (1829–1908) wrote a vision, seemingly as a work of fiction, depicting a last days plague and the Constitution defended among the Saints. Courtesy of the Church History Library.

the *Millennial Star* in February 1883[112] (see Figure 4.4). Evans's vision began with the Protestant Reformation and the founding of the United States as a land of "civil and religious toleration." An angel appeared to direct Evans to the next scene:

> "Son of mortality, look." I looked and beheld a scene most revolting to my senses, from the fact that it was the very reverse of the prosperity and religious freedom I had before witnessed. I saw the representatives of one branch of the republic holding in their hands fetters they themselves had forged. The personage, again addressing me, said, "Knowest thou the meaning of these?" I answered "No." He replied, "These are the chains with which certain sons of the republic, who have tasted of the tree of liberty, desire to bind their fellows. These are they who seek to subvert the cause of human freedom. These seek to enslave one portion of the children of

> freedom who differ with them in religious belief and practice. Know thou, my son, that their object in filthy lucre. They plot to take away human rights, and to destroy the freedom of the soul, to possess the homes of the industrious without fee or reward. Woe unto such, for the vengeance of heaven awaits them."[113]

The scene of conspiring "representatives" seemed to reference the Edmunds Act, which had been signed into law earlier that year. The next scene showed how the repudiation of constitutional principles had destroyed the fabric of American society. The visionary witnessed the rise of factionalism and civil war. "The spirit of bloodshed appeared to possess every heart." The angel comforted him with one final vision of constitutional freedoms being preserved in the West. Specifically, the visionary saw the American flag flying from Ensign Peak. Evans borrowed from the words of John Taylor at the start of the Civil War to describe the new government. "No North, no South, no East, no West, but one unbroken nation whose banner waved for all the world."[114]

Evans seems to have written the vision as a work of fiction. In his personal journal, he did not recount experiencing the vision, but only noted that he had composed the piece for publication. In fact, the opening sentence positioned the vision in the category of literature. "While wrapt in the repose of slumber's soft embrace, perfectly oblivious to every surrounding object, and, to use a Byronic phrase, while the apparently 'still and pulseless world' lay in the same state, my mind was suddenly carried away to the past."[115] When the vision was, in 1886, collected with three other visions in a volume titled *Remarkable Visions*, this first sentence was replaced with one that focused on realism by placing the essay in conversation with current events. "While meditating upon the present position of the Saints and of the false accusations made against them of 'disloyalty,' and of being the 'enemies of mankind,' etc., my mind was suddenly carried away to the past."[116] In 1894, when a third and much revised version—now identified as "a dream," not "a vision"—was published in the *Contributor*, Evans, perhaps now concerned that some had believed his work was an accurate account, concluded with a disclaimer: "I have written the foregoing, which is founded on true principle, under the caption of a dream, partly to instruct and partly to check the folly of reading silly novels now so prevalent."[117]

In the 1894 version, Evans's vision began with the nighttime appearance of an angel. New details explained along what lines the United States would be divided. He saw "wealth is arrayed against labor, labor against wealth." He witnessed how "excited multitudes ran wildly about; strikes increased; lawlessness sought the place of regular government." Violent clashes followed: "Blood flowed down the streets of cities like water. . . . Thousands of bodies lay untombed in the streets." While most of these details had appeared in the Vision of the Plagues' depictions of the apocalyptic city, Evans introduced a new symbol of American unrest: the bombing of national monuments. The Battle Monument in Baltimore appeared in the 1877 vision but only to provide a setting for mass death. Evans described this "ruthless" destruction of "monuments erected to perpetuate the names of the noble and brave" as the rejection or at least the loss of American foundations. This was his example of what he described as "a past in ruins."[118]

Evans's depiction of the last days plague began, as did the Vision of the Plagues, with "an atmosphere tinged with a leaden hue, which was the precursor of an unparalleled plague." He described the new disease in some detail. It began with a "purple spot" located on the victim's cheek or the back of the hand, which increased in size until "it spread over the entire surface of the body, producing certain death." Evans saw terrified mothers throw their infants to the ground as if they were "poisonous reptiles" at the first signs of disease.[119] As the disease progressed in adults, it "rotted the eyes in their sockets and consumed the tongue as would a powerful acid or an intense heat."[120] The description pointed readers to Smith's prophecy of a last days' ailment, which would cause its victims' tongues to "be stayed that they shall not utter against me; and their flesh shall fall from off their bones, and their eyes from their sockets."[121] Evans added that these "wicked men" died "as they stood on their feet, and the birds of prey feasted on their carcasses."[122]

A Final Gathering and a Gentile Invasion on Utah Territory

While the visions previously referred to here emphasized what would occur outside of Utah Territory, another set of apocalyptic visions focused on last days events as they would occur in Utah. With the possible exception of Farnsworth's vision, the most popular of these apocalypses in the later years of the nineteenth century was Newman Bulkley's vision of January 8, 1886 (see Figure 4.5). Bulkley was in his late sixties at the time of his vision. He had been a Mormon since childhood, participated in the Utah War, and was one of the original pioneers of the Mormon settlement in Springville,

Figure 4.5 Photo of Newman Bulkley (1817–1893) whose vision described a future military invasion on Salt Lake City. Courtesy of the Daughters of the Utah Pioneers, Springville, Utah.

Utah.[123] His vision, like many others, occurred in his own bedroom and was connected to sleep. At around 9 o'clock, he dreamed that "the spirit of my dead wife," who had died three years previous, "was hovering round about me." He awoke abruptly and was just as soon enveloped in "the vision of my mind." Bulkley witnessed a session of the Senate deliberating in Washington, D.C., when suddenly the senators "were hurled from the Hall by an unseen power." They "rallied" only to again be thrown from the hall. On their third return to the chambers, the politicians were propelled from the hall with such intensity that several died from the impact. Bulkley watched the survivors emerge with "the name of 'Edmunds' printed in their foreheads."[124] This allusion to Revelation's mark of the beast referenced the Senate's 1882 approval of the anti-polygamy Edmunds Act, depicting the nation's leadership in league with Satan. In the same way that some envisioned Buchanan as the devil's earthly emissary, George F. Edmunds stood in the role of arch-persecutor of the Saints. Thereafter, the vision showed a whirlwind take apart the House of Representatives. The capital city's inhabitants fled.

Bulkley's vision as he recorded it filled gaps in the anonymous 1877 vision. It explained, for example, why the earlier visionary saw Washington, D.C., without any inhabitants. The two visions also similarly depicted gathering refugees desperately fleeing from Babylon's failing structures and violence. In Bulkley's vision, "many thousands of women and children [took] refuge in the timber, hazel rough, or any place where they could conceal themselves from the turmoil that was going on in the States."[125] A rescue party was sent from Salt Lake and brought them safely to Utah. In the 1877 vision, women and children "travelling to the mountains on foot" filled the roads. The visionary found the gender makeup of these last minute gatherers "remarkable."[126] Indeed, it was crucial for the Mormon concept of the millennium.

Latter-day Saints placed great significance on Isaiah's last days prophecy that "in that day seven women shall take hold of one man."[127] In 1852, Orson Pratt defended plural marriage by drawing on this verse as he would many times in the future. He explained that "millions of fathers and brothers will fall upon the battlefield, while mothers, and daughters, and widows will be left to mourn the loss." Many of these women would convert, "flee out from among the nations, and be gathered with the Saints to Zion."[128] John H. Beadle described this prophecy as one of the essential components of Mormon expectations for the last days. He had personally encountered an elderly woman in Utah who expressed her belief that "all the people of America who do not repent will be destroyed now in a few years, so there will be but one man for seven women."[129] The influx of women that would accompany the apocalyptic destruction in the East would then answer Mormon concerns regarding the relative lack of opportunity to live plural marriage among the church membership more generally, given that the current demographics prevented many from practicing this portion of their faith. In addition, the image of women struggling to reach Mormon settlements challenged the critical portrayal of Mormon women forced to remain in

Utah against their will—desperate to leave en masse as they had done with Steptoe's army in 1854.

If one reads Bulkley's vision as a continuation of the anonymous 1877 vision, as seems to have been intended, the subtext was that Mormons would protect women from the gendered violence of the last days. Mormon men were presented in stark opposition to their Gentile counterparts as they sought to protect women and children from the dangers of the eschaton, including the dangers presented by Gentile men, depicted as murderers and rapists.

Bulkley's vision showed that in addition to refugees, a military force would also make the journey to Utah Territory following the destructions in Washington, D.C. The righteous would prepare for this invasion by moving "into valleys as near as possible to the Temples," populating Logan, Manti, St. George, and Salt Lake City.[130] The army surrounded the Saints, preventing their escape. "Then I saw the preparations commence for the entire destruction of the saints, which consisted in their gathering together all the combustible material they could obtain, making a complete wall around this people. It looked to me to be some fifty feet high, and from six to ten rods wide at the bottom."[131] Rather than prepare against this blast in a conventional manner, Mormons received special temple ceremonies and, now endowed with power, were able to turn the bomb back on the invaders. "When the enemy had fired their combustibles, these men, endowed with the Holy Priesthood, walked along, like sentinels on their posts, and waved their hands, and the flames, smoke and ashes that were intended for the destruction of the Saints, turned upon our enemies, and when this combustible matter was consumed and the fire and smoke had cleared away, lo! and behold! the enemies of this people were not to be found."[132]

In 1880, another Mormon visionary, Thomas Harris, had also dreamed of the Saints standing off against a vast army that had surrounded them on all sides. As in Bulkley's vision, the prophecy alluded to the power and protection bestowed in temple rites—the body of Saints each "appeared to be clothed in white robes," evidence of their participation in the temple ordinances. Under the leadership of John Taylor and the Twelve Apostles, the Saints were victorious in the "great struggle."[133] Both Bulkley and Harris linked victory with the specially given power available only to the Saints through their temple ordinances.

While most apocalyptic depictions of a military invasion on Utah Territory promised miraculous divine interventions, the vision of James Booth foresaw an initial season of suffering and martyrdom. In 1874, according to an undated statement, Booth saw Gentile "soldiers on horseback two abreast going westward" along Main Street in Salt Lake City. The men carried strange "instruments of destruction in their arms reaching almost to the ground, similar in appearance to English fire engines made of fine brass." As Booth followed them along Main Street, passing familiar sights, he came to "a large prison with two iron gates towards me, which were very high, with arched spiked tops and arched brickwork above the gates. Between the gates & myself were from two to three hundred (2–300) of our brethren; all without hats. They were very clean & appeared very cheerful. In their midst I beheld the prophet Joseph and his brother Hiram. They looked very much pleased and their complexion was very much fairer than the rest." Booth heard the Holy Spirit's voice inform him that the two Smith martyrs, invisible to the crowd of men, were waiting to greet them "on the other side of the vail."

The soldiers led the prisoners outside of the prison "on the sidewalk in front of the stores" where they had set up their instruments. Booth tried to leave the scene as he heard groans of pain, but swarms of approving "Gentiles" in Salt Lake City's downtown blocked his escape:

> I saw at once that the soldiers and civilian gentiles were butchering our brethren above mentioned. It seemed, they had attached the instruments to their bodies and were pumping the blood out of them, it running into the gutter; where it froze, until it resembled beef suet in consistency but in color like blood. The first man I noticed as being active in butchering was a gentile. He arose from among those whom he had slain and the blood was dripping from his finger ends and from his coattails though he had been lifted out of a pool of blood.

The frightening scene led into a moral lesson about one's willingness to die for the cause. Booth was alarmed when another Latter-day Saint shouted out to the executioners asking them why they did not kill him and Booth who were also Mormons. One of the executioners recommended they flee. The Spirit told Booth to journey to St. George; along the way, he encountered an apparition of Jesus. "As we were looking at each other earnestly, he said: 'Thou wouldst not be afraid to die for my sake, wouldst thou?' Which caused me to tremble and shake before him and said: 'O Lord, thou knowest all things, but I do pray thee, to give me of thy holy spirit, that I may be found true & faithful in all things, even unto death.'" The Lord repeated the question three times before he allowed Booth to continue his journey to St. George. Booth's vision's emphasis on martyrdom reinforced the necessity for the believer to be willing to make the ultimate sacrifice in the last days.

Booth's vision belonged to the class of prophecies that predicted the Saints would first flee southward before they made the final journey to Jackson County. In a final scene, he witnessed Latter-day Saints of all ages making their way toward St. George. The Spirit explained:

> The Latter-day Saints are being murdered in the north for the Gospel's sake and those that are determined to serve God are fleeing to save their lives. But we are only going to be driven to St. George, and there stand still, for we have been driven all we intend to be driven, for there we will stand still and see the salvation of our God or die for Zion's sake.

Booth's vision ended before he was able to witness how God would intervene for the Saints. It stands out from other contemporary examples, as neither depictions of martyrdom, nor of Mormon casualties, were common elements in the visions of the Utah Territory period.

A more substantial but still a minor thread in these visions was instead the Saints' use of violence against their own fair weather adherents. In Farnsworth's and Bulkley's visions, defectors who pledged allegiance to the invading forces were subsequently slaughtered alongside the troops. Harris's vision went further to describe a series of executions taking place after the invasion began in which the Saints united around John Taylor: "As soon as the fainthearted and those who had joined with the wicked saw the power of God they feigned friendship but the day had passed. The power of God manifested itself among the whole Priesthood and deception was impossible and many were destroyed by the Servants of the Lord because they could desern [discern] by the Spirit all that were true to the Kingdom." It was at this point that Harris "felt the final triumph has come."[134]

While the question of how to deal with enemy sympathizers is common in war, these prophecies of future executions suggested the significance of Mormon concerns over loyalty in the rising tensions of the period. Harris's sense that putting to death those who sided with the wicked was a triumph also hinted at how these acts might purify the community of Saints. Nathaniel Jones's dream also included executions designed to remove less faithful Mormons. In it, after the invasion on Salt Lake City, Mormons gathered to Young's mountain retreat. There Young announced, "I thank God that the time which I have prayed for so long has come at last; we will now clean the inside of the platter." The prophet identified "individuals that had been practicing iniquity, telling them the nature of their crimes and penalty. I do not recollect any of the individuals except one who was a woman whom he accused of being a witch. They were all taken out of the canyon and used up."[135]

Harris's and Jones's dreams foresaw the fulfillment of earlier expectations first posited during the Mormon Reformation of 1856–1857. The Reformation was a period of revival in which church leaders called for greater piety, developed a catechism to promote orthodoxy, and required church members to be re-baptized to demonstrate their commitment to reform. The focus was on achieving individual and communal purity.[136] As part of the fiery rhetoric, Young and other church leaders frequently declared that the penalty for sins such as adultery and murder was death. The actual application of what became referred to as blood atonement was never officially enforced. Yet, Latter-day Saints would not have been surprised at Harris's suggestion that Young had prayed for a time when it would be. On March 2, 1856, Young had declared, "The time is coming when justice will be laid to the line and righteousness to the plummet; when we shall take the old broadsword and ask, Are you for God? And if you are not heartily on the Lord's side, you will be hewn down."[137] This envisioned violence informed depictions of the apocalypse.

Young often spoke of the future separation of the righteous and wicked (although he did not always suggest it would come about by violent means) in reference to the Gospels' parable of the goats and the sheep. This biblical framework was also used by Mormon visionaries. Like the purifying violence foreseen by Harris and Jones, schismatic prophet Joseph Morris prophesied of a sorting by means of divinely ordered executions. Morris's revelations foresaw an event in which he and his followers would meet Jesus in Salt Lake City's public square. There, Jesus would grant him "power to discern between the sheep and the goats (so called); and he shall place the sheep on the one side and the goats on the other." The goats would be slain with the aid of "the hosts of heaven," who had accompanied Jesus. Morris viewed this scene as the start of the last battle. He would then go forward with his army of disciples and angels and purge the earth of God's enemies.[138] Morris's vision serves to underscore the ways in which the violence of the apocalypse was no longer simply an event that would take place in the distant United States, but instead came home to roost in what had become the heartland of

Mormonism itself where both the violence of sorting the righteous from the wicked and the military violence of apocalyptic battle are acts that begin and disperse from Salt Lake City.

A Foreign Invasion of the United States

The Saints' Americanism was highlighted in apocalypticism through unconventional manifestations of patriotism. The idea that the Saints would provide military assistance to defend the nation against an imminent foreign invasion seemed untenable after the trek West. However, in the 1870s, this idea was revived when some prophecy enthusiasts embraced a vision attributed to George Washington, which detailed just such a foreign invasion.[139] The vision first appeared in non-Mormon circles in 1861, presumably after the start of the Civil War, and was written by the journalist Charles Wesley Alexander using the pseudonym Wesley Bradshaw.[140] Bradshaw reportedly learned of the vision from one of Washington's aides, who had heard it from Washington. As a literary device, Bradshaw presented a plausible transmission of the vision; however, readers understood from the way the vision was marketed as a "gem of American literature" and the "First Union Story ever written" that it was intended as a patriotic fiction emphasizing the importance of national union.[141]

The vision followed the conventions of apocalyptic literature with an angel guiding "Washington" through various scenes depicting past and future events. Washington was shown in three wars: the Revolutionary War, the Civil War, and a future war. Because the Civil War was only just beginning when Bradshaw composed the vision, one of its central purposes was to prophesy that the Southern revolt would be thwarted. Washington watched as the Civil War came to a close when "a bright angel, on whose brow rested a crown of light, on which was traced the word UNION [*sic*], bearing the American flag, which he placed between the divided nation, and said: 'Remember, ye are brethren!' Instantly the inhabitants, casting from them their weapons, became friends once more, and united around the national standard."[142]

A third war began as forces (symbolically portrayed as thick black clouds) from Europe, Asia, and Africa combined against the United States. In the clouds, Washington "gleamed a dark-red light, by which I saw hordes of armed men. . . . And I dimly saw these vast armies devastate the whole country, and pillage and burn the villages, towns and cities that I had beheld springing up."[143] While American troops fought back, the nation's salvation came via the arrival of the angel with the Union crown and "legions of bright spirits," who "immediately joined the inhabitants of America, who I perceived were well-nigh overcome, but who, immediately taking courage again, closed up their broken ranks, and renewed the battle." Fighting alongside the angelic hosts, America proved victorious. In the wake of the battle, the angel declared: "While the stars remain, and the heaven send down dew upon the earth, so long shall the Republic last." The angel removed his "crown on which still blazen the word UNION [*sic*]" and placed it on the flag, while the citizenry knelt in reverence and said, "Amen."[144]

Despite originating outside the Mormon faith, this (pseudo-) Washington vision does appear to have influenced the genre of apocalypse visions within the Mormon faith tradition. For example, consider Mosiah Hancock, who recalled hearing Smith prophesy in Nauvoo on the topic of a foreign invasion on the United States. In Hancock's memoir, Smith appears to frame his prophesy along the same lines as the Washington vision: Smith first foretold the events of the Civil War and then turned to the last days conflict. Smith continued:

> The United States will spend her strength and means warring in foreign lands until other nations will say, "Let's divide up the lands of the United States," then the people of the U.S. will unite and swear by the blood of their fore-fathers, that the land shall not be divided. Then the country will go to war, and they will fight until one half of the U.S. army will give up, and the rest will continue to struggle. They will keep on until they are very ragged and discouraged, and almost ready to give up—when the boys from the mountains will rush forth in time to save the American Army from defeat and ruin. And they will say, "Brethren, we are glad you have come; give us men, henceforth, who can talk with God." Then you will have friends, but you will save the country when its liberty hangs by a hair, as it were.[145]

The emphasis on the nation coming to be united echoed Washington's vision's emphasis on "UNION." It was as if Hancock had redefined the "legions of bright spirits" that Washington saw defending the nation as a last days Mormon army. Heaven would defend the United States against these invading armies, but it would defend the nation through "the boys from the mountains."

Although Hancock's memory of his conversation with Smith seemed influenced by Washington's vision, the idea that the Saints would defend the nation militarily had originated in Nauvoo, just as Hancock remembered. The Saints, or some among them, already anticipated a time when the United States would petition the Saints for military support and Smith would take the lead of the U.S. Army in his role as lieutenant general.[146] As with other prophecies, Hancock's visions had elements that were dependent on Joseph Smith and elements influenced by more recent prophecy literature—in this case, Washington's vision.

Another vision that evidences the influence of the Washington vision on Mormon apocalypse is that of Charles D. Evans. In 1894, he had portrayed his visionary foreseeing a "foreign power," one that would attempt to "seize the government and supplant it with monarchy." He "stood trembling," but was comforted when he saw "a power arose in the west which declared itself in favor of the constitution in its original form; to this suddenly rising power every lover of constitutional rights and liberties throughout the nation gave hearty support." The war continued with the new government in place. "The struggle was fiercely contested, but the stars and stripes floated in the breeze, and, bidding defiance to all opposition, waved proudly over the land."[147] Evans watched the new government spread as "[c]ities appeared in every direction," and in clear allusion to the rise of Jackson County, "one of which, in the centre of the continent."[148]

Both traditions, of a foreign invasion of the United States or an American invasion on Utah, promised the reversal of powers. The Kingdom of God would rule triumphant as the lone defenders of the Constitution. The messianic angle was also present in both narratives. Either Mormons would preserve the Constitution because there would be none loyal to its precepts, as was the case in Utah invasion narratives, or they would be the only ones able to defend the nation against foreign invaders, thus preserving the Constitution. Although the specific details of these visions differed, their overarching commitment to American patriotism clearly served as a central theme.

These visions were the product of a community of visionaries who narrated their visions in relationship to one another. Even when these apocalyptic visions seemed to present contradicting futures, prophecy enthusiasts tended to see them as adding detail to or complimentary perspectives on the eschaton. The visions shared crucial plot points, such as the destruction of the wicked, the rise of the Kingdom of God, and divine intervention. The greater chronology of these events was well known—it was external to the individual visions themselves, and acted as a kind of comprehensive timeline against which particular visions could be placed. Therefore, a vision did not need to contain all elements of the apocalypse for readers to know what pieces were missing. Where any particular prophet's vision concluded mattered little: The eventual conclusion of Mormonism's apocalyptic schema ended with events most memorably depicted in the final chapter of the Revelation of St. John—the appearance of the New Jerusalem.

Return to Jackson County

One of the most detailed depictions of the New Jerusalem appeared in Parley P. Pratt's popular fictional apocalyptic, *Angel of the Prairies*, first published posthumously in 1880. Pratt's nameless protagonist visited the densely populated city with its "magnificent temple, which, in magnitude and splendor, exceeded everything of the kind before known upon the earth." His angel guide pronounced the edifice "the sanctuary of freedom, the palace of the great King, and the centre of a universal government." He entered the temple through one of its twelve bejeweled gates and was conducted through the courtyard, the outer court, and finally the temple's inner court, the holy of holies. Each area was punctuated with millennial symbolism.[149]

The large courtyard housed an impressive garden, which showcased the natural beauty of animal and plant life "arranged in the most perfect taste, and with an elegance, neatness and beauty, that might well compare with Eden." The temple's outer court was a museum "calculated to impart a world of information on astronomy, geography, history, geometry, theology, etc." A large painting depicted "huge piles of broken iron, and antique weapons of every description, heaped up together in the greatest confusion . . . and men were represented in the act of beating swords into ploughshares and spears into pruning hooks."[150]

> "These," said the Angel of the Prairies, "are the implements of murder and cruelty with which poor, ignorant, mistaken mortals once made war upon each other; but they have long since been laid aside as useless, and the arts of war are no longer studied or practiced on the earth."[151]

The temple's inner court was a vast throne room "with some thousands of noble and dignified personages, all enrobed in white and crowned with authority, power and majesty, as kings and priests presiding among the sons of God." In a central throne sat a divine personage, who Pratt described as "an aged, venerable looking man. His hair was white with age, and his countenance beamed with intelligence and affection indescribable, as if he were the father of the kingdoms and people over which he reigned. He was clad in robes of dazzling whiteness, while a glorious crown rested upon his brow; and a pillar of light above his head, seemed to diffuse over the whole scene a brilliance of glory and grandeur indescribable. There was something in his countenance which seemed to indicate that he had passed long years of struggle and exertion in the achievement of some mighty revolution, and been a man of sorrows and acquainted with grief. But, like the evening sun after a day of clouds and tempest, he seemed to smile with a dignity of repose." Next to him "sat two others scarcely less venerable, and clad and crowned in the same manner" and then an additional twelve separated from the masses of kings and priests. A voice identified the body as "The Grand Presiding Council organized in wisdom, and holding the keys of power to bear rule over all the earth in righteousness."[152]

Pratt's New Jerusalem, while certainly a better literary production than other visions of the time, was envisioned and composed from the same collective imagination. For instance, Evans's vision also described the city's architectural and natural beauty.[153] As in the Revelation of St. John, the city provided the crowning symbol of the millennium, representing the ultimate shift from the reign of Babylon to the reign of Zion. This was the seat of a worldwide government. Yet, while the Saints had an image of what the New Jerusalem would look like when it arrived, they were also preoccupied with how that arrival itself would come about.

Several visionaries reported seeing the rise of the New Jerusalem. The prophet of the 1877 vision witnessed "the states of Illinois, Missouri, and part of Iowa had been swept clean of its inhabitants and the surrounding country was a complete wilderness." In the recently vacated Jackson County, he saw "Twelve men dressed in their temple robes standing in a square with their hands raised, and it was made known to me that they represented the twelve gates of the New Jerusalem." The prophet watched "a multitude of people coming from various directions to take part in the upbuilding of the city and temple and even the angels were on hand to assist in the glorious work. A great cloud arose above them and many of the saints were clothed in their temple robes."[154] Thus, the miraculous and rapid construction of the temple was performed by a workforce of the faithful and angels. The cloud, a symbol identifying God's presence in the Old Testament, marked the Saints' entrance into sacred time. A disembodied voice declared: "Now is established the Kingdom of our God and His Christ which shall no more be thrown down or given to another people."[155]

The scene from the 1877 vision depicted the miraculous way many Mormons had imagined the coming forth of the New Jerusalem with the exception of a peculiar absence of Native American participation. For instance, according to Bulkley's vision, "[T]he remnants went forth and redeemed the land of Zion. I saw the foundation of the Temple laid there, which had the appearance of a bright lustre."[156] Readers who were aware of Latter-day Saint prophecy would know that the term "remnants" referenced the Mormon understanding of the Native Americans as remnant descendants of the twelve tribes of Israel, and that this section of Bulkley's vision thus implied Native Americans would finish the slaughter of Gentiles still in Jackson County before they would begin the construction of the temple. This was the expected chain of events. Yet, the absence of Indians in the 1877 vision seems significant in charting Mormon understandings of the New Jerusalem. Perhaps it was an accidental oversight; however, a de-emphasis on Indians in the prophecy of the New Jerusalem was also apparent in discourses of the era. Brigham Young, in an effort to promote industry and piety, often stressed that the Saints would have to construct the New Jerusalem themselves. God, he explained, "will not send His angels to gather up the rock to build up the New Jerusalem. He will not send His angels from the heavens to go to the mountains to cut the timber and make it into lumber to adorn the city of Zion. He has called upon us to do this work; and if we will let Him work by, through, and with us, He can accomplish it; otherwise we shall fall short, and shall never have the honor of building up Zion on the earth."[157]

Orson Pratt criticized this perspective in 1875 and blamed the interpretation on Book of Mormon illiteracy. "A great many, without reading these things [in the Book of Mormon], have flattered themselves that we are the ones who are going to do all this work. It is not so; we have got to be helpers." The Saints would only "cooperate with the remnants of Joseph in accomplishing this great work."[158] While some may have been ignorant of what the Book of Mormon said about the Indians building the New Jerusalem, this forgetting may have had more to do with the subsequent history of Mormon–Native relations in the West. The Mormons never amassed the number of Native conversions they had anticipated early on. Instead, they found interactions with indigenous peoples in the Great Basin were complicated and unpredictable. From the perspective of the late nineteenth century, Mormons likely found it hard to believe that those they saw as their unreceptive and sometimes hostile neighbors would become their messiahs. Like Orson Pratt, however, there still remained loyal supporters to the traditional Latter-day Saint understanding of Lamanite millennialism, a subject that will be picked up again in the following chapter.

As noted previously, visionaries differed on where they believed the journey to Missouri would begin geographically and what events would immediately precede it. Bulkley described the final exodus in the wake of the Gentile invasion on Salt Lake City:

> During this time, the Temple in Salt Lake City had been completed, and in one of the rooms situated in one of the towers, Jesus and Joseph, with their council, were setting. Then preparations were made for the fifty thousand [who had been endowed in the temple] to go down to the Centre Stake of Zion, with Jesus and Joseph at their head, riding in their Chariots of fire.[159]

Bulkley's image of the resurrected Joseph Smith and Jesus Christ counseling together with the Saints in the Salt Lake Temple hinted at the fulfillment of Malachi's prophecy that the "Lord . . . shall suddenly come to His temple."[160] Christ and Smith's leadership over the exodus to Jackson County responded to other prophecies. One of Smith's revelations said of the Saints' journey, "mine Angel shall go up before you, & also my presence. And in time ye shall possess the goodly land."[161] Bulkley may have also intended to associate the figure of Joseph Smith with the prophesied guide, "a man who shall lead them like as Moses led the children of Israel," who would lead the Saints to Jackson County.[162] Because church leaders had worked to quash speculation on the identity of this messianic figure, non-schismatic prophets rarely spoke of the leaders who would direct the exodus to Missouri.

These concerns notwithstanding, there was a deep Mormon interest in the figure of this last days messiah. Multiple folk hymns and poetry, forms of expression that often allowed more freedom for speculation, addressed the prophecy. The lyrics of "Zions Future," drafted on February 2, 1862, read:

> "A man" will lead the saints,
> With might, from bondage's hold
> The presence of Christ and angels
> Will eclipse "the rod" of old.

> Then vengeance will spread abroad,
> Like a whirlwind, to every shore;
> And Zion, clothed with glory,
> Will reign for ever more.[163]

The songwriter identified only as Ieuan had woven together the language of Smith's February 24, 1834 revelation, as well as reference to "the rod" that some had associated with this figure. Other hymns directly referenced the appearance of the resurrected Joseph Smith. One written by George D. Watt stated:

> There's a good time coming, Saints, a good time coming,
> When Joseph, our beloved seer, will come again, our hearts to cheer,
> In the good time coming.
> And Hyrum, too, with mighty power will rend our bonds asunder,
> Zion's standard plant on every shore, wait a little longer.[164]

The Saints' deliverer from bondage was placed collectively on the resurrected Joseph and Hyrum Smith.

Some influential Saints publicly speculated on the prophecy. Foremost among them stood the apostle Orson Pratt. While he was agnostic as to who would fulfill this role, on March 9, 1873, he posited three possibilities. First, the man like Moses might be Brigham Young, "our present leader," who could miraculously "have his life spared to lead forth his people like a Moses." Second, he might be a "man [who] is now in existence . . . or someone yet to be born."[165] He did not specify in this instance whether the figure would emerge from the church hierarchy or among the laity. Finally, he hypothesized, the man like Moses could be Joseph Smith, as Pratt had initially understood the revelation during Smith's lifetime. "God's arm is not shortened that he cannot raise him up even from the tomb. . . . And if he feels disposed to send him forth as a spiritual personage to lead the camp of Israel to the land of their inheritance, all right."[166]

While the details varied, most visions and exegesis concerning the return to Jackson County depicted the Saints miraculously delivered from Gentile oppression. Recall that Smith's revelation had declared that the Saints, like the Israelites at the time of Moses, "must needs be led out of bondage by power."[167] How this bondage was imagined varied from one representation to another. In 1875, Pratt publicly pondered the prophecy:

> It seems then that this people, at some future time in their sojourn here in this land, may possibly be in bondage greater than they are at the present time. I try to hope for the best, and to think that the bondage we are in and have been in for years, in consequence of the efforts of those who are striving to take away our rights as American citizens, and to trample us down in the dust; I say I have been in hopes that that would be all the bondage that was meant here in this prophecy, but I do not know but what there may be a greater signification to these words.

One possibility, Pratt offered was that "it may be that we shall have our rights completely taken from us."[168]

In 1886, the same year that Bulkley composed his visionary experience, the apostle Moses Thatcher interpreted Smith's prophecy of a return to Jackson County in a discourse in Cache County. While Pratt had been careful to offer multiple possibilities in reference to each element of the prophecy, Thatcher's statement was more definite. Thatcher predicted that the day would soon come when all government offices in the territory would be "in the hands of our enemies" and that the Saints would be "so burdened with taxes that it will be almost more than human nature can endure." Desperate, the Saints would then "cry to the Lord both by night and by day for deliverance." At this time, before 1891, Thatcher explained, "shall that man like unto Moses be raised up and raise us up and lead us out of bondage, back to Jackson County in the state of Mo. There will be no hesitation, everything will be decisive and prompt, the mountains shall tremble before him, and if there be a tree or anything else in the way of their progress it shall be plucked up by the power of God." The man like Moses would be "no other than the Prophet Joseph Smith in his resurrected body."[169]

A member of the congregation in Cache County recorded and published a lengthy excerpt from the discourse, appending a note that stated, "A servant of God holding the power and keys of the holy apostleship does not speak in this manner for mere pastime; there is more in these utterances than we are apt to attach unless we are aided by the spirit of God. They are calculated to cheer the Saints in the time of trial and persecution."[170] When the document circulated among Thatcher's peers in the Quorum of the Twelve, a controversy ensued. George Q. Cannon and later President John Taylor were concerned that Thatcher had taught a new revelation without consulting with the First Presidency, "independent of the question as to the correctness of what he had taught."[171] Thatcher responded, explaining that he had only referred to items revealed by Joseph Smith. Of course, his fellow authorities knew his source material but were concerned with his seemingly authoritative interpretation of the passage's ambiguities.

There were at least three elements of the prophecy that church leaders wanted to leave uncertain. First, was the identity of the man like Moses. Even a footnote in the latest edition of the Doctrine and Covenants warned that "the one referred to in this prophecy is not yet revealed."[172] The identification of the man like Moses as anyone outside of the living prophet minimized the importance of current church leaders. In 1889, apostle Francis M. Lyman declared "this idea of looking for some great man who had been resurrected to come and deliver Zion was erroneous."[173] In 1879, George Q. Cannon addressed those "who have appeared to think that there has been some power lacking" in the current church leadership, "and have manifested a feeling of restlessness, anticipating the rising of someone who should have greater authority than at present exists."[174] He assured them that spiritual gifts and revelation continued among the Saints.

Second, Thatcher had stated that the expected events would come before 1891. While this was the perspective of many Latter-day Saints, church leaders already had some anxiety about dating the eschaton to such a near date. This will be discussed in detail in the following chapter. Finally, church leaders were also disturbed by Thatcher's prediction of further Gentile harassment and bondage. Like Pratt, they preferred to believe that the Saints had already endured the hardship expected of them. In February 1890, apostle Abraham H. Cannon "proclaimed against the encouragement which is given to the feeling that we must go into bondage in order that the Lord may send 'a Moses' to deliver us. I feel that if we will only do as God has commanded, we need go no further into bondage."[175] With so many present difficulties, the authorities attempted to check what seemed to be pessimism about the future.

Ultimately, the hierarchy's statements discouraging definite interpretations of this prophecy provided a foretaste of the more systematic regulations that would take place after statehood. The concerns held by some of the individuals, most importantly George Q. Cannon, provided the impetus to take the next important step in apocalyptic interpretation: that is, the leveling of these concerns. This leveling would take place in several forms, though it often appeared as official retroactive correction of prior popular interpretations. In December 1886, two official statements, one from Moses Thatcher, decried the accuracy and distribution of Thatcher's statement.[176]

American Reception of Mormon Prophecy

There is a long history of Christian suspicion of marginal groups that emphasized the apocalypse. Such groups were often associated with fanaticism and its corollary violence. In the nineteenth century, Americans were aware of Mormon apocalyptic beliefs, just like they knew Mormons championed polygamy and were proponents of theocracy. Benjamin G. Ferris, John W. Gunnison, Thomas Ford, Richard F. Burton, and several other commentators all agreed that apocalypticism was an essential or, in Ferris's words, "the starting-point" of the faith. The American response was largely negative, although this was not always the case.

There was a time during the Civil War when the war prophecy garnered attention and even some support from the non-Mormon press. In 1861, Walter Murray Gibson, a missionary then in California, wrote to Brigham Young, excited that the prophecy was "widely published," having appeared in "nine papers" in the state.[177] According to a September 1862 newspaper article in the *Hartford Daily Courant*, the *Detroit News* had already "warn[ed] the agitators of the terrible evils which they may bring upon the country, and threatens them with the following prophecy." The essay then quoted the entirety of the war prophecy. The *Hartford Daily Courant* reporter clearly took the prophecy seriously. "Anyhow, so far, it is true. Now, negro regiments are to be brought into the army, which will bring the Northern negroes nearer to the slaves, thus bringing on a slave rebellion."[178] The publication of the war prophecy in these and other venues hinted at a larger search to discover a prophetic frame for the Civil War. During the war, newspapers also published alleged prophecies of Nostradamus, apocryphal biblical texts said to apply to current events, and dreams. In 1862, Richard F. Burton sarcastically suggested the Mormon war prophecy should "be found quite as respectable as the 'Visions of an Aged Nun' and 'The Predictions of Sister Rosa Colomba' " from the 1861 collection of Roman Catholic prophecies entitled *Forewarnings: Prophecies on the Church and Revolution, Antichrist, and the Last Times.* While Burton certainly meant to dismiss both the Mormons and his other outlandish examples, he stated that prophecy was "apparently universally and equally diffused" among all people.[179] Mormons were not special in this regard.

It was not the doom Mormons preached that was frightening to many Americans. It was the doomsayers themselves. As John H. Beadle explained, "It is a law of mind that what we prophecy [*sic*] often we soon come to wish for; and if there were no other cause, the tendency of all their preaching and prophesying is to make them look eagerly for the downfall of our Government."[180] That is to say, to those outside the faith, Mormonism's separatist apocalypticism revealed the Saints' anti-American sentiment. Americans sometimes worried that Mormons might try to fulfill their militaristic fantasies of withstanding the U.S. government.

From the time of the Utah War, some believed that Mormons would invade the United States and reclaim Jackson County. In 1857, Young played on such fears, threatening "if they Commence the war I shall not hold the Indians Still by the rist [*sic*] any longer for white men to shoot at them but I shall let them go ahead & do as they please and I shall Carry the war into their own land."[181] The following year, a *New York Times* correspondent, "Mahomet," addressed Mormonism's "Jackson County Millennium," reporting that one church leader had professed that he expected "that the causes that should bring the Saints back to Jackson County, would not be of a hostile nature, but the softening of Gentile feelings towards them." Some Saints claimed they expected to "quietly await some special miracle that shall bring them to Jackson County." However, "Mahomet" found such claims specious, asserting that "the sentiments of the majority of the Mormons . . . point to a bloody end of Gentile domination." The Saints believed "the Lord helps none who will not help themselves" and, as such, were eager to get started overtaking Jackson County.[182]

Discussion of Mormon hostility and violence increased with reports of the Mountain Meadows massacre, the slaying of 120 non-Mormons by Latter-day Saints and Paiutes in Southern Utah in September 1857. In 1870, journalist Wesley Bradshaw reported rumors "that the Mormon Hierarchy have been maturing plans whereby to conduct a war with the United States. It is asserted that they have spies and emissaries at work in every Navy Yard and Arsenal and gun manufactory in the Country, who at a given signal will in case of Expeditions being ordered against Utah, burn or otherwise disable all such stations."[183]

A curious instance of this anxiety was the New York astrologist Harriet M. Van Hoesen, who apparently tried to start her own movement based on her prediction that "the Mormons will rise up against the gentiles and a plague will cut off the wicked" in February 1891. The only safety from the Mormon hordes was in her "house of refuge which she is building for those who will flee to the hills in the dreadful time of danger."[184] Van Hoesen's expectation that Mormons would strike that month may have been based partly on an astrological calculation, but was also likely due to her knowledge of the 1890–1891 prophecy.

In the majority of cases where the non-Mormon press commented on Mormon prophecy in the nineteenth century, it did so in order to illustrate Mormon anti-Americanism. Even if Mormons would never invade, their theocratic expectations remained in opposition to democracy. In 1876, an account of a visit to southern Utah included mention of an elderly prophecy enthusiast. "He said that they (the Mormons) were building up a kingdom in the heart of the United States, that would finally and in the remarkably short time of twenty-five years swallow up, not only the latter Government, but all the Governments of the globe." The old man assured his listener "that I would live to see his prophecy fulfilled; nay, he went so far to assure me that on the authority of revelation to President Young they expected the Savior to Utah within the next fifteen years, there to live and reign with his faithful Saints, the Mormons, who as a matter of course, would all hold offices under him for the space of a thousand years, while we poor outsiders would keep on dying right and left, as usual among ordinary mortals."[185]

The report of Mr. Kelsey's sermon (earlier cited here) described the messianic role of Mormonism following a global war. "That after the people of the United States had destroyed and been destroyed by other nations, they would look around for a man who would lead in quiet and respect to the arms of Christ and the true Church, and would eventually look to Brigham Young, thus fulfilling the prophecy that Brigham Young would eventually be the chief ruler of the United States, and the Mormon the prevailing religion."[186] While these ambitions and expectations were accurate for nineteenth-century Mormonism, the presentation was meant to cast suspicion over the faith.

In other cases, prophecy was depicted as a strategy to dupe credulous converts. A newspaper in Virginia warned readers of one Mormon missionary who made an annual pilgrimage to the area. This missionary had recently convinced a family to flee to Utah based on his prediction of "distressing times in this nation before the close of 1872. Yes, worse than that witnessed in the late civil war."[187] Memorably, John W. Gunnison explained that non-Mormons could use Mormon claims of foreknowledge to their advantage: "If, in a few short years, they see the great city of New York, its people, its temples, and its wealth; go down into the opening earth, and the sea sing a requiem over the grave—if they see the Protestant world become only known in the records of the past—if a guard of angels in glittering armor descend and guide them back in military array across the desert plains—if they hear the groans of the Asiatic nations, dying in frantic battle, in myriads, on the plains of Palestine; then may they know that the testimony of Joseph was of the 'spirit of prophecy.'"[188]

Conclusion

During the Utah Territorial period, hostility characterized the Saints' relationship with the nation. The presence of federal troops and federal marshals fostered these sentiments, as did aggressive legislation that defined the church institution and its most devoted as criminal. The Mormon production and corresponding consumption of prophecy depicting an American apocalypse increased throughout the decade. While Smith's war prophecy formed the basis of this apocalyptic frame previous to the Civil War, after the Civil War, a new set of vernacular apocalypses grew in popularity and updated the Saints' expectations. The Civil War had not led to the collapse of all nations, but the reversal of powers was still on the horizon. The Kingdom of God would stand triumphant preserving the rights of the U.S. Constitution for all people.

Significantly, these later prophecies originated outside of the church's hierarchy. While messianic anticipations were always problematic for the institution, the vast majority of vernacular apocalyptic expectations went unchallenged; church leaders had little reason to do so. They served their purposes well. Prophecy bolstered the church's authority and strengthened the Saints' resolve to endure in the face of American oppression. Meanwhile, this separatist apocalypticism was frightening to non-Mormon Americans and won the Mormons few friends. The millenarian hopes of Mormonism ensured enduring tensions.

5

The Americanization of Mormon Apocalyptic

> Utah's entrance to Statehood again puts in evidence before the country at large that picturesque and ever puzzling people, the Mormons. . . . How will the Saints adjust themselves to the new conditions? Will their old attitude of distrust and suspicion of the government's official representatives undergo, in time, the complete modification essential to the truest patriotism? Will the sense of persecution be ultimately eliminated from their minds? Will they cease to teach their children that the United States once oppressed them and permitted them to be driven forth as wanderers in the desert? In short, will the bitter memories, strong prejudices, and latent antipathies of the present generation die out with the new? Are they to be an integral or extraneous part of an assimilating republic whose extraordinary digestive powers the refuse of many nations has not impaired?
>
> —William Trowbridge Larned[1]

On the morning of January 4, 1896, as George Q. Cannon made his way to visit Wilford Woodruff, he listened to the sounds of celebration: "steam whistles blowing and bells ringing." That morning's news had "filled [him] with delight and thankfulness that at last, after long years of effort and patient waiting, we had been admitted as a sovereign state into the Union and are now clothed with the full powers of citizenship. It is a most auspicious and happy event." He had not forgotten the injustices of the past, but believed that the era of persecution would soon end. "Certainly the Latter-day Saints, who have suffered so much under the bondage of a Territorial form of government, ought to be the most thankful people upon the face of the earth." Cannon believed statehood was a necessary step for the Saints to fulfill

Terrible Revolution. Christopher James Blythe, Oxford University Press (2020). © Oxford University Press.
DOI: 10.1093/oso/9780190080280.001.0001

their destined messianic role for the nation. "To me it has always appeared clear that we never could be the people that the Lord had predicted and we never could perform the work that had been prophesied concerning our uph[o]lding the constitution of the United States, unless we should be recognized as a sovereign state."[2]

William Trowbridge Larned concluded his article, quoted at this chapter's start, commenting on the place of prophecy among Mormons. He was convinced that "this spirit of prophecy and of heavenly help so pervaded the Mormon in thought and action that it was alike a key to his character and his sustaining faith."[3] Larned also saw this emphasis on prophecy as one of the Mormons' peculiarities that would make their transition to genuine patriots difficult. He recounted prophecies attributed to Joseph Smith and Brigham Young throughout the tradition's history. Larned had personally been warned by "an intelligent Mormon woman" to not travel to New York during 1894, since Woodruff had apparently once prophesied that the city would be hit by a tidal wave that year.[4] Both Cannon's and Larned's reflections hint at an awareness that Mormons in the twentieth century would not be able to view prophecy the same way as had Mormons in the nineteenth century. Larned's comments on prophecy were tied into his initial question concerning ending the Mormons' "distrust and suspicion" of government.[5] As if in response to Larned, Cannon's journal entry offered one example of how the Saints' understanding of prophecy could accommodate an American, rather than separatist, perspective.

In the nineteenth century, Mormons understood the world primarily in dualistic terms. They also actively awaited a reversal of powers, which, in turn, fueled their resentment toward the nation and resistance to the process of "Americanization." Church leaders realized that the radical apocalypticism of the past had to be tempered because it stood in the way of assimilation. This chapter examines how the Latter-day Saint hierarchy encouraged church members' acceptance of their new place within the United States through a regulation of vernacular prophecy, and how in doing so, simultaneously redefined what qualified as appropriate religious discourse among lay believers.

While the types of regulation that occurred at the turn of the century were not new, they were consistent, publicized, and more broadly expressed. Developments in Mormon culture modified the nature of official Mormon apocalypticism and, in turn, how the church's leadership permitted individual Mormons to discuss and imagine their eschatological hopes. The changes in Mormon culture included a delayed expectation in the timing of the Second Coming; the waning of dualism; a de-emphasis on apocalyptic geography; and a suspicion toward certain forms of supernaturalism when they originated from the laity. Ultimately, these factors influenced future apocalyptic discourse; however, decades of prophetic statements from official and unofficial sources continued to sustain older ideas of the apocalypse among Latter-day Saints.

Historian Grant Underwood has argued that in Mormonism the "millenarianism of earlier years tends to be preserved by respect for previous prophetic declarations."[6] According to Underwood, this was because when it came to the Saints, "leader and layman alike, are as loath to contradict what an apostle in the 1800s declared as they are to challenge the writings of Paul."[7] Thus, despite the fact that there were major cultural and theological changes underfoot in turn-of-the-century Mormonism, official statements would rarely refute older ideas. The means by which a new generation of leaders modified the more radical elements of nineteenth-century apocalypticism were instead through the condemnation of prophecy that originated among the laity. The church's regulation and rejection of such vernacular prophecy allowed for a careful rebuttal of those aspects of nineteenth-century prophecy that were no longer conducive to the period in which they lived. Just as important, this regulation of vernacular prophecy produced another long-lasting result: The hierarchy, consciously or unconsciously, defined how the average Latter-day Saint participated in and publicly shared their charismatic experiences with others.

Apocalyptic Imminence in the Late Nineteenth Century

During this period of transition, church leaders and lay believers alike began to question the imminence of prophecy's fulfillment. This conversation initially revolved around the contours of the Saints' expectations for the years 1890–1891. The revelation that Christ would not return until Smith was 85 years old (i.e., December 23, 1890) was added to the new edition of the Doctrine and Covenants in 1876.[8] In subsequent years, a number of voices promoted what was hoped for but not actually stated in the revelation: that Christ would return that year. Among those who advocated for this reading of the revelation were church leaders.

In addition to Moses Thatcher's infamous 1886 sermon discussed in the previous chapter, several apostles weighed in on the Smith prophecy. In 1879, Wilford Woodruff told a conference in Arizona, "There will be no United States in the Year 1890."[9] In 1890, the apostle Anthon Lund declared, "We can be sure [the second coming] is in the near future, because the Lord told Joseph Smith . . . that if he lived to be a certain age, he should see His face, which points to [18]91."[10] Orson Pratt appealed to a recent strain of Christian apocalypticism that held the measurements of the Great Pyramid of Giza contained an exact calendar of the most important prophetic dates. Pratt found what he believed to be an error in the measurements of the pyramid's grand gallery as they were recorded by the most prominent advocate for this position, Charles Piazzi Smyth, in his *Our Inheritance in the Great Pyramid.* Once Pratt input the correct measurements, he was able to show a "pyramid date" of April 6, 1830, along with another date that demonstrated "some remarkable phase of the history of the world will be enacted in the year 1891."[11] While not an apostle, Angus McDonald published the influential *Prophetic Numbers* in 1885, which used Daniel's prophecy of weeks to argue that the Saints would possess Jackson County by 1891.[12]

As the prophetic date grew near, the Saints came to modify their expectations. At the October 1890 conference, held only two months before what would have been Smith's 85th birthday, multiple speakers addressed the prophecy. Seventy B. H. Roberts read the text of the revelation and warned the Saints that although he believed "that whatever the Lord has in mind to accomplish in that year will be performed. It may be something, however, that would scarcely create a ripple." Thus, the church should not be surprised if "the greatness of what shall occur in 1891 will not be comprehended until succeeding years."[13] Several speakers argued that each successive year would bring more signs of the times, but too many events remained that needed to occur before the Second Coming for it to take place the following year. George Q. Cannon remarked that he believed "there has been altogether too much agitation" on the timing of the Second Coming. "It is not one year alone; but all the years between us and the coming of our Lord will be big with events. They will be crowded with stupendous occurrences."[14]

The October conference attested to Mormonism's continued emphasis on millenarianism even while the speakers warned against anticipating the Second Coming in 1890–1891. Woodruff, the church president, shared a dream he had of the spirit world where "all seemed to be in a hurry." Later in the dream, Joseph Smith explained that while previous dispensations had sufficient time to prepare for the Second Coming, "we in this dispensation have not had time." Woodruff asked him how much time remained and Smith answered, "That is not revealed to us, nor never will be until the hour comes; but we have much work to do to prepare ourselves for the event."[15] Woodruff noted that he had "always believed from the revelations that we never would know the exact time of the coming of the Son of man; and I am more convinced of this from what the prophet said to me in my dreams."[16] Official discouragement of date-setting was effective, but in many cases, Latter-day Saints had already developed their own alternative explanations for why Jesus would not return in 1890.

Some believed that the prophecy did not refer to the timing of the Second Coming, but rather to a preliminary appearance of Christ to the faithful. In 1886, John M. Whitaker wrote to his friend Anson Call, known for his account of the Rocky Mountain prophecy, to ask whether he had heard "the prophet say what Time the Savior would come to His people, and scenes incident to that time?"[17] In response, Call wrote: "I have never heard him say what year, but I have formed an opinion from his conversation that in 1891 he would make his appearance to certain individuals of the priesthood not to reign as King, but would deliver His people and the Gentile reign would begin to wane and His people would begin to have dominion, and the Law of God would have influence in all the civilized nations of the earth. That the nations would be in commotion at this time."[18] In January 1891, John Steele similarly expected that "if Jesus does not come this year, that some will be privileged to see him in the Temple of the Lord and no doubt the Prophet Joseph Smith also."[19]

Another common response to the prophecy was to push back the date. In 1890, Benjamin F. Johnson, a surviving member of Joseph Smith's Nauvoo inner circle, had already decided it would happen later than many of the Saints assumed. "This is the year to which many have looked as a period for great events. To me it is the middle hour of the night of darkness, before the Millenial [*sic*] dawn or the coming of Christ in His power." Johnson reasoned that just as the Bible had defined a generation as 120 years, the events of the last days would take place over 120 years from the founding of the church in 1830. This would leave the Saints with "another sixty years in which to preach the gospel, gather the saints, redeem the center stake of Zion, build the holy temple, convert the Lamanites, rebuild Jerusalem and for Israel to return from the North." When it came to the promise that Joseph Smith would see Jesus in the flesh during his eighty-fifth year, Johnson speculated, "[W]ho shall say that Joseph, with others who had already obtained their 'White Robes,' did not at that time come fourth [*sic*] through the Resurrection, to see the face of the Saviour as was promised."[20] This idea that Smith's prophecy might only refer to his own introduction to Jesus in the afterlife was common.

There is no indication that Mormons were devastated when Christ did not appear in 1890 or 1891. Many continued to expect the Second Coming would occur in their lifetimes or even in the very near future. Yet, a strain of skepticism and disinterest emerged particularly among younger Saints. In 1894, a Latter-day Saint student at the University of Michigan lamented that many of his generation were "growing indifferent and skeptical. . . . [S]ome begin to think the prophecies of the wicked too strong and that our people wrongly interpret the scriptures and that the destructions will not come in our days."[21] By 1903, Benjamin F. Johnson also noticed the decline in millennial fervour. "We ware [*sic*] over Seventy years ago taught by our leaders to believe that the coming of Christ and the Milinial [*sic*] rein [*sic*] was much nearer *Then*. Than we believe it to be *now*."[22] In 1911, an article in the *Woman's Exponent* compared the "earlier days of the Church, when . . . 'Mormon' Elders quot[ed] from Isaiah and Ezekiel and Daniel and so on" with the present when "some of us have almost forgotten these first lessons in the Latter-Day work; and we only talk of the prevailing every-day topics usually."[23]

By the mid-twentieth century, there were still apocalypticists who predicted imminent eschatological events, but increasingly this sort of rhetoric was considered outside of the mainstream. Church leaders and members still shared the belief that they lived in the last days, but those days could extend generations. The most likely scenario to explain why this shift occurred was not the influence of those who had become jaded with waiting for the apocalypse, but rather that the Saints' need for an imminent reversal of powers was mollified after persecution and prosecution came to an end in the 1890s.

The Decline of Mormon Dualism

At the core of nineteenth-century Mormon discourse lay a vision of humanity as starkly divided between the righteous and the wicked. For Latter-day Saints, the wicked included American political leaders, the legal system, and religious competitors. The church's approach to politics at the end of the nineteenth century provides the clearest examples of their remapping of the world and the corresponding decline of apocalyptic dualism. In 1891, the year after the Manifesto, the church disbanded the Mormon "People's Party," which had until very recently dominated state elections. In turn, leaders encouraged the Saints to affiliate with either the Republican or Democratic parties. The church, which had previously presented the American political system as inherently fraught with divisiveness and thus contrary to the nature of Zion, now pledged their support for the separation of church and state.[24] The collapse of the church's overt influence on politics and Utah's admission as a state in the Union were necessary first steps in the process of Americanization. As the impulse to reject an American identity faded with the increasing cultural and political integration of the Mormons, the Latter-day Saints came to see themselves as patriots—not so different from loyal Americans in other regions of the country. The Spanish-American War cemented this evolving aspect of Mormon identity.

During the Civil War, Mormons remained neutral while professing their loyalty to the Constitution and decrying a flawed federal government. The eagerness by which Latter-day Saints served in the Spanish-American War demonstrated just how far the church had come with fostering what other Americans would recognize as patriotism. However, questions remained regarding how a Mormonism invested in the future millennium could fight in secular wars. At the April 1898 general conference, apostle Franklin D. Richards urged the Saints to see themselves as pacifists enabling the fulfillment of the prophecy that "ev[e]ry man that will not take his sword against his neighbour [*sic*] must needs flee unto Zion for safety."[25] Richards's views mirrored the Mormon position that was dominant during the Civil War, yet, following statehood, his sentiments were clearly in the minority.[26] At the same conference, George Q. Cannon opposed Richards's sentiments:

> I do not want to see our young men get filled with the spirit of war and be eager for the conflict God forbid that such a spirit should prevail in our land, or that we should contribute in any manner to the propagation of a spirit of that kind! But one may say, "Is it not our duty to defend our country and our flag? Is it not our duty to maintain the institutions which the Lord has given to us?" Certainly it is. God has commanded us to be ready to lay down our lives whenever it shall be necessary. . . . If it should be to defend our religion, we have in days past shown our fearlessness in that direction. Speaking generally, our people have not been afraid to lay down their lives for their religion. We should be equally willing, if it should be necessary, to

> lay down our lives for our country, for its institutions, for the preservation of its liberty that these glorious blessings and privileges shall be preserved to all mankind, and especially to those with whom we are immediately connected.[27]

Cannon's position would become the standard LDS view on war thereafter. When the United States entered World War I in 1917, "church leaders showed no disposition to do other than follow the mainstream of national sentiment."[28] That year, Franklin P. Lane, the secretary of the interior, spoke in the Salt Lake Tabernacle. During his discourse, he commented on the day's patriotic festivities: "I have seen inspiring sights before, but never before has one so touched my heart as did your magnificent military parade which I witnessed in the streets of Salt Lake tonight. Oh, how I wish President Wilson himself could have seen it. . . . We saw the streets of Salt Lake lined with the men and women who are giving their sons in response to the call of war and I saw no tears, only smiles, on the faces of those who are making the greatest sacrifice that can be made and seeking it gladly for the sake of liberty."[29] Such a scene was above suspicion; the Mormons' patriotism was unquestionable.

An Americanizing shift occurred even within Latter-day Saint millenarian thought. In 1918, the apostle James Talmage published an article in the *Atlanta Constitution* entitled "Perpetuity of American Nation Assured by Prophecy." He argued that while World War I had taken journalists and politicians around the globe by surprise, Joseph Smith was vindicated in his foresight of an "imminent outpouring of war upon all nations." Talmage explained that the United States had a special destiny and that the Constitution and Declaration of Independence "constitute[d] a pattern by which all governments of the nations shall be shaped." It was partly through this means that prophecies—"that out of this land, which [in] solemn truth is the land of Zion, shall go forth the law of the Lord unto the world at large"—would be fulfilled.[30]

> It is not written in the book of destiny that America shall bow the knee to autocracy; but, to the glorious contrary. It is inscribed in the role of the Divine purpose, that this, the land of Zion, shall be the haven of refuge to the oppressed: "And it shall be said among the wicked: Let us not go up to battle against Zion, for the inhabitants of Zion are terrible; wherefore we cannot stand. And it shall come to pass that the righteous shall be gathered

out from among all nations, and shall come to Zion, singing with songs of everlasting joy" (Doctrine and Covenants 45:70–71).[31]

Only a few years prior, Latter-day Saints would have universally read these verses to mean that the wicked would come to fear the Saints in Zion. Within the context of this new, emergent sense of American patriotism, however, the verses instead came to illustrate America's special place in the grand scheme of things. Mormons were beginning to see the United States as a "redeemer nation" in stark distinction from the separatist rhetoric of the past. According to a newspaper report on a sermon Talmage preached in Iowa on this same theme, he "disclaimed any desire to assert pre-eminence on the part of his people, for they are one, he said, with the mighty citizenry of the country in the determined effort to put down tyranny and establish freedom as the boon of humanity."[32]

Despite the church's sincere efforts at Americanization, the nation's suspicion did not end overnight. Statehood was only the first sign of America's willingness to embrace the repentant Mormon. Historian W. Paul Reeve has demonstrated that it was during this period of transition that the Saints gained acceptance among everyday Americans as "Whites."[33] Regional and denominational antipathy against Mormons remained, but the degree of othering that occurred in the era of polygamy was no more.[34] Mormons recognized this change in American sentiment. In 1937, Mormon prophet Heber J. Grant pronounced that "the day of persecution and of slander and of lying [about Mormonism] has almost disappeared."[35] The following year, he expressed his gladness for "the goodwill and friendship that has developed among all classes of people at home and abroad toward the LDS church during my lifetime. In place of early-day persecution and bitterness we now enjoy high regard and happy associations with all denominations."[36] Of course, there were those who met the end of persecution with skepticism. A particularly skeptical Latter-day Saint, Heber Bennion, decried the church's new position. "Some insist that the Gentiles have repented because they have quit persecuting us, but why have they quit? Is it not that we have surrendered objectionable principles, and joined with them heart and soul in their financial policies, in their politics and social life? What grounds have they for persecuting us after *unconditional surrender*?"[37]

Yet, the vast majority of Saints embraced their newfound acceptance. This shift in the American public's attitude resulted in a corresponding shift among Mormons themselves. The Saints no longer benefited from depicting their fellow Americans or their government as villains. As they remapped their identity onto mainstream America, their previous apocalyptic dualism proved a problematic source of separation from the cultural and geographic communities with which they sought integration. The rhetoric of apocalyptic dualism lost its strength, thus opening up new space for a reworking of the apocalyptic within the early twentieth-century Mormon imagination.

The Gathering

The geographic dimensions of the Mormon apocalypse also evolved during this period of transition. Before the late 1890s, Mormon leaders taught recent converts that it was their religious duty to relocate to the church's headquarters, wherever those headquarters were established at the time. By the end of the century, Saints had gathered within a series of locations: in Ohio, Missouri, Illinois, Utah, and even Mexico and Canada. Latter-day Saints gathered to separate themselves from the lands of the wicked in order to escape divine judgments. They believed God would protect them, but he could only do so if they were not in physical proximity to the targets of his indignation. In the meantime, the Saints gathered to avoid Gentile influences and persecution.

In the late nineteenth century, the church's leadership began to instruct missionaries to de-emphasize the gathering. They recognized the problem of providing employment for all those who might emigrate. George Q. Cannon expressed his hope that while the converts stayed in their countries of origin, their "faith will become stronger, and they will be better able to withstand the trials and difficulties they will have to contend with when they do emigrate to Zion."[38] Gathering to Zion was a major sacrifice and may have been one reason a potential convert was hesitant to be baptized. Historian Thomas G. Alexander described the church's approach on immigration to the West during this period as "an essentially neutral attitude," in which "no inducements were used, but members who decided to emigrate were not stopped."[39] Even in Cannon's 1898 sermon, he had not discarded the notion of gathering, but rather had merely urged new converts to "not be anxious to break up their homes to gather to Zion."[40] Over the coming decades, there were more forceful prohibitions against gathering.[41] Eventually, church leaders redefined Zion to encompass wherever the Saints resided, leaving

Mormons little reason to relocate.[42] They could, in theory, claim the benefits of being a twentieth-century Mormon wherever they lived.

As Zion became an increasingly geographically ambiguous and dislocated concept in Mormon thought, so, too, did Babylon. Instead of calling for the Saints to abandon a literal place, they were commanded to flee "spiritual Babylon," the symbolic site of wickedness.[43] And for the Mormons who did move, leaving behind both the American East as well as European homelands, immigration was no longer understood as a flight from impending destructions. By the mid-twentieth century, Mormons had established congregations in cities they once believed would soon be destroyed. By the end of the twentieth century, belief in location-specific destructions was so removed from Mormon thought that the church built temples in Washington, D.C., Boston, and New York City—cities that were once prominent settings for the apocalypse in Mormon thought.

Latter-day Saints continued to expect that natural disasters, disease, famine, and war would ravage the earth before the Second Coming. Sermons and articles in church periodicals still periodically pointed to global events as "signs of the times." The difference was that Mormon leaders no longer specified which places and peoples were particularly worthy of a display of divine wrath. They were increasingly uncomfortable identifying human suffering with God's chastisement. In October 1923, a month after the devastation of the Great Kantō Earthquake in Japan, James Talmage stated: "What has been called the greatest calamity in history is fresh in our minds. . . . I have only to say that the occurrence of such earthquakes is in accordance with predictions. The Lord forbid that I should assume to pass judgment upon those who are immediately affected, upon those who have lost their lives through such catastrophies [*sic*]. It is beyond the wisdom of men to correctly deduce results by applying general laws or causes to individual cases; and whenever the judgments of the Lord are permitted to fall upon the earth and upon its inhabitants, there are many of the innocent who suffer with the guilty."[44] While nineteenth-century church leaders warned members not to rejoice in the world's suffering, this sort of compassionate reticence to connect tragic events to God's wrath was a novel development. It was a sign that Mormonism was no longer disconnected from the outside world.

Mormons continued to believe that Jackson County would one day be the New Jerusalem. Lorenzo Snow, who served as Mormonism's Prophet, Seer, and Revelator between 1898 and 1901, was particularly emphatic in his belief that a mass return to Jackson County would occur in the near future. On

November 7, 1900, he told a congregation, "There are many here under the sound of my voice, probably a majority who will have to go back to Jackson County and assist in building the temple."[45] That year, the church established a mission office in nearby Kansas City. For many Saints, the church's renewed presence in the region came as a sign that the redemption of Zion was soon to unfold. One of the missionaries explained to a correspondent for the *Chicago Tribune* that the church's plan for the mission was "to lay the foundation of the work which will culminate in the building of the temple certainly to come." There would be "a great many [that] will come here from Utah. . . . Just when we will come to Independence will be hard to say. But that it will be soon is a certainty." The missionary assured the correspondent, "When we come we expect to buy all the land needed for our city, the new Zion."[46] He was correct. While there was not an official gathering to Jackson County in the twentieth century, in 1904, the church purchased a 26-acre lot of land that was originally intended for the Jackson County temple complex.[47] Cultural geographer Craig S. Campbell summed up this transition in Mormonism's relationship with Jackson County as a change "from the idea of an imminent return to a concept of a gradual purchasing of sacred plots and establishing a mission presence there."[48] Despite the potential implications for a Mormon presence in Independence, public discourse surrounding a last days gathering there seemed to quickly dissipate.

For many Latter-day Saints, the end of the literal gathering to the Rocky Mountains also muted the apocalyptic expectations for Utah. Mormons remained aware that prophets had declared the Salt Lake Temple and Ensign Peak as fulfillments of Isaiah's prophecies. However, the average Mormon no longer envisioned a mass scramble to the Rocky Mountains prior to great destructions or mass persecutions occurring elsewhere. Utah already played its role in preserving the Latter-day Saints during a period of intense persecution. A vestige of the gathering remains to this day and is confined to a common fantasy about participating in the events of Adam-Ondi-Ahman and the New Jerusalem in Missouri.

Suspicion toward Vernacular Religious Experience

Another transition that altered Mormon conceptions of the apocalypse was the church's changing relationship to supernaturalism. In 1892, apostle Marriner Merrill referred to "the skepticism which is so common at the present day, even among some who profess to be Saints, concerning things somewhat supernatural."[49] There were numerous reasons for this. The church's first generation was dying at a rapid pace and with them passed the commitment to early Mormon charismata. Perhaps the most significant dynamic to shape twentieth-century Mormon apocalypticism was the hierarchy's growing suspicion of supernaturalism among the laity.

This shift in perspective was particularly detrimental to the popularity of the more dramatic spiritual gifts. That the interpretation of dreams had fallen out of repute was evident by a 1904 observation from Emmeline B. Wells, then editor of *The Woman's Exponent*: "Aunts Presendia [H. Kimball] & Zina [D. H. Young] used to interpret dreams for us but now there is no one to do it"[50] (see Figure 5.1). Visions and tongues had also declined in the new century. In 1904, the *Improvement Era* published a reflection from an early Mormon convert who had recently met a returned missionary who "had never in his life heard anyone speak in tongues."[51] The author noted "the remark was somewhat of a shock to me; because in the early days of the Church—where I was reared—there were so many of the Saints who enjoyed the gifts, and there were none among my acquaintances who had not heard the sweet sound of the gift of tongues." He recalled that the early Saints had considered tongues "the relating of dreams and prophesying, as an essential part of the latter-day gospel."[52] Now these gifts were almost universally absent among the laity. Because these supernatural gifts were the most prominent means by which Mormons brought forth new apocalyptic scenarios, their decline led to the decline of the tradition at large.

There were still those—albeit very few—eager to share their dreams and revelations about the last days. In 1898, the *Deseret News* published an article warning church members of the dangers of vernacular revelations. While the editorial decried modern spiritualism as inherently sinister, it acknowledged "another class of spiritual or mystical manifestations which cannot be set down as evil in their source or tendency, yet which ought not to be relied upon too strongly by members of the Church in weighty matters of faith conduct. To this class belong dreams, visions, prophecies, interpretations of Scripture, etc. that come through unofficial channels." For those that received these revelations, they should be "prized in a spirit of humility and gratitude." However, the article warned members that some "occurrences of this character may originate in sources that are not divine, and even members of the Church may, in consequence, be misled or seriously deceived." They should be careful to "test" and "compare" the manifestations with "the principles

Figure 5.1 Photo of Zina D. Huntington Young (1821–1901), third general Relief Society president and known for her practice of spiritual gifts. After her death and the death of her sister, Presendia Kimball, another prominent woman Emmeline B. Wells declared that no women able to interpret dreams still lived. Courtesy of the Church History Library.

of truth as revealed to and accepted by the Church."[53] The 1898 article concluded succinctly: "Doctrine, prophecy and revelation which come through or are endorsed by the proper authorities of the Church, may be accepted and relied upon implicitly by its members in all the world; but the Saints should be guarded in receiving such instructions through other sources."[54]

Only church leaders could be trusted to discern whether a revelation was legitimate.

Throughout this period, leaders emphasized the potential dangers of charismatic gifts. George Q. Cannon declared a common sentiment of the period: "[I]f angels were to minister unto some men—probably the great bulk of men—it would prove their overthrow, for the reason that they are not fitted to receive those blessings. How often has it been the case in branches of the Church that men and women who have received the gifts of the Spirit have been almost overthrown because of the goodness of God to them!"[55] As Cannon explained, even if a spiritual encounter was legitimate, recipients might also be overcome with pride and come to see themselves as superior to others, including their church leaders. Wilford Woodruff took a different approach in discouraging the Saints from seeking elaborate visions or angelic visitations. He argued that charismatic gifts were inferior to the revelations received by the gift of the Holy Ghost.[56] Church leaders encouraged internalized religious experience, while at times even downplaying their own manifestations, as was the case with Woodruff or in the case of other leaders acknowledging they had never had such experiences but had been guided by the spirit.[57] These approaches highlight an underlying tension within Mormonism: Its claims to legitimacy came through a series of individual supernatural experiences, and yet in order to maintain that legitimacy of the institution during this period of change, practices surrounding individual supernatural experiences needed to be discouraged and even eventually delegitimized.

Yet, apostles continued to recount their own visions and dreams. In doing so, they fortified the implicit idea that such supernatural and charismatic gifts were legitimate only when coming through the appropriate institutionalized channels. In 1896, George Q. Cannon testified before a general conference, "I know that Jesus lives, for I have seen him."[58] In 1900, apostle Marriner Merrill narrated a dream in which he was shown Satan with a company of evil spirits camped outside of the Logan Temple determined to prevent the Saints from performing the sacred rituals there.[59] In 1918, Joseph F. Smith shared a visionary experience he had about the spirit world that would later be canonized in the Doctrine and Covenants.[60] Thus, this period was not characterized by a decline in supernatural experiences among general authorities, but rather was characterized by a decline in the credence such experiences were given when claimed by lay members.[61]

Church leaders actively discouraged public sharing of vernacular prophecy. In July 1933, apostle Joseph Fielding Smith visited Heber J. Grant, then president of the church, to express his concerns with a bishop, Archie Graham, who had given lectures on "his spirit leaving the body" when he suffered from Spanish influenza. His visions of the spirit world were recorded in a statement entitled, "A Visit Beyond the Veil," that may have been circulated during the period.[62] Five days after Smith spoke with Grant, Grant met with Graham for a "long talk." According to Grant's journal: "I assured him I thought it was a mistake for him to go around delivering his lectures. He thanked me and gave me to understand he would discontinue doing this."[63] The result of this kind of active regulation of the gifts meant that the Saints increasingly came to consider the communal sharing of vernacular prophecy and charismata as taboo. In 1938, Joseph Fielding Smith preached against holding special meetings for individuals to "relate remarkable visions or revelations claimed by these individuals to have been given to them. This is wrong."[64]

This was not the end of lay prophecy, but Mormons were increasingly inclined to be suspicious of the vernacular supernatural. Visionaries became hesitant to share their prophecies now outside of the mainstream. The result of this decline in the acceptability of vernacular prophecy among the laity meant that a significant channel through which Mormon apocalypticism had been promulgated was, in essence, shut down. The diminishing evidence for vernacular apocalypticism among the Mormons of this time is not necessarily evidence of a waning belief in the Second Coming, but rather marks a cultural shift surrounding the apocalypse itself. The Mormon concept of the apocalypse shifted into an institutionally regulated space.

A Twentieth-Century Hierarchical Response to Messianic Prophecy

The dominant prophecy discourse promoted by church leaders took on an Americanized perspective. It no longer depended or supported vernacular visions, but instead drew on scripture and accepted statements of Joseph Smith. Few commentators would mention destructions on specific locations. Three major statements issued in 1905, 1913, and 1918, respectively, demonstrated the church's ongoing regulation of vernacular apocalypticism on subjects of messianism, vernacular prophets, and pseudonymous prophecies. These critiques allowed Mormons to alter their perceptions of the apocalypse without disowning the voices of the past.

Many Latter-day Saint apocalypticists outside of the hierarchy condemned this Americanization. In the hands of these critics, prophecy became a tool to protest the direction of the church. An early example of this move is found in Angus McDonald's "The Mormons Have Stepped Down and Out of Celestial Government. The American Indians Have Stepped Up and Into Celestial Government," published in 1892. The four-page tract championed the Ghost Dance movement and the massacre at Wounded Knee as the fulfillment of Lamanite apocalypticism, which signaled, in McDonald's reading, the corresponding divine rejection of the Mormon Church. The pamphlet opened with a criticism of a *Deseret News* headline from January 1892, which read "1890 has passed, and no Messiah has come." McDonald objected: "Had the Church-organ, *The News*, added, 'to us,' the statement would not have misled thousands of its devoted readers."[65] McDonald alluded to stories of a personal visit of the Christian messiah to the followers of a northern Paiute prophet, Wovoka, at Walker Lake, Nevada, in March 1890.

Wovoka, or Jack Wilson as he was known by Whites, had seen a series of visions in the late 1880s. Wovoka's visions, steeped in Christian millenarianism, included his ascension to heaven, where he was taught to instruct Native peoples to live in peace with one another and to perform the communal Ghost Dance. The dances would usher in a utopian era when the earth would be renewed, the messiah would appear, the buffalo would return, the righteous dead would be resurrected, and Whites would no longer oppress Indians. Accounts from Ghost Dance adherents differed on whether this meant Whites would be destroyed, merely left out, or instead integrated into the new order.[66]

Wovoka's devotees congregated in Nevada in 1890, hoping to see "the Indian messiah." Wovoka had told his followers that "Jesus is now upon the earth."[67] The sources contradict one another on the identity of this messiah. Some understood Wovoka to mean that he was the messiah in question. Porcupine, a prominent acolyte, claimed to have seen Wovoka with the stigmata, that is, literally bearing the wounds of the Christian messiah.[68] Most accounts suggest Ghost Dance adherents believed the messiah was a heavenly being outside of the group of believers who appeared to the faithful in vision. Whether this being was Jesus or a distinctive Native messiah was contested.[69] The press covered the Indian "messiah craze." One conspiracy theory even alleged that Mormons, to manipulate the Natives, had arranged for an imposter to pretend to be Jesus Christ.[70]

While many Americans would come to associate the Ghost Dance with violence and fanaticism, Mormons initially saw great significance in reports describing the movement. Mormon leaders seemed conflicted. They hoped that Wovoka's disciples would fulfill Book of Mormon prophecies, but they were also skeptical of or even disturbed by rumors that Jesus had appeared to these non-Mormons. Susa Young Gates, editor of *The Young Woman's Journal*, noted that "few, if any, of our leading Brethren doubt the probability of a certain, if exaggerated, foundation for these stories"[71] (see Figure 5.2). In 1889, when asked for his views on the burgeoning movement, Wilford Woodruff acknowledged the Saints expected the Indians "to receive many manifestations in the last days . . . perhaps of the three Nephites" although he felt the reports did "not inspire us with much confidence." He thought Indians were superstitious—"their tendency, as we understand, is to accept alleged supernatural manifestations with a great deal of credulity." Therefore, he encouraged Mormons to postpone judgment on the matter.[72] Joseph F. Smith also doubted that Ghost Dance adherents had seen Jesus Christ, although he seemed more confident than Woodruff that they had encountered one of the Three Nephites.[73]

Angus McDonald's 1892 pamphlet drew on this initial enthusiasm for the Ghost Dance, but presented the appearance of the messiah to the disciples of Wovoka as the very fulfillment of the Saints' 1890 expectation. That Christ appeared to Natives and not to the Mormons signaled the LDS Church's apostasy. McDonald claimed that those Indians who had attended a particularly important gathering at Walker Lake in March 1890 had been previously "notified by the three Nephites." It was during this meeting that the messiah personally ordained "Twelve Disciples"[74] and invested them with "a dispensation of the Celestial Kingdom of God, the gospel in the covenant of consecration, a perfect oneness in all things."[75] McDonald's assurance that these Native Americans would live the law of consecration was the crux of his argument that they would succeed where the church had failed to live with all things in common. The final united orders—Mormon communal villages—had ceased practicing consecration in the mid-1880s.

McDonald emphasized Mormonism's expectation of last days violence between Gentile and Native. The conflict had already begun with the federal army's slaughter of 150 Sioux performing the Ghost Dance at Wounded Knee. "The massacre of Wounded Knee; the butchery of Sitting Bull; the

Figure 5.2 Susa Young Gates (1856–1933) was the editor of *The Young Woman's Journal* and *Relief Society Magazine*. She was also a collector and advocate of vernacular prophecy. Courtesy of the Church History Library.

imprisonment of Short Bull and others; the breaking up of reservations and the attempts to destroy the treaty stipulations above mentioned by forcing the mark of the Beast, citizenship and statehood, upon the American Indians . . . will ultimately terminate in a war of extermination."[76] Although the term would not be coined for at least two or three decades, McDonald's writings were some of the earliest rumblings of Mormon fundamentalism, a term used to describe the larger movement of individuals, networks, and eventually institutions that rejected one or more aspects of Mormonism's Americanization. The same ideas would be transmitted through the decades by those committed to an 1890 appearance of Jesus. In succeeding decades, some came to believe an "Indian Prophet"—sometimes believed to be one of the "Twelve Disciples"—was leading a group of righteous Native believers somewhere in the Yucatan.

Many prophecy enthusiasts who opposed the church's stance on plural marriage, communalism, and political neutrality championed Smith's November 27, 1832, revelation, published in the Doctrine and Covenants in 1876. Joseph Smith had included the revelation in a letter to W. W. Phelps, then the editor of the church's Missouri-based newspaper, concerning the establishment of Mormon communalism in Jackson County. The relevant portion read:

> And it shall come to pass that I, The Lord God, will send one mighty and strong, holding the scepter of power in his hand, clothed with light for a covering, whose mouth shall utter words, eternal words; while his bowels shall be a fountain of truth, to set in order the house of God, and to arrange by lot the inheritances of the saints whose names are found, and the names of their fathers, and of their children, enrolled in the book of the law of God. While that man, who was called of God and appointed, that putteth forth his hand to steady the ark of God, shall fall by the shaft of death, like as a tree that is smitten by the vivid shaft of lightning.[77]

The revelation promised a messianic figure who would lead the Saints' efforts to live communally and assign them their inheritances (i.e., personal property) in Jackson County. He would "set in order the house of God." A second figure, who was "called of God," would attempt to "steady the ark of God" and would be killed. The revelation compared the second figure to the Levite priest, Uzzah, who unlawfully steadied the Ark of the Covenant—an act against priestly procedure—and was "smote" by the divine and died.[78]

Nineteenth-century dissenters had periodically used the November 27, 1832, revelation to promote their individual movements, but the prophecy would not become a locus of dissent until the early twentieth century. In fundamentalist circles, it was read as a prediction that a messianic figure would emerge outside the usual church hierarchy to replace a fallen (and wicked) church leader. This was especially the case following the Reed Smoot hearing of 1904. After the hearing, several men claimed God had chosen them to replace Joseph F. Smith, the church's sixth president. Individually, they presented themselves as the One Mighty and Strong and Smith as the man who would die while attempting to steady the ark. While this condemnation of Joseph F. Smith may have been partly due to the "second manifesto" (his pronouncement that the church would excommunicate those who participated in further plural marriages), it probably had more to do with the reception of Smith's testimony at the hearing.

Smoot had been elected to the U.S. Senate in 1903 and a year later became the subject of a highly publicized hearing to determine whether he as a Mormon apostle was fit to hold office. The Senate subpoenaed eight of the church's top leaders to answer questions on the nature of the faith and politics.[79] Some Latter-day Saints had expected their prophet would take a dramatic stand against the Saints' accusers. Instead, when it was Joseph F. Smith's turn, he cautiously answered the senators' questions, "minimiz[ing] his role in church government," as a means to rebuff the allegation that the church was involved in a political theocracy in Utah.[80] Smith identified himself as president of the church and, when pressed whether the Saints recognized him as a Prophet, Seer, and Revelator, only acknowledged that he "supposed" that was the case.[81] Some Mormons found one exchange particularly disappointing. When Senator George Frisbie Hoar asked Smith if he had ever had a revelation, he responded in the negative.[82] In context, Smith referred to the type of dialogic revelations that could be added to the Doctrine and Covenants, rather than other forms of inspiration. He identified the most recent revelation as one dictated by John Taylor in 1882, although he agreed that the Manifesto should also be considered a revelation.[83] Critics both within and without the church made much of this exchange. In March 1905, Smith defended his remarks to the Saints:

> For me to say—which was the very end that my critics and my inquisitors were endeavoring to get me to say, in order that I might be led into that trap which they had made for me—to say that God had given to me a revelation upon some new doctrine, or theory, or principle, or precept, or anything to be written, to be observed or handed down as a guide to the Church, would have been untrue. I could not have said that, for He has not done this. But has God revealed to me His mind and His will? Has He made manifest to me a knowledge of His truth by and through the spirit of revelation? Did you ever hear me denying that? No; no man has ever heard me deny that.[84]

Yet, some found Smith's explanation unsatisfying. The Saints expected prophets to receive dramatic visions, dialogic revelation, and theophanies. Smith's candid acknowledgment regarding the types of spiritual experiences he had had seemed to some an admission that he did not measure up to his predecessors.

Samuel Eastman, a convert from Great Britain, would later offer his own cynical, but far from unique, impression of the trial as he read it in the newspaper coverage in Utah:

> The Church heads were critically and keenly questioned as to their being prophets, seers and revelators, and had they ever received such a thing as a divine revelation to their people, and did they really claim to be revelators? I am sorry to say that their answers were largely in the negative on this. If they were truly what they claimed to be here at home among their people, then what a glorious and fitting opportunity they had presented to them of telling the whole government of the United States and the whole nation at large, and in fact the whole civilized world, that they were in very deed what they claimed to be—God's chosen mouthpieces and revelators. What a great testimony they could have borne to this great nation, and this poor, darkened, staggering world! A Paul or a Joseph Smith would have been only too glad to have had such a golden opportunity as they had. I was astonished when I read in the papers the weak and negative answers they gave, and I saw God had not been glorified nor his church on earth honored and extolled by this investigation. I felt saddened and pained over the matter, especially to think this report had gone out all over the nation.[85]

Later that year, Eastman declared himself the One Mighty and Strong. He was one of several to emerge in the early century. As David John, president of the Provo Stake, observed: "Many people have believed or pretended to believe, that elder Joseph F. Smith . . . would be destroyed from the earth, and another man would be appointed to his position as president of the Church."[86] John explained that "writing to this effect," alluding to a 1905 letter written by John T. Clark, another Mighty and Strong, had been "sent to all parts of Utah."[87] He had not exaggerated the popularity of the belief that a messianic figure would soon emerge. There was a constant supply of self-proclaimed candidates eager to fulfill the position. In 1918, Joseph E. Robinson counted five would-be messiahs in California alone since he had taken charge of the California Mission in 1901.[88]

In November 1905, the First Presidency issued a statement to counter the popular messianic interpretation of Smith's revelation. The epistle rebuffed those already leaning toward specific messianic figures, such as Clark and Eastman, and provided alternative ways to understand the prophecy. The statement opened by acknowledging the revelation's popularity. "Perhaps no other passage in the revelations of the Lord, in this dispensation, has given rise to so much speculation as this one." It had been the product of "vain and foolish men to bolster up their vagaries of speculation, and in some cases their pretensions to great power and high positions they were to attain in the Church." The criticism of individuals such as Eastman and Clark was deliberately harsh:

> One would think in such a matter as this that sufficient native modesty would assert itself to restrain a man from announcing himself as the one upon whom such high honors are to be conferred, and who is to exercise such great powers in establishing the Saints in their inheritances; and that even if one suspected, for any reason, that such a position, and such exceptional powers were to be conferred upon him, he would wait until the Lord would clearly indicate to the Church, as well as to himself, that he had been indeed sent of God to do the work of so noble a ministry, as is described in the passage under question. Those, however, who have so far proclaimed themselves as being the "one mighty and strong," have manifested the utmost ignorance of the things of God and the order of the Church. Indeed their insufferable ignorance and egotism have been at the bottom of all their pretensions, and the cause of all the trouble into which they have fallen.[89]

The 1905 statement was crafted to take on not just specific personalities, but the very idea that a messiah would come from outside of the church's hierarchy. These dissenters, the epistle continued, "seem not to have been aware of the fact that the Church of Christ and of the Saints is completely organized, and that when the man who shall be called upon to divide unto the Saints their inheritances comes, he will be designated by the inspiration of the Lord to the proper authorities of the Church, appointed and sustained according to the order provided for the government of the Church . . . the Saints need look for nothing of God's appointing that will be erratic, or irregular, or that smacks of starting over afresh or that would ignore or overthrow the established order of things." Not surprisingly, the First Presidency also took exception with the implication that "the present or some future President of the Church" was the leader, who would be removed by "the shaft of death."[90]

In contrast to these unacceptable interpretations, the 1905 statement offered two possible alternative readings. One interpretation proposed that the prophecy was of historical interest only. The revelation was a warning to Edward Partridge, then bishop of Jackson County, that if he did not fulfill his responsibilities, he would be replaced by another bishop characterized as One Mighty and Strong. The second interpretation, for "those who will insist that the prophecy concerning the coming of 'one mighty and strong' is still to be regarded as relating to the future," proposed that the One Mighty and Strong would be a "future bishop of the Church who will be with the Saints in Zion, Jackson county, Missouri, when the Lord shall establish them in that land."[91] Finally, the epistle warned that the One Mighty and Strong would only be a bishop, not a president of the church, thus ruling out other popular interpretations that the coming figure would be a resurrected Joseph Smith or John the Revelator.[92] The 1905 statement was a comprehensive attempt to suppress interpretations favoring extra-institutional prophets once and for all.

The 1905 statement was not the last time church leaders condemned messianic aspirations among the Saints. In 1909, apostle Joseph Fielding Smith complained about the barrage of mail church leaders received from "false prophets."[93] During the April 1913 general conference, Charles Penrose recalled the time when an aspiring One Mighty and Strong had come to Salt Lake City to take his position at the head of the church. "Sometimes men have come to the president of the Church and claimed to be the person to be raised up 'like unto Moses,' and demanded the keys of the Church. There was one man came, poor fellow, a decrepit kind of being who hung around for several days. He could not get any 'keys' and finally he came and begged for enough money to take him back to the place he came from in the East, and he hobbled out on his wooden leg,—the man 'mighty and strong.' Now I don't say that to ridicule the man, poor fellow, but it illustrates what I am trying to tell you this morning. The Lord has established His Church on the earth, as He has told us, 'in the last days and 'FOR THE LAST TIME.' "[94] In 1917, during a Sunday service in Long Beach, California, Joseph E. Robinson reportedly declared that anyone who "says that a Mighty and Strong is to come has no place among us . . . BUT if he ever comes he will be ordained thru [*sic*] the authorities of the Church."[95]

Prompted by the 1905 statement, local leaders became more vigilant in policing the beliefs and teachings of prophecy enthusiasts in their own congregations. Both Samuel Eastman and John T. Clark were eventually excommunicated. Their supporters were also subject to ecclesiastical sanctions.[96] In 1914, Francis M. Darter, who served as a theological teacher in California, faced criticism "from the leading Brethren of the Church" for "presenting the closing scenes pertaining to the final gathering of our people when Zion of Missouri is redeemed."[97] The Saints' return to Zion would probably not have been as controversial if Darter did not teach that the One Mighty and Strong—who he believed would arise outside of the church's leadership—would lead the expedition. In response to the church's censure, he "agreed to confine my thoughts along these lines to book form." In a book published in 1917, he protested the First Presidency's 1905 statement, which he believed had been unjustly "used against scores of worthy members of both Priesthood and Saints, thruout [*sic*] the stakes of Zion, who have openly declared their belief in these prophecies."[98]

Aspiring prophets did not always have ambitions to lead the church. In 1894, John H. Koyle, a 30-year-old Mormon in Spanish Fork, Utah, claimed the angel Moroni had led him to the site of an ancient Nephite mine—marked with petroglyphs—located near Salem, Utah. The messenger assured him that the mine "would be richer than anything like it in the whole world, but the big, rich deposits of ore he had seen would not be reached and released to them until a time of great world-wide crisis had come when most of the people would be sorely in need of relief."[99] Koyle's story was reminiscent of the region's already expansive mining legends. Specifically, the angel's prophecy followed an idea popular among Mormons that God permitted or prevented the discovery of wealth. Brigham Young had once stated, "People do not know it, but I know there is a seal set upon the treasures of earth; men are allowed to go so far and no farther. I have known places where there were treasures in abundance; but could men get them? No."[100]

In September 1894, Koyle and a small group of friends followed the Nephite's directions and began excavating what they called the Relief Mine (see Figure 5.3). After its incorporation in 1909, the mine attracted prophecy enthusiasts eager to buy stock in the enterprise. In July 1913, church leaders, wary about fraud, sent the apostle and geologist James Talmage to inspect the Relief Mine to ascertain whether it was an authentic enterprise. Talmage was not impressed. He criticized Koyle's plan to drill downward from the top of the mountain, when it seemed to make more sense to work from the

Figure 5.3 Photo of the Relief Mine located in Salem, Utah. Courtesy of Wikimedia Commons.

mountain's side. In his words, "[F]rom the standpoint of geological structure and all the known laws of mineral occurrence their effort is absolutely without promise of success." When the miners shared their faith in Koyle's prophetic gift and the divinity of their work, Talmage responded that he "had made the subject a matter of prayer and had asked to be free from all prejudice or bias and to be able to recognize the facts and the truth, and testified to them that while their free agency was, of course, their own and not to be interfered with by me, that I considered it would be well for them to abandon this work and to take themselves to useful and profitable labor." Curiously, Talmage also saw millenarian significance in the mine. "The predictions of old, that in the last days evil spirits, and even the spirits of devils will be working miracles among the people, are fulfilled."[101]

In September 1913, the First Presidency issued a statement condemning the mine and, in doing so, defined the parameters of acceptable revelatory claims by church members. The statement's opening paragraph reviewed the history of "manifestations from delusive spirits to members of the Church," beginning with Hiram Page's deceptive seer stone. Following a similar approach to the 1905 statement (questioning the character of the supposed revelators themselves), the First Presidency noted that those who brought forth such revelations were flawed in a manner that rendered them susceptible to the "Arch-Deceiver," the devil. Either these would-be prophets were guilty of transgression and were thus easy prey for the adversary or they had succumbed to pride. In this latter case, "[P]eople who pride themselves on their strict observance of the rules and ordinances and ceremonies of the Church are led astray by false spirits, who exercise an influence so imitative of that which proceeds from a Divine source that even these persons, who think they are 'the very elect,' find it difficult to discern the essential difference. Satan himself has transformed himself to be apparently 'an angel of light.' "[102]

Yet, since the First Presidency had no intention of discouraging all forms of revelation, another paragraph outlined the types of charismatic revelations that the Saints should approach with immediate suspicion: "When visions, dreams, tongues, prophecy, impressions or any extraordinary gift or inspiration conveys something out of harmony with the accepted revelations of the Church or contrary to the decisions of its constituted authorities, Latter-day Saints may know that it is not of God, no matter how plausible it may appear."[103] Importantly, this instruction did not oppose spiritual gifts altogether, but rather warned that when such gifts originated from divine sources, they would never oppose church authorities and, following the hierarchical structure of the institution, would or could only be shared and taught to those under one's jurisdiction. "All faithful members are entitled to the inspiration of the Holy Spirit for themselves, their families, and for those over whom they are appointed and ordained to preside."

The statement reaffirmed Smith's revelation concerning Hiram Page, which announced that only the president of the church could receive dialogic revelation for the entire church. "In secular as well as spiritual affairs, Saints may receive Divine guidance and revelation affecting themselves, but this does not convey authority to direct others, and is not to be accepted when contrary to Church covenants, doctrine or discipline, or to known facts, demonstrated truths, or good common sense."[104] The statement relegated believers' dreams, visions, spiritual impressions, displays of glossolalia, and any other form of charismata to the private sphere. Such manifestations might happen—in fact, they should happen in accordance with the church's beliefs about the last days—but they were not to be discussed outside of intimate, domestic circles.

By both promoting revelation and spiritual gifts while simultaneously regulating such events to the private sphere, the church laid claim to the charismatic heritage of primitive Christianity while simultaneously limiting the influence of revelation over the church as a whole when such events occurred among the laity. The 1913 statement, like the earlier 1905 statement against the One Mighty and Strong, proved to be an important weapon in the arsenal of regional church leaders and later for general authorities against dissenting or aspiring prophets. The letters clarified that those movements based on the charismatic visions or revelations of an individual outside of the church hierarchy were necessarily heterodox. As such, local leaders could then act to excommunicate or otherwise marginalize supporters of these types of movements. More importantly, the statements (and the newspaper editorials and general conference sermons that promoted the same message) functioned to instill suspicion: not just of vernacular prophecy, but of all those who would publically claim dramatic charismatic revelation.

Refuting the 1877 Prophecy and White Horse Prophecy

In the first decades of the twentieth century, the hierarchy had responded to messianic revelators and dissenting prophets by laying down rules for proper revelatory practices in the church. The same statement that condemned the Relief Mine placed into question both the validity of Koyle's prophecy itself as well as any attempts to seek an audience for any manifestation that originated with someone who did not hold an ecclesiastical position with the appropriate levels of stewardship and responsibility. Yet, it was not enough to warn against visionaries outside the hierarchy. Many of the most heavily circulated prophecies were allegedly uttered by current or former church leaders. These included most famously prophecies credited to Joseph Smith and popularized by Anson Call, Mosiah Hancock, and Reuben McBride. As the years passed, more and more Saints recorded their recollections of the words of Mormonism's departed visionaries. Prophecies credited to Joseph Smith, Brigham Young, John Taylor, Heber C. Kimball, and Orson Pratt circulated among the faithful. The two most widespread of these prophecies were the December 16, 1877, vision detailing the destructions of American cities ascribed to Joseph F. Smith, discussed in detail in Chapter 4, and what had become the most prominent apocalyptic text—the White Horse Prophecy.

What came to be known as the White Horse Prophecy was recalled by Edwin Rushton from a private conversation with Joseph Smith in May 1843 (see Figure 5.4). Rushton wrote down the White Horse Prophecy sometime after 1890, although he may have shared the narrative previously.[105] He claimed there was only one other present to hear Smith's words, Theodore Turley, who had died in 1871. Whether it was an oral tradition first written in 1890 or a new literary creation, the White Horse Prophecy contained all the essential components of nineteenth-century separatist apocalypticism. One possibility is that Rushton invented a fictive scenario—a personal conversation with the prophet—as a means to frame a comprehensive apocalyptic chronology. It is also possible that Rushton's report of an 1843 conversation is accurate, and he reconstructed this conversation to the best of his abilities and memory. That being said, Rushton could not have recalled the exact words of Smith's lengthy monologue to accurately record them fifty

Figure 5.4 Photo of Edwin Rushton (1824–1904) who drafted the White Horse Prophecy, a reminiscence of a Joseph Smith prophecy reportedly offered in 1843. Frank Esshom, *Pioneers and Prominent Men of Utah* (1913).

years later. An analysis of the text demonstrates that Rushton depended on later sources in drafting the sermon. Historian Don L. Penrod has documented Rushton's borrowing of a full paragraph from Parley P. Pratt's 1844 "A Dialogue Between Joseph Smith and the Devil," as well as several anachronisms in the text.[106]

The prophecy contained nothing objectionable from a nineteenth-century perspective. It was set apart from other prophecies by its comprehensiveness. It conveniently presented in one place content that was scattered across multiple sources. Smith reportedly predicted his own martyrdom, the Saints' exodus to the Rocky Mountains, the raising of an ensign there, and the federal government's persecution of the Saints. From there, the prophecy detailed other familiar scenarios: the collapse of the federal government, the rise of the Kingdom of God, the Saints' offering sanctuary to refugees in the West, the military involvement of Native Americans and African Americans, and the establishment of Zion in Jackson County, Missouri.

The White Horse Prophecy obtained its name from its singular use of the four horsemen of the apocalypse to describe distinct American populations. The White Horse, traditionally identified as Conquest or Jesus Christ, became a symbol of the Mormon people, who would be established as an independent kingdom in the West. Red, Black, and Pale horses (War, Famine, and Death in traditional readings) were interpreted as Native Americans, African Americans, and non-Mormon Euro-Americans.[107] The prophecy predicted an impending American revolution that would splinter the country into factions, leaving no "supreme government." The horrors of America's descent into chaos were illustrated through the usual scenes of familial violence. "Farther [*sic*] would be against Son & Son against the Farther [*sic*] & Mother against the Daughter & Daughter against the Mother the most terrible Scense [*sic*] of Murder and Blood & Rapine that was ever look upon will take Place."[108]

As with other visions, the terrors would send "Hundreds and Thousands of the Honest in Heart to garther [*sic*] not because they were Mormons but because they would not take up the Sword against there Neibors." Echoing the 1877 vision, the refugees would come with just what they could carry in bundles. One of the White Horse Prophecy's singular claims was that the sudden population boom would place Utah in "danger of famine." While the honorable found safety in the Rocky Mountains, the British and French armies arrived in the East to instill order. "The Black Horse will flee to the invadors, and will join with them, for they will fear of becoming again, knowing England did not believe in slavery, fleeing to them, they believed, would make them safe. Armed with British Beyonets [*sic*], the doings of the Black Horse, when they got the Master so." According to Rushton, Smith became disturbed at the view of African Americans slaughtering those who had once enslaved them and "asked the Lord to close the scene." The uprising among former slaves armed by the British seemed to fulfill Smith's war prophecy: "[S]laves shall rise up against their masters, who shall be marshaled and disciplined for war."[109]

Using similar language as previously employed by Eliza R. Snow, Brigham Young, and others, Smith told his 1843 audience that "you will see the Constitution of the United States almost destroyed; it will hang by a thread, as it were, as fine as the finest silk fiber."[110] While the British and French unsuccessfully tried to restore peace in the former United States, the White Horse would send missionaries out to the Pale Horse (non-Mormon Euro-Americans) "to get the Honest among them . . . to Stand By the Constitution of the United States" in the West. There, the Constitution, "as it was given by inspiration of the Lord," was protected by an alliance between "the White Horse" (Mormons) and "the Red Horse" (Native Americans). The Kingdom of God was established among the Saints and all other governments began to pay allegiance to them, the last of which would be the nation of Great Britain. The ten tribes would return, as would Jesus whose initial "coming would be so Natural, that only those who see Him will know He has come, but He will come and give His law unto Zion."

Keeping in mind that Rushton's account of this prophecy is a product of the late nineteenth century, Smith's remarks on the timing of prophecy seem to address the Saints' expectations surrounding 1890. The White Horse Prophecy also addressed Smith's 1832 prophecy that the New Jerusalem "temple shall be reared in this generation." He reportedly told Ruston, "The Temple in Jackson County [would] be Built up in this Generation but the Saints will think there will be no time, to Build it but with all the Great Help you receive you can Put up a great temple." The Saints would discover vast stores of gold in the West and "the Ten Tribes of Israel to Help you Build it." While Native Americans would provide military support for the Saints, the prophecy was conspicuously silent when it came to their participation in the creation of the future Zion. According to a revised draft of the prophecy,

Smith stated, "When you see this land bounded with Iron," apparently alluding to the spread of the railroad across the West, "you may look toward Jackson County."

According to Rushton, Smith concluded his prophecy with two additional warnings. First, he predicted the Chinese would invade "a land beyond the Rockey [*sic*] Mountains."[111] Finally, "the last great Struggle Zion will have to contend with when America will be the Zion of Our God, Called Gog & Magog, led By the Russian Czar his Power will be very great." The revised version of the prophecy identified Gog and Magog as the "nations of the world."[112] This was the Battle of Armageddon. And as with all other contests, the Saints would emerge victorious.

The White Horse Prophecy circulated for at least two decades before it was formally condemned. On the second day of the October 1918 general conference, Joseph Fielding Smith Jr., an apostle, and son of Joseph F. Smith then serving as church president, addressed vernacular prophecies credited to church authorities, focusing on the 1877 vision and White Horse Prophecy in particular.[113] He began by denouncing the 1877 vision that had been credited to his father. The apostle recalled that while visiting congregations,

> my attention has been called, on a number of occasions, to a purported revelation or vision or manifestation, whatever it may be called, supposed to have been received by President Smith sometime in the distant past, in regard to events of great importance dealing with the nations of the earth and the Latter-day Saints. Many things in that purported vision, or revelation, are absurd. My attention has been called to this thing, and good brethren and good sisters have inquired of me to know whether or not there was any truth in that which had come to their attention. It is in printed form; and I have been under the necessity of telling them that there was no truth in it.[114]

Smith then turned to the White Horse Prophecy. As before, he noted that while visiting congregations, he "discovered that people have copies of a purported vision by the Prophet Joseph Smith given in Nauvoo, and some people are circulating this supposed vision, or revelation, or conversation which the prophet is reported to have held with a number of individuals in the city of Nauvoo." The apostle did not bother to relay the content of either vision, but instead articulated how a Latter-day Saint could know whether a revelation or vision was authentic when he or she encountered it:

> I want to say to you, my brethren and sisters, that if you understand the Church articles and covenants, if you will read the scriptures and become familiar with those things which are recorded in the revelations from the Lord, it will not be necessary for you to ask any questions in regard to the authenticity or otherwise of any purported revelation, vision, or manifestation that proceeds out of darkness, concocted in some corner, surreptitiously presented, and not coming through the proper channels of the Church. Let me add that when a revelation comes for the guidance of this people, you may be sure that it will not be presented in some mysterious manner contrary to the order of the Church. It will go forth in such form that the people will understand that it comes from those who are in authority, for it will be sent either to the presidents of stakes and the bishops of the wards over the signatures of the presiding authorities, or it will be published in some of the regular papers or magazines under the control and direction of the Church or it will be presented before such a gathering as this, at a general conference. It will not spring up in some distant part of the Church and be in the hands of some obscure individual without authority, and thus be circulated among the Latter-day Saints. Now, you may remember this.[115]

Smith's statement correlated the truthfulness of a prophecy with where it originated and how it circulated. Mormons could trust periodicals published by the church, epistles distributed by local authorities, and general conference sermons. Important matters would not be broadcast by word of mouth or in the form of independently printed tracts. Regardless of the previous eighty years in which the Saints' individual accounts were standard sources for the collecting of leaders' prophecies, the church of the twentieth century would not depend on uncertain memoirs of "some obscure individual without authority." Smith was adamant that Latter-day Saints should not place confidence in second- and thirdhand accounts of prophets' words.

Immediately following his son's remarks, President Joseph F. Smith Sr. took the stand and reflected on both prophecies:

> This wonderful, mysterious revelation that I have been said to have received a great many years ago, was given in French, and I never knew but two or three words in French in my life; consequently, I could not have been the originator of that revelation.[116] I want you to understand that. I have denied it, I suppose, a hundred times, when I have been inquired of about it. It was

> gotten up by some mysterious person who undertook to create a sensation and lay the responsibility upon me. I am not guilty. When the Lord reveals something to me, I will consider the matter with my brethren, and when it becomes proper, I will let it be known to the people, and not otherwise.[117]

His perspective on the White Horse Prophecy followed in a similar vein, questioning how it was constructed, rather than the content of the vision:

> The ridiculous story about the "red horse," and "the black horse," and "the white horse," and a lot of trash that has been circulated about and printed and sent around as a great revelation given by the Prophet Joseph Smith, is a matter that was gotten up, I understand, some ten years after the death of the Prophet Joseph Smith, by two of our brethren who put together some broken sentences from the Prophet that they may have heard him utter from time to time, and formulated this so called revelation out of it, and it was never spoken by the prophet in the manner in which they have put it forth. It is simply false: that is all there is to it.[118]

Any number of reasons could have aroused the hierarchy's concern with the White Horse Prophecy and 1877 vision of destructions throughout the United States. Only three years after the 1877 revelation was first drafted, Joseph F. Smith had already expressed irritation with rumors that pointed to him as its author and revelator. In a newspaper editorial from November 17, 1880, he clarified: "So far as this pretended vision has been connected with my name it is a fraud. I never had such a vision and am wholly ignorant of its author, and my name has been used in connection with it entirely without my knowledge."[119] Smith's motivation for refuting his authorship of this vision was possibly the same in 1918 as it was in 1880—to correct those who would appropriate a church leader's name for their own agendas. Both 1918 sermons (from Joseph F. Smith and his son, Joseph Fielding Smith) encouraged church members to doubt the authenticity of documents or stories that alleged a special status and did not comply with certain institutional procedures on how new revelation should be presented. There was a proper channel of ecclesiastical communication, even when a document claimed authenticity.

The specific rejection of these two visions while so many others stood unopposed should make us question if it was the content of the visions that bothered Joseph F. Smith and other church leaders. Both the White Horse Prophecy and the vision of American destructions broke the rules articulated at the beginning of this chapter. They presented an apocalyptic geography with destructions devastating the eastern United States while the Mormon corridor escaped largely unscathed. They envisioned a stark dualism between Mormon and non-Mormon. Finally, these visions presented events scheduled to unfold in the near future, presumably in the lives of those who heard them.

Nothing in these visions was foreign to the accepted body of prophecy. They were true to the nineteenth-century apocalyptic worldview from which they emerged. In fact, many elements of the White Horse Prophecy and 1877 prophecy were present in other memoirs, journal entries, or stories from the life of Joseph Smith. Thus, the 1918 statements against pseudonymous prophecies served two purposes. First, they implicitly corrected the depiction of the United States as an object of divine scorn and future wrath. While such ideas had already been questioned with Utah statehood and LDS support of the Spanish-American War, the residue of such sentiments were preserved in prophecy. Second, the 1918 statements were the final step in engendering suspicion toward a prophecy's origin. Church leaders would use these statements to respond not only to reappearances of the White Horse Prophecy and 1877 vision, but also to all vernacular prophecies. Mormons became increasingly cautious not to accept a prophecy as legitimate unless it clearly originated from the institution.

Realizing that these prophecies circulated in manuscript form, Joseph F. Smith and Joseph F. Smith Jr. marked physical copies donated to the church's archives with their objections. Sometime before his death in November 1918, Joseph F. Smith appended a statement to a copy of the White Horse Prophecy in his personal papers: "The foregoing is entirely unreliable and imaginary on the part of Edwin Rushton, who has from memory and an over-wrought enthusiasm and zeal woven it together in his declining years, long after the death of the Prophet. . . . I was *personally well acquainted* with Edwin Rushton and knew him to be an exceedingly visionary man."[120] On the opening pages of three different copies of the White Horse Prophecy, Joseph F. Smith Jr. wrote "not true," "not to be accepted," and "Hold || not authentic."[121] Based on the last entry, it is even possible that at times the church archives did not make these copies available to researchers. Copies of the 1877 prophecy under the title of "A Vision of Joseph F. Smith" were marked with similar phrases: "Not a word of truth in it—Joseph F. Smith," "This letter is not written by Pres. Jos. F. Smith who denied this letter, and is a hoax," "President Smith disclaimed authorship for this. J. F. S." In one copy donated on April 9, 1931, Smith had scratched out the title in pen and added the word "False."[122] Even years after the public condemnation of these prophecies, it remained difficult to control the pseudonymous visions of the past.

At the April 1931 general conference and again in April 1938, Joseph F. Smith Jr. quoted his father's 1918 condemnation of the prophecy. On both occasions, his remarks were prompted by "communications coming from various parts of the Church, asking if certain purported revelations or dreams or visions are reliable and have the endorsement of the Authorities of the Church."[123] Smith may have felt that further statements were needed after one of the Seventies, J. Golden Kimball, preached from a prophecy, "Prophetic Sayings of Heber C. Kimball to Sister Amanda Wilcox," during the October 1930 general conference. While J. Golden Kimball could have drawn from well-documented miracle stories and prophecies associated with Heber C. Kimball, he instead read from the apocalyptic monologue from Wilcox's *Prophetic Sayings*. The document described a conversation Wilcox had with Kimball in 1868, including a shared visionary experience between the two when Kimball assisted her to see the completed Salt Lake Temple by grasping her shoulder. J. Golden Kimball avoided relaying this contextual material, which would have raised suspicion by this period[124] (see Figure 5.5).

The subsequent acceptance of Amanda Wilcox's prophecy, even if only the portions cited by J. Golden Kimball, led to the popularization of ideas that an influx of Gentiles in Salt Lake City would render it "among the wicked cities of the world" and "the western boundaries of the State of Missouri will be swept so clean of its inhabitants that as President Young tells us, 'when we return to that place there will not be as much as a yellow dog to wag his tail.'"[125] This latter prophecy became known as the "yellow dog prophecy" and, while popularized in Wilcox's pamphlet, had been previously credited to Joseph Smith.[126] Perhaps to avoid embarrassing Kimball, no one publicly criticized the sermon. The result has been that numerous orthodox Latter-day Saints have cited this portion of the prophecy, trusting that it came through the proper channels. Except for this setback, the careful institutional regulation of unofficial prophecy has been consistent across the twentieth century to the present.

Figure 5.5 Photo of Amanda H. Wilcox with her husband, Eli Wilcox. Wilcox reported having witnessed a vision, with the assistance of the apostle Heber C. Kimball, in which Salt Lake City became "among the wicked cities of the world." Courtesy of Marjean Wilcox Wright.

Conclusion

In the late nineteenth and early twentieth centuries, the Mormon hierarchy carefully regulated the unruly world of apocalypticism. They dealt with the perpetual issues of date-setting and messianism and other once mainstream ideas that seemed out of place in a church that was now at home in the United States. These anachronisms included the geographic application of Mormonism's Zion–Babylon divide, as well as the question of where the United States fit into prophecy. Was the nation a friend or adversary? It was in these crucial decades of Americanization that church leaders pinpointed unacceptable prophecies, among them the White Horse Prophecy and 1877 vision of devastation in America's cities. If Americanization was to be successful, then the memory of American–Mormon conflict haunting the Saints' millenarian thought would need to be exorcised. And that meant the hierarchy would need to be more hands-on concerning the type of content that could be perpetuated into the new century as well as who was authorized to do such perpetuating.

This shift was the moment when the idea of a vernacular apocalyptic emerged within Mormon consciousness. Mormon prophecy was no longer a communal project.as it had been during the early days of the restoration. Latter-day Saints were taught to understand that there was something dangerous about apocalypticists outside of the hierarchy. This sense of danger countered the religion's underlying sense of egalitarianism and popular accessibility regarding the charismatic: Even if the Saints knew that, following doctrine and scripture, such dreamers and visionaries were supposed to be present among them, and even if having such premonitions was, in theory, a spiritual gift, the end result was a population more inclined to distrust both the content of such charismatic experiences as well as the charismatic process itself. The end result was a culture that claimed authority through charismatic events, but that simultaneously discredited the continuance of such events: Visionaries were supposed to be silent. And yet, this culturally mandated silence did not end LDS charismatic apocalyptic experiences. The final chapter examines how apocalypticism continued into the twentieth and twenty-first centuries.

6
Twentieth- and Twenty-First-Century Apocalyptic Trajectories

> The Constitution of the United States is the political document that guarantees to men their freedom. . . . There is, thus, one great nation on earth that exalts and protects freedom and liberty and the right to worship as one chooses. . . . This is the land of prophecy and of destiny. Here the gospel was restored; here men are free to worship; here they have the talents and the means to carry the word to other nations. This is the Lord's base of operations in the last days. From here the word of truth shall go forth to prepare a people for the Second Coming of the Son of Man.
>
> —Apostle Bruce R. McConkie, 1982[1]

> The Mormon religion is fertile ground for those kinds of anti-government, we-can-take-care-of-ourselves beliefs. . . . There are groups all over Utah waiting for Armageddon. . . . Some of these groups are seeing evidence and signs of the last days in all that is happening around us. . . . They're coming around to the idea that government is the anti-Christ.
>
> —Jimmy Gober, retired ATF officer, 1995[2]

The Persistence of Mormon Apocalypticism

The last days were more complicated after the period of transition. The church's efforts at policing prophecy were never intended to put an end to the tradition's millenarianism, and thus lay members and ecclesiastical authorities continued to share a conviction that they were living in the final dispensation heading toward the millennium. Yet, Mormon representations of the end diverged. In official sources, a moderate millenarianism replaced separatist apocalypticism. Latter-day Saint apostles re-envisioned the United States

Terrible Revolution. Christopher James Blythe, Oxford University Press (2020). © Oxford University Press.
DOI: 10.1093/oso/9780190080280.001.0001

as the Zion of scripture and the nation's enemies as the prophesied end times foes. Apocalypticism endured among Mormon fundamentalists who resisted Americanization and among some devout LDS prophecy enthusiasts who preserved these older models of eschatology while rarely acknowledging (or perhaps were oblivious to) the fact that they were a thorn in the side of the church's hierarchy. This chapter examines how prophecy developed in each of these three networks and, in turn, how these different strains of Mormon apocalyptic influenced one another.

Official Apocalyptic during the Twentieth Century

Even during the era in which church leaders focused on regulating vernacular apocalypticism, World War I demanded integration into the last days schema. It would ultimately prove to be one of the final events to be incorporated.[3] In the previous chapter, I argued that twentieth-century Mormon apocalypticism underwent an Americanizing shift. I showed that, for a time, church leaders increasingly preferred a definition of Zion as the land of America over earlier definitions of a geographically isolated Mormon refuge. In practice, this meant that an increasingly popular way to understand the prophecies of Zion was as prophecies of the United States itself as a nation. The Mormon Zion and the geographic boundaries of the United States were repeatedly conflated such that an understanding of the U.S. as Zion itself took root in the Mormon imagination. Scriptural commentators also returned to Smith's civil war prophecy to position current events. On August 16, 1914, B. H. Roberts announced the fulfillment of that portion of the prophecy that foretold that Great Britain would "call upon other nations, in order to defend themselves against other nations; and then war shall be poured out upon all nations" in the Triple Entente, Triple Alliance, and other European treaties.[4] Roberts referred to Smith's prophecy as the "war program of the last days" and expected that the United States would not have to participate in the Great War because it had already "received her chastisement for her pride, for her injustice and wrong-doing, early in the modern war" (i.e., during the Civil War). He hoped that in the future, when the nations of Europe had come to a "saner state of mind," they would "turn to the United States"—what he called the "larger Zion"—"and out of her counsels find their way to the paths of peace."[5] When the United States entered the war, the idea that millennial prophecies of Zion pertained to the nation assured an Allied success.

Even though Roberts had not foreseen the United States' entrance into the war, his views that the war in Europe would be the final great conflict did not change. He continued to link the Civil War with World War I, insisting that the reason fewer Americans were killed in the war was due to great losses in the Civil War. For Roberts and many other church leaders, the Civil War and Great War in tandem fulfilled the prophecies of violence in the last days. Yet, by the end of the war, these views were contested as Mormon debate surrounding Woodrow Wilson's initiative to establish the League of Nations revealed. For Roberts, the Saints could trust that the League of Nations would achieve its highest ideals and "bring about an everlasting peace."[6] The "war program of the last days" was complete, the prophecy fulfilled, and now the millennium could be realized. In stark contrast, apostle-senator Reed Smoot opposed the League based on a nationalistic reading of prophecy and an assumption that the "war program" was still partially unfulfilled. Responding to a query from League proponent C. N. Lund, he explained that if ratification of the League could lead "to no more wars," then "the revelations given to the Prophet Joseph Smith as recorded in the Doctrine and Covenants are not true." Smoot considered it faithless to believe "that the league of nations will do more for the world than the teachings of the Savior have been able to."[7]

The contention between Mormon leaders reflected the larger controversy about the League occurring throughout the nation. The new body of apocalyptically minded Christian fundamentalists were as suspicious of the League as was Smoot. They saw in the League's promises of global peace a fulfillment of the Book of Revelation's depiction of the rise of a Satanic world government.[8] In contrast, Smoot neither seemed to consider the League inherently evil, nor as a fulfillment of prophecy itself. Rather, he believed the League was doomed to failure because it was an effort to circumvent prophecy.

Smoot's fatalism fascinated the press and the nation as a handbill entitled "Mormon Bible Becomes Issue in League of Nations Fight" began to circulate (see Figure 6.1). In addition to quoting from Smoot's letter to Lund, the handbill also included prophecies from the Book of Mormon concerning American sovereignty and portions of the 1832 war prophecy predicting a "full end of all nations."[9] In September, President Heber J. Grant, a League supporter, opposed the public debate altogether, declaring that "the position of the Church of Jesus Christ of Latter Day Saints is that the standard works of the Church are not opposed to the league of nations." He objected to church members appealing to prophecy to resolve political disagreements.[10]

MORMON BIBLE BECOMES ISSUE IN LEAGUE OF NATIONS FIGHT

Here Are the Prophesies:

Following are some of the Mormon prophesies cited by Senator Smoot to show that "the League of Nations is not divinely inspired and cannot prevent wars." They were published by Joseph Smith, the Mormon prophet, in 1832:

"And I, Nephi, beheld that the Gentiles, that had gone out of captivity, were delivered by the power of God OUT OF THE HANDS OF ALL OTHER NATIONS."—I Nephi, XIII, 19.

"And this land shall be a land of liberty unto the Gentiles, and there shall be NO KINGS upon the land, who shall raise up unto the Gentiles:

"AND I WILL FORTIFY THIS LAND AGAINST ALL OTHER NATIONS."—II Nephi, X, 11-12.

"And whatsoever nation shall uphold such SECRET COMBINATIONS, to get power and gain, until they shall spread over the nation, BEHOLD THEY SHALL BE DESTROYED."—Ether, VIII, 22.

"Behold, this a choice land, and whatsoever nation shall possess it shall be free from bondage, and from captivity, AND FROM ALL OTHER NATIONS UNDER HEAVEN, if they will but serve the God of the land, who is Jesus Christ."—Ether II, 12.

"Verily, thus saith the Lord, concerning the wars that will shortly come to pass, beginning at the rebellion of South Carolina, which will eventually terminate in the death and misery of many souls.

"The days will come that war will be poured out upon all nations beginning at that place. * * *

"And thus, with the sword, by bloodshed, the inhabitants of the earth shall mourn; and with famine, and plague, and earthquakes, and the thunder of Heaven, and the fierce and vivid lightning also, shall the inhabitants of the earth be made to feel the wrath and indignation and chastening hand of an Almighty God, UNTIL THE CONSUMPTION DECREED, HATH MADE A FULL END OF ALL NATIONS."—Doctrine and Covenants, Section 87, verses 1-6.

N. E. A. Staff Special

SALT LAKE CITY, UTAH, Sept. 00—Salt Lake City is the hottest place in the world just now, as far as the League of Nations is concerned.

The unique stand taken by United States Senator Reed Smoot, in basing his opposition to the League upon prophesies and revelations cited from the Book of Mormon, has stirred up a discussion in Mormon circles that is ringing throughout the United States.

Here alone has the religious issue been injected into the contest over the League. Smoot, a Republican in politics, is an apostle of the Mormon church. At the present time, many of the leaders of the church are equally strong Democrats. The idea of a League of Nations to prevent wars has been generally approved of among Mormons.

Its advocates, however, have been thrown into some consternation by Smoot's quoting, from the Book of Mormon, certain passages set down by Joseph Smith in 1832, prophesying a climaxing series of wars until the Lord's second coming on earth.

These passages, says Smoot, make it clear that the League of Nations, as a preventer of wars, will fail.

Strength is added to the claim, in the minds of Mormons, from the fact that in the clearest of these passages, Smith prophesied the outbreak of the Civil War thirty years before it happened, even mentioning South Carolina as the State in which it would start.

The Indian wars were prophesied at the same time. These portions of the Mormon revelations, it is said, have been fully borne out.

A series of meetings that will undoubtedly arouse a high pitch of excitement has been arranged for the Mormon tabernacle by Presiding Bishop C. W. Nibley. At the first, Mormon religious and legal authorities will discuss the League from their respective angles.

President Wilson will speak shortly afterward, and Senator Hiram Johnson of California, opposing the League, will follow at a third session.

Smoot's fire was drawn in his own defense, when C. N. Lund, a Mormon editor of Mt. Pleasant, Utah, wrote him a letter saying:

"It seems to me that in the light of your firm belief in the Divine teachings of the Redeemer of the world, you ought to stand for this covenant whole-heartedly and unreservedly.

"Why can you not see that the same God who inspired Washington and Jefferson and Lincoln does also inspire Woodrow Wilson (not for the sake of the man, but for the sake of the righteous and most holy cause) in this greatest step ever contemplated by the human race?"

Smoot's reply declared that while the nations were sick of war and bankrupt, the whole matter would have to be settled "some time in the future."

"I am not prepared to admit that President Wilson has been inspired of God," Smoot wrote. "I do not believe that God had anything to do with the Shantung matter, nor do I believe He was pleased with the action of President Wilson affecting Fiume or the Saar valley.

"You evidently think that when this covenant is ratified we will have no more wars. Do not be deceived, for such will not be the case. If so, the revelations of Prophet Joseph Smith as recorded in the Doctrine and Covenants are not true.

"I ask you to read the many passages of the Book of Mormon referring to this nation, as well as the many revelations given to the Prophet Joseph Smith, as to the destiny of the same."

Some of the prophesies in question are printed herewith.

Senator Reed Smoot of Utah, who bases his opposition to the League of Nations on the prophesies in the Book of Mormon, published by Joseph Smith in 1832.

Joseph Smith

THE BOOK OF MORMON: AN ACCOUNT WRITTEN BY THE HAND OF MORMON, UPON Plates taken from the Plates of Nephi.

TRANSLATED BY JOSEPH SMITH, Jun.

Title Page of the Book of Mormon

Sen. Reed Smoot

NEA

SAN FRANCISCO, SEPT. 1

Figure 6.1 "Mormon Bible Becomes Issue in League of Nations," 1919. This handbill highlights Senator Reed Smoot's argument that Mormon prophecy opposed U.S. involvement in the League of Nations. Courtesy of Church History Library.

After several years, Smoot's position that violence would continue after World War I became universal among the Saints. However, for a time, some church leaders held to a belief that further conflict and suffering were unnecessary in the wake of the Great War. The world could choose global peace. In October 1921, Seventy Seymour Young reflected: "We have evidently come to the time when there will come through limitation of armaments the security of the world's peace, or we shall go on and on until we repeat—which God forbid—repeat the awful cataclysm of war and destruction such as we witnessed during the world's great war but recently closed."[11] Some, like Young, continued to hope that human agency could bring about the millennial hopes of the Saints.

As more years passed, global disarmament seemed less and less likely. In 1937, J. Reuben Clark, then a counselor in the First Presidency, bemoaned news that European nations were amassing "enormous quantities of raw materials used in war." According to Clark, newspaper reports held that a consensus of "naval and military leaders of all nations believe the next war will look to the extermination of nations, not the destruction of armies; that not alone shall the able-bodied soldiers be cut down, but that innocent babes, their mothers, the aged, decrepit, and infirm are to be slaughtered."[12] The preacher wondered "whether we be not now in the very times foretold by the Savior in his great discourse on the Mount of Olives, and predicted by the prophets from most ancient times. Are not the anti-Christs now walking the earth?"[13] Two years later, when war returned to Europe, he declared, "Nothing is more unrighteous, more unholy, more un-Godly, than man-declared mass slaughter of his fellowman for an unrighteous cause. It has brought down the wrath of the Almighty in all times. God will visit His vengeance upon all who bring it."[14] He—echoing the thoughts of Richards and Roberts—hoped that the United States would remain "the great neutral nation of the earth" and "the only great national moral force and influence for peace left in the world."[15] He believed America could "become the Peacemaker of the world, which is her manifest destiny if she live the law of peace. Believing as we do that America is Zion, we shall then see the beginning of the fulfillment of the prophecy of Isaiah of old 'for out of Zion shall go forth the law.' "[16]

Throughout the war, other church leaders emphasized this concept of American destiny. In April 1944, apostle Charles A. Callis read from the Book of Mormon promises of the "perpetuity of our glorious republic, conditioned upon our obedience to God." He hoped the country would build its defenses to "place it in such a condition of invulnerability that the nations of the earth, as God says in the Doctrine and Covenants, shall say: 'Let us not go up to battle against Zion for the inhabitants of Zion are terrible.' America is Zion, from North to South, from East to West."[17] An earlier generation would have been baffled by the claim that amassing weapons was a prophetic characteristic of Zion as much as they would have been by the identification of the United States as Zion. Neither position seems to have continued long after World War II. Certainly, church leaders continued to talk about American destiny and patriotically supported each successive conflict. Yet, by 1945, some Mormon leaders questioned whether a true parallel between the United States and Zion was possible given the identity of Zion as a last days refuge from violence. Clark described the atomic bombings of Hiroshima and Nagasaki as the "crowning savagery of the war." "We Americans," he preached, "wiped out hundreds of thousands of civilian population with the atom bomb in Japan, few if any of the ordinary civilians being any more responsible for the war than we were in aiding America. Military men are now saying that the atom bomb was a mistake. It was more than that: it was a world tragedy."[18] And America's savagery was not limited to their deeds during the war; Clark was also horrified at the development of biological weaponry.

Clark continued, "Thus we in America are now deliberately searching out and developing the most savage, murderous means of exterminating peoples that Satan can plant in our minds. We do it not only shamelessly, but with a boast. God will not forgive us for this. If we are to avoid extermination, if the world is not to be wiped out, we must find some way to curb the fiendish ingenuity of men who have apparently no fear of God, man, or the devil, and who are willing to plot and plan and invent instrumentalities that will wipe out all the flesh of the earth."[19] American exceptionalism would still appear in Mormon discourse throughout the next several decades, but the violence of the midcentury rendered the concept of America as millennial Zion untenable.

The atomic bomb changed the way American Christians imagined the apocalypse. Historian Paul Boyer observed that "prophecy interpreters [before 1945] typically envisioned this 'burning day' in naturalistic terms—earthquakes, comets, volcanic eruptions—or as eschatological event beyond human understanding . . . with the coming of the atomic bomb, everything changed: it seemed that man himself had, in the throes of war, stumbled on the means of his own prophesied doom."[20] Americans quickly came to accept that they, too, would not always be immune to nuclear attacks. In the words of apostle John A. Widtsoe: "We imagine our cities, homes, and loved ones, laid low by an irresistible, merciless force. A helpless, hopeless gloom clouds the future. A fear never known before stalks the footsteps of thinking people."[21] J. Reuben Clark instructed his children that "when the first atomic bomb is dropped here in America," they were to relocate to the family ranch "and stay until it is over."[22] It took the violence of World War II for such to happen, but Mormon leaders no longer assured their flock that the nation would go unscathed from future violence.

After World War II, American Saints joined their countrymen in decrying Communism abroad and signs of socialism at home. It was in this Cold War context that some LDS leaders began to share a prophecy that the U.S. Constitution would be imperiled. Apostle Ezra Taft Benson, known for his controversial anti-Communism, frequently invoked Smith's uncanonized prophecy of the Saints redeeming the Constitution while also pointing to the Book of Mormon's depiction of conspiracy preceding the collapse of nations. He preached that church members had a responsibility to defend the Constitution, despite the fact that the nation had "apostatized in various degrees from different constitutional principles."[23] In a representative statement from 1965, he warned that "many of the prophecies referring to America's preservation are conditional. That is, if we do our duty we can be preserved, and if not then we shall be destroyed. This means that a good deal of the responsibility lies with the priesthood of this Church as to what happens to America and as to how much tragedy can be avoided."[24] By the 1990s, the rhetoric regarding the Saints' role in defending the American Constitution declined as church leaders focused on internationalization.

In fact, the Constitution prophecy is a fascinating exception to mid- to late- twentieth-century church leaders' approaches to millenarianism. These more recent authorities rarely attempted to line up prophecies with world events. Instead, when they spoke of apocalyptic prophecies, they limited their remarks to scriptural commentary. Historian Grant Underwood has emphasized the continuity in Mormon millenarian thought from the nineteenth century to the present by examining the writings of apostle Bruce R. McConkie, who, in 1981, "published the longest work ever written by a Latter-day Saint on eschatological matters": *The Millennial Messiah.* For Underwood, what is "striking is how little McConkie's millennial treatise differs from those written during Mormonism's first generation. The same supernatural biological and geological changes anticipated then are expected today, including the abolishment of infant mortality, the herbivorization of carnivores, the unification of continental landmasses, and the commingling of mortals and resurrected immortals. That such views seemed plausible in the early nineteenth century is perhaps not surprising. That they are still maintained today provides dramatic testimony of the degree to which LDS millenarianism in particular and Mormonism in general have resisted the encroachments of modernity."[25] Indeed, McConkie even presented Christ's millennial rule as encompassing the direction of both church and state.[26] Perhaps because the association of Mormonism with theocracy was no longer a vital part of American criticisms of the church, he did not hesitate to champion such views. There are moments in his *Millennial Messiah* in which he contradicts early ideas (e.g., the return of the ten tribes from the north; the

American Indians' role in building the New Jerusalem), but these are few and far between.

Even when it came to Armageddon, the apostle-scholar depicted it in all its "horror and brimstone and blood and fire."[27] McConkie's descriptions of Armageddon revealed the *Millennial Messiah* as a late Cold War interpretation of Mormonism's master narrative. Like evangelical apocalypticists writing at the time, he interpreted scripture through the lens of modern technology. Ancient descriptions of battle were references to nuclear war and "atomic fallout."[28] Vague imagery from the visions of the prophet Joel seemed to be imperfect attempts to describe tanks, trucks, helicopters, airplanes, and intercontinental ballistic missiles.[29] McConkie identified Russia and the United States (aligned with Israel) as the two sides of the last days conflict.

Millennial Messiah was illustrative of a broader trend thoroughly established among church leaders by the mid-twentieth century to avoid drawing on nineteenth-century voices, especially nineteenth-century interpreters of the apocalypse. In McConkie's words, his goal was "to set forth what the scriptures themselves, as properly interpreted, have to say about the great and coming day."[30] With the exception of Joseph Smith's canonized prophecies, quotations from nineteenth-century general authorities, including Orson Pratt, Orson Hyde, and Parley P. Pratt, were completely absent from his work.[31] McConkie's preference for a sola scriptura approach to apocalypticism allowed for a re-invention of Latter-day Saint expectations.

In consequence, the apocalypse had become delocalized and depersonalized as it became more universal. The Saints and their immediate enemies were no longer the epicenter of the last days narrative. Natural disasters, plagues, and violence would occur around the world. The Battle of Armageddon, which was described frequently in an American context, was now securely back in Palestine. The American continent remained important as the site of the New Jerusalem.[32] The United States remained significant in its role as redeemer nation, assuring the continuation of freedom throughout the globe and acting as a launching pad for the Gospel. Americans were no longer the oppressors of God's people. They were sanctified because of their heritage of democracy, but also because the nation housed the Lord's church. With the Americanization of Mormon millenarianism fully in place with World War I, it no longer made sense to focus on the plight of Mormon refugees winding their way through a post-apocalyptic American landscape. The prophet would appoint some Saints, whom McConkie called "delegates," to relocate to Jackson County, but they would do so in an orderly fashion as their "services are needed."[33] McConkie did not tell the story of a Mormon people besieged or of Native American uprisings. While he listed San Francisco, Chicago, and New York among the world's cities that would be destroyed as part of the "fall of Babylon," he also included London, Paris, Berlin, Moscow, Tokyo, and São Paulo.[34] This geographic reorientation of Mormon apocalypticism proved politically and culturally normative within the social and religious currents of mid-twentieth-century America. By situating the Battle of Armageddon on the other side of the world in the state of Israel, McConkie's apocalyptic scenario fit closely with larger geographic expectations of twentieth-century American evangelicals. They, too, tended to believe it would be the Soviets that would lead the last days invasion on the Holy Land. Since they no longer perceived themselves as a political entity, Latter-day Saints came to see their participation in the last days confined largely to fulfilling a parallel set of prophecies. Namely, Latter-day Saints prepared for the Second Coming through missionary work, temple work, righteous living, and emergency preparation. They would no longer emphasize last days persecution, martyrdom, or fleeing Babylon—ideas that resonated with nineteenth-century Saints but were out of place in the twentieth century.

As the twentieth century advanced, leaders addressed their sermons to a church membership that dreaded the arrival of the apocalypse more than they hopefully anticipated it. Numerous sermons were devoted to assuring the church that the righteous have no cause for fear. This rhetoric of reassurance stood in stark contrast to leaders' perception of nineteenth-century Latter-day Saints. In a discourse preached on April 2, 1854, Jedediah Grant spoke of a different type of fear among Latter-day Saints: the fear that "they would not live to see the fulfillment of the prophecies." In the same sermon, he assured those Saints that they "may now dismiss their fears, and dispense with all their anxiety in relation to the predicted events . . . for they are rolling in with such rapidity . . . as to exceed even our most sanguine expectations." He explained that "the Latter-day Saints are perfectly calm and serene among all the convulsions of the earth—the turmoils, strife, war, pestilence, famine, and distress of nations" because they were privy to prophecy.[35]

That nineteenth-century Saints were more comfortable with Armageddon than their twentieth-century counterparts should come as no surprise. After all, the early Saints had physically removed themselves from the apocalypse. Destructions would overrun the American continent—among the lands they had fled—but they were safe in Zion. Likewise, the early Saints saw themselves as the victims of a tyrannical power structure. For nineteenth-century

Saints, the apocalypse would herald the reversal of powers and finally put an end to their oppression.

The situation was vastly different in the twentieth century. The Mormon apocalyptic imagination once centered on scenes of what would happen to non-Mormons in distant cities, but after the transition into the twentieth century, God's wrath could seem indiscriminate in its breadth and scope. As such, many Latter-day Saints became alienated from the hope once inherent in their eschatology. This alienation and the declining discussion of apocalyptic in church settings would drive many to the teachings of Mormon apocalypticists outside of the church hierarchy, and even outside the church itself.

Mormon Fundamentalism

In the first decades of the twentieth century, apocalypticism prospered among those who believed the church had strayed from the original teachings of the faith. Such fundamentalist Mormons bristled at changes in ritual and theology and particularly with what they saw as the church's pandering to the state. Mormon fundamentalism in its various forms was the clearest twentieth-century continuation of nineteenth-century Mormon apocalypticism. In the hands of Mormon fundamentalists, apocalypticism developed in fascinating ways in response to the Americanization of the LDS Church. Prophecy enthusiasts in Mormon fundamentalism have been influential throughout modern Mormonism. Indeed, prophecy enthusiasts throughout Mormonism seem to have cross-pollinated one another's thought. Throughout the twentieth century, the writings of Francis M. Darter, Ogden Kraut, and others had a wide circulation that placed them in the hands of many mainstream Latter-day Saints. Orthodox Latter-day Saints were often unaware of the authors' fundamentalist affiliations, as was initially the case with both Darter and Kraut.

Apocalyptic was a constant element in early fundamentalist literature through the republication of nineteenth-century prophecies and the publication of new prophecies that continued traditional themes of resistance to oppressive government, the destruction of the wicked, places of refuge, and an eventual return to Jackson County. While prophecy that supported the church could also include these themes, Mormon fundamentalism differed most strikingly in its inclusion of an LDS apostasy and subsequent messianic "setting in order." These texts might be new, coming directly from dissenting prophets like John T. Clark or Samuel Eastman, or present as statements credited to earlier church leaders. A typical early Mormon fundamentalist apocalyptic text might describe how a church leader had predicted the church would abandon plural marriage to avoid persecution or foresee wicked leaders in the church's future. This apostasy would be resolved when the One Mighty and Strong would emerge to replace the church's corrupt leadership with the righteous. Fundamentalist apocalypticism drew on the traditional elements and sources of the apocalyptic within the faith, such as Joseph Smith's 1832 prophecy of the One Mighty and Strong, but reworked the details of their interpretation in order to provide support for their belief in an apostatized mainstream Mormonism.

Lorin C. Woolley became the most prominent Mormon fundamentalist voice in part because of his appeal to prophecy-telling. He shared experiences assisting church leaders who were hiding from law enforcement during "the raid" in the 1880s. Woolley had provided security for John Taylor while the prophet stayed at his father's home in Centerville, Utah. Reportedly, while stationed outside Taylor's room late one evening in the fall of 1886, Woolley overheard Taylor converse with Joseph Smith and Jesus Christ. The following day, Taylor told those at the home about the spiritual manifestation, including what the celestial beings had revealed to him about coming events in Utah. The church would reject plural marriage, Taylor predicted, following which "'apostacy [*sic*] and whoredom would be rampant in the Church.' He said that in the time of the seventh president of this Church, the Church would go into bondage both temporally and spiritually and in that day (the day of bondage) the One Mighty and Strong spoken of in the 85th Section of the Doctrine and Covenants would come."[36] Woolley later clarified that the One Mighty and Strong would be Joseph Smith, who would return in a resurrected state.[37]

"The Lorin Woolley Story," as it became known, provided those who believed that the church had gone astray in the 1890s with a narrative to make sense of the past decades. The prophet John Taylor had foreseen the church's wavering and had made sure that if church leaders ended polygamy, there would be those outside the hierarchy who could rightfully perpetuate it without their explicit permission. For this reason, according to Woolley, Taylor conferred on those in attendance at the fall 1886 meeting with the authority to perform plural marriages and made them swear they would ensure a child was born to a polygamous union each year until Christ's Second

Coming. This commission was at the core of Mormon fundamentalism, and Woolley later organized a council of apostles to whom he passed on this charge.[38]

Woolley was also an apocalyptic visionary in his own right. In August 1932, he told his council about a dream or vision of "what was about to happen." In it, he was shown "turmoil in all parts of eastern continent—rape, murder, disease, and devastation, reaching from there to here; Congress in turmoil, fighting each other, terrifying one another; spots in the intermountain region infected, but carnage not so general. The power of the Priesthood here will save the country from utter destruction."[39] On other occasions, he described visions of modern warfare, focusing on airplanes that "would devastate and destroy cities and villages, and highways."[40] Foreign invaders would take the Pacific coast before they were stopped by forces "from the inward country." European forces would invade the East and would "burn and destroy and kill" everything in their path until they reached the Missouri River. These armies would eventually be thwarted by prayer circles. Woolley saw three groups of elders in Canada, the United States, and Mexico whose prayers would keep the final assault at bay.[41] Woolley's visions utilized tropes and imagery that placed him squarely within the tradition of Mormon apocalypticism, even as his commitment to a narrative designed to present an alternative, authorized practice of polygamy broke with the hierarchy of the church. His prophecies are a key example of the ways in which once normative apocalyptic ideas began to share space with non-normative Mormonism.

Other fundamentalist voices contributed to the apocalyptic map of the twentieth century, as was the case with the Mexico-based Church of the Firstborn of the Fullness of Times founded by the sons of Alma Dayer LeBaron in 1955. LeBaron had decades previously proclaimed himself the One Mighty and Strong. While there would eventually be debates on which of his sons he had appointed as his successor, five of the seven brothers accepted that Joel was the rightful prophet of the new church. Shortly after the church was organized, Joel dictated a revelation declaring that he was a modern-day Moses sent to "deliver my people from bondage." In the voice of the Deity, it commanded the fundamentalist leader, Rulon C. Allred, to organize for the fundamentalists' relocation to "a land of Zion . . . Colonia LeBaron in the land of Mexico."[42] The apocalyptic message of the Church of the Firstborn revolved around a vision the elder LeBaron experienced in 1910, in which he saw 100 years into the future of Mexico. The then current revolution of 1910 would subside and the nation would prosper with improvements to infrastructure, agriculture, and education. "Toward the end of the vision, the people were better looking, of larger stature, and well dressed." Meanwhile, LeBaron "saw the entire nation of the United States swept with destruction from coast to coast." Mexico was "somewhat affected" by the destructions, but went largely unscathed. By the end of the vision, it appeared Mexico was "a garden of Eden" and "the millennial reign of peace had commenced."[43] The Church of the Firstborn urged their converts to follow the vision's warning and relocate to Mexico. One of the church's apostles Ervil LeBaron warned, "The faithful scarcely have time to gather to the places of safety in the land of the Lamanites before these judgments come."[44] The LeBarons saw their colony in Chihuahua, Mexico, as the fulfillment of other early Mormon prophecies of the Saints' preliminary gathering in the South before the final exodus to Jackson County. Members of the Church of the Firstborn expected they were the ones who would one day return to Jackson County as these prophecies anticipated.

Other Mormon fundamentalists flocked to a variety of places of refuge in the twentieth century—usually in the rural intermountain West. The most famous of these locations was the Arizona town of Short Creek, where fundamentalists gathered in 1935 to avoid prosecution. Fundamentalist leader Joseph W. Musser predicted the commune would from its "very small beginning . . . grow to fill the whole earth."[45] Woolley had identified the spot as the site of the Book of Mormon city Bountiful, "where the Savior made his visit to the Nephites upon this continent."[46] He foresaw the landscape transforming to accommodate a great influx of people. "It is a choice land. One acre there will prove as productive as five acres in other parts of Utah. One well there will develop enough water for a thousand acres. Here is one place water will bubble up in the desert, as spoken of by Isaiah."[47] Other fundamentalists relocated near Salem, Utah, where John H. Koyle predicted a city of refuge, the "White City," would be built near the Relief Mine.[48]

In 1994, the newly organized True and Living Church of Jesus Christ of Saints of the Last Days singled out the town of Manti in the Sanpete Valley as the final gathering place. For the previous two years or more, a study group had coalesced around James Harmston and others, to consider nineteenth-century Mormon distinctives, ultra-conservative politics, and apocalyptic prophecy. Early members would frequently testify about how God had inspired them to move to Manti. Even before the church officially formed, one believer began to tell others about having seen a vision of a military force intent on entering the valley through one of the mountain passes. Echoing nineteenth-century apocalyptic, he watched as a group of Latter-day Saint men in their temple robes defended the valley through prayer. In response, rocks rained down on the invaders, freeing the faithful from potential oppression and blocking the passage. Another former member, who had long since grown cynical of the idea, recalled Harmston's teachings that "God was going to place a protective dome of sorts over Manti. The town would become a latter-day Shekinah, that is, a placed [*sic*] protected by the divine presence. . . . Sentries would guard the gates to keep out the unworthy. . . . When the armies of the world attacked us—as you can bet those jealous infidels were sure to do—no problem. Armed only with faith as a grain of mustard seed, all the righteous men of Manti needed to do was command a mountain or two to bury their attackers."[49] Manti was the ultimate place of refuge.

Fundamentalists produced a variety of committed communities within a wide, if western, geographic range. While the specific landscapes varied from Mexico to Arizona and Utah (among others), the emphasis on relative geographic isolation reinforced notions of nineteenth-century Mormon identity in which the land set the people apart, marking them as a refuge from apocalyptic violence.

From the wave of messiahs in the first decade of the twentieth century, fundamentalist apocalypticism revolved around the prophecy of the One Mighty and Strong and the removal of corrupt church leaders. By the mid-twentieth century, most believed, like Woolley, that Joseph Smith would fulfill this role himself in a resurrected state, but new prophets also claimed to be this messiah, as was the case with both LeBaron and Harmston. Fundamentalists often described a last days messianic figure conflating the figures of the One Mighty and Strong and the man like Moses, who would deliver the Saints from a future bondage.[50] Among fundamentalists, the church's "bondage" consisted of financial debt, specifically the 1931 mortgage of the Temple Block to Chase National Bank, as well as the Manifesto, which prohibited them from living their religion.[51]

Fundamentalists imagined different possibilities for how the Lord would set the church in order. In one vision, John H. Koyle saw a future general conference during which Joseph Smith would appear and dismiss the current general authorities before personally appointing new leaders.[52] Others anticipated this reversal of power being brought about through a violent takeover. Like John T. Clark and Samuel Eastman, they believed it was a church president who would one day "fall by the shaft of death," as predicted in Smith's 1832 prophecy.[53] Some fundamentalists similarly interpreted another prophecy in the extracanonical Testament of Levi, which stated, "After that the Lord hath sent Vengeance upon them in the Priesthood, then will God raise up a new Priest, unto whom all the Lord's word shall be opened."[54] While Woolley and his successors in the largest fundamentalist groups discouraged animosity toward church leaders, many awaited the final showdown. Harmston once announced that LDS Church leaders, whom he called "those hypocritical jackasses," would be "called into accountability." Speaking of the LDS apostle Boyd K. Packer, he prophesied "in the name of the living God" that at this future meeting, "that man's skin is going to be turned as black as coal before he makes his departure. And how I do know that? Because I am the one that's going to make it that way!"[55] Such statements demonstrated both a sense of moral superiority from the fundamentalist perspective as well as an acceptance of violence as a means to return the church to this same morality from which it had fallen.

Related to these judgments on the church and its leaders, fundamentalist visionaries often warned that Salt Lake City and other Utah population centers would not be safe during the coming destructions. In 1995, Harmston pronounced, "The LDS church in Salt Lake City will be completely destroyed. It will fall like a rock in one day."[56] In 1983, another fundamentalist who identified himself as the One Mighty and Strong, Frank Miller, predicted that the Salt Lake Valley "will be cleansed by earthquake and plague."[57] These expectations built on the visions of Amanda Wilcox and the 1877 vision that included wickedness, devastation, and disease in Salt Lake City. This was particularly evident in fundamentalist B. Harvey Allred's graphic depiction of the destructions in the valley:

> An east wind of overwhelming fury shall come upon this land, a land hitherto preserved by its mountains from the wind's fierce blasts. It shall level to the earth the habitations and magnificent works of the ungodly and those who blaspheme God's holy name among this people; and floods of gushing waters shall pile them in heaps upon the low places in the midst of their valleys. Pestilence and diseases shall take hold upon the wicked, and their bodies shall lie strewn upon the broken earth, an unbearable stench therefrom shall afflict the living. By heaven's flaming sheets of lightning shall their bodies be burned as chaff thrown from a summer's threshing floor.[58]

While it was common for apocalypticists (even of the fundamentalist variety) to expect that Utah would escape with minimal damages, some, like Allred, made little distinction between the destructions they predicted would occur in the West and those they predicted would occur in the East.

One component of nineteenth-century apocalyptic chronology that completely disappeared in mainstream Mormonism was the concept of an American military invasion on Utah. Its absence made sense given that Latter-day Saints no longer saw the federal government as their oppressors. Tensions with the American state had largely dissipated in the first decades of the twentieth century. On the other hand, fundamentalists still lived in tension with political and legal authorities. Males were prosecuted into the 1950s. Officials from Arizona raided Short Creek in 1953, placing 263 children in foster homes.[59] For Mormon fundamentalists, the state remained the oppressor, and that oppression often took the form of potential state-led violence. As already noted in the prior discussion, the True and Living Church anticipated a standoff with troops entering the Sanpete Valley. Woolley also pointed to the protective powers of communal prayer in his prophecies concerning a last days invasion. In 1934, Koyle prophesied that the government "will send an army out here worse than Johnston's Army to put us down." Fundamentalist author Norman C. Pierce printed this prophecy from Koyle next to the prophecy of Stephen M. Farnsworth and Newman Bulkley.[60] He believed one of the great tests of the last days was "The Test of the Army," which would decide whether the Saints will "embrace the arm of the Lord for protection and defy the U.S. Army, or will . . . embrace the strong arm of the flesh represented by 100,000 able bodied soldiers."[61] Koyle predicted that one-third of the Mormons would pledge loyalty to the army before the righteous would defeat their invaders by "Priesthood Power."[62] The reliance on power in the form of priesthood during these prophesied invasions and concerns with internal loyalty during this last battle echoed similar prophecies around the time of the Utah War.

In 1988, one family of fundamentalists believed they were literally participating in this last days struggle during a twelve-day standoff with law enforcement on their property. The conflict began nine years earlier with an original standoff between John Singer, the family patriarch, after the state sought to take custody of Singer's children. Singer was shot and killed on January 18, 1979. After his death, Vickie Singer, John's widow, had a revelation that he would be resurrected and return as the One Mighty and Strong.[63] Every year on the anniversary of his death, the family flew a version of the Kingdom of God flag that Singer had designed over their home. Vickie explained: "It stands for freedom and God-given rights. He loved that flag. It has the Star of David on it and 13 stripes which stand for the thirteen tribes of Israel. The star in the middle represents Christ. It will fly in honor of what he stood for and died for."[64]

The full nationalistic implications of this symbol would be more apparent when this flag was again hoisted over the Singer home during the 1988 standoff. Addam Swapp, Singer's son-in-law, dictated a revelation on December 26, 1987, that explicitly prepared him for a physical confrontation:

> I give unto you a commandment, that you go out to battle against this church and government. . . . They will be utterly destroyed and none will remain on the face of this land, and I the Lord God will support you and multiply your Priesthood greatly that you will fight valiantly for me, for your arm will be my arm, and I will let the sword fall in your behalf. Behold I will bring your enemy under your feet and you will trample underfoot many people, and I will preserve you by the power of my Spirit.[65]

Swapp was told to "stand and fight manfully with great courage" and "fear not for your life or your families [*sic*] lives for they are in my hands."[66] On January 16, 1988, Swapp bombed an empty Latter-day Saint building and then planted a pole (or spear) in the earth with nine feathers attached, each feather representing a year since Singer was killed. The next day, the siege began and the family raised their version of the Kingdom of God flag. From there, Vickie wrote to the governor of Utah, explaining, "We fly the banner of the kingdom of God from our rooftop. It is the Ensign flag that was flown by the Saints when they first entered the valley, still living by the precepts restored through the Prophet Joseph Smith. It is our standard. We cannot give ourselves into the hands of the STATE officials."[67]

The Singers understood their conflict with the state through their nationalist expectation that the United States must fall before the Kingdom of God could be established. Echoing the Utah War, the law enforcement present seemed to be aware that they were participating in just such a contest. After the SWAT team took control of the property and arrested the adult members of the family, "the officers went up on our roof and took down the flag, as if they felt threatened by it."[68] Four years later, Vickie reflected on a movie that had been made about their experience. She criticized much of the content and the portrayal of the family, but she "appreciate[d]" a scene showing the "flag of the Kingdom of God waving gloriously over our home, which kingdom will once again be restored to earth in righteousness, allowing liberty for all."[69] The flag had symbolically tied their experience—their uncompromising separatist zeal—with the Mormon past.

Unlike the Singers, most fundamentalists did not anticipate they would be soldiers in the final battle. Fundamentalists remembered the Native Americans as harbingers of the nation's apocalypse even after this belief had dissipated among mainstream LDS after the period of transition. The authors of *Laman Manasseh Victorious*, a fundamentalist text published in 1931, retold the dream of a friend who reported seeing numerous stars emerge in the sky, which represented the rise and fall of different nations. "Then looking to the Southwest, he saw millions of pale stars and a large one moved in majesty and set himself in the midst of the other groups. The pale stars formed themselves in military order around him." He then noticed that they were not actually stars as he had first thought, but rather arrowheads. An Indian woman, who had appeared to interpret his vision, told him, "[T]hey will drip blood shortly." She explained that the "large star you see is a mighty man among my brethren of the Lamanites. Those pale stars are the myriads of the Lamanites who will hear and follow him."[70] For these fundamentalist authors, Native Americans would bring about retributive violence on the nation. In this case, they were led by a prophet among them, thus perhaps implying they were knowingly coming to the aid of their Latter-day Saint counterparts. Yet, as in all models of Latter-day Saint Amerindian apocalypticism, they had their own scores to settle over stolen property and past Euro-American atrocities.

In the 1980s, Frank Miller published a vision in which he and a friend were assaulted by marauding Native peoples. His friend was murdered, but a woman among his attackers intervened before they could kill Miller. The Native woman explained to him that she could only do so once and then, as in the previous example, interpreted the scene for the visionary's understanding. "These young braves have made a covenant one with another, that they will put to death any white person who they come across. It is their desire to claim back this their land of inheritance from the white man, who has driven and persecuted them through the years."[71] In another vision, Miller saw an army made up of troops from South America and Mexico invading the United States. "As far as the eye could see, stretched this vast ocean of moving hate. They carried whatever weapons of war they could find, from pitch forks, swords and spears, to automatic weapons." The only ones who would survive the impending assault were those who would gather to places of refuge where "the Indians would have a superstition given to them, which would prevent them from shedding blood there."[72] Writing from the perspective of the Cold War, Miller presumed the invasion occurred at the behest of a Communist plot. In each of these fundamentalist visions, the Native body served as a site through which the final battles of the apocalypse would be realized.

Another recurring feature of Mormon fundamentalist prophecy that again continued to be utilized in the twentieth century, growing out of its use in nineteenth-century Mormonism, was that of date-setting. In 1931, Francis M. Darter's full-length study of pyramidology, *Our Bible in Stone*, was particularly illustrative of this tendency. According to Darter, while the Hebrew Bible seemed to suggest that 1940 was "the extreme limit for the Second Coming of Christ," his research into the Great Pyramid had convinced him that it was possible to place the event in 1936[73] (see Figure 6.2). Darter would later amend these dates. In his short pamphlet "Amazing L.D.S. Prophetic

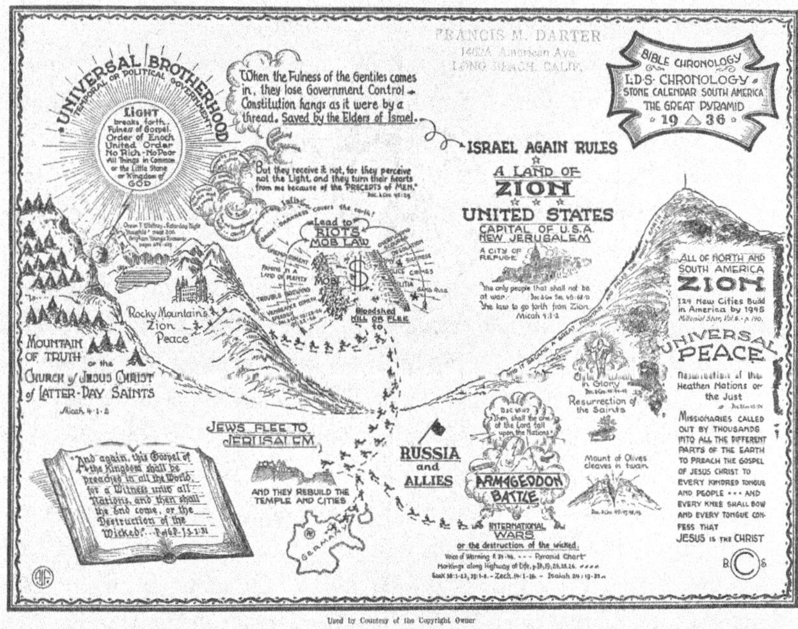

Figure 6.2 Francis M. Darter, "Bible Chronology," featured in his book *The Time of the End.* Darter was one of the most prolific prophecy enthusiasts of the early twentieth century. This image depicts his chronology of the last days based on his reading of scripture and his study of the measurements of the Pyramid of Giza.

Dates," he pinpointed the timing of the millennium to 1960 and the return of Jesus Christ to 1967.[74] Many Latter-day Saints assumed that something dramatic—perhaps the Second Coming itself—would occur before or during the year 2000 CE, an event next discussed in more detail. This belief was reflected in expectations of a rapture-like event among the Fundamentalist Church of Jesus Christ of Latter-day Saints. The church's prophet, Rulon Jeffs, had predicted that a select group he had organized in June 1999 would be "caught up when the judgments of God go over the earth, then we will be let down again."[75] James Harmston placed the Savior's return nine months later in March 2000.

On March 17, 2000, Harmston recorded a dialogue between himself and one of the Three Nephites, whom he identified as Jeremiah, in which he outlined his expectations for the next two weeks. He wanted Jeremiah to confirm that his anticipations were accurate—perhaps a needed reassurance after a previously unfulfilled date-setting.[76] Harmston's hyper-detailed prophecy demonstrated how fundamentalist apocalyptic drew on popular themes from the nineteenth century, while also developing singular motifs—many of which were shared throughout the larger fundamentalist movement.

The document included ten numbered events, summarized here. On March 25, Harmston intended to meet for prayer with his inner circle—what he called the Church of the Firstborn. At this time, the Three Nephites would "step through the veil and speak to us" and Harmston would be "called to my father's presence" and be translated (made immortal) and "receive instructions necessary to perform my assigned tasks." The next day, he would bring "some of my brethren of the Church of the Firstborn" to a hill behind the Manti Temple, where the community had found petroglyphs linking the site with Moroni's travels, and there he would "invoke the 'plague' of cleansing upon the Sanpete Valley." Some who had been specifically "marked" would immediately die and the ensuing "panic and chaos" would prompt the rest of the non-True and Living Church inhabitants of Manti to "flee the valley." The faithful would then walk to the Manti Temple, where they would "take possession of it by the power of the Fullness of the Holy Priesthood." On Monday, March 27, they would hold a meeting to dedicate the Manti Temple before the "Father, Son and Witness Testator" would perform a ritual to cause the building to emit light. Then, "We expect the Resurrected Christ to suddenly come to His Temple then and we shall greet Him with shouts of joy and love." He would translate all the faithful Saints and then there would be a "great reunion" where the faithful would meet with the angels of heaven. By

Thursday, after three days of instruction in the temple, the Manti believers would travel to the Salt Lake Temple to meet with the general authorities of the LDS Church and "rebuke them for their apostasy, rebellion to God and deception of God's children." Harmston expected it would "be overwhelming and then we will let them suffer until they meet in their general conference."

During general conference, the True and Living Church leadership and their "counterparts from the other side of the veil" would appear before the LDS Saints and "finally release their wicked leadership and collapse the entire structure of the LDS Church before their very eyes and the television viewers from around the world." Within twenty-four hours, they would "take up our assigned places along the Wasatch Front and openly in view of the inhabitants to execute the Priesthood Ordinances that will destroy by 'natural calamity' their 'Babylonian Empire' which will destroy and all of their idols and false hopes." They would then return to the "Shekinah" in Manti and begin the work of "bringing survivors to Christ." After Harmston went through his ten points, Jeremiah assured him: "[T]hese events will transpire."[77]

Harmston's blueprint for the final moments of the apocalypse shared much in common with nineteenth-century apocalyptic. Keeping in mind that in Harmston's thought, he was a reincarnation of Joseph Smith, the scenarios outlined here correspond neatly with Newman Bulkley's vision, in which Joseph Smith meets with Jesus Christ in the temple and then the faithful armed with the authority of the temple rites are able to lay waste to the wicked. Plagues and natural disasters cannot harm the faithful gathered in the place of refuge. Yet, whereas Bulkley and other visionaries saw the U.S. government as their ultimate foes, Harmston's vision reflected fundamentalism's growing animosity toward the LDS Church. The ultimate enemy of the faithful was not a corrupt government but a corrupt church. The idea of setting things in order in such a public manner echoed Koyle's prophecy in which church leaders were replaced during general conference. The idea that this dramatic reversal of powers would be televised was a modern rendition, but one that captured a broader fundamentalist sentiment that the setting in order would definitively determine the question as to who led God's work.

Yet, even if the immediate conflict would be against rival ecclesiastical leaders, the True and Living Church and other fundamentalists also ultimately viewed the U.S. political system as corrupt, and thus anticipated the inauguration of a political state in addition to the dismantling of the LDS Church's hierarchy. A painting by Kaziah May Hancock, a former member of the True and Living Church and a current evangelical Christian, depicted these last days events.[78] While Harmston preaches on the hill in front of the Manti Temple, another man plants the church's rendition of the Kingdom of God flag. The flag, like the one flown above the Singers' home, pointed to the ultimate vision of a millennial kingdom free from oppression by either ecclesiastical or governmental powers.

Vernacular Prophecy: Pseudonymous Prophecy

Apocalypticism also continued among those who saw themselves as supporters of the current direction of church leadership. As Latter-day Saints became less receptive to new visionaries, apocalypticists focused their resources on publishing anthologies of older prophecies, often including one or two that had been opposed by church leaders. While some compilers may not have been aware of institutional refutations of these and other texts, others openly defended their decision to publish them.

In 1931, Robert W. and Elisabeth A. Smith published *The Last Days*, a prophecy compilation similar to the late-nineteenth-century "Remarkable Visions" collections. The Smiths were not selective in what they included, printing environmental warnings from scientists and dire reports of international affairs alongside the usual Latter-day Saint prophecies. They petitioned readers for additional prophecies from LDS Church authorities and continued to update and republish the collection in new editions. The Smiths sought to convince their readers that the apocalypse was imminent by the sheer "weight of evidence presented,"[79] but avoided criticism by professing to not "vouch for nor discredit the prophecies" they published.[80] Periodically, advertisements for *The Last Days* in newspapers warned of imminent cataclysm. The book was apparently a bestseller with "constant requests for new editions."[81] The tenth edition appeared in 1948, and after a twenty-year hiatus, a final eleventh edition was published in 1968.[82]

Robert Smith, an advocate of the White Horse Prophecy, which he called "a sacred relic of the Prophet Joseph Smith." He claimed to be "the first person to present [it] in any book," complaining that many had reproduced his copy with its accompanying notes in pamphlet form. He tried to demonstrate that the version he printed was accurate by tracing its origins to Edwin Rushton. His own copy had come from Rushton's son-in-law, C. N. Christensen. Later, he was able to compare his copy to one that Rushton had given to church patriarch John Smith. Robert Smith decided to publish the eleventh edition of the *Last Days* after confirming his was an "exact copy"—presumably operating under the idea that uniformity seemed to authenticate the prophecy.[83]

In 1962, Duane S. Crowther, another prophecy enthusiast, included a twenty-two-page defense of the White Horse Prophecy in his *Prophecy: Key to the Future*. Taking on those who challenged "the claim that the Prophet made the prophecy,"[84] he presented the text in one column and in a second column quoted from church leaders who appeared to have made the same prediction. He concluded with eight numbered "Observations Concerning the Prophecy," arguing that Rushton's account conformed to Smith's revelations, scriptural prophecies, and the history of the nineteenth century (i.e., the revelation seemed to have been fulfilled).[85]

Crowther conceded that the portion "pertaining to foreign nations and their relationship to the Church during the [future] period of internal conflict in the United States are generally unsubstantiated. This is the area which refers to the 'Horses.'"[86] Perhaps not coincidentally, this was also the passage that Joseph F. Smith had labeled nonsense. Thus, Crowther's concession made it possible for his readers to accept both the revelation and the official statement against it. He concluded by noting that "while it is impossible to say with certainty that the prophecy is valid and that it *was* made by Joseph Smith, the overwhelming weight of the evidence at hand causes the author to be of that opinion."[87] The work of the Smiths and Crowther—along with Norman Pierce's *3½ Years* (1968) and Ogden Kraut's *Vision of the Latter Days* (1970)—played a significant role in keeping the White Horse Prophecy in circulation.

When it came to the 1877 prophecy, apocalypticists defended its authenticity by arguing for alternative authors. Since the critique against the 1877 vision was largely based on the fact that it had been incorrectly credited to Joseph F. Smith, Wilford Woodruff seemed the most reasonable alternative candidate. Based on Woodruff's transcription of the dream into his personal journal, his biographer Matthias Cowley assumed that Woodruff himself was the author. Cowley even quoted from portions of the prophecy he assigned to Woodruff in his 1909 work, *Wilford Woodruff: His Life and Labors*.[88] Following its appearance in Woodruff's biography, the prophecy was generally accepted as his dream until Assistant Church Historian Richard Turley published a critique of this claim as part of a larger study of Mormon forgeries. The crux of Turley's argument against Woodruff's authorship was that he did not speak French and thus could not have been reading the scriptures in French before bed, as the narrator of the 1877 prophecy did. In addition,

Turley argued that although Woodruff recorded the vision in first person, the fact that he pointed to a space in the text that seemed to have been intended as the place to insert the prophet's name if he acquired it.[89]

Roger K. Young, a prophecy enthusiast who will be discussed in more detail here, rebutted the finality of Turley's conclusion. Young acknowledged that Woodruff was an improbable author, but proposed John Taylor as a fitting candidate. At the time of the vision, Taylor was the senior apostle, had served a mission in France, and had even been in charge of the French translation of the Mormon scriptures. Young argued that the dream even conformed to the language of John Taylor. He also argued, in a manner similar to Crowther's defense of the White Horse Prophecy, that the prophecy was dated to the right time period and that it had already been partially fulfilled. He incorrectly claimed that "it has never received a refutation by the Church, especially by Joseph Fielding Smith, who spent a good portion of his time refuting fraudulent visions and prophecies."[90] It is possible that Young did not know of the prior refutations. Perhaps the question of authorship left church leaders without a definitive way to refer to the vision, and thus made it difficult to disavow the prophecy in a way that the Saints could associate the disavowal with the intended vision.

While the White Horse Prophecy and the 1877 vision remain the best known pseudonymous prophecies, as the twentieth century progressed, there were a few significant additions to this corpus. The "Horseshoe" or "Lunt Home" Prophecy was a rare example of a prophecy recorded in the mid-twentieth century that garnered sufficient attention to attract the condemnation of church leaders. On June 28, 1951, Edward Lunt recorded an affidavit testifying that John Taylor had, while staying at the family home in Cedar City, relayed a lengthy prophecy to Edward's mother, Sarah Ann Lunt. Sarah regularly discussed the prophecy with family members. The features, themes, and tropes provided a familiar example of the vernacular apocalyptic; there was little novel about the prophecy.

The Horseshoe Prophecy echoed the prediction credited to Joseph Smith that the Saints would travel from Utah to the South and then on to Jackson County. Taylor reportedly foretold the destruction of railroads, which would force the Saints to return as they had come. In Jackson County, "civilization will become entirely extinct" previous to the Saints' arrival. Yet, the Horseshoe Prophecy differed from other prophecies in that it focused on future devastation in Salt Lake City and the surrounding areas. Previously in the majority of the nineteenth-century prophecies, when an invading army appeared in Salt Lake City, God and the priesthood prevented the destruction of the Saints. According to Lunt, Taylor's vision was dramatically distinct: He had seen a future when the Saints would become "quite indifferent to the counsel and advice of the authorities of the church, and were more interested in the accumulation of wealth than they were in living their religion." While the average Mormon had turned from God, "he saw that war had been started, and that so great was the destruction of life within the city that blood ran down the gutters as though it were streams of water, and the violence was such that it would cause the destruction of the beautiful city." The righteous would flee the city and "remove the church records across the Colorado river." Taylor warned Sarah Ann Lunt: "If you are alive at that time, be sure that you are not behind the Church records, because after the Church records leave and are made secure, the very powers of hell would be turned loose, and there will be such destruction that there will be but little life remain, —not only in Salt Lake City, but in adjoining cities also."[91]

Lunt's account spread largely through photocopies and its inclusion in prophecy anthologies. By 1968, in the midst of increasing racial tensions in the United States, a new variant of the prophecy emerged with a fresh paragraph attached to the text. The interpolation attributed the streams of blood on Salt Lake City's streets to racial violence:

> The Negro people will make many demands upon the white people of America and gain them all, concerning "civil rights", except that the Mormon Church will not allow them to hold the Priesthood. Since the Church will be the last holdout to their wishes, they will descend upon Salt Lake City in droves, to demonstrate and force their will upon the Church. When they arrive a militia will meet them west of the city to prevent their entrance; but it will be quickly overcome by the numbers of Negroes. These marching intruders will enter the city and break through to Temple Square. They will knockdown the doors of the Temple (east), enter and desecrate the Temple, even to the ravishing of women therein. When the people of the city shall hear of this, they shall gather themselves together and in their anger wipeout the intruders to the degree that blood will flow freely down the gutters of Salt Lake City.[92]

The timing of this interpolation suggests the possibility that it was connected to a rumor campaign headed by local members of the John Birch Society that there would be a race riot in Salt Lake City during the October 1965 general conference. The National Association for the Advancement of Colored People (NAACP) discounted the rumors, yet news of race riots in other American cities fomented panic in Utah.[93]

Folklorist William Wilson recorded two informants who relayed this portion of the prophecy as they had heard it. The first was a professional church education instructor who claimed "that it was common knowledge among teachers in the church educational system that a confrontation with Black Panthers was going to take place in the streets of Salt Lake City and that this would be a fulfillment of the prophecy that Blacks would wreak havoc in the streets of Zion. He said that this prophecy was given to President Taylor. It was common knowledge from reliable sources [he said] that Blacks and hippies were arming themselves in the canyons east of the city and that the FBI had uncovered plans by revolutionaries to hit Salt Lake City with a violence campaign." Wilson identified his second informant as a "stockbroker who claimed he did not believe the part [of the Horseshoe Prophecy] about Negroes." According to the statement of this second informant, "John Taylor is supposed to have said that the Negroes will march to the west and that they will tear down the gates to the temple, ravage the women therein, and destroy and desecrate the temple. Then the Mormon boys will pick up their deer rifles and destroy the Negroes, and that's when the blood will run down the street."[94] Although many met the claims of a Utah-based race war with suspicion, the timely additions obtained a greater notoriety than the original vision itself.

On March 30, 1970, the First Presidency under the direction of Harold B. Lee issued a statement criticizing the Horseshoe Prophecy on eight points. Because the revelation claimed to originate with John Taylor, the church carefully dismantled the reliability of Lunt's account altogether. Specifically, the notice stated that the Horseshoe Prophecy varied in each of its versions and that only one of these versions contained the reference to the future racial unrest in Salt Lake City. The statement concluded by chocking up the prophecy as "just another evidence of the cleverly designed motives of individuals who seize upon the emotionalism of our present day to get publicity, and to further agitate the feelings of Church members on matters which must be left to the wisdom of the Lord and His guidance, which are under His divine control."[95] Prophecy enthusiasts tended to heed Lee's condemnation of the prophecy's later interpolation, while still regarding the original affidavit as legitimate.[96]

So far as written texts are concerned, only one other prophecy credited to a church leader has entered the corpus of popular prophecy literature: a nuclear war prophecy credited to George Albert Smith. On at least three occasions between October 1988 and March 1989, David Hughes Horne recorded his memory from the postwar 1940s when Smith, then the Latter-day Saint prophet, visited his childhood home. Smith was both a neighbor and a cousin, so such encounters were apparently not unusual. The prophet reportedly told the family: "I have had a troublesome vision of another great and terrible war that made the war just ended look like a training exercise, and people died like flies. It began at a time when the Soviet Union's military might dwarfed that of the United States, and we, that is the United States, would have missiles that carried an atomic bomb in Europe." Horne recalled that Smith stated that the "worst time of the depression will seem like a Sunday School picnic when compared with how conditions will be after that great war." In 1964, Horne would hear BYU professor Sidney Sperry say that he had once approached George Albert Smith after a conference and found him "woefully mutter[ing] as he looked over the congregation, 'They'll die like flies.'"[97] While Horne's depiction of Smith's horror at the apocalypse—foreseeing the slaughter of the faithful by nuclear weapons—does not seem to fit the typical optimism then expressed by church leaders concerning the survival of church members in the last days, the prophecy does align with vernacular apocalypticism's ability to give voice to the fears inhabiting the contemporary cultural consciousness. Thus, this popular vision clearly manifested the nuclear fears that were increasingly prevalent throughout the United States during the 1980s.

Vernacular Prophecy: Calculating Armageddon from the Cold War to the Year 2000

Joanna Brooks, who grew up in southern California, recalled the prominent role nuclear war played for her family in her popular memoir, *The Book of Mormon Girl*. She described how her mother pointed out probable local targets for Russian nukes, promising that their deaths would be quick. The history of Mormon authorities encouraging church members to store a year's supply of food and other necessities for future hardships grew out of economic anxieties following the Great Depression. Brooks depicted how this counsel took an apocalyptic undercurrent by itemizing for the reader the family's survival gear for each child and grownup along with the supplies that filled the cupboards in the garage: "Industrial-size water barrels lined the back of our house . . . in case a nuclear attack or ash falling from the skies made the swimming pool unfit to drink."[98]

Brooks's family were far from the only ones who expected that their food storage and emergency preparations would be used in the apocalypse. A popular story from the era described an encounter between a nameless but usually female Latter-day Saint—sometimes a church employee—and the prophet Spencer W. Kimball. Kimball asked the woman if she had her food storage and when she replied in the negative, Kimball responded in similar but distinct ways. "If you knew what I knew, you would get it soon."[99] "He said if she knew what he did she would be out buying it now."[100] Or even, "If you don't have it now, it's too late."[101] One variant claimed the prophet recommended the woman sell her family home and use the money on food storage.[102] In another account, the woman had planned a nice wedding: "If you knew what I knew, you would be using your money for other purposes."[103] In yet another account, when the woman encountered Kimball, she was carrying Christmas gifts: "If you knew what I knew, you would return the gifts and use the money for a year's supply."[104] And in a final account, the woman had recently married and Kimball told her, "If you knew what I knew, you would sell your ring and buy food storage."[105]

Other stories recounted Latter-day Saints being warned by divine messengers—usually, one of the Three Nephites—to prioritize the purchase of food storage. Frequently, the story held that LDS motorists picked up a hitchhiker who during the trip asked them, "Do you have your two-year supply?" or declared, "Get your food storage," before disappearing from the car.[106] These narratives all clearly centered around a specific apprehension: that it was possible to disrupt and destabilize the system of food production and distribution, and that this disruption would be dangerous without adequate preparation. So, while Brooks's family were no doubt zealots among Latter-day Saints, the culture of anxiety in Mormonism produced by this apprehension created a space in which such preparations were not only emphasized, but made sense.

While there are no records of such ominous warnings being imparted by other contemporary church leaders as those depicted in the stories of Spencer W. Kimball, it is likely not coincidental that so many of these accounts circulated in 1977, a year after one general authority had called on the Saints to prioritize food storage. In the April 1976 general conference, the Seventy Vaughn J. Featherstone preached solely on the subject of food storage and declared that "one year from today we ought to have a year's supply of food in all active—and many inactive—members' homes in the Church." He recommended that food storage should take precedence over Christmas, new clothes, and vacations. Featherstone suggested the sale of "luxury possessions" and cutting down on expenses to buy the supplies.[107] As we will see, Featherstone himself believed the Second Coming was imminent, but he did not explicitly connect the apocalypse with his counsel to collect survival essentials. Food storage would be useful in times of emergency regardless of eschatology after all. On the ground, the apocalypse was the lens by which many Saints understood their church's encouragement to prepare for hardships, particularly in an era of Cold War apprehensions.

Brooks also recalled believing that her family might trek through the apocalypse to Jackson County. "We grew up always ready to abandon this world, to take our small backpacks of bottled water, freeze-dried food, first-aid kits, and candles, and simply walk away, walk as far as Missouri if we had to, if that was where the New Jerusalem would be built."[108] While the vast majority of Mormons, and even the majority of committed preppers among them, only fantasized about this journey, some Mormons have actually relocated to Missouri in hopes to be there ahead of the larger exodus of Saints.[109] In 1979, the recurring emphasis on Missouri among some segments of the church membership raised enough concern that the church's periodical, *The Ensign*, published an article tackling "Missouri myths." The author, Graham Doxey, argued that the gathering to Missouri was yet future and was unlikely to include all church members. Doxey urged believers to await word from the "living prophet," whose "vision is both perfect and sufficient for our day."[110] There was definitely a spectrum of last days zeal. Brooks's family were deeply immersed in apocalyptic preparations, but they never left the grid or relocated in response to prophecy.

The average Latter-day Saint was more likely to take an interest in the last days as the century moved forward. Based on the wealth of apocalyptic discussions in the 1980s and 1990s, it is reasonable to think that the year 2000 should have had more of an impact on Latter-day Saints than it did. Joseph Smith had interpreted John the Revelator's vision of Christ opening a book sealed with seven seals as the unfolding of the history of the world. The seven seals represented "seven thousand years of its continuance or its temporal existence."[111] According to a traditional reading of biblical chronologies, the world began in 4000 BCE. The millennium, ushered in by the Second

Coming, would begin at the opening of the seventh thousand-year period or in 2000 CE. Many Mormons came to believe that April 6 was a seal's start date because of a popular twentieth-century LDS belief that Jesus' birth occurred on April 6, 1 CE, corresponding to the opening of the fifth seal. Thus, many apocalypticists accepted April 6, 2000, as a date of great significance in the apocalyptic timeline.

Rumors that a church leader had hinted at the timing of the Second Coming were increasingly commonplace as the new millennium gradually approached. One set of legends recorded in the 1960s alleged that David O. McKay, then the Latter-day Saint prophet, had prayed about the date of the Second Coming while in the Salt Lake Temple. One account collected in 1961 and preserved in Brigham Young University's folklore archives stated, "There have been rumors going around the church of a vision President McKay had in the temple not long ago. It consisted of his inquiring of the Lord as to how close we are to the Millennium. It is said that when he came out of the temple he was very pale and made the statement, 'Even I didn't think it was this close.'"[112] A second account, collected by a Brigham Young University student, was more expansive:

> This story was related to me by Lueda Baggley, whose uncle was one of the men asked to attend the conference held for all mission presidents about a year ago. On the last day of the conference, all of the people were waiting for President McKay to come so that they could all go through the temple. They waited quite a while for him, and soon became quite concerned because the appointed time for meeting had passed. When he finally arrived, Lueda's uncle said that he had tears in his eyes. He told the people that he had been pleading with the Lord for more time for the people. That the Lord specifically told him three things of major importance. First, the people were to watch for Russia; second, the people were to build up their food supplies, third, the people were to become more righteous and humble themselves.[113]

In 1978, one commentator drafted his "speculation" on the timing of the Parousia based on an alleged statement from apostle Gordon B. Hinckley, who had told a group of missionaries in South Africa that the Second Coming would occur on April 6 and would occur on a Sabbath. The apocalyptic commentator plotted out when each April 6 would fall on a Sunday up to the end of the century. He found three Sundays that fell on April 6: in 1980, 1986, 1997, respectively. He reasoned, "1980 seems too soon and 1997 too late. The year 1986 could be the one we're looking for."[114] When Hinckley was first asked whether he had made the statement as reported, he simply retorted, "Of course not—I know better than that." However, after he realized the "speculation" document was circulating widely among Latter-day Saints, he publicly "set the record straight" in a March 1979 devotional at Brigham Young University.[115]

Four years later, another document that claimed to originate with a general authority began to circulate among the Saints. However, unlike Hinckley's alleged assertions about the Second Coming, this document was legitimate. On April 6, 1983, Seventy Vaughn J. Featherstone wrote a letter to "my beloved fellow saints in the twenty-first century," which was to be deposited in a time capsule associated with the dedication of a temple in Atlanta, Georgia. Featherstone expected these future believers who would read his letter to "have witnessed the Second Coming of Christ, the day for which we have long awaited."[116] The assumption that the year 2000 was the timing of the scheduled Parousia was widespread.

Church leaders continued to refuse to speculate about the timing of the Second Coming and often—like Joseph Smith in 1844—suggested it would come generations from the time in question. While standing by Smith's seven-thousand-year history of the earth, Bruce R. McConkie explained, "We, of course, cannot tell with certainty how many years passed from the fall of Adam to the birth of Jesus, nor whether the number of years counted by our present calendar has been tabulated without error."[117] Leaders have frequently discouraged members from speculating on the timing of the Second Coming and instead encouraged them to seek personal righteousness for when the day would finally arrive. These repeated protests of church leaders hint at how widespread they believed the actual expectations for the year 2000 were.

Church Sunday schools regularly assigned curriculum on the signs of the times and the Second Coming. Yet, during the last decade of the twentieth century, those who desired something beyond the general discussion of scripture available in church meetings or McConkie's *Millennial Messiah* could find it in new voices. In 1991, Avraham Gileadi's *The Last Days: Types and Shadows from the Bible and the Book of Mormon* was published by the church-owned Deseret Book and quickly became a bestseller. Gileadi was an Old Testament scholar whose books came with the endorsement of professors of scripture from Brigham Young University, including the highly revered Hugh Nibley. Gileadi's first book, a translation of Isaiah with commentary based on the Book of Mormon, appeared in 1988 with little controversy, until reviewers zeroed in on Gileadi's emphasis on a last days messiah: the Davidic servant, a prophetic forerunner to the Second Coming. While Gileadi's expectations of a last days king held little immediate risk to the composition of the church, such claims had persistently provided the basis for a schism in Latter-day Saint history. After being on sale for only a month, *The Last Days* had nearly sold its first printing of 8,649 copies when Deseret Book decided to withdraw it from circulation, citing excessive complaints.[118] According to one report, "LDS general authority Deseret Book board members apparently decided to pull the book due to reports that some members were making dramatic career changes and had moved to remote locales because of the book's apocalyptic tone."[119] Gileadi's writings were only one part of the larger apocalyptic movement that was gaining traction in the late twentieth century. He stood out for his popularity.

Ronald Garff was another apocalypticist whose work quickly gained attention and eventual notoriety. Garff had produced a set of three videotapes, "Today Through Armageddon," in which he lectured on the events of the last days, providing actual dates. Joanne Hanks, former Mormon and member of the True and Living Church, would cite a videotape series that was almost certainly "Today Through Armageddon" as the start of her family's fascination with the end of the world. A friend of her husband "raved" about the series, claiming that "they revealed secret knowledge about the Second Coming of Christ."[120] Hanks described Garff, whom she called "the nerdy fellow," "weaving together passages from the Bible, Book of Mormon, and other Mormon scriptures . . . [and] demonstrated step by step and diagram by diagram, that he knew when the Second Coming of Christ would happen. It wasn't just soon. It was alarmingly soon."[121] She was convinced by the end of the series, but ultimately decided to throw away the videos because she was aware the church frowned on this type of speculation "and instead to remain worthy on general principle."[122] The Hanks' interest drew them back, however and they "replaced the videos, devoured books on the subject, and searched out clandestine meetings with the like-minded."[123] As it was for thousands of other Latter-day Saints, for the Hanks, the early 1990s was a time of apocalyptic preparations and study. Garff had tapped into a significant enough consumer base that sales from the series provided for his livelihood. When local leaders instructed him to stop selling "Today through Armageddon," he told reporters that he had to "make up my mind. . . . Do I want to keep my church membership, or do I want to eat?"[124]

There is no question that the church was concerned with the growing apocalyptic marketplace. Garff was warned he could lose his membership and, in 1993, Gileadi was excommunicated. The deeper concern was with apocalypticism's confluence with survivalism and ultraconservative politics. This confluence had a mobilizing effect on radicals. The Gulf War had already created an uptick in American apocalyptic fears, which was made all the more combustible with George H. W. Bush's infamous declaration of a "New World Order." The president's rhetoric inadvertently tapped into a vein of conspiracy theory focused on the dangers of internationalism to American sovereignty.[125] Historian Michael Barkun detailed the major themes within the movement:

> The systematic conversion of republican institutions by a federal government utilizing emergency powers; the gradual subordination of the United States to a world government operating through the United Nations; the creation of sinister new military and paramilitary forces, including governmental mobilization of urban youth gangs; the permanent stationing of foreign troops on U.S. soil; the widespread use of black helicopters to transport the tyranny's operatives; the confiscation of privately owned guns; the incarceration of so-called patriots in concentration camps run by FEMA; the implantation of microchips and other advanced technology for surveillance and mind control; the replacement of Christianity with a New Age world religion; and, finally, the manipulation of the entire apparatus by a hidden hierarchy of conspirators operating through secret societies.[126]

While not all late-twentieth-century American apocalypticists subscribed to each of these ideas, they often subscribed to some of them. This included many Mormon apocalypticists who began to read their own narrative through these influences.

In the summer of 1990, Sterling Allen organized the American Study Group as a community to discuss far-right politics from a Mormon perspective. By the fall of 1991, the group was approximately 5,000 members strong and believed the United States was on the verge of a Soviet invasion. In the meantime, they were incensed at Bush's "New World Order," believing the president intended to scrap the Constitution in favor of an international government. A September 1991 newspaper article paraphrased a lecture sponsored by the Midvale Utah chapter of the American Study Group. The speaker declared: "The wise should establish a food reserve in their homes, learn hunting and gardening skills and become less dependent on government for support. . . . Bomb shelters would help—as would a refuge in the mountains, fully stocked with arms and supplies."[127] Some members were more prepared than others, including some who were establishing "places of refuge" and some who were building bomb shelters.

That the merger between prophetic and political beliefs resonated with an even larger population of Mormons was evident by the results of the 1992 presidential election. Populist candidate Bo Gritz, an LDS convert, obtained nearly 28,000 votes in Utah. He campaigned on "abolishing the IRS, eliminating foreign aid, prohibiting foreign ownership of American soil and opposing global government."[128] Gritz unabashedly drew on apocalyptic rhetoric, such as when he warned, "We must return America to God through a revival of Christian ethics or lose our birthright to an international federation founded in Atheism and the Anti-Christ."[129] Latter-day Saint leaders grew concerned with grassroots efforts to promote Gritz's candidacy and instructed him "not to accept invitations to speak in church buildings." According to Gritz, church leaders went so far as to instruct members not to support his campaign.[130]

Speakers at the October 1992 general conference took on the Saints' mounting apocalypticism. Apostle Boyd K. Packer denounced those "among us now who have not been regularly ordained by the heads of the Church and who tell of impending political and economic chaos, the end of the world. . . . They are misleading members to gather to colonies or cults."[131] Apostle M. Russell Ballard warned the Saints to not "be caught up in extreme preparations."[132] In November, many leaders from rural Utah where apocalypticism was particularly a concern met to discuss how they should respond to "troublesome ideologies." Emerging from this meeting were three documents aimed to assist regional leaders in the identification of extremists and dangerous beliefs.[133]

Likely the most important among them was the "Profile of the Splinter Group Members or Others with Troublesome Ideologies," which was reportedly used by at least six stake presidents "as a guide for excommunications."[134] In some instances, the profile listed traits shared by many staunchly conservative Latter-day Saints that would have generated little controversy: membership in the John Birch Society, homeschooling, food storage, and a belief "that the government is corrupt." Yet in context, the list was clearly concerned with the extremism associated with survivalism, apocalypticism, and fundamentalist leanings. These potentially unsafe Saints did not just have food storage, but rather were "inordinately preoccupied with food storage." They did not just expect the Second Coming, but had "a preoccupation with the end of the world and the events preceding the coming of the Savior." They seemed to have little regard for the authority of their church leaders. Some met with fundamentalist leaders. The profile identified certain influential figures around which this network of believers coalesced. "They listen to tapes such as the 'Bo Gritz' tapes and others about such topics as Armageddon." "They read the books of Avraham Gileadi and other materials which are unapproved by the Church."[135] Many met in "study groups," which they valued to such an extent that when asked to stop, "they tell you [i.e., Church leaders] straight out they will have to take the matter to the Lord to see what He tells them before they will agree." The profile noted "that many of these people reportedly have visions and dreams which they share with group members but not priesthood leaders." As always, the threat of charismatic revelation shared among church members was a cause for concern, as was establishing communities of like-minded believers outside of the church-sponsored congregation.

The points by which dangerous extremism was identified were not necessarily in and of themselves warning flags when considered individually, but when they were considered together as a group, they painted a portrait of apostasy. Considering such persons a danger to the flock, church leaders felt justified in trying to root them out. This more authoritarian approach to regulation was covered in November 29, 1992, when the *Salt Lake Tribune* ran an article asserting that the church was "purging hundreds of Mormon dissidents who Church officials say are preoccupied unduly with Armageddon." A church spokesman characterized the idea that the church was conducting a "purge" as an exaggeration, but acknowledged that "LDS Church leaders increasingly have been concerned about ultraconservative 'super patriots' and survivalists, many of whom have quit their jobs and moved their families to mountain retreats."[136]

Ultimately, the church's efforts to police apocalypticists had mixed results. On one hand, they inadvertently strengthened the ranks of fundamentalist communities, like Jim Harmston's True and Living Church, which consisted of marginalized apocalypticists. The message of the True and Living Church would attract thousands to weekend instructional retreats, known as "the Models," and hundreds would migrate to Sanpete Valley to participate in the apocalypse. Such large-scale mobilization and effectiveness were exactly the sort of dissent the church had hoped to prevent. On the other hand, the church's efforts effectively discouraged members from becoming consumed in apocalyptic culture. As Tara Westover's recent memoir *Educated* suggests, Y2K fears had very little impact on Latter-day Saints even in rural areas where such fears prospered. Westover's father was a committed survivalist who raised his family off the grid, but, according to his daughter, by 2000 no one took his survivalist warnings seriously.[137] Indeed, there were no significant movements radicalizing church members at the turn of the millennium, in part, due to the institutional regulation from the previous decade.

Vernacular Prophecy: Sharing the Sacred

Returning to the beginning of the century, the regulation of apocalyptic during the period of transition marginalized and limited the influence of prophecy enthusiasts and visionaries. Without a forum in church periodicals, visionaries turned to a small number of independent publishers, such as Robert and Elizabeth Smith's Pyramid Press. Lerona Wilson did just that, publishing her visions with the Smiths in 1915 and 1933.[138] Other visionaries such as Alma D. Erickson did not publish their manifestations until much later.[139] Even when the count includes unpublished visions that circulated informally, there began to be fewer manifestations revolving around destructions preceding the eschaton.

One possible explanation for the absence of a substantial record of apocalyptic dreams and visions from the mid-twentieth century is that these manifestations shifted in their emphasis from destructions and refuge to genealogy and temple work. Visionaries like Archie Graham, Heber Q. Hale, and even Lerona Wilson foregrounded their knowledge of the afterlife and the essential nature of temple rites over warnings of Armageddon.[140] Of course, the urgency through which these visionaries promoted temple work also came with last days overtones: ordinances needed to be performed in preparation for the Savior's return. And it is important to note that this early diminishing of the apocalyptic in the twentieth century did not last: Later in the century, apocalyptic themes experienced a resurgence.

What the regulation of apocalypticism most successfully accomplished among everyday Latter-day Saints was the relegation of these conversations to private settings. Latter-day Saints came to accept that such topics had inherent dangers and acted accordingly. Apostle Boyd K. Packer offered one of the most revealing reflections of the Latter-day Saint concern over sharing sacred experiences. He warned:

> Personal spiritual experiences should be treated with care. Dreams and visions and visitations are not uncommon in the Church and are a part of all that the Lord has revealed in this dispensation. Thus a worthy Church member may be the recipient of a marvelous spiritual experience. I have come to know that these experiences are personal and are to be kept private. Recipients should ponder them in their heart and not talk lightly about them.[141]

At the same time, these experiences were designed to be shared—albeit rarely—under the condition that the recipient feels spiritually moved to do so. "We may be prompted on occasion to tell of our spiritual experiences, but generally we should regard them as sacred." Personal revelations belonged to the recipient as a special type of secret that was only shared under supernatural guidance. While there were benefits of mutual edification and social bonding that came with sharing such intimate details of one's encounter with the divine, doing so also came with the risk that these manifestations would be considered of little importance by the hearer.[142] Packer recommended that such "experiences which involve dreams or visions or visitations might be recorded and put away in family records to serve as a testimony and an inspiration to our descendants in the generations ahead."[143] These manifestations are to be "put away" or concealed to preserve their sanctity and rightfully divulged only after one receives an additional spiritual prompting to do so. One's family and posterity are uniquely privileged to access these personal revelations.

Packer also weighed in on the ethics and conditions of sharing someone else's experience that they had entrusted to you. He posited different rules for historic and contemporary manifestations. In the former case, "it is not out of order . . . to present some experiences from those who have lived in years past." When it came to contemporary sharing, he explained:

> I made a rule for myself a number of years ago with reference to this subject. When someone relates a spiritual experience to me, personally or in a small, intimate group, I make it a rigid rule not to talk about it thereafter. I assume that it was told to me in a moment of trust and confidence, and therefore I never talk about it. If, however, on some future occasion

> I hear that individual talk about it in public in a large gathering, or where a number of people are present, then I know that it has been stated publicly and I can feel free under the right circumstances to relate it. But I know many, many sacred and important things that have been related to me by others that I will not discuss unless I am privileged to do so under the rule stated above.[144]

Packer's rules focused on maintaining confidences and recognizing the privileged status of being entrusted with a spiritual experience.

Scott Mitchell, an LDS graduate student at the University of Missouri-Columbia, studying LDS women's visions of their future children reached a similar conclusion. Folklorist Margaret Brady had claimed that women widely shared these visions "not only . . . within close family groups, but they are most frequently told in Relief Society meetings, as personal testimony during church services, and as didactic anecdotes in classes for young adults."[145] They did so, according to Brady, to garner status within the community. This claim puzzled Mitchell since, as a life-long Mormon, he had yet to hear such a story. Ultimately, as he sought informants, he discovered that the average Latter-day Saint was hesitant to share these stories. Those who had heard the stories secondhand encouraged Mitchell to interview the person who had told them the story, rather than to record their version of the story outright. His own family members proved the most cooperative informants. Mitchell concluded that accounts of these experiences were told in limited circles and that Mormon men often felt they were simply not entitled to repeat these narratives.[146] Latter-day Saints shared Packer's sentiments that there should be caution when sharing the experiences of another.

It was in "small, intimate groups" and "personal" conversations that Mormon apocalyptic endured in everyday interactions between Saints and where it continues to thrive until this day. Yet, because skepticism of vernacular apocalyptic is far-reaching, small intimate circles may have their own tensions in place. I witnessed such a scene in 2013 when in a small café in Provo, Utah, I sat down to lunch with my wife and two friends—both LDS women in their thirties. During our engagement, conversation turned to a recent lecture one of the women had attended. She was moved by the lecturer's telling of a near-death experience that had allowed him to share insights about the afterlife, as well as details about the Second Coming. For my friend, hearing this person's story was a spiritual experience itself; however, understanding its potential to ignite controversy, she prefaced her remarks by stating that none of the speaker's revelations contradicted official church doctrine. The other friend who had been listening intently looked down uncomfortably. She queried why God would share a revelation of that magnitude with this man rather than one of his prophets. While any Latter-day Saint might have such an experience, this visionary had violated the taboo of sharing his experiences widely. For a moment, our believing friend nervously defended the right of a Latter-day Saint to testify of his or her personal experiences that confirmed church doctrine. The lunch continued, but both of our friends seemed quieter in the wake of the awkward exchange.

Even a family setting could contain these same tensions. In 1982, Barbara Hill, a Latter-day Saint college student in Utah, explained how "apocalyptic stories hold a strange place" in her family:

> My father tends to be very skeptical about them. He always says, "Yes, and if you don't like that one, wait a week and there will be a new rumor going around." According to him, it's all pure conjecture. He very rarely tells the story himself, but when he does mention them, it is usually because he is ridiculing them for how silly and far out they are. As a result, we don't tell these stories much when he is around. Conversely, my mom is a great believer in a lot of this apocalyptic lore. She has done a lot of studying in the prophecies of Isaiah and Ezekiel, and can see how these prophecies are being fulfilled.[147]

Hill's mother, a prophecy enthusiast, shared apocalyptic stories with her daughter, suggesting that while she avoided the topic with her spouse, she managed to find relationships that would allow for just these sorts of interactions and sharing, such as her relationship with her child.

With the advent of the Internet, these circles—"small, intimate groups"—could take on nontraditional forms. By the mid-1990s, online communities consisting of Latter-day Saints sharing dreams, visions, and prophecies were thriving. The largest of these communities, "Another Voice of Warning" [LDSAVOW], has thousands of paid subscribers. The website includes a classifieds section where users can buy anything from camping equipment to assault rifles to land in remote parts of Utah. The site owner publishes reports of current events and how they pertain to prophecy. Most importantly, its discussion boards serve as a hub for the collection of hundreds of individually submitted dreams and visions, along with more general last days talk. Like the apocalyptic imaginary of the nineteenth century, these dreams echo and build on one another with scenarios of impending famine, disease, nuclear war, foreign invasions, and other calamities that will strike the United States. The community is steeped in survivalism, and as such, much discussion focuses on food storage and other forms of preparation.

Like their early Mormon counterparts, these visionaries prophesy of last days events in local contexts. A collection of these reports published by the site founder, Roger K. Young, contains many dreams focused on locations in the American Northwest, Idaho, Georgia, and Utah. A typical account includes individuals being called to a church meeting, where the faithful are told to flee more populated areas and relocate to remote Latter-day Saint communities with basic needs and a tent. They refer to this future gathering as the "call out." LDSAVOW and Young's writings have popularized the idea of last days tent cities—an echo of the Vision of the Plagues discussed in Chapter 5. Members of AVOW consider themselves faithful members of the church, and the website prominently displays a warning against promoting apostate agendas.

In one of his works, Young addressed Latter-day Saint suspicions of apocalyptic dreams and visions head on:

> All of these dreams and visions are of special importance and significance to the individuals to whom they are given. It is they who are then responsible for the understanding and application of the message of such dreams and visions in their lives. Occasionally, we find that some of this revelation has some significance to others beyond the receiving individual, their families, or their direct responsibility. Of course, we are very blessed when such a dream or vision is recorded and then an inspired interpretation is given by either a heavenly messenger or by one with prophetic or apostolic authority. It helps clarify things so well. However, this is often not available.[148]

Young assures his readers that he does not intend for these revelations to be understood as "official" or church-sponsored in any sense. They are only binding on the individuals who received them. However, he disagrees with the "currently popular belief among the Gentile members that only church leaders can have dreams or visions that might have interest to others. . . . [I]t is a true principle that only priesthood leaders can have revelation that can command those under their stewardship. The distinction between commanding others or just informing others is the key point."[149] He warns that individuals who read his compilation should "ponder, pray about, and decide if there is any relevance or importance for themselves and their family."[150] Despite his popularity, Young explicitly denies that he claims to be a visionary or inspired interpreter of last days events. For this reason, he presents the visions in whole, "for each individual reader to discern for himself their validity and whether or not there might be some relevance to himself and his particular situation."[151] The caution by which community members share their visions and the sincere effort to distinguish themselves from schismatic prophecy movements comes in response to the general perception that such views are heterodox. The potential of such skepticism is a constant undercurrent of the modern Latter-day Saint's experience sharing personal revelation, whether that sharing occurs in private or public contexts.

Vernacular Apocalypticism and Near-Death Experiences

In the twenty-first century, lay visionaries became celebrities in what was increasingly referred to as LDS "prepper" circles. In the nineteenth century, folk prophets recorded short accounts of their prophecies that they then published as broadsheets or in small pamphlets. Few of these visionaries sought to establish themselves as public figures and rarely provided additional commentary on their experiences. In contrast, the most prolific contemporary visionaries have published full-length books and afterward continued to interact with their readers through additional writings, podcasts, interviews, and public lectures. It is to these personalities we now turn our attention.

For decades, the best-known lay prophecies have been presented in the form of first-person near-death experience (NDE) accounts. In 1992, the writings of an active Mormon, Betty Jean Eadie, became the first national NDE bestseller. Eadie's *Embraced by the Light* was initially marketed with a flyer branding the work "Of Special Interest to Members of the Church of Jesus Christ of Latter-day Saints."[152] The first printing of 20,000 copies sold in ten days, largely from sales in Utah.[153] Eadie dealt with the afterlife, rather than the apocalypse. However, a decade later, NDE literature made an apocalyptic-turn.

The earliest of these apocalyptic NDE visionaries was Gayle Smith, who, in 1996, began to share her experiences on Utah radio programs. She eventually authored a short account entitled *Gayle's Story: One Woman's Visions of the End Days in America*. While Smith's initial NDE took place in 1969, it was not until 1993 that she began to see visions of a "cleansing" of the

Saints in Utah. She described a sequence of events that would start with an economic collapse and then be followed ten days later with one and then another major earthquake along the Wasatch front. While other visionaries had described the breakdown of social ties in eastern cities, Smith's vision was set apart by its portrayal of violence, cannibalism, and rape occurring in the Mormon homeland. She reflected on desperation's power to corrupt and decivilize. "People just go crazy and they start rioting, looting and killing because they are angry. . . . There is nothing to eat so people kill others because they are hungry. After a time they begin to kill because they enjoy it. All of them become very depraved. I saw these marauding bands doing awful sadistic sexual acts, cannibalism, eating people while they are still alive and kicking."[154] Smith "said seeing and anticipating the horrible deeds done by these people turned sub-human is far more frightening to her than seeing the natural calamities she has seen and believes will come."[155] In the resulting chaos, the government—specifically, the Federal Emergency Management Agency (FEMA)—would institute marital law, confiscate firearms and food storage, and outlaw prayer and religious gathering. Those who resisted the new laws, including a curfew and travel restrictions, would face concentration camps or death squads. Meanwhile, the government would unleash a plague on the populace and a nuclear device would explode in Salt Lake City. Russia would invade from the east, while China would invade from the west.

Smith addressed "the mark of the beast," a physical mark on the right hand or forehead, that, according to Revelation, the tyrannical government of the last days would force on its citizens. "No man might buy or sell, save he that had the mark, or the name of the beast, or the number of his name . . . his number is Six hundred threescore and six."[156] Smith's vision is one of very few instances when the mark of the beast appeared in Mormon sources, especially in its original economic context. Smith, echoing evangelical apocalypticists, identified the mark as a "computer chip" that would record a person's vital information and track their movements. There would be an eighteen-digit number connected to each chip, beginning with 666 "which represents the world government," another three-digit national code, a three-digit area code, and concluding with the individual's Social Security number.[157] Similar details had appeared in the writings of earlier non-Mormon prophecy enthusiasts, who suggested the mark would consist of an eighteen-digit code (i.e., 6 + 6 + 6), including the combination of the Social Security number and the expanded zip code.[158]

Smith is noteworthy for being the only NDE visionary who gained wide appeal while also depicting the church in adversarial terms. The church, she claimed, would yield to the reign of the Antichrist in order to avoid persecution. Leaders would order members to turn over their food storage, which they would then give to the government. When they did so, Latter-day Saints would be obliged to receive the mark of the beast and deny Christ. Those who resisted would be beheaded. The Saints' food storage would be redistributed to those who had taken the mark. Smith was distressed that the church would be complicit with the Beast, but was "told that it is very important that I warn people of this!"[159] Years later, Smith would be excommunicated, possibly due to later allegations that the Mormon prophet Thomas S. Monson had raped her.[160] As a result, her visions are not as popular among LDS prophecy enthusiasts as they once were, but they do still occasionally appear in collections or discussions of the last days. Mechelle McDermott's popular anthology *The Great Gathering* quotes from Gayle Smith, but a parenthetical note does state: "[D]ream was when she was in full standing, currently excommunicated."[161]

Sarah Menet, an LDS convert, also depended on radio programming to disseminate word of her 1979 NDE before she put her story into print. Her memoir *There Is No Death* focused on descriptions of the spirit world in the vein of *Embraced by the Light*, with only one chapter describing a vision of the apocalypse. This portion of Menet's vision shared much in common with Smith's vision, but Menet's began with a missile strike—an Iranian nuclear missile launched from Libya striking Israel. Her attention turned to the United States, where she witnessed what she would later understand was the collapse of the Twin Towers. An economic crisis would follow before bioterrorist attacks would occur in four American cities: New York, Los Angeles, San Francisco, and Salt Lake City. Reminiscent of Charles D. Evans's portrayal of a future disease that began with a purple spot on the hands or face, this disease "started with white blisters, some of the size of a dime, appearing on the hands, arms, and faces of the victims. The blisters developed into white sores, apparently filled with pus. Those with the disease would stumble around for weeks and fall over dead." A second "flu-like" disease left sufferers bleeding from their "nose, mouth, eyes, and ears." Those taken with the second illness, Menet believed, were more fortunate because they died quicker deaths with less suffering than those who contracted the first disease.

Like Gayle Smith, Menet saw rioting and violence throughout America's cities. Marauding gangs targeted those trying to escape into the countryside.

Food and water became scarce after a lengthy winter and the contamination of the water supply. Like Smith, Menet was disturbed by the way this suffering turned some into vicious predators:

> It seemed that some of them had lost their minds and went around in these gangs killing people just for the sake of killing; others did so for food or to gain some material possessions from their victims. Those who were killing for no reason were like beasts—animals completely out of control as they raped, looted, burned, and butchered people. I saw these gangs go into the homes of those who were hiding. They would drag them out of their hiding places and commit unspeakable horrors.
>
> And unnatural fear and hatred came over many people. Some family ties that once existed between husbands and wives and parents and children no longer mattered. They only cared about individual survival. Men would kill their wives and children for food or water. Mothers would kill their children.[162]

Civil unrest accounted for more deaths than the earthquakes and other natural disasters combined. In Menet's future America, the only safety to be found was in "cities of light," where the righteous had gathered to protect and care for one another. Menet saw twenty or thirty of these cities scattered across the western United States, along with "three or four" of them being in the East. There, individuals lived "in tents of all kinds, many of which were no more than blankets held up by poles." They had plenty of food and supplies and "car[ed] more for each other than for themselves." The roving killers avoided these refuges and sought "easier targets" for their violence.[163]

Nuclear explosions occurred throughout the nation, including "a small mushroom cloud form north of Salt Lake City without the aid of a missile"—an interesting echo from Smith's vision.[164] An invasion of Russian and Chinese troops followed, with some of the Russians parachuting into Utah. "I did not see much of this war but was impressed that it was short in duration and that the Russian and Chinese armies were defeated and withdrew. No explanation regarding how or why was received."[165] Menet's vision continued with images of earthquakes, tidal waves, more diseases, and meteors. At the end of her NDE, she was given the choice of whether to return to her body or remain in the afterlife. Ultimately, Menet chose to return to mortality in order to prepare her children for the coming disasters.[166]

Other NDE books followed Menet's *There Is No Death*, but none achieved the same degree of influence until John Pontius's *Visions of Glory: One Man's Astonishing Account of the Last Days*, published in 2012, and Julie Rowe's *A Greater Tomorrow*, published in 2014. Pontius's *Visions of Glory* relayed the experiences of a friend pseudonymously identified as "Spencer," whose visions also came as part of a series of near-death experiences. Perhaps more than any other example of modern Mormon apocalyptic, *Visions of Glory* echoed themes from a century before. This may have been partly due to the involvement of Pontius, who organized and massaged many hours of interviews into the first-person narrative of *Visions of Glory* and was also fully conversant with the history of prophecy. What is certain is that these similarities did not escape Pontius, who included an appendix of nineteenth-century visions: the 1877 vision credited to John Taylor, Sols Guardisto's vision, the Vision of the Plagues, George Washington's vision, and the 1894 variant of Charles D. Evans's vision.[167]

"Spencer's" visions, like many NDE accounts, began with a guided tour of the spirit world. He was eventually permitted to see the apocalypse as he was transported "as if I were in a fast helicopter, close to the earth." The devastation began in autumn with a "massive earthquake" in Salt Lake City. The next spring, a series of earthquakes struck the West Coast. In another two months, more earthquakes hit the central United States. "Spencer" flew to the northeastern United States that had been safe from earthquakes but not from a "biological attack" that devastated the region. "I saw bodies stacked in town squares and cities abandoned because of the stench of death." According to Pontius, "Spencer" was unaware of similar depictions in the 1877 vision at the time he saw his vision, but when he learned of it, he was "startled." Like Menet and Smith, he also saw "marauding bands of people plundering and stealing in every major city." He believed they murdered to "preserve remaining resources for themselves," comparing their actions to "survivors in a lifeboat throwing the weakest among them overboard to leave enough food and water for the strongest." His flight over the United States ended with seeing the arrival of tens of thousands of armed foreign troops. In an only slightly veiled acknowledgment that "Spencer" believed these were UN peacekeeping forces, Pontius wrote, "They wore blue-green helmets, and I assumed they were international relief troops." The last thing "Spencer" saw in this segment of his vision was uprisings against the foreign military in California.[168]

After this flyover experience, "Spencer" became "a participant in the vision," foreseeing what would happen to him personally during the destructions as if it was occurring to him in the present. He was in Salt Lake City at the time of the first earthquake and the subsequent flooding of the city. His vision differed from others, including his own initial flyover, in that his emphasis was not on the impact of the disaster but rather on efforts to assist others in the chaos. Those who had food storage, a small minority of church members, shared freely with those in need. The church was crippled immediately after the earthquake but recovered and successfully organized relief efforts to such a degree that it rivaled the foreign troops that had come to provide aid. Eventually, in a stark departure from Gayle Smith's vision, the foreign troops would persecute the church, because its organization stood in the way of their "primary goal . . . to establish their own government in place of federal and local governments." The troops initiated new laws that declared the church must stay out of civic concerns. They falsely accused, arrested, and even executed leaders. It was after this period that the biological attack—a plague that wiped out 25 percent of the globe—and the troops of the "new world order" increased their efforts to "assert greater and greater control, including establishing martial law and suspending civil liberties."[169]

According to "Spencer," church members rallied during the plague, miraculously healing the ill and reclaiming Temple Square. The turning point in "Spencer's" vision was the fall general conference when the resurrected Joseph Smith appeared to the assembled Saints. He announced that the events of Adam-Ondi-Ahman had already occurred a few weeks before. Then Smith reviewed the gatherings to Salt Lake City and other "cities of Zion" throughout the world. When he finished his discourse, Joseph Smith introduced Jesus Christ, whose very presence empowered the Saints to fulfill their last days missions—in some cases, as with "Spencer," the individuals were translated or made immortal.[170] From there, "Spencer" received an assignment to join a company that would journey to a gathering of the Saints in Cardston, Canada.[171] When they arrived in Cardston, the refuge that Sol Guardisto had seen in the 1920s was already in operation, with 20,000 Saints present.[172] "Spencer" lived in Cardston for a time until he eventually left with a small company heading toward Missouri. His account ended with visions of the New Jerusalem Temple, the return of the lost tribes of Israel and the city of Enoch, as well as the Second Coming.[173] There is little question that this volume contained the largest single account of an apocalyptic vision in Latter-day Saint history.

Recognizing that his account of "Spencer's" vision would attract controversy, John Pontius crafted the book's introduction to address the naysayers. He carefully laid out "Spencer's" orthodox credentials as "a lifelong member" who currently volunteered in the temple and had held positions in "bishoprics, high councils, stake positions, and many other callings."[174] He recounted "Spencer's" ruminations about sharing such a sacred personal experience. "Spencer" had spent years "constrained to silence" until he shared some of his experiences with a confidant among the Twelve Apostles who acknowledged that what he had shared with him was "from God" but advised him to "treasure it up in [his] heart, write it down, and not speak of it until the Lord told [him] to."[175] After this apostle's death, "Spencer" was visited by an angel, who told him that a man named John would come into his life who would "understand you and your visions. You can tell him all you have experienced. He will help you understand them as well. Just be patient until then." Eight years later, "Spencer" met John Pontius and they recorded his story.[176]

Pontius made the case that his book was not at odds with the church's policies on sharing prophetic revelation. "What you are about to read is, to my thinking, the most comprehensive and powerful insight into the latter days that has come to an average person. It is not scripture and should not be considered such. It is not prophetic for anyone but Spencer himself. It is simply an account of how the Lord has prepared one humble man, my friend Spencer, for his latter-day mission. You and I are just blessed to be the fly on the wall, so to speak."[177] The categorization of "Spencer's" visions as personal revelation is perhaps dubious since it announced imminent disasters that his readers would ignore at their own peril. Yet, Pontius defined them as "personal"—the kind of manifestation that members should expect to receive. From his perspective, God revealed to "Spencer" what would happen to him, and learning details about what would happen to others was more of a byproduct of that personal manifestation. Pontius went a step further to suggest that some portions of the vision were potentially symbolic and that even "Spencer" was unclear on "what every part of it means even to him."[178] Pontius seemed to assure his audience that he did not intend to compel them to accept "Spencer's" account or his interpretation.

Pontius described "Spencer" with adjectives like "average" and "humble" to stave off accusations that "Spencer" was seeking position or status. When critics eventually took on the book, they did so by alleging inconsistencies between "Spencer's" eschatology and LDS scripture, and, of course, criticizing the heteropraxy in sharing a revelation of this kind. Greg Smith, a writer for the independent Latter-day Saint organization FairMormon, accused "Spencer" of having "fall[en] victim to the great seduction of apocalyptic thinking—*he* sees the truth which others cannot see. *He* is among the chosen to whom God reveals the truth, while others continue blind. *He* is part of a spiritual elite within the Church, both because he has such things revealed to him, and because he believes properly while others do not" (emphasis in the original). Even if his account did not contradict scripture, such a vision "should not be disclosed publicly without the President of the Church's approval."[179] Of course, if these sorts of critiques presented a significant challenge to "Spencer's" credibility, they did not negatively impact sales of Pontius's book. When a second edition was published in 2017, a banner was printed on the cover advertising over 100,000 copies sold—phenomenal sales for an LDS book.

Julie Rowe is another visionary whose last days message has garnered a large audience among Latter-day Saints. Her NDE occurred in 2004, at which time she met an ancestor—initially identified only as John but later revealed to be John the Revelator—who guided her through a series of afterlife visions before showing her the apocalypse. She witnessed future church leaders urging the faithful to prepare for difficult times and after some time that "the invitation came from the prophet for Church members to gather at camps that had been prepared as places of refuge."[180] Rowe saw that the church would make use of campgrounds and other undeveloped properties in order to establish tent cities. After the "callout," most church members stubbornly refused to evacuate their homes, leaving themselves subject to the forces of the apocalypse. Rowe's vision included all the major elements of Mormon eschatology: an economic collapse, rioting, wars throughout the globe, plague, and persecution. America was the center of much of this destruction. Like Smith, Menet, and "Spencer," Rowe witnessed biological weapons released in the nation's cities. She saw the "Statue of Liberty bombed, and the statue's arm holding the torch fell, with a huge wave covering it."[181] An earthquake "twisted the Arch in St. Louis as if it were soft pretzel."[182] Utah would certainly not be exempt from this sort of disaster. Rowe "saw a huge earthquake hit Utah, devastating thousands and destroying most of Utah Valley and the Salt Lake Valley. . . . Water sprang up from the ground, causing severe flooding, mudslides and other destruction. Houses literally fell off the mountains, and others were sucked into the ground as the earth trembled and quaked."[183]

Like "Spencer," Rowe saw UN troops establish a government in the United States and institute martial law. While these initial foreign troops professed that they were only there to aid the struggling nation, other troops from Russia, China, "and some of what I believe were North Korean troops" invaded.[184] Like Gayle Smith, Rowe saw that the new government "required a microchip to be implanted in the hands or foreheads of those who sought food, water, clothing, or shelter."[185] It was in this setting that she saw Americans would "recognize the need to fight for the Constitution and for their freedom," which led to uprisings.[186] Even among those who had found safety in the camps, people enlisted to fight.

Rowe's depiction of armed resistance is a considerable departure point from *Visions of Glory*, which portrayed rebellion against the oppressive government as contrary to God's will. In contrast, Rowe saw God inspiring Latter-day Saint participation in a last days revolution—much like that depicted in the White Horse Prophecy. She saw that "men and women were called upon to fight for the freedom of the American people and for the Constitution of the United States of America."[187] In her second book, Rowe revealed that while she was not sure how the war would conclude, she knew that it came about "in a miraculous way—through the efforts of the Elders of Israel and the hand of the Lord—the enemy was vanquished from the land."[188] She would continue to discuss the thirteen-month war in later venues, eventually revealing that she would "help lead those elders of Israel as a Joan of Arc figure." In her words: "I witness and testify to you of my mission in this as the gifts the Lord has given me to help the elders [who] are called by their brethren to stand forth and to come to the defense of the Constitution and freedoms of the United States of America."[189]

According to Rowe, during the chaos, there was safety available in the camps, especially among those camps where the residents had begun to live the law of consecration. These camps were called—as they were in Menet's vision—Cities of Light, and Rowe explained that they were illuminated by a "literal light from God."[190] Enemy troops and marauding bands tried to infiltrate these communities but "could not penetrate an invisible shield or barrier that had been placed around the outskirts of the camp to protect the Saints." If they continued to try to broach the boundaries of the camp, they were "struck down by a force that was so powerful they died instantly."[191] The vision echoed the pillar of light that accompanied the Hebrew exodus from Egypt, as well as Isaiah's prediction that "the Lord will create upon every dwelling place of mount Zion, and upon her assemblies, a cloud and smoke by day, and the shining of a flaming fire by night: for upon all the glory shall be a defence [*sic*]."[192] This theme of the holy light providing defense resonated in modern Mormon apocalyptic to such an extent that it appeared in Rowe's visions, in the "shekinah" that James Harmston expected to encompass the Sanpete Valley, and as a pillar of light in "Spencer's" visions that would lead the journey to Jackson County and protect the faithful along the way.

Controversies involving Rowe began in the summer of 2015. In August, the church's seminaries and institutes of religion, which provide curriculum and courses for Latter-day Saint high school and college students, added Rowe's book to a list of "spurious materials" that instructors should not share with students. The following month, the *Salt Lake Tribune* reported a dramatic increase in the sales of food storage and emergency supplies in Utah.[193] In some Mormon prepper circles, there was a growing expectation that an event of importance was imminent based on a blood moon that would happen on September 28, 2015. The *Tribune* reporting was a bit jumbled, but the anxiety or anticipation around September was real. Evangelical preacher John Hagee had popularized an idea that the correlation between four blood moons and the feasts of the Hebrew calendar served as signs of the last days. The first blood moon would be on April 15, 2014, coinciding with the Jewish Passover and the fourth moon would occur on September 28, 2015, coinciding with the celebration of the Feast of Tabernacles.[194] To be sure, the tetrad, as it was called, had its advocates among Mormon apocalypticists, but if Rowe believed that it was related to the end, she did not say so directly, though there was a general sense of immediacy throughout her writings.

In October 2015, Rowe began the Greater Tomorrow Relief Fund, a 501c non-profit, geared toward offering "relief to those who may suffer from natural disasters or civil unrest on a global scale." The website does not explicitly link the movement to the church, but prominently displays Rowe's photograph with an explanation of her prophecies.[195] In a podcast, she explained that since her NDE, she had known she would "one day have warehouses of supplies—have safehouses and other things." A key element of her "personal mission" was to assist refugees during "the tribulations" as they make their way across the country. Unlike typical relief agencies, its purpose was limited to use for the apocalypse alone. Because Rowe has seen "where the natural disasters are or will be as well as where the foreign troops are and where the enemy will come and where we will be in battle and things like that," she can locate the right places to purchase properties and store supplies.[196] Rowe's most recent publication recounts the miraculous ways individuals who aid with this endeavor have come into her life.

The similarities between the last days scenarios of Rowe, "Spencer," Menet, and Smith have allowed for them to be read as corroborating one another despite points of divergence among them.[197] Each of these visionaries foresaw Utah-based earthquakes at the start of a series of destructive events that would strike the nation. While such an emphasis was bound to resonate with those familiar with earthquake predictions in the scripture, it also spoke to the anxiety of a populace that is regularly urged to prepare for massive earthquakes along the Wasatch Front.[198] In April 2016, Rowe predicted what she called the "Wasatch Wakeup," an early morning earthquake in northern Utah that would prod people to take seriously the last days warnings. On May 5, 2016, she was a guest on *The Bryan Hyde Show*, a radio program, when she was "triggered . . . into a state of vision." She told the listeners that the earthquake was "imminent" and would happen previous to the forthcoming election. In response, many of Rowe's supporters accelerated their preparedness efforts, and as she would later recall, "I knew of some individuals who had invested a significant amount in emergency supplies who began to have regrets and started selling some of their investments."[199]

Even before Rowe made these predictions that did not occur when expected, "Spencer" seems to have received greater acceptance among the general Mormon populace. There are any number of reasons why this might be the case. For starters, "Spencer's" appeal could be related to the initial publication of his prophecies. While he used an established author, John Pontius, who published with a mainstream LDS press, Rowe wrote under her own name, was a first-time author, and published with a press that specialized in last days fiction and near-death experience books. Additionally, Rowe had been directly involved with online prepper communities before she published her book, something that may have caused some Latter-day Saints concerned with questions of orthodoxy to question her message.[200] While neither book was carried in the largest LDS bookstore chain, *Visions of Glory* received much wider distribution. It is also true that Latter-day Saints are more prone to give credence to the voices of men since those who are officially recognized as Prophets, Seers, and Revelators are exclusively male. I suspect that cultural assumptions about gender likely relate to a tendency to dismiss Rowe.

Yet, I am convinced that gender and publisher choice are less important than the distinct ways in how Rowe and "Spencer" performed the role of visionary. "Spencer's" anonymity creates a prophetic mystique that Rowe's availability cannot duplicate. He has not monetized his story beyond the book nor sought to mobilize people. He has appeared in private venues to share details from his experiences, but has avoided the spotlight. In contrast, Rowe—regardless of her motivations—has been something of an entrepreneur of apocalypticism. Within four years of publishing *A Greater Tomorrow*, she has produced three follow-ups. She has promoted her message via media interviews, her personal blog and podcasts, including *The Julie Rowe Show* on YouTube. The messianic undertones in her earliest work and the explicit claim to be a "Joan of Arc figure" in the last days battle are exactly the sort of details that Latter-day Saints have come to see as unacceptable when it comes to sharing personal revelation. The financial dimensions of Rowe's project can be particularly controversial for Latter-day Saints, who subscribe to a lay clergy. As a result, efforts by individuals to collect donations and potentially accrue a salary seems to smack of "priestcraft."

On May 26, 2019, Julie Rowe published a podcast that included an announcement indicating she had been excommunicated from the LDS Church a month previously. According to Rowe, the court was called after her local stake president had been contacted by a regional leader concerned with Rowe's podcasts and her energy work business. The charges included "Apostasy, teaching false doctrine, priestcraft, and defaming the good name of the church." Rowe announced that her excommunication was the result of corrupt men who had "infiltrated" the church's leadership. She prophesied that church leaders would eventually visit her where she would be living in Idaho after the destructions in Salt Lake City and seek her forgiveness.[201]

The apocalyptic personalities discussed in this section are the most visible and prolific participants in—and really the spokesmen for—a movement of Latter-day Saint visionaries. While the movement has gained momentum from a modern American prepper subculture, it pulls from motifs and concepts that have survived from the nineteenth century, which have now been translated across time in order to address a distinct set of twenty-first-century anxieties. The Internet has created structures that have allowed the widespread distribution of their manifestations, but it has also facilitated others' ability to dispute their claims, opening them up to ongoing debate. Just as folk prophets have come to employ different strategies to ensure that others recognize them as orthodox speakers, the Latter-day Saint laity has developed a recognition of cues by which they judge visionaries. A century of regulation has emphasized caution when sharing revelatory experiences, a reluctance for personal celebrity, and a proper reverence for church leaders.

Conclusion

Increasing church regulation of apocalypticism in the twentieth century severed the phenomenon into multiple strains, each of which engaged the master narrative in distinctive ways across time. While commentators, whether general authorities or the solo dreamer, remained connected to Joseph Smith's millenarian portrayal of the last days, they also continuously adapted the last days scenarios and re-imagined the players involved. Hierarchical voices placed the United States as the Zion of prophecy, in which they saw the church as playing a crucial part. They modified expectations to promote a moderate millenarianism in stark contrast to the separatist apocalypticism of the Mormon past. Mormon fundamentalists, in contrast, have preserved this separatist apocalypticism just as they have remained embattled with the state. In such communities, tensions of American citizenship remain. In addition, they have been compelled to fit the church into their expectations for the reversal of powers. In contrast to the separatist apocalypticism of the fundamentalists, the vernacular apocalypticism of non-hierarchical members of the Church of Jesus Christ of Latter-day Saints remained supportive of the direction of the institution. Among these voices are those who—while often malleable to the criticisms of church leaders relating to specifics—have preserved the methods and intensity of nineteenth-century Mormon apocalypticism. Yet, influenced by the direction of the modern church, they now frequently write as conservative American patriots, aiming their expectations of destructions at liberal political movements or nebulous future tyrannies.

Afterword

Apocalypticism in the "Mormon Moment"

Widespread interest in Mormons was already on the rise when journalists coined the expression "Mormon moment" to describe the surge of attention that came with the debut of *The Book of Mormon* on Broadway and Mitt Romney's second presidential campaign. Throughout this era, whether it was to explain Elizabeth Smart's kidnapping, Cliven Bundy's standoff, or Glenn Beck's constitutionalism, prophecy and apocalypticism accompanied news coverage of the Latter-day Saints. At times, such beliefs became the focus of media attention, as was the case in the fall of 2015. This news cycle was particularly relevant for our study given that journalists not only covered a rise in apocalyptic belief but also in many cases, they followed the church's efforts to distance the institution from such ideas. Headlines read: "Mormon Church Issues Call for Calm as 'Blood Moon' Sparks Apocalypse Fears," "Mormon Leaders Reassure Faithful: Sunday's 'Blood Moon' Isn't Sign of Apocalypse," and "LDS Church Dismisses 'Blood Moon' Worries."[1] Twenty-first-century Americans have had ample opportunity to learn about Latter-day Saints' peculiar last days beliefs. Meanwhile, the church's public relations arm has stayed busy refuting the official nature of these prophecies.

Latter-day Saint politicians were particularly vulnerable to the specter of prophecies that the righteous among the Saints would preserve the nation in a future constitutional crisis. On November 3, 2006, the *Wall Street Journal* published "White Horse in the White House," which discussed what leading Utah Republicans and teachers at Brigham Young University thought of the prophecy.[2] Unfortunately, the article, like countless others over the next decade, perpetuated the mistaken notion that the prophecy suggesting the Constitution would "hang by a thread, as it were, as fine as the finest silk fiber" was synonymous with the White Horse Prophecy, rather than that the prophecy appeared in the White Horse Prophecy as well as numerous other mainstream Latter-day Saint discourses. (We'll address the effects of this confusion in the discussion that follows.)

Terrible Revolution. Christopher James Blythe, Oxford University Press (2020). © Oxford University Press.
DOI: 10.1093/oso/9780190080280.001.0001

Figure A.1 John Scott, *The Last Judgment*, a mural included in the Washington, D.C., Temple in 1974. © By Intellectual Reserve, Inc.

The press continued. On June 4, 2007, the *Salt Lake Tribune* opened the doors for further coverage of Romney and political messianism with an article entitled "Romney Candidacy has Resurrected Last Days Prophecy of Mormon Saving the Constitution."[3] In 2010, between Romney's campaigns, the *Huffington Post* documented an exchange between Beck and Orrin Hatch that invoked the rhetoric of constitutional crisis and, according to the writer, was designed to "send a coded message to the nation's six million Mormons—or at least those Mormons who believe in what Latter-day Saints call 'the White Horse Prophecy.' "[4] When Mitt Romney secured the Republican nomination for the 2012 presidential election, the media continued to refer to the White Horse Prophecy, sometimes even with the assumption that their readers were already aware of its contents. Echoes of the nation's earlier scandal involving Latter-day Saint apocalypticism appear in these portrayals. In many cases, the White Horse Prophecy's presence in the national press was only a partly concealed attempt to marginalize the Latter-day Saint faith and "its" candidate. Commentary on the prophecy played off a long history of American fears about organized religion's pursuit of a national theocracy.[5]

This was most blatant in 2012 with Sally Denton's editorial "Romney and the White Horse Prophecy" at Salon.com, in which she argued that Romney was unfit for office because he "has an underlying religious conception of the presidency and the American government." While recognizing the Constitution prohibited a religious test for candidates, she aroused a suspicion against Romney's Mormonism, alleging that the candidate's conception of prophecy and government could not allow for a separation between church and state. She acknowledged that Romney had denied belief in the White Horse Prophecy, but oddly asserted it was essential to probe the issue in order to understand "the man, the mission and the candidacy." Against this background, it became clear that Romney was trying to scramble for "the office of the American presidency . . . the ultimate ecclesiastical position to which a Mormon leader might aspire." Doubling down on this idea that his rise to the presidency was Romney's secret personal religious mission, she suggested that he had been selected for the role of Mormonism's religio-political messiah from his youth. To do so, she rehashed the claim of a former Mormon, Michael Moody, that Mitt was known "only half jokingly, as the 'One Mighty and Strong' " during his college days at Brigham Young University.[6] If Romney believed there was a divine plan to place him as a Latter-day Saint in the presidency and good Latter-day Saints follow the commands of the church's hierarchy, then the church would assume control of the nation.

Denton's claims did not go unchallenged. Nathan B. Oman, associate professor of law at the University of William & Mary and practicing Mormon, referred to Denton as an "alarmist" and argued that her attempts to portray "Romney's candidacy [as] part of some sinister Mormon plot" were based on a shallow understanding of Latter-day Saint history.[7] Erika Fry, writing for the *Columbia Journalism Review*, referred to Denton's piece as a "sinister and conspiracy-minded account," which "compels readers to be afraid of Mormons and their secret designs."[8] My personal favorite response was Yair Rosenberg's "Protocols of the Elders" in the *Tablet*, which compared the conspiracy theories surrounding Romney's election (including Denton's "casting the prophecy as a cornerstone of Mormon identity or Romney's worldview") to the long history of anti-Semitic theories claiming a secretive Jewish agenda.[9]

The popular association of the Constitution prophecy with the White Horse Prophecy led to a lack of clarity in the press. Because commentators were unaware of the full content of the White Horse Prophecy, some presumed that the "white horse" referred to a heroic champion who would single-handedly defend the Constitution—what one columnist referred to as a "Mormon white knight."[10] Of course, the Constitution prophecy (and the White Horse Prophecy, for that matter) spoke of a Latter-day Saint intervention but seemingly as a community rather than from a messiah among them. This misunderstanding contributed to conspiratorial uses of the White Horse Prophecy. When Romney responded to questions about the prophecy for the *Salt Lake Tribune* in 2007, he seems to have had this same idea in mind, stating that he had not "heard [his] name associated with it or anything of that nature."[11]

This is not to say that some Latter-day Saints had not, in the nineteenth century, longed for their prophet to be recognized as the head of state. The reversal of powers was at the heart of Mormon apocalyptic. While they used strategies of resettlement and isolation to avoid persecution in the present, they longed for their re-integration into the state as defenders of the republic's ideals. While these prophecies threatened and provoked outsiders, they never spoke of an aggressive theocratic takeover through military or political means. The White Horse Prophecy and so many other nineteenth-century apocalyptic texts were about messianism, foreseeing the "terrible revolution" and a post-apocalyptic world in which the righteous citizens of the once great United States would seek their help to revive the republic. When the world had turned upside down and Mormons were politically in control, they envisioned restoring the constitutional rights of all Americans.

The conflation of the Constitution prophecy with the White Horse Prophecy was also advantageous to the church and Latter-day Saint political candidates. They could now disavow the White Horse Prophecy without having to delve into that portion of the prophecy that had actually been championed by church leaders throughout the tradition's history. It saved them from having to explain, or even understand, the complicated history of Mormon political messianism. The church issued a statement asserting that "the so-called 'White Horse Prophecy' is based on accounts that have not been substantiated by historical research and is not embraced as Church doctrine."[12] Presumably, they meant that one could not trace the 1902 text of the White Horse Prophecy to the lifetime of Joseph Smith. It seems doubtful the public relations department was aware of Smith's prophecy that Latter-day Saints would intercede during a constitutional crisis in a contemporary 1840 account.

When Romney was asked for his thoughts on the White Horse Prophecy, he also declared it was "not official church doctrine," explaining: "There are a lot of things that are speculation and discussion by church members and even church leaders that aren't official church doctrine. I don't put that at the heart of my religious belief."[13] It does not matter whether he knew that the Constitution prophecy existed independent of the White Horse Prophecy. Romney was able to marginalize the prophecy by categorizing it as "speculation" instead of "official doctrine." He continued the discourse of a century before—first perpetrated through the authority of church statements—in which such items were relegated to the unofficial. It was something that was spoken among church members and even leaders, but it was not "official" or at the "heart" of his belief. While the very construction of the "unofficial" in twentieth-century Latter-day Saint rhetoric set the stage for this sort of repudiation, it is likewise interesting that he like so many other Saints knew the White Horse Prophecy was unofficial and had been declared such by church leaders. The White Horse Prophecy had become a useful scapegoat—a substitute for more nuanced conversation—that served to disavow the worldview of apocalyptic separatism that once was at the center of Latter-day Saint belief.

The voices that are strangely absent from this public discussion are those of Latter-day Saints who still anticipate the "terrible revolution" of nineteenth-century prophecy. I have documented the echoes of these views among prophecy enthusiasts to the present. To be sure, these believers face stigma if they do not follow the cultural codes of prophecy articulated in official church statements. That means they usually share the church's rejection of the White Horse Prophecy or at least take a complicated view on the subject. Yet, while church leaders focus on a moderate depoliticized millenarian discourse, the American apocalypse continues to find an audience among a segment of Latter-day Saints.

Notes

Introduction

1. White Horse Prophecy, in Don L. Penrod, "Edwin Rushton as the Source of the White Horse Prophecy," *BYU Studies* 49, no. 3 (2010): 123.
2. Vision, December 16, 1844, in *Wilford Woodruff's Journal* 7: 421.
3. Significant texts on the development of ideas of priesthood and Church leadership in the nineteenth century include William G. Hartley, *My Fellow Servants: Essays on the History of the Priesthood* (Provo, UT: BYU Studies, 2010); Gregory A. Prince, *Power from on High: The Development of Mormon Priesthood* (Salt Lake City, UT: Signature Books, 1995); and D. Michael Quinn, *Mormon Hierarchy: Origins of Power* (Salt Lake City, UT: Signature Books, 1994).
4. John J. Collins, *The Apocalyptic Imagination: An Introduction to Jewish Apocalyptic Literature*, 2nd ed. (Grand Rapids, MI: William B. Eerdmans Publishing Company, 1998 [1984]), 5.
5. Collins, *The Apocalyptic Imagination*, 8.
6. Catherine Wessinger, "Millennial Glossary," in *The Oxford Handbook of Millennialism*, ed. Catherine Wessinger (New York: Oxford University Press, 2011), 718.
7. Kathleen Flake, "Translating Time: The Nature and Function of Joseph Smith's Narrative Canon," *Journal of Religion* 87, no. 4 (October 2007): 500.
8. Flake, "Translating Time," 497.
9. Grant Underwood, *The Millenarian World of Early* Mormonism (Chicago: University of Illinois Press, 1993), 76.
10. See David D. Hall, ed., *Lived Religion in America: Toward a History of Practice* (Princeton, NJ: Princeton University Press, 1997).
11. One key exception is Laurel Thatcher Ulrich's *A House Full of Females: Plural Marriage and Women's Rights in Early Mormonism, 1835–1870*, written with an eye toward the "writings of ordinary people" (New York: Knopf, 2017), xxiv.
12. For representative works, see Hector Lee, *The Three Nephites: The Substance and Significance of the Legend in Folklore* (Albuquerque: University of New Mexico Press, 1949); William A. Wilson, *The Marrow of Human Experience: Essays on Folklore*, ed. Jill Terry Rudy (Logan, UT: Utah State University Press, 2006); Austin and Alta Fife, *Saints of Sage & Saddle: Folklore among the Mormons* (Bloomington: Indiana University Press, 1956).
13. Tom Mould and Eric A. Eliason, "The State of Mormon Folklore Studies," *Mormon Studies Review* 1 (2014): 41.
14. William A. Wilson, "The Study of Mormon Folklore: An Uncertain Mirror for Truth," in Wilson, *The Marrow of Human Experience*, 185.

15. William A. Wilson, "What's True in Mormon Folklore? The Contribution of Folklore to Mormon Studies," *Arrington Annual Lecture Series* (2007): 8–9.
16. See Flake, "Translating Time"; Samuel Morris Brown, *In Heaven as It Is on Earth: Joseph Smith and the Early Mormon Conquest of Death* (New York: Oxford University Press, 2012).
17. Jared Farmer, *On Zion's Mount: Mormons, Indians, and the American Landscape* (Cambridge, MA: Harvard University Press, 2008).
18. Alan Dundes, *Interpreting Folklore* (Bloomington: Indiana University Press, 1980), 2.
19. Leonard Norman Primiano, "Vernacular Religion and the Search for Method in Religious Folklife," *Western Folklore* 54, no. 1 (January 1995): 38.
20. Primiano, "Vernacular Religion and the Search for Method," 39.
21. Primiano, "Vernacular Religion and the Search for Method," 44.
22. David D. Hall, *Worlds of Wonder, Days of Judgment: Popular Religious Beliefs in Early New England* (New York: Alfred A. Knopf, 1989), 11.
23. Christopher James Blythe, "The Exorcism of Isaac Russell: Diabolism and Nineteenth-century Mormon Identity Formation," *Journal of Religion* 98, no. 3 (July 2018): 305–326.
24. Christopher James Blythe, "The One Mighty and Strong(s): Messianism and the Rise of MormonFundamentalism," in Newell Bringhurst and Craig Foster, *The Persistence of Polygamy: Fundamentalist Mormon Polygamy from 1890 to the Present* (JohnWhitmer Books, 2015), 112–143.

Chapter 1

1. Joseph Smith, Revelation, January 2, 1831, in *The Joseph Smith Papers, Documents*, Vol. 1: *July 1828–June 1831*, ed. Michael Hubbard MacKay, Gerrit J. Dirkmaat, Grant Underwood, Robert J. Woodford, and William G. Hartley (Salt Lake City, UT: The Church Historian's Press, 2013), 232 [D&C 38:29]. Future references to the Documents series of the Joseph Smith Papers will be referenced with a "D" followed by the volume number.
2. Joseph Smith, History [ca. June–October 1839], draft, in *The Joseph Smith Papers, Histories*, Vol. 1: *Joseph Smith Histories, 1832–1844*, ed. Karen Lynn Davidson, David J. Whittaker, Mark Ashurst-McGee, and Richard L. Jensen, 1:220, Draft 2 [Joseph Smith History 1:30]. Future references to the Histories series of the Joseph Smith Papers will be referenced with a "H" followed by the volume number.
3. Joseph Smith, History [ca. June–October 1839], draft, in *JSP* H1:222, Draft 2 [Joseph Smith History 1:33]. The original manuscript identifies the angel's name as Nephi; however, earlier and later accounts refer to the angel as Moroni. For a discussion of this discrepancy in the manuscripts, see *JSP* H1:223n56; Dan Vogel, ed., *History of Joseph Smith and the Church of Jesus Christ of Latter-day Saints: A Source and Text-Critical Edition* (Salt Lake City, UT: The Smith-Petit Foundation, 2015), 1:12, fn12.

4. Orson Pratt, *A[n] Interesting Account of Several Remarkable Visions, and of the Late Discovery of Ancient American Records* (Edinburgh, 1840), 7. According to Grant Underwood, "this statement highlights the essential link between what early Latter-day Saints considered the *raison d'etre* of Mormonism and the millennial dream" (Grant Underwood, "Apocalyptic Anticipations: Mormon Millenarianism in the Early Years," *Communal Societies* 37, no. 1 (2017): 83).
5. Joseph Smith, History [ca. June–October 1839], draft, in *JSP* H1:224, Draft 2 [Joseph Smith History 1:36–38].
6. Joel 2:28–32.
7. Joseph Smith, History [ca. June–October 1839], draft, in *JSP* H1:226, Draft 2 [Joseph Smith History 1:43].
8. Joseph Smith, History [ca. June–October 1839], draft, in *JSP* H1:226–230, Draft 2 [Joseph Smith History 1:44–47].
9. Richard Bushman, *Joseph Smith: Rough Stone Rolling* (New York: Alfred A. Knopf, 2005), 45–59.
10. Joseph Smith, History [ca. June–October 1839], draft, in *JSP* H1:222, Draft 2 [Joseph Smith History 1:34].
11. Revelation 14:6.
12. Joseph Smith, Revelation, November 3, 1831, in *The Joseph Smith Papers: Documents*, Vol. 2: *July 1831–January 1833*, ed. Matthew C. Godfrey, Mark Ashurst-McGee, Grant Underwood, Robert J. Woodford, and William G. Hartley (Salt Lake City, UT: The Church Historian's Press, 2013), 119 [D&C 133:36]. The correlation between Moroni and John's angel was also noted by Orson Pratt in 1840, when he wrote that the coming forth of the Book of Mormon "revealed by the angel . . . fulfill[ed] the vision of John, which he beheld on the Isle of Patmos" (Orson Pratt, *A[n] Interesting Account of Several Remarkable Visions*, 30).
13. "Synopsis of the History of Heber Chase Kimball," in History of Brigham Young, Book G, 1857–1859, pp. 128–129, CHL.
14. Richard S. Van Wagoner, ed., *The Complete Discourses of Brigham Young* (Salt Lake City, UT: Signature Books, 2010), 1:65.
15. 1 Nephi 1.13.
16. Grant Hardy, *Understanding the Book of Mormon: A Reader's Guide* (New York: Oxford University Press, 2010), 76.
17. 1 Nephi 12:1–2.
18. 1 Nephi 12:4.
19. 1 Nephi 12:11.
20. Hardy, *Understanding the Book of Mormon*, 298.
21. Jared Hickman, "The Book of Mormon as Amerindian Apocalypse," *American Literature* 86, no. 3 (September 2014): 429–461.
22. 1 Nephi 13:3–5.
23. 1 Nephi 13:4–9.
24. 1 Nephi 13:28–29.

25. Nephi was forbidden from recording the conclusion of his vision because John the Revelator had been specially chosen to "write the remainder of these things . . . [and] also write concerning the end of the world" (1 Nephi 14:21–22).
26. Later Mormon commentators have condemned this correlation. Stephen E. Robinson, "Early Christianity and 1 Nephi 13-14," in *The Book of Mormon: First Nephi, The Doctrinal Foundation*, ed. Monte S. Nyman and Charles D. Tate Jr. (Provo, UT: Religious Studies Center, Brigham Young University, 1988), 177–191.
27. Christopher C. Jones and Stephen J. Fleming, "'Except among that Portion of Mankind,' Early Mormon Conceptions of the Apostasy," in *Standing Apart: Mormon Historical Consciousness and the Concept of Apostasy*, ed. Miranda Wilcox and John D. Young (New York: Oxford University Press, 2014), 63.
28. 1 Nephi 13:12.
29. 1 Nephi 13:13.
30. 1 Nephi 13:17.
31. 1 Nephi 13:19.
32. Joseph Smith, Revelation, December 16–17, 1833, in *The Joseph Smith Papers: Documents*, Vol. 3: *February 1833–March 1834*, ed. Gerrit J. Dirkmaat, Brent M. Rogers, Grant Underwood, Robert J. Woodford, and William G. Hartley (Salt Lake City, UT: The Church Historian's Press, 2014), 395 [D&C 101:80].
33. 2 Nephi 1:5–6.
34. 1 Nephi 1:9.
35. Ether 2: 8–9.
36. Ether 13:5.
37. Revelation, ca. March 7, 1831, in *JSP* D1:280 [D&C 45:66].
38. Joseph Smith, Discourse, ca. July 19, 1840, in *JSP* D7:341.
39. See Nicholas Guyatt, *Providence and the Invention of the United States, 1607–1876* (New York: Cambridge University Press, 2007).
40. Quoted in *The Libro de las Profecias of Christopher Columbus*, trans. Delno C. West and August Kling (Gainesville: University of Florida Press, 1991), 54.
41. Quoted in *The Libro de las Profecias*, 60.
42. *The Libro de Las Profecias*, 61–62.
43. Avihu Zakai, *Exile and Kingdom: History and Apocalypse in the Puritan Migration to America* (New York: Cambridge University Press, 1992), 144–147.
44. Cotton Mather, *Theopolis Americana: An Essay on the Golden Street of the Holy City* (Boston, B. Green, 1710), 34.
45. Reiner Smolinski, "Israel Redivivus: The Eschatological Limits of Puritan Typology in New England," *The New England Quarterly* 63, no. 3 (September 1990): 361–368.
46. William Twiss, Letter to Joseph Mede, March 2, 1634, in *The Works of the Pious and Profoundly-Learned Joseph Mede* (London, 1672 [1665]), 799.
47. Joseph Mede, Letter to William Twiss, March 23, 1634, in *The Works of the Pious and Profoundly-Learned Joseph Mede*, 800.
48. See, for example, Cotton Mather, *Magnalia Christi Americana: or, the Ecclesiastical History of New-England* (London, 1702), 46.

49. Samuel Sewall, *Phaenomena quaedam Apocalyptica* (1697); Menasseh Ben-Israel, *The Hope of Israel* (1650); Thomas Thorowgood, *Jewes in America* (1650); see also Jeffrey K. Jue, *Heaven Upon Earth: Joseph Mede (1586–1638) and the Legacy of Millenarianism* (Netherlands: Springer, 2006), 187–188.
50. The complete verse reads: "Surely the isles shall wait for me, and the ships of Tarshish first, to bring thy sons from far, their silver and their gold with them, unto the name of the LORD thy God, and to the Holy One of Israel, because he hath glorified thee" (Isaiah 60:9).
51. *Some Thoughts Concerning the Present Revival of Religion in New Englad*, in *Works of Jonathan Edwards*, Vol.: *Great Awakening*, ed. C. C. Goen (New Haven, CT: Yale University Press, 1970), 353–355).
52. See Ernest Lee Tuveson, *Redeemer Nation: The Idea of America's Millennial Role* (Chicago: University of Chicago Press, 1968).
53. Guyatt, *Providence and the Invention of the United States*, 107.
54. Nathan O. Hatch, *The Sacred Cause of Liberty: Republican Thought and the Millennium in Revolutionary New England* (New Haven, CT: Yale University Press, 1977), 23–24.
55. For a concise introduction to the history and lore connected with the lost ten tribes, see Eric Maroney, *The Other Zions: The Lost Histories of Jewish Nations* (New York: Rowman & Littlefield Publishers, 2010), 19–30.
56. 2 Esdras 13:41–42.
57. Carla Gardina Pestana, *Protestant Empire: Religion and the Making of the British Atlantic World* (Philadelphia: University of Pennsylvania Press, 2009), 92–93.
58. Eran Shalev, *American Zion: The Old Testament as a Political Text from the Revolution to the Civil War* (New Haven, CT: Yale University Press, 2013), 127.
59. Elias Boudinot, *A Star in the West, or, A Humble Attempt to Discover the Long Lost Ten Tribes of Israel* (Trenton, NJ: D. Fenton, S. Huntchinson, and J. Dunham, 1816), 297–298.
60. Underwood, *The Millenarian World of Early Mormonism*, 63.
61. Mark Ashurst-McGee, "Zion Rising: Joseph Smith's Early Social and Political Thought" (PhD diss., Arizona State University, 2008), 154.
62. Hickman, "The Book of Mormon," 429–461.
63. Hickman, "The Book of Mormon," 430.
64. 3 Nephi 21:22.
65. Hickman, "The Book of Mormon," 451.
66. 3 Nephi 21:12.
67. See Richard Slotkin, *Regeneration through Violence: The Mythology of the American Frontier, 1600–1860* (Norman: University of Oklahoma Press, 1973), 85–86; 105–106.
68. Gregory Evans Dowd, *A Spirited Resistance: The North American Indian Struggle for Unity, 1745–1815* (Baltimore: John Hopkins University Press, 1992), 128–129; Lee Irwin, *Coming Down from Above: Prophecy, Resistance, and Renewal in Native American Religions* (Norman: University of Oklahoma Press, 2008), 195–196, 205–206.
69. Parley P. Pratt, *A Voice of Warning* (New York, 1837), 190–191.

70. For a more thorough discussion of the Latter-day Saints complicated relationship with Native peoples, see W. Paul Reeve, *Religion of a Different Color: Race and the Mormon Struggle for Whiteness* (New York: Oxford University Press, 2015), 52–105.
71. Pratt, *A Voice of Warning*, 65–66.
72. Discourse, between ca. 26 June and 2 July 1839, as reported by Willard Richards, in *JSP* D6:524.
73. Gary Shepherd and Gordon Shepherd, *Binding Earth and Heaven: Patriarchal Blessings in the Prophetic Development of Early Mormonism* (University Park: The Pennsylvania State University Press, 2012), 62.
74. Armand L. Mauss, *All Abraham's Children: Changing Mormon Conceptions of Race and Lineage* (Chicago: University of Illinois Press, 2003), 9.
75. Joseph Smith, Revelation, November 3, 1831, in *JSP* D2:118 [D&C 133:26–27, 32].
76. Isaiah 24:20. See Phebe Woodruff, Letter to Wilford Woodruff, July 2, 1840, CHL.
77. Benjamin F. Johnson, *My Life's Review: Autobiography of Benjamin Franklin Johnson* (Provo, UT: Grandin Book Company, 1997), 82–83.
78. "Extract from the Prophecy of Enoch," *The Evening and the Morning Star*, August 1832. This text would later appear as part of the Book of Moses in the Pearl of Great Price.
79. *Joseph Smith's New Translation of the Bible: Original Manuscripts*, ed. Scott H. Faulring, Kent P. Jackson, and Robert J. Matthews (Provo, UT: Religious Studies Center, 2004), 117.
80. Revelation, September 1830-B, in *JSP* D1:186 [D&C 28:9]. When this revelation was published in the Book of Commandments in 1833, the reference "among the Lamanites" was altered to "on the borders by the Lamanites" (Book of Commandments 30:9).
81. Joseph Smith, Revelation, July 20, 1831, in *JSP* D2:7–8 [D&C 57:2–3].
82. Joseph Smith, Revelation, June 22, 1834, in *The Joseph Smith Papers: Documents*, Vol. 4: *April 1834–September 1835*, ed. Matthew C. Godfrey, Brenden W. Rensink, Alex D. Smith, Max H. Parkin, and Alexander L. Baugh (Salt Lake City, UT: The Church Historian's Press, 2016), 74 [D&C 105:13–14].
83. Joseph Smith, Revelation, ca. March 7, 1831, in *JSP* D1:277 [D&C 45:31].
84. Joseph Smith, Revelation, ca. March 7 1831, in *JSP* D1:280 [D&C 45:68].
85. Joseph Smith, Letter to Noah C. Saxton, January 4, 1833, in *JSP* D2:355.
86. Joseph Smith, Discourse, between ca. 26 June and 4 August 1839–A, in *The Joseph Smith Papers: Documents*, Vol. 6: *February 1838–August* 1839, ed. Mark Ashurst-McGee, David W. Grua, Elizabeth A. Kuehn, Brenden W. Rensink, and Alexander L. Baugh (Salt Lake City, UT: The Church Historian's Press, 2017), 547.
87. *Journal of Discourses* 2:147.
88. Revelation 21:9.
89. Elaine H. Pagels, *Revelations: Visions, Prophecy, and Politics in the Book of Revelation* (New York: Penguin Books, 2012), 34–35.
90. Revelation 18:2–4.
91. Joseph Smith, Revelation, September 1830–A, in *JSP* D1:179 [D&C 29:8].
92. Joseph Smith, Revelation, November 3, 1831, in *JSP* D2:117 [D&C 133:14].

93. Underwood, *The Millenarian World of Early Mormonism*, 29.
94. Joseph Smith, Revelation, December 27–28, 1832, in *JSP* D2:342 [D&C 88:88].
95. Joseph Smith, Revelation, ca. 7 March 1831, in *JSP* D1:279 [D&C 45:63].
96. Joseph Smith, Revelation, December 25, 1832, in *JSP* D2:330 [D&C 87:4].
97. Joseph Smith, Revelation, December 25, 1832, in *JSP* D2:330 [D&C 87:1].
98. Joseph Smith, Revelation, December 25, 1832, in *JSP* D2:330 [D&C 87:4].
99. Joseph Smith, Revelation, December 25, 1832, in *JSP* D2:331 [D&C 87:6].
100. Joseph Smith, Journal, April 2, 1843, in *The Joseph Smith Papers: Journals*, Vol. 2: *December 1841–April 1843*, ed. Andrew H. Hedges, Alex D. Smith, and Richard Lloyd Anderson (Salt Lake City, UT: The Church Historian's Press, 2011), 324 [D&C 130:13]. Future references to the Journals series of the Joseph Smith Papers will be referenced with a "J" followed by the volume number.
101. Joseph Smith, Journal, April 2, 1843, in *JSP* J2:324 [D&C 130:12].
102. Malachi 3:1.
103. Joseph Smith, Visions, 3 April 1836, in *The Joseph Smith Papers: Documents*, Vol. 5: *October 1835–January 1838*, ed. Brent M. Rogers, Elizabeth A. Kuehn, Christian K. Hamburger, Max H. Parkin, Alexander L. Baugh, and Steven C. Harper (Salt Lake City, UT: The Church Historian's Press, 2017), 224–229 [D&C 110].
104. Trever Anderson, "Doctrine and Covenants Section 110: From Vision to Canonization" (master's thesis, BYU, 2010), 1–9.
105. Daniel 7:13–14.
106. Collins, *The Apocalyptic Imagination*, 101.
107. See Joseph Smith, Revelation, ca. August 1835, in *JSP* D4:411 [D&C 27:11]; Doctrine and Covenants (1835) 78:3 [D&C 78:15–16].
108. Joseph Smith, Journal, May 19, 1838, in *The Joseph Smith Papers: Journals*, Vol. 1: *1832–1839*, ed. Dean C. Jessee, Mark Ashurst-McGee, and Richard L. Jensen (Salt Lake City, UT: The Church Historian's Press, 2008), 271.
109. Zechariah 12:10, 14.
110. Revelation, ca. March 7, 1831, in *JSP* D1:278–279 [D&C 45:51–52].
111. Joseph Smith, Revelation, December 7, 1830, in *JSP*, D1:221 [D&C 35:15].
112. Minutes, Discourse, and Blessings, February 14–15, 1835, in *JSP* D4.225.
113. *The Midnight Cry*, June 15, 1843. For an explanation of this calculation, see David L. Rowe, *God's Strange Work: William Miller and the End of the World* (Grand Rapids, MI: William B. Eerdsmans Publishing Company, 2008), 105–106. For a discussion of Mormon critiques of Miller, see Underwood, *The Millenarian World of Early Mormonism*, 120–121; Smith was not alone in leveling this criticism against Miller's dates. See Ernest R. Sandeen, *The Roots of Fundamentalism: British and American Millenarianism, 1800–1930* (Chicago: University of Chicago Press, 1970), 52.
114. Joseph Smith, Journal, April 2, 1843, in *JSP* J2:325.
115. Joseph Smith, Journal, April 6, 1843, in *JSP* J2:338.
116. Richard Lloyd Anderson, "Joseph Smith and the Millenarian Time Table," *BYU Studies* 3, nos. 3 and 4 (Spring/Summer 1961): 61.
117. Joseph Smith, Journal, March 10, 1844, in *Joseph Smith Papers: Journals*, Vol. 3: *May 1843–June 1844* (Salt Lake City, UT: The Church Historian's Press, 2015), 200.

118. Joseph Smith, Journal, November 13, 1833, in *JSP* J1:16–18.
119. Matthew 24:30.
120. Joseph Smith, Letter to "the Editor of the Times and Seasons," *Times and Seasons*, March 1, 1843.
121. Joseph Smith, Journal, April 6, 1843, in *JSP* J2:339.
122. Joseph Smith, Revelation, December 16–17, 1833, in *JSP* D3:391 [D&C 101:23–25].
123. Joseph Smith, "Church History," *Times and Seasons*, March 1, 1842.
124. Underwood, *The Millenarian World of Early Mormonism*, 40–41.
125. Joseph Smith, Revelation, December 27–28, 1832, in *JSP* D2:345 [D&C 88:110–115].
126. For a reproduction of the "Nauvoo Charter," see Act to Incorporate the City of Nauvoo, December 16, 1840, in *The Joseph Smith Papers: Documents*, Vol. 7: *September 1839–January 1841*, ed. Matthew C. Godfrey, Spencer W. McBride, Alex D. Smith, and Christopher James Blythe (Salt Lake City, UT: The Church Historian's Press, 2018), 472–488.
127. Joseph Smith, Sidney Rigdon, and Hyrum Smith, "A Proclamation to the Saints Scattered Abroad," *Times and Seasons*, January 15, 1841.
128. Philip Barlow, "Shifting Ground and the Third Transformation of Mormonism," in *Perspectives on American Religion and Culture*, ed. Peter W. Williams (Malden, MA: Blackwell Publishers, 1999), 141.
129. Marvin S. Hill, *Quest for Refuge: The Mormon Flight from American Pluralism* (Salt Lake City, UT: Signature Books, 1989), 93.
130. Josiah Quincy, *Figures of the Past, From the Leaves of Old Journals* (Boston, 1883), 390.
131. Wandle Mace, Autobiography [expanded], MS 1189, p. 120, CHL.
132. Revelation 12:7, Joseph Smith translation.
133. Perrigrine Sessions, Reminiscences and Diaries, p. [44], CHL.
134. Malachi 4: 5–6.
135. J–oseph Smith, Discourse, October 3, 1841, in *Times and Seasons*, October 15, 1841; Obadiah 1:21.
136. Malachi 3:3; Joseph Smith, Instruction on Priesthood, ca. October 5, 1840, in *JSP* D7:440.
137. Devery S. Anderson, "The Anointed Quorum in Nauvoo, 1842–45," *Journal of Mormon History* 29, no. 2 (Fall 2003): 152.
138. Joseph Smith, Revelation, July 12, 1843, Revelations Collection, ca. 1829–1876, CHL.
139. Joseph Smith, Discourse, August 23, 1843, Franklin Dewey Richards, Scriptural Items, ca. 1841–1844 [p. 36], CHL.
140. Revelation 7:1–3.
141. Brown, *In Heaven as It Is on Earth*, 147.
142. Joseph Smith, Discourse, August 13, 1843-A, as reported by Franklin D. Richards, https://www.josephsmithpapers.org/the-papers/documents/1843.
143. *Manuscript History of the Church*, E-1, p. 1875; see also Wilford Woodruff, Journal, February 4, 1844, in *Wilford Woodruff's Journal* 2:348.
144. Wandle Mace, Autobiography, MS 1924, p. 131. This is a different version of Mace's autobiography than the one previously cited.

145. *Words of Joseph Smith: The Contemporary Accounts of the Nauvoo Discourses of the Prophet Joseph*, ed. Andrew F. Ehat and Lyndon W. Cook (Provo, UT: Religious Studies Center, 1980), 233.
146. For a discussion of the Mormon influence in regional politics, see Glen Leonard, *Nauvoo: A Place of Peace, a People of Promise* (Salt Lake City/Provo, UT: Deseret Book Company/Brigham Young University Press, 2002), 289–300.
147. JS and Elias Higbee, Letter to Hyrum Smith and the High Council, December 5, 1839, in *JSP* D7:69.
148. Spencer W. McBride, "When Joseph Smith Met Martin Van Buren: Mormonism and the Politics of American Religious Liberty," *Church History: Studies in Christianity and Culture* 85, no. 1 (March 2016): 156.
149. Joseph Smith, Discourse, ca. July 19, 1840, in *JSP* D7:342.
150. Richard E. Bennett, Susan Easton Black, and Donald Q. Cannon, *The Nauvoo Legion in Illinois: A History of the Mormon Militia, 1841–1846* (Norman, OK: The Arthur H. Clark Company, 2010), 115.
151. Joseph Smith, Journal, March 11, 1843, in *JSP* J2:306.
152. Joseph Smith, Journal, March 11, 1843, in *JSP* J2:324.
153. Joseph Smith, History, 1838–1856, E-1 [July 1, 1843–April 30, 1844], 1936, https://www.josephsmithpapers.org/the-papers/histories/jspph3. See also Michael Scott Van Wagenen, *The Texas Republic and the Mormon Kingdom of God* (College Station: Texas A&M University Press, 2002), 26–27.
154. "Who Shall Be Our Next President?," *Times and Seasons*, October 1, 1843.
155. Joseph Smith, Letter to John C. Calhoun, Lewis Cass, Henry Clay, Richard M. Johnson, and Martin Van Buren, November 4, 1843, https://www.josephsmithpapers.org/the-papers/documents/1843.
156. Henry Clay, Letter to Joseph Smith, November 15, 1843; John C. Calhoun, Letter to Joseph Smith, December 2, 1843; Lewis Cass, Letter to Joseph Smith, December 9, 1843, https://www.josephsmithpapers.org/the-papers/documents/1843.
157. Bushman, *Joseph Smith: Rough Stone Rolling*, 517.
158. Bushman, *Joseph Smith: Rough Stone Rolling*, 7.
159. Bushman, *Joseph Smith: Rough Stone Rolling*, 8.
160. Daniel 2:44.
161. *Journal of Discourses* 24:241.
162. "The Government of God," *Times and Seasons*, July 15, 1842.
163. "The Government of God."
164. Council of Fifty, Minutes, March 14, 1844, in *The Joseph Smith Papers: Administrative Records*, Vol. 1: *Council of Fifty, Minutes, March 1844–January 1846*, ed. Matthew J. Grow, Ronald K. Esplin, Mark Ashurst-McGee, Gerrit J. Dirkmaat, and Jeffrey D. Mahas (Salt Lake City, UT: The Church Historian's Press, 2016), 48.
165. D. Michael Quinn, "The Council of Fifty and Its Members, 1844–1945," *BYU Studies* 20, no. 2 (Winter 1980), 167.
166. Quinn, *Mormon Hierarchy: Origins of Power*, 230–231.
167. George Miller, Letter to "Dear Brother," June 28, 1855, in H. W. Mills, "De Tal Palo Tal Astilla," *Annual Publication of the Historical Society of Southern California* 10, no. 3 (1917): 132.

168. Council of Fifty, Minutes, March 11, 1844, in *JSP* A1:40.
169. Council of Fifty, Minutes, April 18, 1844, in *JSP* A1:127–128.
170. Council of Fifty, Minutes, April 11, 1844, in *JSP* A1:96.
171. Steven H. Heath, "The Sacred Shout," *Dialogue: A Journal of Mormon Thought* 19, no. 3 (Fall 1986): 118. It was especially fitting since Smith had imagined this shout as occurring among "shining seraphs around thy throne" (Prayer of Dedication, March 27, 1836, in *JSP* D5:206 [D&C 109:79.])
172. "It is not wisdom to use the term 'king' all the while. Let us use the term 'proper source' instead of 'king' and it will be all understood and no person can take advantage" (Council of Fifty, Minutes, April 18, 1844, in *JSP* A1:128).
173. Lyman Wight and Heber C. Kimball, Letter to Joseph Smith, June 19–24, 1844, https://www.josephsmithpapers.org/the-papers/documents/1844.
174. Reuben G. Miller, *James J. Strang, Weighed in the Balance of Truth and Found Wanting: His claims as First President of the Melchisedek Priesthood Refuted* (Burlington, WI, 1846), 12.
175. Joseph Smith, Journal, March 10, 1844, in *JSP* J3:201.
176. Quinn, "The Council of Fifty and Its Members," 165.
177. Council of Fifty, Minutes, April 18, 1844, in *JSP* A1:110–111.
178. Council of Fifty, Minutes, April 18, 1844, in *JSP* A1:111.
179. Council of Fifty, Minutes, April 18, 1844, in *JSP* A1:111.
180. Council of Fifty, Minutes, April 25, 1844, in *JSP* A1:137.
181. Joseph Smith, Editorial, *Times and Seasons*, April 15, 1844. See also Patrick Q. Mason, "God and the People: Theodemocracy in Nineteenth-Century Mormonism," *Journal of Church and State* 53, no. 3 (Summer 2011): 349–375.
182. Johnson, *My Life's Review*, 87.
183. Council of Fifty, Minutes, April 11, 1844, in *JSP* A1:97.
184. Terryl L. Givens, *Viper on the Hearth: Mormons, Myths, and the Construction of Heresy* (New York: Oxford University Press, 1997), 131–132; see also J. Spencer Fluhman, "The 'American Mahomet': Joseph Smith, Muhammad, and the Problem of Prophets in Antebellum America," *Journal of Mormon History* 34, no. 3 (Summer 2008): 23–45.
185. Council of Fifty, Minutes, April 18, 1844, in *JSP* A1:121.
186. William Clayton, Journal, April 18, 1844, in *An Intimate Chronicle: The Journals of William Clayton*, ed. George D. Smith (Salt Lake City, UT: Signature Books, 1991), 131.
187. Joseph Smith, Revelation, September 1830-B, in *JSP* D1:186 [D&C 28:11].
188. Provo Utah Central Stake General Minutes 1849–1977, April 6, 1856, CHL.
189. Joseph Smith, Revelation, September 1830-B, in *JSP* D1:185 [D&C 28:2.]
190. Joseph Smith, Revelation, September 1830-B, in *JSP* D1:185 [D&C 28:5.]
191. See Bushman, *Joseph Smith: Rough Stone Rolling*, 120–122.
192. David Whitmer, *An Address to All Believers in Christ* (Richmond, MO, 1887), 32–33.
193. Joseph Smith, Letter to William W. Phelps, July 31, 1832, in *JSP*, D2:266.
194. John S. Dinger, ed., *The Nauvoo City and High Council Minutes* (Salt Lake City, UT: Signature Books, 2011), 455.

195. *History, 1838–1856*, Vol. D-1: *August 1, 1842–July 1, 1843*, p. 1522, https://www.josephsmithpapers.org/the-papers/histories/jspph3.
196. "To the Elders of the Church of Jesus Christ of Latter Day Saints, to the churches scattered abroad, and to all the saints," *Times and Seasons*, November 1839.
197. Discourse, April 8, 1843, as reported by William Clayton–B, https://www.josephsmithpapers.org/the-papers/documents/1843.
198. *Words of Joseph Smith*, 187; Smith had held this view at least since March 1832, when he presented a revealed exegesis of several passages in Revelation (Joseph Smith, Answers to Questions, between ca. March 4 and 20, 1832, *JSP* D2:208–213 [D&C 77]).
199. Joseph Smith, Journal, April 8, 1843, in *JSP* J2:347.

Chapter 2

1. Wilford Woodruff, Journal, July 18, 1844, in *Wilford Woodruff's Journal* 2:424–425.
2. See Brown, *In Heaven as It is On Earth*, 36–37, 48–50.
3. Jan Shipps, *Mormonism: The Story of a New Religious Tradition* (Urbana: University of Illinois Press, 1985), 60.
4. Genesis 19:24. See, for example, Wilford Woodruff, Journal, November 1, 1845, in *Wilford Woodruff's Journal* 2:610.
5. Doctrine and Covenants (1844) 111:1 [D&C 135:1].
6. The quote from Hyrum Smith has partially deteriorated from Taylor's later account; however, the same quote appeared in an announcement of the martyrdom that appeared in the 1845 Doctrine and Covenants (John Taylor, Martyrdom Account, Historian's Office History of the Church (draft) 1845–1867, CR 100 92, p. 48, CHL; Doctrine and Covenants (1844) 111 [D&C 135]).
7. John Taylor, Martyrdom Account, Historian's Office History of the Church (draft) 1845–1867, p. 51, CHL.
8. Council of Fifty, Minutes, Events of June 1844, in *JSP* A1:201. Although Mormons placed importance on Smith's willingness to sacrifice his life, they placed less significance on the classic image of the "voluntary martyr." Such a willing figure appears in the Book of Mormon and the biblical text, but in practice Mormons did not see one's status as a martyr jeopardized by self-defense.
9. Leonard, *Nauvoo*, 397.
10. The former opinion may be found in Bushman, *Joseph Smith: Rough Stone Rolling*, 549–550, and Leonard, *Nauvoo*, 397–398. The latter opinion is championed by historians Robert S. Wicks and Fred R. Foister, who include at least ten sources to defend their position. See *Joseph and Junius: Presidential Politics and the Assassination of the First Mormon Prophet* (Logan: Utah State University Press, 2005), 179–180.
11. Council of Fifty, Minutes, Events of June 1844, in *JSP* A1:201–202; William M. Daniels, Affidavit, Hancock County, Illinois, July 4, 1844, Joseph Smith Office Papers, CHL.
12. Mary Elizabeth Rollins Lightner, Remarks, April 14, 1905, p. 3, CHL.

13. For example, after June 27, 1844, Mormons saw John Taylor as a "living martyr," whose "blood [at Carthage] was then mingled with the blood of the martyred Prophet and Patriarch." Quoted in B. H. Roberts, *The Life of John Taylor* (Salt Lake City, UT: George Q. Cannon & Sons, 1892), 413–414.
14. Charles Buck, *A Theological Dictionary*, 2nd American ed. (Philadelphia, 1823), 342.
15. E. L. F., "Martyrs," *The Child's Friend and Family Magazine*, September 1, 1845.
16. The volume had decreased in popularity over the nineteenth century. An 1884 commentator noted that "Foxes 'Book of the Martyrs' was more of a classic with our fathers than with the present generation" (*Friends Review*, August 16, 1884).
17. Edward Stevenson, *Reminiscences of Joseph, the Prophet, and the Coming Forth of the Book of Mormon* (Salt Lake City, 1893), 5–6.
18. P[arley] P. Pratt, "Cry of the Martyrs," *Times and Seasons*, September 2, 1844.
19. Susan Juster describes martyrdom as an "interpretive category" in "What's 'Sacred' About Violence in Early America?," *Common Place* 6, no. 1 (October 2005), http://www.common-place.org/vol-06/no-01/juster/index.shtml.
20. Eliza R. Snow, Letter to Isaac Streator, February 22, 1839, CHL.
21. Revelation 17:6.
22. Revelation 18:6, 8.
23. Revelation 6:10.
24. Revelation 6:11.
25. "A Word to the Saints," *Times and Seasons*, November 1839, emphasis mine.
26. Doctrine and Covenants (1844) 111:3, 5 [D&C 135:3, 5].
27. Johnson, *My Life's Review*, 91.
28. Arza Adams, Diary and Reminiscences, p. [42], CHL.
29. "Night of Martyrdom," *Frontier Guardian [Council Bluffs, Iowa]*, June 27, 1849.
30. *Life of Mosiah Lyman Hancock*, comp. Amy E. Baird, Victoria H. Jackson, and Laura L. Wassell, pp. 29–30, CHL.
31. Joseph Fielding, "'They Might Have Known He Was Not a Fallen Prophet'": The Nauvoo Journal of Joseph Fielding," ed. Andrew F. Ehat, *BYU Studies* 19, no. 2 (Winter 1979): 152.
32. Sarah DeArmon Pea Rich, Autobiography and Journal, 1885–1890, p. 63, CHL.
33. Gilbert Belnap, Autobiography, 1856, p. [87], CHL.
34. *The Life of Mary A. Rich*, p. 17, CHL.
35. Joseph Hovey, Autobiography, p. 29, CHL.
36. *The Life of Mary Rich*, p. 17.
37. *Life of Mosiah Lyman Hancock*, 30.
38. Lyman Littlefield, *Reminiscences of Latter-day Saints* (Logan: The Utah Journal Co., 1888), 163.
39. Sally Randall, Letter to "Dear Friends," July 1, 1844, Sally Randall Letters, 1843–1852, CHL.
40. In the letter of then recently disenchanted Mormon Sarah Scott, to her devout mother in Massachusetts, she claimed that Smith himself had claimed he would be protected for at least five years. "Joseph also prophesied on the stand a year ago last conference that he could not be killed within five years from that time; that they could not

kill him till the Temple would be completed, for that he had received an unconditional promise from the Almighty concerning his days, and he set Earth and Hell at defiance; and then said, putting his hand on his head, they never could kill this Child. But now that he is killed some of the Church say that he said: unless he gave himself up. My husband was there at the time and says there was no conditions whatever, and many others testify to the same thing." Sarah Scott, Letter to "My Dear Father and Mother," July 22, 1844, in George F. Partridge, ed., "The Death of a Mormon Dictator: Letters of Massachusetts Mormons, 1843–1848," *The New England Quarterly* 9, no. 4 (December 1936): 597.

41. Isaac Scott, Letter to His In-laws, in Partridge, "The Death of a Mormon Dictator," 600.
42. Minutes, October 6–9, 1843, https://www.josephsmithpapers.org/the-papers/documents/1843.
43. Wilford Woodruff, Journal, July 28, 1844, in *Wilford Woodruff's Journal* 2:431. An excerpt from a letter Smith wrote while incarcerated was later canonized in Mormon scripture, because it seemed to allude to this same foresight. The excerpt may be found in Doctrine and Covenants 122. See Kathleen Flake, "Joseph Smith's Letter from Liberty Jail: A Study of Canonization," *Journal of Religion* 92, no. 4 (October 2012): 517.
44. Nauvoo Relief Society, Minutes, April 28, 1842, in Jill Mulvay Derr, Carol Cornwall Madsen, Kate Holbrook, and Matthew J. Grow, eds., *The First Fifty Years of the Relief Society: Key Documents in Latter-day Saint Women's History* (Salt Lake City, UT: The Church Historian's Press, 2016), 56.
45. R. Laurence Moore, *Religious Outsiders and the Making of Americans*, 34. Moore exaggerates the uniformity of such statements across Smith's lifetime. While early in his ministry the Mormon prophet often spoke of persecutions, he claimed divine protection that would enable him to withstand his enemies until his ministry was complete. These were optimistic statements predicting his well-being in the face of danger, which had been threatened by incarceration and mob violence, rather than predictions of his approaching demise.
46. See Bushman, *Joseph Smith: Rough Stone Rolling*, 542–543.
47. Parley P. Pratt, "Proclamation to the Church of Jesus Christ of Latter-day Saints," *Millennial Star*, March 1845.
48. Fielding, "'They Might Have Known He Was Not a Fallen Prophet,'" 153–154.
49. Minutes, October 6–9, 1843.
50. Johnson, *My Life's Review*, 87.
51. Benjamin G. Ferris, *Utah and the Mormons: The History, Government, Doctrines, Customs and Prospects of Latter-day Saints* (New York: Harper & Brothers, 1854), 110.
52. John D. Lee, Journal, July 1840, p. 20, CHL.
53. William Clayton Journal, quoted in Bushman, *Joseph Smith: Rough Stone Rolling*, 574.
54. Wandle Mace, Autobiography, MS 1924, p. 110.
55. In actuality, the non-Mormon residents of Carthage had already fled when they received word of the deed. Leonard, *Nauvoo*, 399.
56. Fielding, "'They Might Have Known He Was Not a Fallen Prophet,'" 152.

57. Vilate Kimball, Letter to Heber C. Kimball, June 30, 1844, in Ronald K. Esplin, "Life in Nauvoo, June, 1844: Vilate Kimball's Martyrdom Letters," *BYU Studies* 19, no. 2 (Winter 1979): 238–239.
58. Sally Randall, Letter to "Dear Friends," July 1, 1844.
59. See Parley P. Pratt, "Cry of the Martyrs," *Times and Seasons*, September 2, 1844.
60. Randall, Letter to "Dear Friends," July 1, 1844; see also *Chicago Times*, November 20, 1875.
61. This chapter had recently been on Smith's mind. On June 15, 1844, Smith's journal reads, "examin[in]g Benj[amin] West's paitig [painting] of death on the pale horse—which has been exhibit[in]g in my readi[n]g room—for 3 days" (Joseph Smith, Journal, June 15, 1844, in *JSP* J3:284). For a discussion of this exhibit, see Noel A. Carmack, "Of Prophets and Pale Horses: Joseph Smith, Benjamin West, and the American Millenarian Tradition," *Dialogue: A Journal of Mormon Thought* 29, no. 3 (Fall 1996): 174–176.
62. Wilford Woodruff, August 18, 1844, in *Wilford Woodruff's Journal* 2:446.
63. "Conference Minutes," *Times and Seasons*, November 1, 1845.
64. W. W. Phelps, "The Joseph/Hyrum Smith Funeral Sermon," ed. Richard Van Wagoner and Steven C. Walker, *BYU Studies* 23, no. 1 (Winter 1983): 15–16.
65. "The ruffian, of whom I have spoken, who set him against the well-curb, now secured a bowie knife for the purpose of severing his head from his body. He raised the knife and was in the attitude of striking, when a light, so sudden and powerful burst from the heavens upon the bloody scene, (passing its vivid chain between Joseph and his murderers,) that they were struck with terrified awe and filled with consternation. This light, in its appearance and potency, baffles all powers of description. The arm of the ruffian, that held the knife, fell powerless; the muskets of the four, who fired, fell to the ground, and they all stood like marble statues, not having power to move a single limb of their bodies." William Daniels's account as reproduced in Lyman O. Littlefield, *The Martyrs* (Salt Lake City, UT: The Juvenile Instructor Office, 1882), 81.
66. Helen Mar Whitney recalled that "their bodies had been kept hidden till this time upon Joseph's premises and closely guarded, as there had been large sums of money offered for them by different parties to speculate upon" ("Scenes in Nauvoo," *Woman's Exponent*, June 1, 1883). Stories about those seeking the remains endured into the next century. In 1915, the grand-daughter of a young non-Mormon woman living in Illinois at the time recalled learning that "[t]he solgers [*sic*] wanted Joseph Smiths [*sic*] head for they thought he was a smart man and wanted his head" (Evalina Gurule, Letter to N. B. Lundwall, January 18, 1915, Nels B. Lundwall Correspondence, 1915, CHL).
67. Isaac Lewis Manning, Statement, November 6, 1903, CHL.
68. For a discussion of the complex history and multiple burial sites of Joseph and Hyrum Smith, see Barbara J. Hands Bernauer, *Still "Side by Side": The Final Burial of Joseph and Hyrum Smith* (Kansas City, MO: Arrow Press, 2001).
69. John C. Bennett, Letter to James Strang, April 2, 1846, James Jesse Strang Collection, Beinecke Rare Book and Manuscript Library, Yale University.
70. Joseph Smith, Journal, April 16, 1843, in *JSP* J2:359. For a discussion of the Smith family tomb, see Joseph Johnstun, "'To Lie in Yonder Tomb': The Tomb and Burial of Joseph Smith," *Mormon Historical Studies* 6, no. 2 (Fall 2005): 163–180.

71. "Conference Minutes," *Times and Seasons*, November 1, 1845.
72. Joseph Heywood [and John Fullmer], Letter to Brigham Young, October 16, 1846, CHL.
73. "Gleanings about John D. Lee," compiled by Edna Lee Brimhall, account collected July 15, 1931, p. 58, Leonard J. Arrington Papers, Utah State University Special Collections, Logan, UT.
74. According to Worth Kilgrow, Patriarch Harrison Sperry claimed to have personally "saw the bodies, with a few other trusted ones, lying in their caskets, side by side." Although this was said to have occurred in 1848, Sperry "said they looked very natural, almost as tho[ugh] asleep." Robert Shrewsbury Affidavit, in *Reminiscences of John W. Woolley and Lorin C. Woolley*, 3rd ed., ed. comp. Rhea A. Kunz (Payson, UT: Latter Day Publications, 2007), 125.
75. For information on this conclusion and the William Carter family story, see Lee Wiles, "Monogamy Underground: The Burial of Mormon Plural Marriage in the Graves of Joseph and Emma Smith," *Journal of Mormon History* 39, no. 3 (Summer 2013): 19–23.
76. *The Autobiography of Parley Parker Pratt*, ed. Parley P. Pratt [Jr.] (New York, 1874), 371.
77. William Appleby, Autobiography and Journal, p. 282, CHL.
78. *Journal of Discourses* 4:285–286.
79. Appleby, Autobiography and Journal, 282.
80. Appleby, Autobiography and Journal, 282.
81. Van Wagoner, ed., *The Complete Discourses of Brigham Young*, 2:853.
82. The author has borrowed the term "secondary savior" to describe Joseph Smith from Brown, *In Heaven as It Is On Earth*, 296–297.
83. Appleby, Autobiography and Journal, 288.
84. Appleby, Autobiography and Journal, 288.
85. Appleby, Autobiography and Journal, 288.
86. "Prophetic Sayings of Heber C. Kimball to Amanda H. Wilcox," Susa Young Gates Papers, CHL. Other variants of the vision have been collected in "Amanda Wilcox's accounts of the prophecies of Heber C. Kimball, circa 1904," CHL. Also published as Amanda H. Wilcox, *Prophetic Sayings of Heber C. Kimball to Sister Amanda Wilcox* (n.p./n.d.).
87. Newman Bulkley, *A Vision as Seen by Newman Bulkley, on the Night of 8th January, 1886, in Springville, UT* (Springville, 1886), 6–7.
88. Both William Clayton and non-Mormon sheriff, Jacob Backenstos, put together incomplete lists of the killers, the former including twenty-eight names and the latter eighty-nine. For the relative merits of these and later lists, see Debra Marsh, "Respectable Assassins: A Collective Biography and Socio-Economic Study of the Carthage Mob" (master's thesis, University of Utah, 2009), 21–30.
89. Michael Homer, *Joseph's Temples: The Dynamic Relationship between Freemasonry and Mormonism* (Salt Lake City: University of Utah Press, 2014), 148–150.
90. Bushman, *Joseph Smith: Rough Stone Rolling*, 450.
91. Kenneth W. Godfrey, "Joseph Smith and the Masons," *The Journal of the Illinois Historical Society* 64, no. 1 (Spring 1971): 79.

92. "The Murder," *Times and Seasons*, July 15, 1844.
93. Zina D. H. Young, "Woman's Mass Meeting," *Woman's Exponent*, December 1, 1878.
94. Helen Mar Whitney Kimball, "Life Incidents," *Woman's Exponent*, March 15, 1881; Whitney claimed to cite this from her father's diary, although it is possible the quote is her own reconstruction of her father's sentiments.
95. Wilford Woodruff, Journal, August 19, 1860, in *Wilford Woodruff's Journal* 5:482–483; for a discussion of Young's motives in this assertion, see Robert S. Wicks and Fred R. Foister, *Joseph and Junius: Presidential Politics and the Assassination of the First Mormon Prophet*, 253.
96. See, for example, "Sidney Rigdon Esq.," *Times and Seasons*, November 1, 1844.
97. This is evident from criticisms that he intended to hold a dance in the dining room of the Nauvoo Mansion "which was still stained with the blood which flowed from Joseph and Hyrum, as their bodies lay in said room preparatory to burial." *Manuscript History of the Church*, 13:41.
98. See John Dinger, "'A Mean Conspirator' or 'The Noblest of Men': William Marks' Expulsion from Nauvoo," *John Whitmer Historical Association Journal* 34, no. 2 (Fall/Winter 2014): 12–38.
99. Thomas Ford, *A History of Illinois from Its Commencement in 1818 to 1847* (Chicago: S.C. Griggs and Co., 1854), 360.
100. [W. W. Phelps,] "Joseph Smith," *Times and Seasons*, August 1, 1844.
101. Parley P. Pratt, Willard Richards, John Taylor, and W. W. Phelps, "To the Saints Abroad," *Times and Seasons*, July 15, 1844.
102. *Journal of Discourses* 12:121.
103. Thomas Ford, Letter to Willard Richards and W. W. Phelps, July 22, 1844, Willard Richards Journal and Papers, CHL.
104. Matthew 27:25.
105. "Speech of Elder Orson Hyde, Delivered Sunday, June 15, 1845," *Times and Seasons*, August 15, 1845.
106. Clayton, *An Intimate Chronicle*, 552.
107. Brown, *In Heaven as It Is On Earth*, 290.
108. Allen J. Stout, Reminiscence and Journal, p. 22, CHL.
109. William Clayton, Journal, July 7, 1844, in Clayton, *An Intimate Chronicle*, 138.
110. Leonard, *Nauvoo*, 388.
111. H. Michael Marquardt, ed., *Early Patriarchal Blessings of the Church of Jesus Christ of Latter-day Saints* (Salt Lake City, UT: The Smith-Pettit Foundation, 2007), 338.
112. Council of Fifty, Minutes, March 11, 1845, in *JSP* A1:306.
113. Council of Fifty, Minutes, March 11, 1845, in *JSP* A1:310.
114. Council of Fifty, Minutes, March 11, 1845, in *JSP* A1:311.
115. Joseph Smith, Revelation, July 19, 1841 [D&C 124:106], https://www.josephsmithpapers.org/the-papers/documents/.
116. See Samuel R. Weber, "'Shake off the Dust of Thy Feet': The Rise and Fall of Mormon Ritual Cursing," *Dialogue: A Journal of Mormon Thought* 46, no. 1 (Spring 2013): 108–132.
117. Mark 6:11.

118. Joseph Smith, Revelation, September 22–23, 1832, in *JSP* D2:301 [D&C 84:92].
119. Joseph Smith, Revelation, August 8, 1831, in *JSP* D2:37 [D&C 60:14].
120. Joseph Smith, Revelation, August 8, 1831, in *JSP* D2:37 [D&C 60:15].
121. Orson Hyde, Journal, September 16, 1832, CHL.
122. In the Kirtland Temple, individuals had their feet washed in a similar but not identical rite, re-enacting Christ washing the feet of his apostles. However, rather than the emphasis be placed on the wicked, the rite was performed to cleanse the recipient "from the blood of this generation" (Doctrine and Covenants (1835) 7:45–46 [D&C 88:138]).
123. Weber, " 'Shake off the Dust of Thy Feet,' " 114.
124. "An Epistle of the High Council of the Church of Jesus Christ of Latter-day Saints, in Nauvoo," *Times and Seasons*, June 1, 1842.
125. Joseph Smith, Revelation, July 1830-A, in *JSP* D1:159 [D&C 24:16].
126. D&C 132:47.
127. Eugene England, ed., "George Laub's Nauvoo Journal," *BYU Studies* 18, no. 2 (Winter 1978): 160.
128. Chapman Duncan, Reminiscences, p. 7, CHL.
129. Joseph Fielding Journal, p. 12, CHL.
130. Joseph Smith, Revelation, September 22–23, 1832, in *JSP* D2:303–304 [D&C 84:114–115].
131. Joseph Smith, Discourse, March 10, 1844, as reported by Wilford Woodruff. https://www.josephsmithpapers.org/the-papers/documents/.
132. Charles C. Rich and Heber C. Kimball, "History of David W. Patten," *Millennial Star*, July 9, 1864.
133. Clayton, Journal, June 19, 1845, in Clayton, *An Intimate Chronicle*, 168.
134. Heber C. Kimball, *On the Potter's Wheel: The Diaries of Heber C. Kimball*, ed. Stanley Kimball (Salt Lake City, UT: Signature Books, 1987), 125.
135. Wilford Woodruff, Journal, August 27, 1844, in *Wilford Woodruff's Journal* 2:457.
136. Ford, *A History of Illinois*, 360–361.
137. Wilford Woodruff, Journal, November 2, 1845, in *Wilford Woodruff's Journal* 2:611.
138. Warren Foote, Autobiography, p. 76, CHL.
139. Nels B. Lundwall, *The Fate of the Persecutors of the Prophet Joseph Smith* (Salt Lake City, UT: Bookcraft, 1952).
140. See Dallin H. Oaks and Marvin S. Hill, *Carthage Conspiracy: The Trial of the Accused Assassins of Joseph Smith* (Urbana: University of Illinois Press, 1975), 219; Marsh, "Respectable Assassins"; for a treatment of these stories in light of a broader American folklore of curses, see Richard C. Poulsen, "Fate of the Persecutors of Joseph Smith: Transmutations of an American Myth," *Dialogue: A Journal of Mormon Thought* 11 (Winter 1978): 63–70.
141. See Poulsen, "Fate of the Persecutors of Joseph Smith."
142. Orson Hyde, *Speech of Elder Orson Hyde Delivered Before the High Priests Quorum in Nauvoo, April 27, 1845, Upon the Course and Conduct of Mr. Sidney Rigdon* (City of Joseph [Nauvoo], IL: John Taylor, 1845), 5. One member of the mob had allegedly

declared that "he saw the two martyrs always before him!" (*Autobiography of Parley Parker Pratt*, 476).

143. Brigham Young Minutes, June 1, 1845, Arrington Papers.
144. The role of ghosts in the punishment of their victims is a well-known trope appearing throughout Western literature and perhaps most memorably in the works of William Shakespeare, of which many nineteenth-century Mormons were familiar.
145. Pratt, *Key to the Science of Theology*, 119.
146. Pratt, *Key to the Science of Theology*, 120.
147. Pratt, *Key to the Science of Theology*, 121–122.
148. "Speech of Elder Orson Hyde, Delivered Sunday, June 15, 1845," *Times and Seasons*, August 15, 1845. In this sermon, Hyde envisioned the haunting of the murderers: "Murder and garments rolled in blood are continually before their eyes."
149. Manuscript History of the Church 14:270, CHL.
150. Like other examples of Mormon lore dating back to the nineteenth century, this idea was popularized in an often read piece of early Mormon literature. See Lycurgus A. Wilson, *The Life of David W. Patten: The First Apostolic Martyr* (Salt Lake City, UT: Deseret News, 1904), 45–47. For a discussion of the legend of the Wandering Jew, see Galit Hasan-Rokem and Alan Dundes, *The Wandering Jew: Essays in the Interpretation of a Christian Legend* (Bloomington: Indiana University Press, 1986).
151. Abraham O. Smoot, Letter to Joseph F. Smith in Wilson, *Life of David W. Patten*, 46.
152. Job 1:7. For a discussion of this and other Latter-day Saint encounters with Cain, see Matthew Bowman, "A Mormon Bigfoot: David Patten's Cain and the Conception of Evil in LDS Folklore," *Journal of Mormon History* 33, no. 3 (Fall 2007): 62–82.
153. "Speech of Elder Orson Hyde, Delivered Sunday, June 15, 1845," *Times and Seasons*, August 15, 1845.
154. Matilda C. Giauque Steed, "The Suffering of One of the Assassins," in Lundwall, *The Fate of the Persecutors of Joseph Smith*, 311.
155. Littlefield, *The Martyrs*, 111.
156. Thomas Nichols, "A Mobocrat Roams Western Sheep Ranges," in Lundwall, *The Fate of the Persecutors of Joseph Smith*, 298.
157. Genesis 4:15.
158. George A. Smith, Letter, October 18, 1849, *Millennial Star*, April 15, 1850.
159. *Journal of Discourses* 8:357.
160. *Journal of Discourses* 9:102.
161. *Autobiography of Parley Parker Pratt*, 475–476.
162. *Autobiography of Parley Parker Pratt*, 477.
163. J. C. Cox, "Thirteen Mobocrats Meet a Common Fate," in Lundwall, *The Fate of the Persecutors of Joseph Smith*, 296.
164. Littlefield, *The Martyrs*, 109.
165. Joseph Smith, Revelation, September 1830-A, in *JSP* D1:180 [D&C 29:18–20].
166. Zechariah 14:12.
167. Revelation 19:17–18.
168. Brown, *In Heaven as It Is On Earth*, 37.

169. "Conference Minutes," *Times and Seasons*, November 1, 1845.
170. Miller, *James J. Strang, Weighed in the Balance of Truth and Found Wanting*, 22.
171. "Conference Minutes," *Times and Seasons*, November 1, 1845.
172. Joseph Hovey, Autobiography, p. 58. Kimball seems to have alluded to a tradition that Smith's blood could not be removed from the floorboards of the jail. See Brian Q. Cannon, "'Long Shall His Blood . . . Stain Illinois': The Carthage Jail in Mormon Memory," *Mormon Historical Studies* 10, no. 1 (Spring 2009): 1–19.
173. Hill, *Quest for Refuge*, 175.
174. Brigham Young, "To the Brethren of the Church of Jesus Christ of Latter Day Saints Scattered Abroad Throughout the United States," *Times and Seasons*, November 1, 1845.
175. Young, "To the Brethren of the Church."
176. Young, "To the Brethren of the Church."
177. Underwood, *The Millenarian World of Early Mormonism*, 29.
178. Joseph Hovey, Autobiography, pp. 68–69, CHL.
179. Underwood, *The Millenarian World of Early Mormonism*, 67–68, emphasis in the original.
180. "Conference Minutes," *Times and Seasons*, November 1, 1845.
181. "Hymn 282," *A Collection of Sacred Hymns for the Church of Jesus Christ of Latter-day Saints, in Europe*, 5th ed. (Liverpool, 1847), 339.
182. For a discussion of this issue, see Lori Elaine Taylor, "Telling Stories about Mormons and Indians" (PhD diss., State University of New York at Buffalo, 2000), 211–228.
183. William B. Pace, Autobiography, pp. [2–3], CHL. This statement was credited to Smith's final sermon to the Nauvoo Legion, which Pace erroneously dated to June 22, 1844, although it actually occurred four days prior. He recorded this entry from minutes drafted by Alfred Bell, "taken on the spot by him, and supposed to be very correct." Bell's minutes have not survived, but Pace's entry bears similarities to the other known accounts of the June 18, 1844, sermon. See the only extant primary sources in *Words of Joseph Smith*, 383–384, and the reconstructed account in *History of the Church* 6:498–500. The context in which this statement appears in Pace's account is a prophesied event in the Rocky Mountains in which "you will be called upon to go forth and call upon the free men from Maine to gather themselves in the strongholds of the Rocky Mountains." In the only other account where this appears, Smith "called for all philanthropic men from Main[e] to the Rocky Mountains & from the East & the west & from the North & the south to the help of this people. . . . " What seems to have been remembered as an appeal during the intense period previous to Carthage is remembered in Pace's entry as a prophecy predicting a future day.
184. Joseph Lee Robinson, Autobiography and Journals, 1883–1892, p. 17, CHL.
185. Marquardt, *Early Patriarchal Blessings*, 244.
186. Sally Randall, Letter to "Dear parents and Brothers and Sisters," January 15, 1845, Sally Randall Letters, 1843–1852, CHL.
187. "Reply to the Preston Chronicle," *Millennial Star*, July 1841.

188. During an investigation of this community led by Alpheus Cutler, one of their leaders explained that "a part of their mission was to bring the Indians and Missourians in collision" (Orson Hyde, George A. Smith, and Ezra T. Benson, Report to "Presidents Brigham Young, Heber C Kimball, Willard Richards, and the Authorities of the Church of Jesus Christ of Latter Day Saints in Zion," April 5, 1849).
189. Clayton, Journal, December 21, 1845, in Clayton, *An Intimate Chronicle*, 220–221.
190. Clayton, *An Intimate Chronicle*, 251.
191. Clayton, *An Intimate Chronicle*, 221.
192. Clayton, *An Intimate Chronicle*, 222.
193. *Journal of Discourses* 2:32.
194. Fielding, " 'They Might Have Known He Was Not a Fallen Prophet,' " 159.
195. Fielding, " 'They Might Have Known He Was Not a Fallen Prophet,' " 159. This incident would become a well-known episode in Mormon history/legend, in which another man, William Miller, pretended to be Brigham Young, in order to allow his escape. Everyone worked together to fool the marshals, until in Carthage, a former Mormon realized the ruse.
196. Clayton, *An Intimate Chronicle*, 226.
197. Colleen McDannell, *Material Christianity: Religion and Popular Culture in America* (New Haven, CT: Yale University Press, 1995), 220.
198. Quoted in McDannell, *Material Christianity*, 297–298. A note on the original manuscript reads, "This note is not to be accepted as authentic. JFB [JFS]."
199. Clayton, *An Intimate Chronicle*, 223.
200. Clayton, *An Intimate Chronicle*, 224.
201. Clayton, *An Intimate Chronicle*, 224.
202. Oliver Huntington reported hearing from John Taylor that Smith had told him that "he did not want his garments to be exposed to the sneers and jeers of his enemies" (Oliver B. Huntington, *History of the Life of Oliver B. Huntington*, 48, CHL).
203. Sarah G. Richards, Letter to Zina Huntington, September 20, 1890, Sarah G. Richards Reminiscenses, CHL.
204. Clayton, *An Intimate Chronicle*, 224.
205. Clayton, *An Intimate Chronicle*, 223.
206. For a taste of these stories, see Polly Aird, Jeff Nichols, and Will Bagley, eds., *Playing with Shadows: Voices of Dissent in the Mormon West* (Norman, OK: The Arthur H. Clark Company, 2001), 106.
207. Ferris, *Utah and the Mormons*, 312.
208. Bulkley, *A Vision as Seen by Newman Bulkley*, 5–6.
209. Bulkley, *A Vision as Seen by Newman Bulkley*, 5.
210. Fielding, " 'They Might Have Known He Was Not a Fallen Prophet,' "165.
211. Fielding, " 'They Might Have Known He Was Not a Fallen Prophet,' " 165–166.
212. Will Bagley, ed., *The Pioneer Camp of the Saints: The 1846 and 1847 Mormon Trail Journals of Thomas Bullock* (Spokane, WA: The Arthur H. Clark Co., 1997), 67.
213. Horace Whitney, Journal, October 14, 1846, CHL.
214. Mary Richards, Letter to Samuel W. Richards, September–October, 1846, in *Winter Quarters: The 1846–1847 Life Writings of Mary Haskin Parker Richards*, ed. Maurine

Carr Ward (Logan: Utah State University Press, 1996), 97. This addendum to the letter was written on October 10, 1846.

215. Quoted in Matthew McBride, *A House for the Most High: The Story of the Original Nauvoo Temple* (Salt Lake City, UT: Signature Books, 2007), 324.
216. Fielding, "'They Might Have Known He Was Not a Fallen Prophet,'" 166.
217. Hall, *Worlds of Wonder, Days of Judgment*, 241.

Chapter 3

1. G[eorge] P. Dykes, *The City of Refuge* [ca. 1865].
2. Malachi 3:1.
3. On July 6, 1844, William Clayton recorded a journal entry stating that there were "already 4 or 5 men pointed out as [Smith's] successors" (Clayton, Journal, July 6, 1844, in Clayton, *An Intimate Chronicle*, 137).
4. Minutes, August 8, 1844, Historians Office General Church Minutes, 1839–1877, CHL.
5. General Church Minutes, December 27, 1847, CHL.
6. For a more extensive conversation on this position, see Christopher James Blythe, "'Would to God, Brethren, I Could Tell You Who I Am!': Nineteenth-Century Mormonisms and the Apotheosis of Joseph Smith," *Nova Religio* 18, no. 2 (November 2014): 5–27.
7. "Minutes of a Conference in Pittsburgh, October 12, 1845," *Latter Day Saint's Messenger and Advocate*, October 15, 1845.
8. Van Wagoner, *Sidney Rigdon*, 359–396.
9. The original document is at Yale's Beinecke Rare Book and Manuscript Library. See also "Letter from Joseph Smith to James J. Strang," *Voree Herald*, January 1846, 1:1. For a discussion of the letter and questions concerning its authenticity, see Charles Eberstadt, "A Letter That Founded a Kingdom," *Autograph Collectors' Journal* 3, no. 1 (October 1950): 2–5, 32.
10. For a discussion of Strangite membership statistics, see Vickie Speek, "From Strangites to Reorganized Latter Day Saints: Transformations in Midwestern Mormonism, 1856–1879," ed. Newell G. Bringhurst and John C. Hamer, *Scattering of the Saints: Schism within Mormonism* (Independence, MO: John Whitmer Books, 2007), 142–146.
11. Kyle R. Walker, *William B. Smith: In the Shadow of a Prophet* (Salt Lake City, UT: Greg Kofford Books, 2015), 353–354.
12. William Smith, "A Revelation given to Selah Lane and others, March 19, 1849," *Melchizedek & Aaronic Herald*, May 1, 1849.
13. "A Proclamation," *Zion's Harbinger and Baneemy's Organ*, January 1849.
14. Joseph Smith, Letter to William W. Phelps, November 27, 1832, in *JSP* D2:319–320.
15. Joseph Smith, Revelation, February 24, 1834, *JSP* D3:460 [D&C 103:16.]
16. Wilford Woodruff, Journal, March 8, 1857, in *Wilford Woodruff's Journal* 5:30–31.
17. Wilford Woodruff, Journal, August 23, 1862, in *Wilford Woodruff's Journal* 6:71.

18. Joseph Smith, Revelation, July 19, 1841, D&C 124:32.
19. Council Minutes, February 4, 1860, MSS 2394, Box 1, Folder 2, 51, Church of Jesus Christ (Cutlerite) Papers, L. Tom Perry Special Collections.
20. Church Minutes, January 6, 1861, Box 1, Folder 3, 87, Church of Jesus Christ (Cutlerite) Papers.
21. Joseph Smith III, *Memoirs of Joseph Smith III*, ed. Mary Audentia Smith Anderson and Richard P. Howard (Independence, MO: Herald Publishing House, 1979), 98–99.
22. Church Minutes, Box 1, Folder 3, 87–88, Church of Jesus Christ (Cutlerite) Papers.
23. Lyman Wight, *An address by way of an abridged account and journal of my life from February 1844 up to April 1844, with an appeal to the Latter-day Saints* (1848), 3–4; Council of Fifty, Minutes, May 6, 1844, in *JSP* A1:155–158.
24. Lyman Wight to Sanford Porter, 7 December 1855, 37, Lyman Wight Letterbook, Community of Christ Library-Archives. See also Lyman Wight to the *Northern Islander*, July 1855, 24, Lyman Wight Letterbook, Community of Christ Library-Archives, Independence, MO.
25. Lyman Wight, Letter to William Smith, July 26, 1849, *Melchizedek and Aaronic Herald*, September 1849.
26. "Letter from Joseph Smith to James J. Strang," *Voree Herald*, January 1846.
27. "Letter from Joseph Smith to James Strang."
28. "The Translation of the Plates Made by the Prophet James by Urim and Thummim, September 18, 1845," *Voree Herald*, January 1846.
29. S. P. Bacon, "Voree," *Gospel Herald*, November 29, 1849.
30. James Strang, Revelation, July 8, 1846, in "Revelation," *Voree Herald*, September 1846.
31. "Hyde's Revelation," *Voree Herald*, April 1846. A slightly different variant of this curse may be found in Autobiography of Isaac C. Haight, typescript, HBLL, http://www.boap.org/LDS/Early-Saints/IHaight.html.
32. The revelation was first published as a broadside under the title ""He that hath ears to hear, let him hear what the Spirit saith unto the Churches." See also Orson Hyde, Letter to the Editor, April 5, 1846, *Millennial Star*, May 15, 1846.
33. Richard E. Bennett, *We'll Find the Place: The Mormon Exodus 1846–1848* (Norman: Oklahoma University Press, 2009), 243. First published in 1999 by Deseret Book.
34. John G. Turner, *Brigham Young: Pioneer Prophet* (Cambridge, MA: The Belknap Press of Harvard University Press, 2012), 167–169.
35. Joseph Smith, Journal, February 23, 1844, in *JSP* J3:182.
36. *Journal of Discourses* 10:252.
37. Farmer, *On Zion's Mount*, 143–144.
38. John D. Lee, Journal, January 13, 1846, CHL.
39. Isaiah 2:2–3.
40. Isaiah 5:26.
41. *Wilford Woodruff's Journal* 3:107.
42. Council of Fifty, Minutes, March 11, 1844, in *JSP* A1:42.
43. Council Minutes, February 26, 1847, Historian's Office General Church Minutes, 1839–1877, CHL.

44. John D. Lee, Journal, January 13, 1846.
45. Two months later, on March 3, 1846, Orson Hyde alluded to Young's vision in a Nauvoo sermon. "Joseph is as much our president as he ever was. . . . Suppose he had appeared to the 12 & held a flag waving it & saying go Westward—& s[aid] when I drop that flag—stop." Minutes of Meeting, quoted in Walker, "'A Banner is Unfurled,'" 74.
46. *Journal of Discourses* 13:85.
47. Council Minutes, February 26, 1847, Historian's Office General Church Minutes, 1839–1877, CHL.
48. Wilford Woodruff, Journal, May 29, 1847, in *Wilford Woodruff's Journal* 3:188.
49. Benjamin F. Johnson, Letter to Dimick B. Huntington, January 16, 1901, CHL.
50. See D. Michael Quinn, "The Flag of the Kingdom of God," *BYU Studies* 14, no. 1 (1973): 107.
51. Orson Hyde, Letter to Samuel Brannan, September 5, 1846, CHL; for further discussion of this flag and a published image, see Will Bagley, *Scoundrel's Tale: The Samuel Brannan Papers* (Spokane, WA: Arthur H. Clark Company, 1999), 155–156.
52. William J. Johnstun, Dream, 1867 [5–6], CHL.
53. Don Maguire Journal, Second Narrative (July 1877; June 29, 1878), 21, quoted in Quinn, "The Flag of the Kingdom of God," 111–112.
54. William C. A. Smoot, "Remarks at the American Party Banquet," *Salt Lake Tribune*, March 18, 1910. For a debate over this issue, see Walker, "'A Banner is Unfurled,'" 80–81.
55. "The Temple," *Millennial Star*, February 19, 1853.
56. *Journal of Discourses* 1:133.
57. "Who Designed the Temple?," *Deseret News Weekly*, April 23, 1892.
58. See, for example, Wilford Woodruff Journal, August 23, 1862, in *Wilford Woodruff's Journal* 6:71.
59. Wilford Woodruff, Journal, May 13, 1847, in *Wilford Woodruff's Journal* 3:175.
60. Benjamin Brown, Journal, p. 26, CHL.
61. "Prophetic Sayings of Heber C. Kimball to Amanda H. Wilcox," Susa Young Gates Papers, CHL.
62. Stephen C. Taysom, *Shakers, Mormons, and Religious Worlds. Conflicting Visions, Contested Boundaries* (Bloomington: Indiana University Press, 2011), 86–87.
63. This entry was written by Thomas Bullock in Manuscript History of the Church, D 1, p. 1362, and first published in "History of Joseph Smith," *Deseret News*, November 7, 1855. See Dan Vogel, ed., *History of Joseph Smith and the Church of Jesus Christ of Latter-day Saints: A Source- and Text-Critical Edition* (Salt Lake City, UT: Smith-Pettit Foundation, 2015) 5:79, fn91. See Taysom, *Shakers, Mormons, and Religious Worlds*, 215, fn127.
64. Anson Call, Statement, ca. 1854, CHL. A more polished account appears in Edward William Tullidge, *Tullidge's Histories*, Vol. 2 (Salt Lake City, UT: Juvenile Instructor, 1889), 271–272.
65. Lewis Clark Christian, "Mormon Foreknowledge of the West," *BYU Studies* 21, no. 4 (Fall 1981): 406.
66. Oliver B. Huntington, "Prophecy," *Young Woman's Journal*, April 1891; see also Oliver B. Huntington Journal, February 24, 1883, HBLL.

67. Stephen M. Farnsworth, Letter to Orson Hyde, August 2, 1857, CHL.
68. *Washington's Vision, Mother Shipton's Prophecy, and S. W. Farnsworth's Vision* (Salt Lake City, 1877), 8. Farnsworth was erroneously referred to in this pamphlet as "S. W.," rather than "S.M."
69. *Journal of Discourses* 5:142.
70. Farnsworth, Letter to Orson Hyde, August 2, 1857.
71. Farnsworth, Letter to Orson Hyde, August 2, 1857.
72. "A Vision as Seen by Stephen M. Farnsworth, In Nauvoo, Ill." (Bloomington, UT, 1886), 5–6.
73. *Washington's Vision, Mother Shipton's Prophecy, and S. W. Farnsworth's Vision*, 8; Farnsworth, Letter to Orson Hyde, August 2, 1857, CHL.
74. Farnsworth, Letter to Orson Hyde, August 2, 1857.
75. *Journal of Discourses* 5:142–143.
76. Provo Utah Central Stake Melchizedek Priesthood Minutes and Records, p. 45, CHL.
77. Terryl Givens, *By the Hand of Mormon: The American Scripture that Launched a New World Religion* (New York: Oxford University Press), 99.
78. See Kenneth W. Godfrey, "The Zelph Story," *BYU Studies* 29, no. 2 (1989): 31–56.
79. Joseph Smith, Letter to Emma Smith, June 4, 1834, in *JSP* D4:57.
80. See Bushman, *Joseph Smith: Rough Stone Rolling*, 489–490. See Don Bradley and Mark Ashurst-McGee, "Joseph Smith and the Kinderhook Plates," in *A Reason for Faith: Navigating LDS Doctrine and Church History*, ed. Laura Harris Hales (Provo, UT: BYU Religious Studies Center, 2016), 93–115. Parley Parker Pratt, Letter to John Van Cott, May 7, 1843, CHL.
81. "The Far West," *Evening and Morning Star*, October 1832.
82. Charles Thompson, *Evidences in Proof of the Book of Mormon* (Batavia, NY, 1841), 102–105.
83. Darryl V. Caterine, *Haunted Ground: Journeys through a Paranormal America* (Santa Barbara, CA: Praeger, 2011), 128.
84. Lyman Wight, Letter to William Smith, July 26, 1849, in *Melchisedek and Aaronic Herald*, September 1849.
85. Wilford Woodruff, December 20, 1846, in *Wilford Woodruff's Journal* 3:101.
86. Willard Richards, Journal, March 14, 1846, CHL.
87. *Journal of Discourses* 11:84.
88. W. Paul Reeve, "'As Ugly as Evil' and 'As Wicked as Hell': Gadianton Robbers and the Legend Process among the Mormons," *Journal of Mormon History* (Fall 2001): 145.
89. William Appleby, Autobiography and Journal, January 29, 1850.
90. Robert L. Campbell, Diary, January 8, 1850, CHL.
91. For a discussion of Phelps's proclivity toward translation, see Samuel Brown, "The Translator and the Ghostwriter: Joseph Smith and W. W. Phelps," *Journal of Mormon History* 34, no. 1 (Winter 2008): 26–62.
92. For one twentieth-century Mormon's thoughts on the site, see James Roy Harris Sr., *Southwestern American Indian Rock Art and the Book of Mormon* (Orem, UT: James Roy Harris Sr., 1991), 81–89.

93. J[ohn]. W[illiams]. Gunnison, *The Mormons, or Latter-day Saints, in the Valley of the Great Salt Lake: A history of their Rise and Progress, Peculiar Doctrines, Present Condition, and Prospects* (Philadelphia, 1852), 62
94. Brigham D. Madsen, *Exploring the Great Salt Lake: The Stansbury Expedition of 1849–50* (Salt Lake City: University of Utah Press, 1989), 312–313.
95. Charles D. Evans, "The Fate of Moroni," 1897, CHL.
96. Whitney, *Life of Heber C. Kimball*, 446–447; see also Barbara Lee Hargis, "A Folk History of the Manti Temple: A Study of the Folklore and Traditions Connected with the Settlement of Manti, Utah and the Building of the Temple" (master's thesis, BYU, 1968).
97. David H. Cannon Jr., Affidavit, October 14, 1942, quoted in Kirk M. Curtis, "History of the St. George Temple" (master's thesis, BYU, 1964), 24–26.
98. Charles L. Walker, Journal, January 26, 1881, in *Diary of Charles L. Walker*, ed. A. Karl Larson and Katharine Miles Larson (Logan: Utah State University Press, 1980), 2:526.
99. Diagram Showing Moroni's Travels, undated, CHL.
100. Diagram Showing Moroni's Travels.
101. Mormon historian Ardis E. Parshall has argued against the accuracy of this tradition based partly on this point. See November 18, 2010, http://www.keepapitchinin.org/2010/11/18/moronis-purported-rambles/.
102. 3 Nephi 28:7.
103. Lee, *The Three Nephites*, 30–31.
104. *Journal of Discourses* 2:264.
105. "Vision of Arapine on the night of the 4th of Feb 1855," Brigham Young Office Files, CHL. See also David Grua, "Arapeen, the Ute Prophet," *Juvenile Instructor*, November 26, 2013, http://juvenileinstructor.org/arapeen-the-ute-prophet/.
106. George Washington Hill, "An Indian Vision," *Juvenile Instructor* 12, January 1877, 11.
107. Van Wagoner, *The Complete Discourses of Brigham Young*, 2:930; Reeve, *Religion of a Different Color*, 93.
108. *Journal of Discourses* 17.301.
109. "A Journal of the travels of President Brigham Young and company from Great Salt Lake City, Utah Territory to Fort Limhi in Oregon Territory, 1857," p. 52, CHL.
110. Ira Ames, Autobiography and Journal, 1858, [p. 40], CHL.
111. Nathan V. Jones, Dream, October 5, 1857, CHL. The only known copy of Jones's dream dates to February 18, 1863, and was copied by James W. Cummings from an earlier version presumably in Jones's hand. Jones requested Cummings to make this copy and present it to the apostle George A. Smith.
112. High Priests Quorum Minutes, January 3, 1858, Cottonwood Stake Melchizedek Priesthood Minutes and Records, 1907–1950, CHL.
113. See Richard D. Poll, "The Move South," *BYU Studies* 29, no. 4 (1989): 65–88.
114. Santiago, "Seeking a Refuge in the Desert," *Contributor*, May 1890, 249. Clifford Stott identifies "Santiago" as a pseudonym for James Martineau (Clifford Lyle Stott,

Search for Sanctuary: Brigham Young and the White Mountain Expedition (Salt Lake City: University of Utah Press, 1984), 261, fn14).

115. Santiago, "Seeking a Refuge in the Desert II," *Contributor* 11 (June 1890): 299.
116. "Southern Exploring Company Journals and Chart, 1858 April–June," p. 17, CHL.
117. *The Life Story of Mosiah Lyman Hancock*, 28, CHL.
118. 4 Nephi 1:3, 25.
119. Charles L. Walker, Journal, January 26, 1881, in *Diary of Charles L. Walker*, 2:525.
120. Collected copies of a prophecy by John Taylor as told by Edward Lunt, undated, CHL.
121. The impact of this prophecy is discussed in John C. Lehr, "Polygamy, Patrimony, and Prophecy": The Mormon Colonization of Cardston," *Dialogue: A Journal of Mormon Thought* 21 (Winter 1988): 114–121.
122. Charles O. Card, *The Diaries of Charles Ora Card: The Canadian Years, 1886–1903*, ed. Donald G. Godfrey and Brigham Y. Card (Salt Lake City: University of Utah Press, 1993), 30–31.
123. Parley P. Pratt, *A Letter to the Queen of England, Touching the Signs of the Times, and the Political Destiny of the World* (Manchester, England, 1841).
124. Card, *The Diaries of Charles Ora Card*, 97.
125. "Sols Guardisto, Letter to Mrs. and Mr. John M. Brown, Circa 1922," MS 8848, CHL.

Chapter 4

1. Ferris, *Utah and the Mormons*, 201–202.
2. "Conference Minutes," *Times and Seasons*, November 1, 1845.
3. Brent M. Rogers, *Unpopular Sovereignty: Mormons and the Federal Management of Early Utah Territory* (Lincoln: University of Nebraska Press, 2017), 43.
4. Rogers, *Unpopular Sovereignty*, 44.
5. "The First Epistle of Orson Pratt," *The Seer*, January 1853.
6. *The Pearl of Great Price* (Liverpool: F.D. Richards, 1851).
7. *Journal of Discourses* 8:58. Pratt even possessed a manuscript copy. (Scott C. Esplin, "'Have We Not Had a Prophet Among Us?' Joseph Smith 's Civil War Prophecy," in *Civil War Saints*, ed. Kenneth L. Alford (Salt Lake City, UT: Religious Studies Center, 2012), 44–45.
8. "War," *The Seer*, April 1854. See also Joseph Smith, Revelation, December 25 1832, in *JSP* D2:328–331.
9. "War."
10. "War."
11. "War."
12. "War."
13. "War."
14. William P. MacKinnon, "Sex, Subalterns, and Steptoe: Army Behavior, Mormon Rage, and Utah War Anxieties," *Utah Historical Quarterly* 76 (Summer 2008): 227–246.
15. Laurel Thatcher Ulrich, "Runaway Wives, 1830–1860," *Journal of Mormon History* 42, no. 2 (April 2016): 5.

16. Van Wagoner, *The Complete Discourses of Brigham Young*, 2:989–990.
17. Turner, *Brigham Young*, 245–246; *Journal of Discourses* 2:309–317.
18. Rogers, *Unpopular Sovereignty*, 144–145.
19. Rogers, *Unpopular Sovereignty*, 162–163.
20. Rogers, *Unpopular Sovereignty*, 194–195.
21. George Q. Cannon, Journal, September 16, 1858, The Church Historian's Press, http://www.churchhistorianspress.org/george-q-cannon/.
22. Quoted in Turner, *Brigham Young*, 297.
23. John D. Lee, Journal, July 8, 1858, in *A Mormon Chronicle: The Diaries of John D. Lee, 1848–1876* (San Marino, CA: Huntington Library, 1955), 1:175.
24. Jesse Gove, Letter to Maria Gove, June 18, 1858, in *The Utah Expedition, 1857–1858: Letters of Capt. Jesse A. Gove, 10th Inf., U.S.A. of Concord, N.H., to Mrs. Gove and Special Correspondence of the New York* Herald, ed. Otis G. Hammond (Concord: New Hampshire Historical Society, 1928), 175.
25. *Memoirs of John R. Young: Utah Pioneer, 1847* (Salt Lake City, UT: The Deseret News Press, 1920), 115.
26. Heber C. Kimball, Memorandum Book, 1848–1864, CHL.
27. Donald R. Moorman, with Gene A. Sessions, *Camp Floyd and the Mormons: The Utah War* (Salt Lake City: University of Utah Press, 1992), 273, 276.
28. Charles L. Walker, Journal, August 2, 1861, in Walker, *Diary of Charles L. Walker*, 1:191.
29. Ezekiel 38:22.
30. Revelation 16:14, 19:13–21.
31. Ezekiel 39:17–20; Revelation 19:17.
32. *Journal of Discourses* 5:139.
33. Revelation 12:16.
34. *Journal of Discourses* 7:50.
35. *Journal of Discourses* 2:251. See also 2 Kings 19:35, 6:14–17.
36. Wilford Woodruff, Journal, March 12, 1858, in *Wilford Woodruff's Journal* 5:175.
37. George Q. Cannon, Journal, 22 September 1858.
38. Wilford Woodruff, Journal, February 3, 1858, in *Wilford Woodruff's Journal* 5:162.
39. For an analysis of this and poetry from the Utah War, see Trenton B. Olsen, "Conflict of Church and State: Two Latter-day Saint Poets' Perspectives on the Utah War of 1857–1858," *Intermountain West Journal of Religious Studies* 1, no. 1 (2009): 2–22. The complete lyrics may be found on pp. 20–21.
40. "President Buchanan and Utah," *Millennial Star*, January 16, 1858.
41. *Journal of Discourses* 9:182.
42. *Journal of Discourses* 2:182.
43. J[ohn]. H. Beadle, *Life in Utah; or the Mysteries and Crimes of Mormonism* (Philadelphia: National Publishing Company, 1870), 301.
44. Brigham Young, Office Journal, July 9, 1861, CHL. See Brett D. Dowdle, "'What Means This Carnage?': The Civil War in Mormon Thought," in *Civil War Saints*, ed. Kenneth L. Alford (Provo, UT: Religious Studies Center, 2012), 118.
45. "Celebration," *Deseret News*, July 10, 1861.

46. "Celebration."
47. William H. Miles, Letter to Walter Murray Gibson, December 3, 1860, Brigham Young Incoming Correspondence, 1839–1877, Box 27, Folder 17, CHL.
48. Pratt, "War," 241.
49. Dowdle, "'What Means This Carnage?,'" 110, fn21.
50. Manti Ward General Minutes, June 2, 1861, CHL.
51. Mount Pleasant Minutes, March 8, 1861, CHL.
52. Hyde had first taught this idea by 1845. (See Van Wagoner, *The Complete Discourses of Brigham Young*, 1:117.)
53. Frederick Douglass, "American Apocalypse" Sermon, June 16, 1861, in *The Frederick Douglass Papers: Speeches, Debates and Interviews, 1855–1863*, ed. John W. Blassingame (New Haven, CT: Yale University Press, 1986), 3:437.
54. *Prophetic Times* 1 (1863):22, Quoted in Sandeen, *The Roots of Fundamentalism*, 97.
55. Guyatt, *Providence and the Invention of the United States*, 6.
56. For a study of apocalyptic surrounding the Civil War, see James H. Moorhead, *American Apocalypse: Yankee Protestants and the Civil War, 1860–1869* (New Haven, CT: Yale University Press, 1978); Ben Wright and Zachary W. Dresser, eds., *Apocalypse and the Millennium in the American Civil War Era* (Baton Rouge: Louisiana State University Press, 2013).
57. Roy P. Basler, ed., *Collected Works of Abraham Lincoln* (New Brunswick, NJ: Rutgers University Press, 1953), 8:333.
58. See Guyatt, *Providence and the Invention of the United States*, 279–282.
59. Provo Utah Central Stake Melchizedek Priesthood Minutes and Records, February 21, 1858, CHL.
60. Joseph Smith, Revelation, February 24, 1834, in *JSP D*3:460 [D&C 103:11]; Isaiah 51:3.
61. Richard Bennett, "'We Know No North, No South, No East, No West': Mormon Interpretations of the Civil War, 1861–1865," *Mormon Historical Studies* 10, no. 1 (Spring 2009): 60.
62. "As It Is," *Deseret News*, November 18, 1863.
63. Hannah Peck Meacham, Letter to Mariah D. Funk, November 1, 1863, Mariah D. Funk, Correspondence 1863–1880, CHL.
64. Charles L. Walker, Journal, November 9, 1864, in *Diary of Charles L. Walker*, 1:245.
65. Beadle, *Life in Utah*, 307.
66. *Journal of Discourses* 9:143.
67. Henry J. Doremus, Letter to "Dear Uncle," June 1, 1865, Henry J. Doremus Correspondence, 1852–1870, CHL.
68. "Mormon Prophecy," *The Daily Cleveland Herald*, March 19, 1866.
69. Interview with David Whitmer, *Deseret News*, August 21, 1878.
70. Nephi Packard, Letter to A. Milton Musser, July 24, 1896, A. Milton Musser Papers, CHL.
71. Joseph Smith, Revelation, December 25, 1832, in *JSP* D2:330 [D&C 87:4].
72. T. B. H. Stenhouse, *The Rocky Mountain Saints: A Full and Complete History of the Mormons* (New York: D. Appleton and Company, 1873), 421.
73. Beadle, *Life in Utah*, 306.

74. Sarah Barringer Gordon, *The Mormon Question: Polygamy and Constitutional Conflict in Nineteenth-century America* (Chapel Hill: University of North Carolina Press, 2002), 81.
75. Gordon, *The Mormon Question*, 120–122.
76. Gordon, *The Mormon Question*, 149.
77. *A Mormon Mother: An Autobiography of Annie Clark Tanner*, 4th ed. (Salt Lake City: University of Utah Tanner Trust Fund, 2006), 75.
78. Wilford Woodruff, Revelation, January 26, 1880, in *Wilford Woodruff's Journal* 7:615.
79. *Wilford Woodruff's Journal* 7:616.
80. Wilford Woodruff, Journal, December 28, 1880, in *Wilford Woodruff's Journal* 7:611; Journal, January 19, 1881, in *Wilford Woodruff's Journal* 8:6–7.
81. D. Michael Quinn has suggested that John Steele dictated this vision and sent it to Woodruff, who was serving as the church historian. (D. Michael Quinn, *The Mormon Hierarchy: Extensions of Power* (Salt Lake City, UT: Signature Books, 1997), 774.)
82. *Steele Family Papers* (1989), 1277. Copy located at the L. Tom Perry Special Collections. This author is indebted to Jonathan Stapley for pointing him to this source.
83. Wilford Woodruff, Journal, June 15, 1878, in *Wilford Woodruff's Journal* 7:419–423.
84. Joseph F. Smith, "A Fraud," *Deseret Evening News*, November 17, 1880.
85. Wilford Woodruff, Journal, June 15, 1878, in *Wilford Woodruff's Journal* 7:420. The complete vision is included on pp. 419–423. Other versions, including those credited to Joseph F. Smith, are available in "Dreams of Wilford Woodruff, December 16, 1877," CHL.
86. *Wilford Woodruff's Journal* 7:420.
87. *Wilford Woodruff's Journal* 7:421.
88. *Wilford Woodruff's Journal* 7:421.
89. This variant appears in several instances included in "Dreams of Wilford Woodruff, December 16, 1877," is entitled, "A ~~Vision Given to~~ Dream Had By Wilford Woodruff, December 16, 1877." The variant transcribed in Wilford Woodruff's journal states only that the men robbed the women of their valuables, leaving out the references to rape and murder.
90. *Wilford Woodruff's Journal* 7:422.
91. *Wilford Woodruff's Journal* 7:422.
92. Stuart Lasine, "Jehoram and the Cannibal Mothers (2 Kings 6:24–33): Solomon's Judgment in an Inverted World," *Journal for the Study of the Old Testament* 50 (1991): 39.
93. Jeff Berglund, *Cannibal Fictions: American Explorations of Colonialism, Race, Gender, and Sexuality* (Madison: University of Wisconsin Press, 2006), 29–76.
94. Revelation, ca. March 7 1831, in *JSP* D1:277 [D&C 45:31].
95. Isaiah 28:18.
96. "The Cholera," *The Evening and Morning Star*, September 1832. For Mormon understandings of the disease, see also Robert T. Divett, "His Chastening Rod: Cholera Epidemics and the Mormons," *Dialogue: A Journal of Mormon Thought* 12, no. 3 (1979): 6–15.

97. Charles E. Rosenberg, *The Cholera Years: The United States in 1832, 1849, and 1866* (Chicago: The University of Chicago Press, 1987 [1962]), 40–43.
98. Rosenberg, *The Cholera Years*, 3.
99. James Moyle, Reminiscence, 1886, typescript, p. 11, CHL.
100. "The Destroyer is upon the Waters," *Millennial Star*, July 1, 1849.
101. "Remarkable Dreams," *Contributor: A Monthly Magazine of Home Literature*, August 1884.
102. "Remarkable Dreams."
103. "Remarkable Dreams."
104. Hill, *Quest for Refuge*, 17.
105. Drew Gilpin Faust, *This Republic of Suffering: Death and the American Civil War* (New York: Alfred A. Knopf, 2008), 73.
106. Brett Mizelle, *Pig* (London: Reaktion Books, 2011), 55–57.
107. Michael A. Ross, "Justice Miller's Reconstruction: The Slaughter-House Cases, Health Codes, and Civil Rights in New Orleans, 1861–1873," *The Journal of Southern History* 64, no. 4 (November 1998): 649–676.
108. *Journal of Discourses* 12:198.
109. This event appears in all three synoptic gospels. See Mark 5:1–20; Matthew 8:28–34; Luke 8:26–39.
110. *Journal of Discourses* 8:251.
111. "Remarkable Dreams."
112. C[harles] D. E[vans], "A Vision," *Millennial Star*, February 19, 1883.
113. Evans, "A Vision.
114. Evans, "A Vision."
115. Evans, "A Vision."
116. *Remarkable Visions* (Salt Lake City, UT: Jos. Hyrum, Parry, & Co., 1886), 19.
117. Charles D. Evans, "A Dream," *Contributor*, August 1894.
118. Evans, "A Dream."
119. Evans, "A Dream."
120. Evans, "A Dream."
121. Joseph Smith, Revelation, September 1830-A, in *JSP* D1:180 [D&C 29:19].
122. Evans, "A Dream."
123. Newman Bulkley and Ina Bulkley, Autobiography and Biography of Newman Bulkley, ca. 1950, CHL.
124. Bulkley, *A Vision as Seen by Newman Bulkley*, 1–2.
125. Bulkley, *A Vision as Seen by Newman Bulkley*, 2.
126. *Wilford Woodruff's Journal* 7:420.
127. Isaiah 4:1.
128. Orson Pratt, "Celestial Marriage," *The Seer*, April 1853.
129. Beadle, *Life in Utah*, 300.
130. Bulkley, *A Vision as Seen by Newman Bulkley*, 3.
131. Bulkley, *A Vision as Seen by Newman Bulkley*, 5.
132. Bulkley, *A Vision as Seen by Newman Bulkley*, 5–6.
133. "A Dream by Thomas Harris," October 1, 1880, CHL.

134. "A Dream by Thomas Harris."
135. Nathan V. Jones, Dreams, October 1857, CHL.
136. One of the strongest treatments of the Reformation appears in Taysom, *Shakers, Mormons, and Religious Worlds*, 169–194.
137. *Journal of Discourses* 13:226.
138. Joseph Morris, *The "Spirit Prevails"* (San Francisco: J.A. Dove & Co., 1886), 31. (See Chapter 21:6–7.)
139. It first appeared in *Millennial Star*, May 15, 1876. For more on the influence of the vision in Mormon culture, see Ardis E. Parshall, "What George Washington Didn't Say about Barack Obama in the *Relief Society Magazine*, the *Saints' Herald*, or Even the *Millennial Star*," *Keepapitchinin*, September 23, 2008.
140. An early publication of Washington's vision appeared in the *Philadelphia Inquirer*, June 24, 1861. See J. L. Bell, "The Truth of Washington's Vision," *Boston 1775*, December 30, 2006.
141. See advertisement in *The Soldier's Casket*, February 1865.
142. *Washington's Vision* (Philadelphia, 1864), 14.
143. *Washington's Vision*, 14.
144. *Washington's Vision*, 15.
145. *The Life of Mosiah Hancock*, 29.
146. Joseph Smith, Journal, April 2, 1843, in *JSP* J2:324.
147. Evans, "A Dream."
148. Evans, "A Dream."
149. Parley P. Pratt, *The Angel of the Prairies; A Dream of the Future* (Salt Lake City, UT: Deseret News Printing and Publishing Establishment, 1880), 11–12.
150. Pratt, *The Angel of the Prairies*, 12–13.
151. Pratt, *The Angel of the Prairies*, 13.
152. Pratt, *The Angel of the Prairies*, 13–14.
153. Evans, "A Dream."
154. "A Dream Had by Wilford Woodruff, December 16, 1877."
155. "A Dream Had by Wilford Woodruff, December 16, 1877."
156. Bulkley, *A Vision as Seen by Newman Bulkley*, 6–7.
157. *Journal of Discourses* 13:313.
158. *Journal of Discourses* 17:301.
159. Bulkley, *A Vision as Seen by Newman Bulkley*, 6.
160. Malachi 3:1.
161. Joseph Smith, Revelation, February 24, 1834, in *JSP* D3:461 [D&C 103:20].
162. Joseph Smith, Revelation, February 24, 1834, in *JSP* D3:460 [D&C 103:16].
163. "Zion's Future," in "Ieuan," *The Beehive Songster Being a Collection of Original Songs* (Salt Lake City, The Daily Telegraph Office, 1868), 23–24.
164. Untitled, in William Wiles, *The Mountain Warbler* (Salt Lake City: Deseret News Book, 1872), 65–66.
165. *Journal of Discourses* 17:362.
166. *Journal of Discourses* 17:363.
167. Joseph Smith, Revelation, February 24, 1834, in *JSP* D3:461 [D&C 103:17].

168. *Journal of Discourses* 17:303.
169. George Q. Cannon, Journal, July 19, 1886.
170. "Words Spoke by Moses Thatcher at Lewiston, Cache County, 1886," in *Testimony of Important Witnesses as Given in the Proceedings Before the Committee on Privileges and Elections of the United States Senate in the Matter of the Protest Against the Right of Hon. Reed Smoot, A Senator from the State of Utah, to Hold His Seat* (Salt Lake City, UT: Salt Lake Tribune Publishing Company, 1905), 160.
171. George Q. Cannon, Journal, July 22, 1886.
172. Doctrine and Covenants (1876) 103:16, note l.
173. Abraham H. Cannon, Journal, October 7, 1889, in *An Apostle's Record: The Journals of Abraham H. Cannon*, ed. Dennis B. Horne (Clearfield, UT: Gnolaum Books, 2004), 99.
174. *Journal of Discourses* 21:269.
175. Abraham H. Cannon, Journal, February 1, 1890, in *An Apostle's Record*, 132.
176. "An Unauthorized Publication," *Deseret News*, December 1, 1886; Moses Thatcher, "Notice," *Deseret News*, December 1, 1886.
177. Walter Murray Gibson, Letter to Brigham Young, June 8, 1861, Box 28, Folder 6, CR 1234 1, Brigham Young Office Files, CHL.
178. "A Mormon Prophecy," *Hartford Daily Courant*, September 16, 1862.
179. Henry D. Langdon, ed., *Forewarnings: Prophecies on the Church and Revolution, Antichrist, and the Last Times*, 4th ed. (London: Burns and Lambert, 1861), 359.
180. Beadle, *Life in Utah*, 307.
181. Wilford Woodruff Journal, September 13, 1857, in *Wilford Woodruff's Journal* 5:97.
182. "The Mormons," *New York Times*, March 2, 1858.
183. Wesley Bradshaw, *Brigham Young's Daughter* (Philadelphia: C. W. Alexander, 1870), 73.
184. "The Devil Coming: Remarkable Prophecy of an Astrologist," *San Francisco Chronicle*, December 14, 1890.
185. "Southern Utah," *St. Louis Globe-Democrat*, June 25, 1876.
186. "Mormon Prophecy," *The Daily Cleveland Herald*, March 19, 1866.
187. *The Atlanta Daily Sun*, July 15, 1871.
188. Gunnison, *The Mormons*, 165.

Chapter 5

1. William Trowbridge Larned, "The Rocky Mountain Prophets," *Lippincott's Monthly Magazine* 60 (September 1897): 382.
2. George Q. Cannon, Journal, January 4, 1896.
3. Larned, "The Rocky Mountain Prophets," 385.
4. Larned, "The Rocky Mountain Prophets," 393.
5. Larned, "The Rocky Mountain Prophets," 382.
6. Underwood, *The Millenarian World of Early Mormonism*, 141.
7. Underwood, *The Millenarian World of Early Mormonism*, 141.
8. This section, based on Joseph Smith's April 2, 1843, statement, appeared as Section 130 of the 1876 Doctrine and Covenants.

9. Eastern Arizona Stake General Minutes, 1879–1886, September 27, 1879, CHL.
10. The County Register, August 28, 1890, in Lawrence G. Coates, "The Mormons and the Ghost Dance," *Dialogue: A Journal of Mormon Thought* 18, no. 4 (Winter 1985): 107.
11. "The Great Prophetic Pyramid—An Important Discovery by Prof. O. Pratt, Sen.," *Millennial Star*, May 5, 1879.
12. Angus McDonald, *Prophetic Numbers; or the Rise, Progress and Future Destiny of the "Mormons"* (Salt Lake City, UT: W.M. Egan, 1885), 53–54.
13. *Collected Discourses* 2:105–106.
14. *Collected Discourses* 2:120–121.
15. "General Conference," *The Latter-day Saints' Millennial Star*, October 27, 1890.
16. "General Conference."
17. John M. Whitaker, Letter to Anson Call, January 22, 1886, CHL.
18. Anson Call, Letter to John M. Whitaker, January 30, 1886, CHL.
19. John Steele, Letter to "Dear Father and Mother," January 11, 1891, CHL.
20. Johnson, *My Life's Review*, 319–320.
21. Quoted in Thomas W. Simpson, *American Universities and the Birth of Modern Mormonism* (Chapel Hill: University of North Carolina Press, 2016), 51.
22. Benjamin F. Johnson, Letter to George F. Gibbs, Benjamin F. Johnson Papers, CHL.
23. "The Fulfillment of Prophecy," *Woman's Exponent*, July 1911.
24. See Thomas G. Alexander, *Mormonism in Transition: A History of the Latter-day Saints, 1890–1930* (Urbana: University of Illinois Press, 1986), 7–9. The First Presidency issued the "Political Manifesto" in 1896, which further assured the nation of the church's avoidance of political involvement (Leonard J. Arrington and Davis Bitton, *The Mormon Experience: A History of the Latter-day Saints*, 2nd ed. (Urbana: University of Illinois Press, 1992 [1977]), 249).
25. Revelation, ca. March 7, 1831, in *JSP* D1:280 [D&C 45:68].
26. *Sixty-Eighth Annual Conference of the Church of Jesus Christ of Latter-day Saints* (Salt Lake City, UT: Deseret News Publishing Co., 1898), 80–83.
27. *Sixty-Eighth Annual Conference*, 87; see also D. Michael Quinn, "The Mormon Church and the Spanish-American War: An End to Selective Pacifism," *Dialogue: A Journal of Mormon Thought* 17, no. 4 (Winter 1984). 24–25.
28. Leonard J. Arrington and Bitton, *The Mormon Experience*, 252.
29. Quoted in Allan Kent Powell, "Utah's War Machine: The Utah Council of Defense, 1917–1919," in *Utah and the Great War: The Beehive State and the World War I Experience*, ed. Allan Kent Powell (Salt Lake City: University of Utah Press, 2016), 113.
30. James E. Talmage, "Perpetuity of American Nation Assured by Prophecy," *San Francisco Chronicle*, September 15, 1918.
31. Talmage, "Perpetuity of American Nation Assured by Prophecy."
32. "Mormons and the World War: Dr. James E. Talmage in Davenport Lecture Tells of Their Patriotism," *Quad-City Times*, August 25, 1918.
33. Reeve, *Religion of a Different Color*, conclusion.
34. Patrick Q. Mason, *The Mormon Menace: Violence and Anti-Mormonism in the Postbellum South* (New York: Oxford University Press, 2011). 192–193.
35. Heber J. Grant, "A Message to the Youth of the Church," *Improvement Era*, August 1937.

36. Heber J. Grant, *Salt Lake Tribune,* November 22, 1938.
37. Heber Bennion, *Gospel Problems* ([ca. 1920]), 17.
38. *Sixty-Ninth Semi-Annual Conference of the Church of Jesus Christ of Latter-day Saints* (Salt Lake City, UT: Deseret News Publishing Co., 1898), 4.
39. Alexander, *Mormonism in Transition*, 289–290.
40. *Sixty-Ninth Semi-Annual Conference*, 4.
41. See, for example, "Stay Where you are!" *Millennial Star*, September 15, 1921.
42. *One Hundred Forty-Second Annual Conference of the Church of Jesus Christ of Latter-day Saints* ([Salt Lake City, UT]: Deseret News Press, 1972), 6–7.
43. Jan Shipps, *Sojourner in the Promised Land: Forty Years Among the Mormons* (Urbana: University of Illinois Press, 2000), 261.
44. *Ninety-Fourth Semi-Annual Conference of the Church of Jesus Christ of Latter-day Saints* (Salt Lake City, UT: Church of Jesus Christ of Latter-day Saints, 1923), 51–52.
45. John M. Whitaker, Journal, November 7, 1900, CHL.
46. "Mormons Plan Return to Old Home," *Chicago Tribune*, August 19, 1900.
47. R. Jean Addams, "The Bullion, Beck, and Champion Mining Company and the Redemption of Zion," *Journal of Mormon History* 40, no. 2 (Spring 2014): 219.
48. Craig S. Campbell, *Images of the New Jerusalem: Latter Day Saint Faction Interpretations of Independence, Missouri* (Knoxville: University of Tennessee Press, 2004), 151.
49. Marriner Merrill, *Juvenile Instructor*, October 15, 1892.
50. Emmeline B. Wells, Diary, January 9, 1904, L. Tom Perry Special Collections, BYU.
51. Dr. James X. Allen, "Passing of the Gift of Tongues," *Improvement Era*, December 1904.
52. Allen, "Passing of the Gift of Tongues."
53. "In Relation to the Mystical," *Deseret Evening News*, March 26, 1898.
54. "In Relation to the Mystical."
55. "Discourses," *Deseret Weekly*, March 23, 1889.
56. "Discourses."
57. For instance, see Abraham H. Cannon's discourse in *Collected Discourses* 2:22; Heber J. Grant, Diary, May 30, 1890, in *The Diaries of Heber J. Grant, 1880–1945, Abridged* (Salt Lake City, UT: Privately Published, 2010), 93–94.
58. George Q. Cannon, Discourse, *Deseret Weekly*, October 31, 1896.
59. Alexander, *Mormonism in Transition*, 295.
60. This vision is currently included as the final section 138 of the LDS Doctrine and Covenants.
61. For another interpretation of charismata among general authorities during the period of transition, see Quinn, *Mormon Hierarchy: Extensions of Power*, 1–6.
62. Archie J. Graham, "A Visit Beyond the Veil, Undated," CHL.
63. Grant, Diary, July 21, 1933, and July 26, 1933, in *The Diaries of Heber J. Grant*, 298.
64. *One Hundred Eighth Annual Conference of the Church of Jesus Christ of Latter-day Saints* (Salt Lake City, UT: Church of Jesus Christ of Latter-day Saints, 1938), 65.
65. Angus McDonald, *The Mormons Have Stepped Down and Out of Celestial Government. The American Indians Have Stepped Up and Into Celestial Government*, 1.

66. Gregory Smoak, *Ghost Dances and Identity: Prophetic Religion and American Indian Ethnogenesis in the Nineteenth Century* (Los Angeles: University of California Press, 2006), 165–171.
67. James Mooney, *The Ghost Dance Religion and the Sioux Outbreak of 1890* (Washington, DC: Government Printing Office, 1896), 781.
68. Smoak, *Ghost Dances and Identity*, 168–169.
69. Louis S. Warren, *God's Red Son: The Ghost Dance Religion and the Making of Modern American* (New York: Basic Books, 2017), 262–263.
70. Coates, "Mormons and the Ghost Dance," 108.
71. Susa Y. Gates, "The Editor's Department," *Young Woman's Journal*, September, 1890.
72. Wilford Woodruff, Letter to George Terry, May 25, 1889, quoted in Lawrence G. Coates, "Mormons and the Ghost Dance," 102.
73. Joseph F. Smith, "The Messiah Craze," *Young Woman's Journal*, March, 1891, 270.
74. The wording "Twelve Disciples" rather than "Twelve Apostles" pulls from the Book of Mormon's distinction between Christ selecting Twelve Apostles in the Old World, but Twelve Disciples in the New.
75. McDonald, *The Mormons Have Stepped Down and Out of Celestial Government*, 3.
76. McDonald, *The Mormons Have Stepped Down and Out of Celestial Government*, 4.
77. Joseph Smith, Letter to William W. Phelps, November 27, 1832, in *JSP* D2:319–320 [D&C 85:6–8]. This revelation first appeared in "Let Every Man Learn His Duty," *Evening and Morning Star*, January 1833.
78. See 2 Samuel 6:6–7; 1 Chronicles 13:9–10. For a discussion of how Latter-day Saint churches have interpreted this revelation, see Bill Shepard, "To Set in Order the House of God": The Search for the Elusive "One Mighty and Strong," *Dialogue: A Journal of Mormon Thought* 39, no. 3 (Fall 2006): 19.
79. Kathleen Flake, *The Politics of American Religious Identity: The Seating of Senator Reed Smoot, Mormon Apostle* (Chapel Hill: University of North Carolina Press, 2004), 51.
80. Flake, *The Politics of American Religious Identity*, 95.
81. Flake, *The Politics of American Religious Identity*, 95.
82. *Testimony of President Joseph F. Smith of the Mormon Church and Senator Reed Smoot* (Salt Lake City, UT: Salt Lake Tribune Publishing, 1905), 177
83. *Testimony of President Joseph F. Smith*, 165.
84. "President Joseph F. Smith on Revelation," *Millennial Star*, April 6, 1905.
85. Samuel Eastman, *A Brief Memoir of My Life* (1930), 11.
86. Quoted in Flake, *The Politics of American Religious Identity*, 98.
87. Flake, *The Politics of American Religious Identity*, 98.
88. *Eighty-Ninth Semi-Annual Conference of the Church of Jesus Christ of Latter-day Saints* (Salt Lake City, UT: Deseret News, 1918), 119–120. See also Brian C. Hales, "John T. Clark: The One Mighty and Strong," *Dialogue: A Journal of Mormon Thought* 39, no. 3 (Fall 2006): 49.
89. Joseph F. Smith, John R. Winder, and Anthon H. Lund, "The One Mighty and Strong," *Deseret Evening News*, November 11, 1905.
90. Smith, Winder, and Lund, "The One Mighty and Strong."

91. Smith, Winder, and Lund, "The One Mighty and Strong."
92. Smith, Winder, and Lund, "The One Mighty and Strong."
93. *The Eightieth Semi-Annual Conference of the Church of Jesus Christ of Latter-day Saints* (Salt Lake City, UT: Deseret News, 1909), 8.
94. *Eighty-Third Annual Conference of the Church of Jesus Christ of Latter-day Saints* (Salt Lake City, UT: Deseret News, 1913), 62–63, emphasis in the original.
95. Francis M. Darter, *The Lord's Strange Work* (Long Beach, CA: Self-Published, 1917), 49.
96. "Excerpts from the Journal of Nathaniel Baldwin," 1. Copy of typescript in the possession of the author. Originals of Baldwin's journals are available at the University of Utah Special Collections.
97. "Excerpts from the Journal of Nathaniel Baldwin," 3.
98. "Excerpts from the Journal of Nathaniel Baldwin," 30.
99. Norman C. Pierce, *The Dream Mine Story*, rev. ed. (Salt Lake City, UT: Self-Published, 1972), 7.
100. *Journal of Discourses* 19:39.
101. James E. Talmage, Diary, July 16, 1913, CHL.
102. Joseph F. Smith, Anthon H. Lund, and Charles W. Penrose, "A Warning Voice: To the Officers and Members of the Church of Jesus Christ of Latter-day Saints," *Improvement Era* 16 (September 1913).
103. Smith, Lund, and Penrose, "A Warning Voice."
104. Smith, Lund, and Penrose, "A Warning Voice."
105. Don L. Penrod, "Edwin Rushton as the Source of the White Horse Prophecy," *BYU Studies* 49, no. 3 (2010): 75–84.
106. Penrod, "Edwin Rushton as the Source of the White Horse Prophecy," 82.
107. White Horse Prophecy, CHL.
108. White Horse Prophecy.
109. Joseph Smith, Revelation, December 25, 1832, in *JSP* D2:330 [D&C 87:4].
110. White Horse Prophecy.
111. White Horse Prophecy.
112. White Horse Prophecy, Revised Version.
113. To distinguish him from his father, Joseph F. Smith Jr. became referred to as Joseph Fielding Smith. This text uses the latter name.
114. *Eighty-Ninth Semi-Annual Conference*, 54–55.
115. *Eighty-Ninth Semi-Annual Conference*, 55.
116. The revelation was not actually in French; however, the revelator commented that he had been reading the Doctrine and Covenants in French at the time of the vision.
117. *Eighty-Ninth Semi-Annual Conference*, 57.
118. *Eighty-Ninth Semi-Annual Conference*, 57–58.
119. Joseph F. Smith, "A Fraud," *Deseret Evening News*, November 17, 1880.
120. Joseph F. Smith, "Edwin Rushton's Vagaries," Joseph F. Smith Papers, CHL.
121. See "Collected Copies of the White Horse Prophecy [ca. 1902–1970]," CHL.
122. "Dreams of Wilford Woodruff, 1877 December 16," CHL.

123. *One Hundred and First Annual Conference of the Church of Jesus Christ of Latter-day Saints* (Salt Lake City, UT: Church of Jesus Christ of Latter-day Saints, 1931), 68–69; *One Hundred and Eighth Annual Conference*, 64–65.
124. "Prophetic Sayings of Heber C. Kimball to Sister Amanda H. Wilcox," Susa Young Gates Papers, ca. 1870–1933, CHL.
125. *One Hundredth Annual Conference of the Church of Jesus Christ of Latter-day Saints* (Salt Lake City, UT: Church of Jesus Christ of Latter-day Saints, 1930), 59.
126. One Latter-day Saint, George Burkett, recalled, "I heard Joseph Smith say in my house when in Clay County that when we returned there [Jackson County] there not would be a dog to wag his tail or move his tongue against us" (George Burkett, Letter to "Dear Children," December 18, 1870, CHL).

Chapter 6

1. Bruce R. McConkie, *The Millennial Messiah: The Second Coming of the Son of Man* (Salt Lake City, UT: Deseret Book Company, 1982), 94–95.
2. Mike Carter, "Utah Brand of Militia Tied to State's Dominant Culture," *The [Provo] Daily Herald*, May 13, 1995.
3. A later exception would include the relocation of Jewish populations to Palestine and the creation of the state of Israel, as well as the opening of regions for Latter-day Saint missionary work.
4. B. H. Roberts, "A Mormon View of the World War of 1914: Fulfillment of Joseph Smith's Prophecies of 1832," *Liahona: The Elders' Journal*, October 20, 1914.
5. Roberts, "A Mormon View of the World War of 1914."
6. "League is Only Plan for Universal Peace Says Roberts," *Myton Free Press*, June 19, 1919.
7. "Senator Smoot Declares for Treaty Reservations," *The Salt Lake Herald-Republican*, August 24, 1919.
8. Robert C. Fuller, *Naming the Antichrist: The History of an American Obsession* (New York: Oxford University Press, 1995), 160–161; Markku Ruotsila, "Conservative American Protestantism in the League of Nations Controversy," *Church History* 72, no. 3 (September 2003): 593–616.
9. *Mormon Bible Becomes Issue in League of Nations Fight* (San Francisco: Pacific NEA Bureau, [1919]).
10. Heber J. Grant, "The Treaty of Peace-Restoration of the Gospel," Discourse, September 21, 1919, *Improvement Era*, December 1919.
11. *Ninety-Second Semi-Annual Conference of the Church of Jesus Christ of Latter-day Saints* (Salt Lake City, UT: Church of Jesus Christ of Latter-day Saints, 1921), 196.
12. *One Hundred Seventh Annual Conference of the Church of Jesus Christ of Latter-day Saints* (Salt Lake City, UT: Church of Jesus Christ of Latter-day Saints, 1937), 23–24.
13. *One Hundred Seventh Annual Conference*, 25.

14. *One Hundred Tenth Semi-Annual Conference of the Church of Jesus Christ of Latter-day Saints* (Salt Lake City, UT: Church of Jesus Christ of Latter-day Saints, 1939), 11.
15. *One Hundred Tenth Semi-Annual Conference*, 15.
16. *One Hundred Tenth Semi-Annual Conference*, 17.
17. *One Hundred Fourteenth Annual Conference of the Church of Jesus Christ of Latter-day Saints* (Salt Lake City, UT: Church of Jesus Christ of Latter-day Saints, 1944), 133.
18. *One Hundred Seventeenth Semi-Annual Conference of the Church of Jesus Christ of Latter-day Saints* (Salt Lake City, UT: Church of Jesus Christ of Latter-day Saints, 1946), 88.
19. *One Hundred Seventeenth Semi-Annual Conference*, 89.
20. Paul Boyer, *When Time Shall Be No More: Prophecy Belief in Modern American Culture* (Cambridge, MA: The Belknap Press of Harvard University Press, 1992), 115; see also Spencer R. Weart, *The Rise of Nuclear Fear* (Cambridge, MA: Harvard University Press, 2012), 57. An earlier version of Weart's book appeared as *Nuclear Fear: A History in Images*, 1988.
21. John A. Widtsoe, *Faith Under the Atomic Bomb*, Address, April 7, 1946, p. 1.
22. Harold B. Lee, "President J. Reuben Clark Jr.: An Appreciation on his Ninetieth Birthday, September 1871–September 1961," *Improvement Era*, September 1961.
23. *Official Report of the One Hundred Fifty-Seventh Semiannual General Conference of the Church of Jesus Christ of Latter-day Saints* (Salt Lake City, UT: Church of Jesus Christ of Latter-day Saints, 1987), 5.
24. *One Hundred Thirty-Fifth Annual Conference of the Church of Jesus Christ of Latter-day Saints* (Salt Lake City, UT: Church of Jesus Christ of Latter-day Saints, 1965), 125.
25. Underwood, *The Millenarian World of Early Mormonism*, 141.
26. McConkie, *The Millennial Messiah*, 311.
27. McConkie, *The Millennial Messiah*, 463.
28. McConkie, *The Millennial Messiah*, 455.
29. McConkie, *The Millennial Messiah*, 456.
30. McConkie, *The Millennial Messiah*, xxii.
31. Bruce R. McConkie once participated in a question-and-answer session with the faculty of Brigham Young University. During this meeting, he acknowledged his hesitance to cite other Mormon authorities in his work. His son remembered that McConkie explained, "Last week I quoted Parley P. Pratt for the first time in my life. I did it because I could square what he said with the scriptures and because he said it better than I could have." Joseph Fielding McConkie and Richard Neitzel Holzapfel, "Becoming Master Teachers," *Religious Educator* 12, no. 1 (2011): 154.
32. McConkie, *The Millennial Messiah*, 303–305.
33. McConkie, *The Millennial Messiah*, 294.
34. McConkie, *The Millennial Messiah*, 445.
35. *Journal of Discourses* 2:146–147.
36. Joseph Musser and J. Leslie Broadbent, *Supplement to the New and Everlasting Covenant of Marriage* (1934), 61.
37. Joseph Musser, Journal, August 13, 1922, copy in this author's possession.

38. Brian C. Hales, *Modern Polygamy and Mormon Fundamentalism: The Generations after the Manifesto* (Salt Lake City, UT: Greg Kofford Books, 2006), 195–198.
39. Joseph Musser, Book of Remembrance, August 16, 1932, p. 33, copy in this author's possession.
40. Moroni Jessop, Testimony of Moroni Jessop, p. 28, copy in this author's possession.
41. Joseph Musser, Book of Remembrance, February 17, 1932, p. 12.
42. "Revelation given to Rulon C. Allred through the medium of Joel F. LeBaron: the morning of the first day of October, in the year of our Lord 1955, at the home of Price W. Johnson, Salt Lake City, Utah," CHL.
43. Verlan M. LeBaron, *The LeBaron Story* (Juarez, Chihuahua, Mexico: Keels & Co, 1981), 35.
44. Quoted in Lyle O. Wright, "Origins and Development of the Church of the Firstborn of the Fullness of Times" (master's thesis, BYU, 1963), 153.
45. Joseph Musser, Journal, May 10, 1935.
46. Testimony of Moroni Jessop, p. 18, copy in this author's possession.
47. Joseph Musser, Book of Remembrance, February 17, 1932, pp. 11–12.
48. Norman C. Pierce, *The Dream Mine Story* (Salt Lake City, 1958), 64; see "Dream Mine Excerpts Concerning the Prophet John Koyle and the Relief Mine near Salem, Utah; Excerpts of Revelations found in The Second Book of Commandments," http://www.2bc.info/pdf.
49. Joanne Hanks, *"It's Not About the Sex" My Ass: Confessions of an Ex-Mormon Ex-Polygamist Ex-Wife* (Lulu.com, 2012), 34–35.
50. For example, Lorin C. Woolley's recounting of Taylor's prophecy of the One Mighty and Strong referred to this bondage.
51. Jessop, Testimony of Moroni Jessop, pp. 36–37; "Temple Block Sold," pamphlet republished in Rhea Allred Kunz, *Reminiscences of John W. and Lorin C. Woolley*, 3rd ed. (Payson, UT: Latter Day Publications, 2007), 4:14–19.
52. Pierce, *The Dream Mine Story*, 69.
53. Joseph Smith, Letter to William W. Phelps, November 27, 1832, in *JSP* D2:319–320 [D&C 85:8].
54. See Francis M. Darter, *The Testament of Levi, the Son of Jacob* (Salt Lake City, UT: Deseret News Press, 1937); Clyde Neilson, *Levi's Eighth Priest or Zion's Deliverer* (Holladay, UT, 1941); Clyde Neilson, *Mormon Apostasy: Levi Predicts Corruption in Heber J. Grant's Administration* (Holladay, UT, undated).
55. Dan Egan, "Hex, Wives, and Videotape: Polygamist Leader Shaking Up Manti," *Salt Lake Tribune*, April 26, 1998.
56. Becky Johns, "The Manti Mormons: The Rise of the Latest Mormon Church," *Sunstone*, June 1996.
57. Frank Miller, *The Salt Lake Valley Cleansing, The Indian Vision, The Law of Judgement* (Laveen, AZ: Thenco, 1988), 2.
58. B. Harvey Allred, *A Leaf in Review of the Words and Acts of God and Man Relative to the Fullness of the Gospel*, 2nd rev. ed. (Draper, UT: Review & Preview, 1980 [1933]), 209.

59. Martha Sonntag Bradley, *Kidnapped from that Land: The Government Raids on Short Creek Polygamists* (Salt Lake City, UT: University of Utah Press, 1993), ix–x.
60. Norman C. Pierce, *The 3½ Years* (1963), 171–179.
61. Pierce, *The 3½ Years*, 171.
62. Pierce, *The 3½ Years*, 176.
63. David Fleisher and David M. Freedman, *Death of an American: The Killing of John Singer* (New York: Continuum Publishing Company, 1983), 205–207.
64. "'It's been a hard year . . . we've missed him a great deal,'" *The Park Record*, January 17, 1980.
65. Addam Swapp, Revelation, December 26, 1987, quoted in Ogden Kraut, "The Singer/Swapp Siege: Revelation or Retaliation?" *Sunstone*, November 1988.
66. Addam Swapp, Revelation, December 26, 1987.
67. Vickie Singer, Letter to Governor Bangerter, January 27, 1988, quoted in Vickie Singer, *Vickie Singer Tells Her Story* (March 1992), 48–49. Copy in this author's possession.
68. Singer, *Vickie Singer Tells Her Story*, 23.
69. Singer, *Vickie Singer Tells Her Story*, 36.
70. William K. Ray, *Laman Manassah Victorious: A Message of Salvation and Redemption to His People Israel, First to Ephraim and Manasseh* (Idaho Falls, ID, 1931), 137–138.
71. Miller, *The Salt Lake Valley Cleansing*, 4.
72. Miller, *The Salt Lake Valley Cleansing*, 5–6.
73. Francis M. Darter, *Our Bible in Stone, Its Divine Purpose, and Present Day Message, The Mystery of the Ages Revealed* (Salt Lake City, UT: Deseret News, 1931), 144.
74. F. M. Darter, *Amazing L.D.S. Prophetic Dates* (Salt Lake City, 1959).
75. Quoted in Benjamin G. Bistline, *Colorado City Polygamists: An Inside Look for the Outsider* (Scottsdale, AZ: Agreka Books, 2004), 187.
76. In 1998, three former members of the True and Living Church sued the church for $264,390 they had donated because Jim Harmston had "promised them a face-to-face meeting with Jesus Christ but never delivered" (Kristen Moulton, "Ex-members Sue Church Based in Manti," *The Daily Herald*, April 9, 1998).
77. James Harmston, Dialogue with Jeremiah, untitled, March 17, 2000, copy in this author's possession.
78. This painting appeared in "As Christ Fails to Appear, TLC Members Sue Church," *Sunstone*, September 2005.
79. Robert W. Smith and Elizabeth A. Smith, *The "Last Days": A compilation of prophecies pertinent to the present gathered from secular and religious sources embracing George Washington's vision and others of a prophetic nature with excerpts from prophetic writings of Joseph Smith Jr.* (Salt Lake City, UT: Pyramid Press, 1931), p. d.
80. "Wednesday's the Day," *Salt Lake Tribune*, November 14, 1948.
81. Robert W. Smith, *Scriptural and Secular Prophecies Pertaining to the Last Days*, 11th ed. (Salt Lake City, UT: Superior Publishing, 1968), 5.
82. Robert W. Smith, *Scriptural and Secular Prophecies Pertaining to the Last Days*, 10th ed. (Salt Lake City, UT: Pyramid Press, 1948); Smith, *Scriptural and Secular Prophecies*, 11th ed.
83. Smith, *Scriptural and Secular Prophecies*, 11th ed., 4.

84. Duane S. Crowther, *Prophecy: Key to the Future* (Salt Lake City, UT: Bookcraft, 1962), 301.
85. Crowther, *Prophecy*, 321–322.
86. Crowther, *Prophecy*, 322.
87. Crowther, *Prophecy*, 322.
88. See Matthias Cowley, *Wilford Woodruff: His Life and Labors* (Salt Lake City, UT: Deseret News, 1909), 505.
89. Richard Turley, *Victims: The LDS Church and the Mark Hofmann Case* (Chicago: University of Illinois, 1992), 17.
90. Roger K. Young, *Dreams and Visions of the Last Days*, 2nd ed. (Rigby, ID: Celestial Publications, 2008), 134.
91. "Collected copies of a prophecy by John Taylor as told by Edward Lunt, undated," CHL.
92. "Collected copies of a prophecy by John Taylor as told by Edward Lunt, undated," CHL. This variant was dated to February 1969.
93. D. Michael Quinn, "Ezra Taft Benson and Mormon Political Conflicts," *Dialogue: A Journal of Mormon Thought* 26, no. 2 (Summer 1993): 35–39.
94. William A. Wilson, "The Paradox of Mormon Folklore," *BYU Studies* 17, no. 1 (Autumn 1976): 44–45.
95. Quoted in Don L. Penrod, "Critical Analysis of Certain Apocryphal Reports in the Church of Jesus Christ of Latter-day Saints as Related by Members of the Church" (master's thesis, BYU, 1971), 49–50.
96. The later variant does not appear in any of the significant prophecy collections.
97. Vision of George Albert Smith, October 20, 1988, CHL.
98. Joanna Brooks, *The Book of Mormon Girl: A Memoir of an American Faith* (New York: Free Press, 2012), 29–31.
99. Kathy Hutchinson, collected by Donald Smurthwaite, "Warning in the Elevator Version 3," February 3, 1977, Character Legends, William A. Wilson Folklore Archives [WFA], L. Tom Perry Special Collections, Brigham Young University.
100. Barbara May, collected by Marlene Joyner, "Kimball story food storage," February 1977, Character Legends, WFA.
101. Shelley Bradburn, collected by Scott Adams, "Food storage (President Kimball) It's too late," February 27, 1977, Character Legends, WFA.
102. Scott C. Parkinson, collected by Gordon Irving, untitled, January 9, 1977, Character Legends, WFA.
103. Scott Madsen, collected by Donald Smurthwaite, "Warning in the elevator," January 29, 1977, Character Legends, WFA.
104. Ralph Zobell, collected by Donald Smurthwaite, "Warning in the elevator version 2," undated, Character Legends, WFA.
105. Beth Wagner, collected by Rodney Call, "Food Storage," October 14, 1977, Character Legends, WFA.
106. Legend cycle, Food storage motorist, Supernatural Religious Legends, WFA.
107. Vaughn J. Featherstone, "Food Storage," *Ensign*, May 1976.
108. Brooks, *The Book of Mormon Girl*, 43.

109. In 2014, one of this author's students who had recently finished a mission to Missouri recalled that she visited one family who had purposefully designed their home for future guests who would need to stay. She recalled that the family had a supply of extra toothbrushes.
110. Graham W. Doxey, "Missouri Myths," *Ensign*, April 1979.
111. Joseph Smith, Answers to Questions, between ca. March 4 and 20, 1832, in *JSP* D2:211 [D&C 77:6].
112. Gerald Mass, collected by self, untitled, May 12, 1961, Supernatural Religious Legends, WFA. Mass included a disclaimer: "In checking on this I found that this was a rumor and nothing more. This story can definitely be labelled as false."
113. Lueda Baggley, collected by Linda Bradshaw, untitled legend about David O. McKay, undated, Supernatural Religious Legends, WFA.
114. "The Second Coming of Christ, Pure Speculation by Darwin Smith. October, 1978," p. 1, CHL.
115. Gordon B. Hinckley, "We Need Not Fear His Coming," *BYU Devotional*, March 26, 1979, https://speeches.byu.edu/talks/gordon-b-hinckley_need-not-fear-coming/.
116. Vaughn J. Featherstone, Letter "To My Beloved Fellow Saints in the Twenty-First Century," April 6, 1983, CHL. For context, see Elder John E. Enslen, Letter "To Any Who May Be Interested," February 15, 2010, CHL.
117. McConkie, *The Millennial Messiah*, 31.
118. Peggy Fletcher Stack, "LDS Scholar's Book Pulled, Sparks 'Davidic' Debate," *Salt Lake Tribune*, July 11, 1991.
119. "Bomb of Gileadi," *Sunstone*, September 1991.
120. Hanks, *"It's Not About the Sex,"* 29–30>.
121. Hanks, *"It's Not About the Sex,"* 30.
122. Hanks, *"It's Not About the Sex,"* 31.
123. Hanks, *"It's Not About the Sex,"* 32.
124. Chris Jorgensen, "Mormons' End-of-World Talk Could End LDS Membership," *Salt Lake Tribune*, December 2, 1992.
125. Michael Barkun, *A Culture of Conspiracy: Apocalyptic Visions in Contemporary America* (Berkeley: University of California Press, 2003), 40.
126. Barkun, *A Culture of Conspiracy*, 39–40.
127. "Group Prepares for the End," *Daily Spectrum*, September 3, 1991.
128. "Calendars of Doom," *The Economist*, December 19, 1992.
129. Linda Ashton, "Candidate Used Stanfoff to Capitalize on His Theme of 'God, Guns, and Gritz,'" *Deseret News*, September 3, 1992.
130. Bo Gritz, "Salt Lake City 'N Me," *Center for Action Monthly Newsletter*, November 1994.
131. *Official Report of the One Hundred Sixty-Second Semiannual General Conference of the Church of Jesus Christ of Latter-day Saints* (Salt Lake City, UT: Church of Jesus Christ of Latter-day Saints, 1992), 102.
132. *Official Report of the One Hundred Sixty-Second Semiannual General Conference*, 42–43.
133. The documents were entitled "Profile of the Splinter Group Members or Others with Troublesome Ideologies," "Dealing with Apostate and Splinter Groups," and

"Our Challenge to Keep the Doctrine of the Church Pure." Copies in this author's possession.

134. Chris Jorgensen and Peggy Fletcher Stack, "It's Judgment Day for Far Right: LDS Church Purges Survivalists," *Salt Lake Tribune*, November 29, 1992.
135. "Profile of the Splinter Group Members or Others with Troublesome Ideologies," copy in this author's possession.
136. Jorgensen and Stack, "It's Judgment Day for Far Right."
137. Tara Westover, *Educated: A Memoir* (New York: Random House, 2018), 84–85.
138. Lerona A. Wilson (written by her husband, Joseph E. Wilson), *An Open Vision* (Salt Lake City, 1915); Lerona Abigail Martin Wilson, *Life After Death: Personal Experiences* (Salt Lake City, UT: Pyramid Press, 1933).
139. Alma D. Erickson, *Personal revelation given to Alma D. Erickson in the early 1930's regarding the great and dreadful day of the Lord*, undated. Two copies available in in the Church History Library.
140. Archie J. Graham, "A Visit Beyond the Veil, Undated," CHL; Heber Q. Hale, "A Heavenly Manifestation, 1920," CHL; Martin Wilson, *Life After Death: Personal Experiences*.
141. Boyd K. Packer, *Mine Errand from the Lord: Selections from the Sermons and Writings of Boyd K. Packer* (Salt Lake City, UT: Deseret Book, 2008), 134.
142. Tom Mould, *Still, the Small Voice: Narrative, Personal Revelation, and the Mormon Folk Tradition* (Logan, UT: Utah State University Press, 2011), 61–76.
143. Packer, *Mine Errand from the Lord*, 134.
144. Packer, *Mine Errand from the Lord*, 134–136.
145. Margaret K. Brady, "Transformations of Power: Mormon Women's Visionary Narratives." *Journal of American Folklore* 100 (October–December 1987): 466.
146. Scott Mitchell, "'You Have No Right to Do Such A Thing': An Insider Study of Entitlement of Spirit Child Narratives in Mormon Communities" (master's thesis, University of Missouri—Columbia, 2004), 30.
147. Barbara Hill, collected by Jeanne Hill, "Apocalypse," May 17, 1882, Supernatural Religious Legends, WFA.
148. Young, *Dreams and Visions of the Last Days*, 25.
149. Young, *Dreams and Visions of the Last Days*, 27.
150. Young, *Dreams and Visions of the Last Days*, 19.
151. Young, *Dreams and Visions of the Last Days*, 28.
152. Quoted in Massimo Introvigne, "Embraced by the Church? Betty Eadie, Near-Death Experiences, and Mormonism," *Dialogue: A Journal of Mormon Thought* 29, no, 3 (Fall 1996): 105.
153. Introvigne, "Embraced by the Church?," 105, 107.
154. Gayle Smith, *Gayle's Story: One Woman's Visions of the End Days in America*, Version 2.0 (March 3, 1999), p. 16. Copy in this author's possession.
155. "A Report of Gayle Smith's Visions of What Could Happen to the Now Peaceful Valleys Along the Wasatch Front," October 1998, http://www.greaterthings.com.
156. Revelation 13:17–18.
157. Smith, *Gayle's Story*, 19–20. For a discussion of these ideas in evangelical apocalyptic culture, see Fuller, *Naming the Antichrist*, 179–182.

158. Boyer, *When Time Shall Be No More*, 285.
159. Smith, *Gayle's Story*, 19.
160. Paul Drockton, "Utah Woman Accuses Mormon Prophet of Attempted Rape," copy in the possession of the author.
161. Mechelle McDermott, *The Great Gathering* (2015), 82.
162. Sarah Menet, *There Is No Death: The Extraordinary True Experience of Sarah LeNelle Menet*, 2nd ed. (Philipsburg, MT: Mountain Top Publishing, 2003 [2002]), 66–67.
163. Menet, *There Is No Death*, 67–68.
164. Menet, *There Is No Death*, 69.
165. Menet, *There Is No Death*, 70.
166. Menet, *There Is No Death*, 73.
167. John Pontius, *Visions of Glory: One Man's Astonishing Account of the Last Days*, 5th anniv. ed. (Springville, UT: CFI, 2017), appendix. The first edition was published in 2012.
168. Pontius, *Visions of Glory*, 106–109.
169. Pontius, *Visions of Glory*, 110–117.
170. Pontius, *Visions of Glory*, 127–136.
171. Pontius, *Visions of Glory*, 137.
172. Pontius, *Visions of Glory*, 148.
173. Pontius, *Visions of Glory*, chapters 8 and 9.
174. Pontius, *Visions of Glory*, xv.
175. Pontius, *Visions of Glory*, xx–xxi.
176. Pontius, *Visions of Glory*, xxi–xxii.
177. Pontius, *Visions of Glory*, xxii.
178. Pontius, *Visions of Glory*, xviii.
179. " 'Spenser's' Visions of Glory," book review, https://www.fairmormon.org/archive/publications/spencers-visions-of-glory.
180. Julie Rowe, *A Greater Tomorrow: My Journey Beyond the Veil* (Provo, UT: Spring Creek Book Company, 2014), 111.
181. Rowe, *A Greater Tomorrow*, 130.
182. Rowe, *A Greater Tomorrow*, 129.
183. Rowe, *A Greater Tomorrow*, 128.
184. Rowe, *A Greater Tomorrow*, 135.
185. Rowe, *A Greater Tomorrow*, 126. Interestingly, Pontius, writing from "Spencer's" perspective, noted, "In all of my visions, I never saw a mark upon people, or heard people talking of being forced to receive a mark or microchip in order to buy and sell." He somewhat cryptically acknowledged the possibility that Social Security numbers might be related to the mark of the beast: "It was already true that we each had a number to our name, and that number was required for any large transaction, such as buying a home or obtaining credit. That may have been part of the mark." Yet, he did see a spiritual marking tied into the "counterculture of political correctness . . . and the assault on Christian values and traditions" (Pontius, *Visions of Glory*, 123).
186. Rowe, *A Greater Tomorrow*, 127.

187. Rowe, *A Greater Tomorrow*, 137.
188. Julie Rowe, *The Time Is Now* (Provo, UT: Spring Creek Book Company, 2014), 125–126.
189. "#29—New Jerusalem," *The Julie Rowe Show*, August 22, 2017.
190. Rowe, *A Greater Tomorrow*, 138.
191. Rowe, *A Greater Tomorrow*, 146.
192. Isaiah 4:5.
193. Peggy Fletcher Stack, "Some Mormons stocking up amid fears that doomsday could come this month," *Salt Lake Tribune*, September 15, 2015.
194. John Hagee, *Four Blood Moons: Something Is About to Change* (Brentwood, TN: Worthy Publishing, 2013), chapter 16.
195. Greater Tomorrow Relief Fund homepage, http://www.greatertomorrowfund.org.
196. "#8—The Gathering and GTRF," *The Julie Rowe Show*, May 31, 2017.
197. One of the most popular collections of last days apocalyptic in Mechelle McDermott, *The Great Gathering*, which includes summaries and comparisons throughout.
198. Be Ready Utah, "Earthquake," https://www.utah.gov/beready/family/earthquake.html.
199. Julie Rowe with Eric J. Smith, *Rising Above the Flames: My Untold Story* (Provo, UT: Spring Creek Book Company, 2018), 4.
200. Rowe, *Rising Above the Flames*, 132.
201. Julie Rowe, "#77—Unrighteous Dominion," May 26, 2019, YouTube video.

Afterword

1. "Mormon Church Issues Call for Calm as 'Blood Moon' Sparks Apocalypse Fears," *The Guardian*, September 26, 2015; Daniel Politi, "Mormon Leaders Reassure Faithful: Sunday's 'Blood Moon' Isn't Sign of Apocalypse," *Slate*, September 26, 2015; Brady McCombs, "LDS Church Dismisses 'Blood Moon' Worries," *Deseret News*, September 26, 2015.
2. "White Horse in the White House," *Wall Street Journal*, November 3, 2006.
3. "Romney Candidacy has resurrected last days prophecy of Mormon saving the Constitution," *Salt Lake Tribune*, June 4, 2007.
4. Dana Milbank, "Mormon Prophecy Behind Glenn Beck's Message," *Huffington Post*, October 5, 2010.
5. For a nuanced discussion of the place that religion played in Romney's campaigns and the corresponding media coverage, see J. B. Haws, *The Mormon Image in the American Mind: Fifty Years of Public Perception* (New York: Oxford University Press, 2013), chapters 9 and 10.
6. "Romney and the White Horse Prophecy," *Salon*, January 29, 2012.
7. Nathan B. Oman, "The Mormon Plot That Wasn't," *New York Daily News*, February 1, 2012.
8. "Romney and the 'Mormon Moment,'" *Columbia Journalism Review*, March 2, 2012.
9. Yair Rosenberg, "Protocols of the Elders," *Tablet*, February 16, 2012.

10. Maureen Dowd, "Mitt's White Horse Pulls Up Lame," *New York Times*, January 31, 2015.
11. "Romney Candidacy has resurrected last days prophecy of Mormon saving the Constitution," *Salt Lake Tribune*, June 4, 2007.
12. "Church Statement on 'White Horse Prophecy' and Political Neutrality," January 6, 2010, https://www.mormonnewsroom.org/blog/church-statement-on-white-horse-prophecy-and-political-neutrality.
13. "Romney Candidacy has resurrected last days prophecy."

Index

Figures are indicated by *f* following the page number

For the benefit of digital users, indexed terms that span two pages (e.g., 52–53) may, on occasion, appear on only one of those pages.